SHAKESPEARE
THE PLAYER

Shakespeare the player? A bearded Shakespeare in profile from a
miniature by George Vertue, dated 1754 (from the collection of Lois A.
Gaeta, photograph supplied by courtesy of the Shakespeare Centre
Library, Stratford-upon-Avon)

SHAKESPEARE THE PLAYER

A LIFE IN THE THEATRE

JOHN SOUTHWORTH

SUTTON PUBLISHING

This book was first published in 2000 by
Sutton Publishing Limited · Phoenix Mill
Thrupp · Stroud · Gloucestershire · GL5 2BU

This paperback edition first published in 2002

British Library Cataloguing in Publication Data
A catalogue record for this book is available from the British
Library

ISBN 0 7509 3060 8

Typeset in 10.5/11.5pt Plantin.
Typesetting and origination by
Sutton Publishing Limited.
Printed and bound in Great Britain by
J.H. Haynes & Co. Ltd, Sparkford.

Contents

	Acknowledgements	vii
1	*The Invisible Man*	1
2	*Killing the Calf*	13
3	*The Apprentice*	22
4	*Admiral's Man*	30
5	*The Rose, 1592*	46
6	*The Player Poet*	58
7	*Chamberlain's Man*	84
8	*He that Plays the King*	115
9	*The Globe, 1599–1601*	142
10	*Travelling Man*	175
11	*King's Man*	204
12	*Blackfriars*	228
13	*The Man Shakespeare*	249

Contents

Appendices

A   Recollections of Marlowe, Kyd and Peele
in Shakespeare's early plays   256

B   Conjectural programme of performances
of 'harey the vi' at the Rose in 1592/3   266

C   Correspondences in word, image or thought
between Shakespeare's plays of 1593/4 and
the Sonnets   268

D   Conjectural doubling plots for *Romeo and Juliet*,
Henry V and *Troilus and Cressida*   272

Abbreviations   278

Notes   280

Further Reading   319

Index   320

Acknowledgements

I am indebted for the data on which my book is based to all those scholars who have toiled so devotedly in the field of research to establish the facts as we presently know them, especially Sir Edmund Chambers, whose six volumes of his *Elizabethan Stage* and *William Shakespeare* – from which I quote throughout, as acknowledged in the notes – have provided an invaluable source of reference.

I am likewise indebted to the many libraries that have assisted my studies, and here I want to make special mention of my friends at the Central Ipswich Branch of Suffolk Libraries (my home library) who have been so unfailingly helpful in obtaining the books I have needed through the Inter-Library Loan Scheme, and in meeting my other enquiries.

In the interpretation of the plays, I have learnt as much from the directors and actors I have worked with in productions of the plays down the years as I have from books. My greatest debt of all is to Michael Saint-Denis, Glen Byam Shaw and George Devine, my former teachers at the Old Vic School, to whom the book is dedicated in affectionate memory.

A final word of acknowledgement is due to those libraries and museums that have kindly supplied photographs for the book's illustrations, and given me permission to reproduce them. Particular acknowledgement is made in the captions. In the few instances where I have been unable to trace the copyright owners, I offer apologies and assurance of future correction, if they will kindly get in touch with me.

John Southworth
Ipswich, November 2002

The Droeshout engraving, 1623 (Folger Shakespeare Library, Washington, DC)

ONE

The Invisible Man

The eyes that stare blankly out at us from the familiar Droeshout portrait of Shakespeare have little to tell us of the player that he was – or indeed of the man, however we choose to regard him. This should not surprise us. The artist's depiction of his features must have borne a reasonable likeness or it would not have been passed by Shakespeare's former fellows, Heminges and Condell, for inclusion in the First Folio of 1623, which they edited; but Droeshout had been only fifteen when Shakespeare died in 1616 and he is unlikely to have known him well, if at all.[1] He had probably based his engraving on an earlier portrait or sketch and, if so, whatever life the original may have had was lost in the copying.

But in fairness to Droeshout, we should bear in mind what Heminges and Condell's purpose had been in commissioning the portrait, which was to embellish a first collected edition of their friend's plays with an appropriately dignified image of their author. Shakespeare's renown as player and man of the theatre was not in question – not among those who had known him personally or had seen him perform; his reputation as dramatic poet was yet to be established. Seven years earlier in a bid to secure scholarly recognition for his own dramatic achievements, Ben Jonson had published his plays in a similarly impressive folio volume, which may have prompted Heminges and Condell to do the same for their former fellow. As they explain in their prefatory letters, the Shakespeare folio was intended as both memorial and rescue mission: 'to keepe the memory of so worthy a Friend, & Fellow alive, as was our SHAKESPEARE'; but also because whereas before 'you [the readers] were abus'd with deverse stolne, and surreptitious copies, maimed, and deformed by the frauds and stealthes of injurious imposters, that expos'd them: even those are now offer'd to your view cur'd, and perfect in their limbes; and all the rest, absolute in their numbers, as he conceived them'.[2] (The 'rest', it should be said, comprised no less than eighteen plays that had never before appeared in print, including *The Tempest, Twelfth Night* and *Macbeth*, which, but for Heminges and Condell's initiative in searching out Shakespeare's manuscripts and the company's prompt books, might easily, probably would, have been lost for ever.) But, like Jonson, they would also have had a larger end in view. For the paradox is that at the highest point of their achievement in the English dramatic renaissance of the sixteenth and early seventeenth centuries, the status of playwrights had never been so low, or plays so little regarded as a literary form.

In 1605, at the lowest ebb of his fortunes, the proudly assertive Jonson, committed to prison with George Chapman for their part in the writing of a play called *Eastward Ho!* that had given offence to the authorities, was so far obliged to bow to the common opinion as to write cringingly to the Earl of Salisbury that the cause of their incarceration – '(would I could name some worthier) . . . is, a (the word irks me that our Fortunes hath necessitated us to so despised a course) a play, my Lord'.[3] In founding his now famous Oxford library in the years that followed, Sir Thomas Bodley was insistent on excluding plays from the newly published books that he wished to assemble on its shelves. Writing to the Bodleian's librarian in 1611/12, Sir Thomas assures him that even if 'some little profit might be reaped (which God knows is very little) out of some of our playbooks, the benefit thereof will nothing near countervail the harm that the scandal will bring unto the library when it shall be given out that we stuff it full of baggage books . . .'. In another letter, he puts playbooks in the same category of ephemera as almanacs and proclamations, and refers to them collectively as 'riff-raffs'. The 'baggage books' and 'riff-raffs' he thus dismisses as unworthy of attention would have included newly published quarto editions of plays by both Shakespeare and Jonson.[4] Even so cultured and frequent a playgoer as the poet John Donne, writing in 1604 or 1605 (years in which *Hamlet* and *Othello* were in performance at the Globe), does not even mention Shakespeare's name or that of any other dramatist in a catalogue of thirty-four works by thirty different authors of the time. As Professor Bentley concludes, 'he did not consider plays in the category of serious literature'.[5] Nor even, it would appear, of literature at all in the usual sense. Though Shakespeare the player, Shakespeare the theatre director and part-owner, would certainly have been known to him, Shakespeare the playwright and dramatic poet was seemingly invisible to him.

Plays of the period were, of course, written to be performed: heard, not read. Throughout the whole of the seventeenth century – and in spite of first Jonson's, then Heminges and Condell's, best editorial endeavours – plays continued to be primarily regarded not as books and thus belonging to literature, but as public events in which a story was enacted by means of spoken words and the movement and gestures of actors on a stage to an audience assembled at a particular time and place. They existed temporally – in the two to three hours' traffic of the stage – not spatially in the way that a book exists and can be handled and shelved. In the theatre, the words were of great importance; at no period of theatrical history have they been of *more* importance (one went to hear a play, not see it); but they were written by their author to be memorised by actors, and came into their true, intended form only when spoken. We need to remember, too, that Shakespeare was one of those actors; he was writing for himself as a performer as well as for his fellows.

In this respect, the medium in which Shakespeare and other dramatists of the period worked – that of the popular theatre – had continuity with, and was itself an almost unique survival of, the age-old oral culture that had been dominant throughout the Middle Ages. By Shakespeare's time that popular culture of the harper-poets and itinerant interluders was in rapid disintegration and retreat before the advance of literacy and an increasing availability of printed books;[6] a profound shift in the cultural climate that had been in slow, inexorable progress since the fourteenth century but was then brought to a critical stage by more recent religious changes. The Bible – previously reserved as reading matter to a Latin-speaking elite and communicated to an illiterate laity in the form of pictorial images, liturgical ritual and religious drama (all providing an essentially communal experience) – now became in its English translations generally available and subject to individual interpretation. The altar, where an action was performed and a sacrifice offered, gave place in importance to the pulpit, from which the scriptures were read and expounded, and to the chained Bible which people were encouraged to read for themselves – an essentially private act. In the religious compromise effected by the Elizabethan church settlement, the Eucharist survived, but more perhaps as a service to be read than as an action to be *done*, with the altar replaced by a removable table. The great *Corpus Christi* cycles of plays, that had survived long enough for Shakespeare to have seen at least one of them at Coventry, did not simply fall out of favour, as was once believed, but were actively suppressed in the interests of the new Protestant orthodoxy by an alliance of secular and ecclesiastical powers that within thirty years of Shakespeare's death was to close and demolish the theatres.[7] So far as the medium of Shakespeare's expression was concerned, it was an end-game that he and his fellows were playing.

Shakespeare's plays (and those of his fellow dramatists) were no more written for publication than were the *Corpus Christi* cycles or later morality plays and interludes, and their survival as texts was to prove just as chancy. Not only were they aimed at performance, rather than publication, but their publication was, in most circumstances, firmly resisted by the companies for which they had been written, including the Chamberlain's (later, King's) Men, in which Shakespeare became a sharer. This was because, in the absence of any enforceable copyright other than that of the stationers who printed them, the effect of such publication was to make the texts of the plays freely available for performance by rival companies to the financial loss of those who had commissioned and first performed them. (The plays belonged, not to the author, but to the company. Hence the importance of the playbook, and the book-keeper who was responsible for it.) Nevertheless, as we know, some of Shakespeare's more popular plays *did* find their way into print during his lifetime, for the most part in pirated editions, 'maimed and deformed', as Heminges and Condell put it, 'by the frauds and stealthes of injurious imposters', and it was in response to that specific situation that they had mounted their rescue mission. In normal circumstances, only when a play was thought to have exhausted its immediate potential in the theatre and had been dropped from the current repertoire was its publication authorised by the company concerned as a disposable capital asset.

But there was another, more telling reason for Shakespeare having remained invisible to so many of his contemporaries. It was not just the ephemerality of the medium in which he worked or the low status accorded to dramatists among other authors, but a deep-seated disdain on the part of the educated and armorial classes of his day, especially the literati among them, for all those who, like himself and his fellows, earned their living in the realm of public entertainment, whether as musicians, actors or playwrights. Quite simply, they were regarded as 'below the salt', to be patronised perhaps, but otherwise excluded from respectable society. Here was the real source of that discredit which Bodley believed would reflect upon his new library by the admittance of playbooks – irrespective of their quality. It was embodied in the vagrancy laws of the period where minstrels and players were routinely cited together as 'rogues and vagabonds', subject to a whipping if caught on the road without the protection afforded by their acceptance of a nominal, but nonetheless menial, status as servants of the monarch or other great lord. Quite apart from the extreme views of Puritans such as Stubbs and Gosson, for whom acting itself was an offence against God, and players the 'Devil's brood', such attitudes were a commonplace of moderate contemporary opinion.

Once, it may have been otherwise. 'Plaier', John de la Casa admits in 1615, 'was ever the life of dead poesie, and in those times, that Philosophy taught us morall precepts [he means the classical era], these acted the same in publicke showes'; but 'Player is now a name of contempt, for times corrupt men with vice, and vice is growne to a height of government'; for 'Players, Poets, and Parasites', he goes on, 'doe now in a man joyne hands [in Shakespeare? In Marlowe and Jonson, who at one time had also been players?]; and as Lucifer fell from heaven through pride: these have fallen from credit through folly: so that to chast eares they are as odious as filthy pictures are offensive to modest eyes'.[8]

Here, perhaps, are those 'public means which public manners breeds' referred to by Shakespeare himself in Sonnet 111:

> Thence comes it that my name receives a brand,
> And almost thence my nature is subdued
> To what it works in, like the dyer's hand.

Or, as Shakespeare's friend and admirer, John Davies of Hereford, was to bluntly express it in 1603, 'the stage doth staine pure gentle bloud'.[9] The same snobbish disdain for the occupation of player was to fester on until comparatively recent times.

The publication of the First Folio was not only, then, a work of fellowly piety to preserve the text of Shakespeare's plays and rescue them from the pirates; it also implied a claim for recognition of his genius as a dramatic poet, which, seven years after his death, remained largely unacknowledged. And the engraving Heminges and Condell commissioned Droeshout to make for it was designed to promote a reformed image of Shakespeare as poet and man of letters in circumvention of the contemporary prejudice against him as public entertainer. In the immediate term, their efforts met with only limited success;[10] but, as the book found its way into libraries (the earliest reference is to a copy bound by the Bodleian in 1624), it was to light a long fuse to an explosion of scholarly interest and a still-thriving academic industry – all centred, naturally enough, on the plays as literary texts. It is the Droeshout engraving – the only authenticated, contemporary portrait we possess – that has dominated the imagination of the book's users ever since.

The Droeshout engraving is immediately followed in the First Folio by Ben Jonson's tribute to his dead colleague and friend and, as if in acknowledgement of its limitations, the reader is urged by him to 'look/Not on his picture, but his book'.

The memorial bust of Shakespeare in Stratford church (of uncertain date but installed by 1623 at the latest) reinforces this message. (See Plate 2.) Beneath a carving of the now familiar figure, holding a quill in his right hand and resting his left on a sheet of paper, the passer-by is enjoined to stay, and

READ IF THOU CANST, WHOM ENVIOUS DEATH HATH PLAST,
WITH IN THIS MONUMENT SHAKSPEARE: WITH WHOME,
QUICK NATURE DIDE: WHOSE NAME DOTH DECK $\overset{S}{Y}$ TOMBE,
FAR MORE THEN COST: SIEH ALL, $\overset{T}{Y}$ HE HATH WRITT,
LEAVES LIVING ART, BUT PAGE, TO SERVE HIS WITT.

The inscription is misspelt and over-punctuated; nor does Shakespeare lie 'with in this monument' but under the floor of the church some yards away, but its purport is identical to that of Jonson's epitaph. If we seek the soul of Shakespeare, his 'living art', we have nowhere left to look but to the pages of his book; in that time and place, the theatre was not considered an acceptable option.

A long succession of biographers and scholars have since applied this advice in the most literal way by searching the speeches of the fictional characters he created, and the changing themes of his plays, for clues to Shakespeare's inner, emotional life, or his political and religious opinions. The method is not altogether without interest or value; but the material available to this kind of research is so large and so various that, like the Bible, it can be used selectively to support a multiplicity of contradictory views. So prone is it to subjective bias that all too often the portrait that emerges is found to be more reflective of the researchers' own preconceptions and prejudices, and of the values and assumptions of the period in which they are writing, than it is of Shakespeare; these look for Shakespeare in the mirror of his book and see only a cloudy image of themselves. In so far as such enquiries proceed from a belief that in writing his plays Shakespeare was primarily engaged in a form of self-expression, rather than in responding to the practical needs of the theatres he served and the changing demands and tastes of the public with whom he was in constant touch in the most intimate way possible – as an actor on the stage – they rest on a fallacious premise. This is not to deny that, like all great poets and writers, Shakespeare was able to mould whatever material came his way to an aesthetic expression of his own unique experience of life and of the world around him, or to do so in words that at their finest and best reach to universal truths; but, by definition, such intuitive insights are not to be found on the surface of his mimetic inventions; and unless we start from a true appreciation of his initial motivations in putting pen to paper, of choosing one theme, one treatment of a theme, one story rather than another, and always with a particular end in view – a play for a specific group of actors to perform in a specific theatre at a specific time that would give pleasure to a specific audience – we go badly astray. In search of his 'living art', we discover only a life. And is it really Shakespeare's?

Those unwilling or unable to accept the plain fact of his profession as player, or its necessary implications, have found 'evidence' for a whole series of alternative occupations to fill the so-called 'lost years' of his youth and early manhood: schoolmaster, soldier, sailor, butcher, glover, dyer, scrivener, lawyer, barber-surgeon – nothing is too far-fetched if it can serve to postpone the moment of his emergence, 'exelent in the qualitie he professes', as player. Others would avoid that moment of truth altogether by attributing the plays to some other contemporary figure considered to be more fitted by birth and education to be their author. Sir Francis Bacon, the earls of Rutland, Derby, Southampton and Oxford have been among the leading contenders for the coveted title. The mystery these set out to solve is of their own making, and the effect of their conjectures merely to muddy the waters of genuine research.

For those who focus on Shakespeare's poetry in isolation from the dramatic uses to which he put it, there is no mystery; or rather the mystery is seen as endemic to the nature of poetry itself, for as Keats explained in a letter,

> . . . the poetical Character . . . is not itself – it has no self – it is every thing and nothing. It has no character – it enjoys light and shade; it lives in gusts, be it foul or fair, high or low, rich or poor, mean or elevated. . . . A poet is the most unpoetical of anything in existence; because he has no identity – he is continually in and filling some other Body. The Sun, the Moon, the Sea and Men and Women who are creatures of impulse are poetical and have about them an unchangeable attribute – the poet has none; no identity – he is certainly the most unpoetical of all God's creatures. . . .[11]

For Jorge Luis Borges likewise, 'There was no one in him; behind his face (which even through the bad paintings of those times resembles no other) and his words, which were copious, fantastic and stormy, there was only a bit of coldness, a dream dreamt by no one'. But Borges situates this quality of 'negative capability' not in Shakespeare's nature as poet, but in his predestined profession as actor. 'No one', he goes on to assert, has ever been so many men as this man who like the Egyptian Proteus could exhaust all the guises of reality. At times he would leave a confession hidden away in some corner of his work, certain that it would not be deciphered; Richard affirms that in his person he plays the part of many and Iago claims with curious words 'I am not what I am'.[12]

And certainly, if part of his peculiar genius as dramatist and poet lay in his capacity to identify with the thoughts and feelings of his characters, and to speak with their voices out of the situations in which he had placed them, that authorial gift cannot have been wholly unconnected with the actor's ability – which, as a senior member of the leading company of his day, he would also have enjoyed – to identify with the characters he played and to make the words of the playwright his own – which in his case, of course, they normally *were*. It is this protean component in Shakespeare's identity that leads so many biographers astray and confuses the critics.

I have said that in publishing the First Folio, Heminges and Condell had planted the seed for an extraordinary, if belated, awakening of scholarly interest in the plays, but the repercussions of it were to spread much further afield.

By the time of Shakespeare's death in 1616, the theatre to which he had contributed so greatly was already in decline; in 1642 the playhouses were closed by government decree, and were to remain closed for the nineteen long years of the interregnum, during which time they fell into ruin and were demolished. The companies disbanded and, apart from occasional scratch performances in private houses, makeshift booths or taverns, theatrical activity came to an end. Much that is now obscure and confusing in Shakespeare's life story is directly attributable to this break in tradition. When, at his restoration in 1660, Charles II licensed the building of two new theatres in the capital, they were of a very different type from those that Shakespeare had known and written for, and his plays had only a fitful presence in them. When occasionally revived, it was usually in 'improved' (that is to say, mutilated) versions that their author would have had difficulty in recognising as his own.

It was not, then, principally through the theatre that the great upsurge of interest in, and admiration for, his plays was mediated, but rather through publication of a long and continuing series of revised, annotated editions of the First Folio, to which many of the most learned men of the late seventeenth and eighteenth centuries contributed. And as more popular versions of these proliferated in the nineteenth century (lacking notes but often lavishly illustrated by imagined scenes from the plays), the 'book', to which Jonson had recommended the reader to look rather than its author's portrait, came to occupy an honoured place beside the Bible in every Victorian home. And the higher that Shakespeare's reputation as poet and author rose to a pinnacle of universal praise as National Bard, patriotic spokesman, secular prophet and moral exemplar, the more desirable it became to distance him from his theatrical roots and from his occupation as player; while Baconian eccentrics balked at any such connection, these were simply passed over by the mass of biographers as an incidental circumstance of his social situation at a particular period of his life that he was soon to transcend. The tendency was to delay his adoption of the base trade to as late as possible and contrive his retirement from it as early as possible.

In 1908, Thomas Hardy, replying to an appeal for a donation to a Shakespeare memorial that was to take the form of a national theatre, was able to reply that he did not think that Shakespeare

appertains particularly to the theatrical world nowadays, if ever he did. His distinction as a minister of the theatre is infinitesimal beside his distinction as a poet, man of letters, and seer of life, and that his expression of himself was cast in the form of words for actors and not in the form of books to be read was an accident of his social circumstances that he himself despised.[13]

Recent scholarship, to which we are indebted for more detailed information about the theatrical conditions in which the plays were conceived and first performed than was previously available and, from the beginning of the twentieth century, the restoration to the plays in the theatre of a fuller, more accurate text and a better understanding and respect on the part of actors and directors for Shakespeare's intentions and methods in writing them, has gone some way to restore the balance. No one today would write about Shakespeare's plays without paying at least lip service to the theatrical context of their original creation or seek to deny (as Hardy did) its relevance to a more complete appreciation of them as works of art.

But the pattern of late entry to the players' profession and early retirement from it first set by Shakespeare's early biographers on the basis of imperfect knowledge and Warwickshire legend persists. And as the Droeshout engraving and the Stratford monument have continued to cast their baleful gaze over subsequent generations of readers, and a great, still burgeoning quantity of academic writing – ranging in quality from the brilliantly perceptive to the near-lunatic and barely comprehensible – has descended on the plays considered primarily as texts to be studied rather than as plays to be enjoyed, Shakespeare the player and man of the theatre has remained in the shadows. While literally millions of words have been devoted to authorial and textual problems, few have thought it worthwhile or necessary to treat in any detail of Shakespeare's consecutive career as player, or the possible ways in which his experience as an actor may have influenced his writing. The situation that confronted Heminges and Condell in 1623 has thus been exactly reversed. The unacknowledged dramatist whose reputation they sought to promote in face of scholarly neglect has come to occupy nearly all of the frame while the player and man of the theatre whose memory they revered is relegated to the margins.

Does any of this really matter? True, we do not know for certain how good a player Shakespeare was and, for the most part, can only conjecture as to the roles that he played. Again, the art of the actor, however accomplished, and the art of the theatre in general of which he was undoubtedly a master, are essentially ephemeral and, to that extent, beyond our recall. In these circumstances, it is not to be wondered at that his supreme achievement as dramatic poet, for which we have the firm evidence of the printed plays, is seen as of greater importance than any necessarily speculative estimate of his histrionic skills. But from an historical and biographical point of view, it is surely necessary to an adequate understanding of the period, the society in which he lived, and his place within it, to seek an authentic portrait of the man in the fullness of his being; and how can we hope to do this without taking due account of his professional occupation during much the greater part of his life – the occupation by which he was mainly known to his contemporaries? Rob a man of his profession or 'quality' (as the actor's profession was termed in his time) and you rob him of an essential part of his identity. And this is perhaps more true of the actor than anyone else. But there is another objection to those who regard Shakespeare's occupation as player as more or less peripheral to an appreciation of his genius as 'poet, man of letters, and seer of life'; for, in attempting to separate the two – the man from his works, the works from the context and original purpose of their creation – you distort and obscure the meaning of the works themselves.

Here, precisely, is the vacuum that lies at the heart of so much biographical and academic writing about Shakespeare, past and present. And how deeply alienating it can be to those who are brought to approach his plays for the first time in preparing for school examinations, when the incomparable music of his verses is reduced to numbered, chopped-up parcels of dead learning. 'Explain and discuss'!

Certainly, unless we place this fact of his occupation at the centre of our consideration of his life and works, we are left with an insoluble enigma; of how a well-educated but inexperienced young man from a small Warwickshire town with no theatrical background or training came to have such command of theatrical ways and means, such knowledge and understanding of the poetic and dramatic techniques of his predecessors and contemporaries as, in his earliest-known works, to have surpassed them in achievement and, in a few short years, gone on to write the greatest plays in the language.

To get to grips with the man himself, we have to go behind the literary legend, the invisible man of the Droeshout portrait and the Stratford monument; to make a big leap of historical imagination to put ourselves into that pre-literary, theatrical world that Shakespeare actually inhabited, when the words that he wrote in his London lodgings, or in the snatched intervals of repose on his visits home or on tour, were words to be acted, words for himself and his fellows to speak and be heard from a stage. This I attempt from the perspective of a fellow performer, a latter-day working actor, in the chapters that follow.

TWO

Killing the Calf

As all that is known with any degree of certainty concerning Shakespeare, is – *that he was born at Stratford upon Avon, – married and had children there, – went to London, where he commenced actor, and wrote poems and plays, – returned to Stratford, made his will, died, and was buried*, – I must confess my readiness to combat every unfounded supposition respecting the particular occurrences of his life.

George Steevens in a letter to Malone[1]

Half a century passed after Shakespeare's death before anyone thought it worthwhile to publish an account of his life. In the meantime, the country had been torn apart by civil war, the theatres closed and destroyed, and the world he had known turned upside down. The first such account (too brief to be described as anything more than a biographical sketch) was that of Thomas Fuller in his *History of the Worthies of England* (1662). Though Shakespeare's second daughter Judith had lived on until the Restoration, and there must then have been others in both Stratford and London who remembered him and would have been able to supply at least some outline of his early life and career, the normally assiduous Fuller appears to have taken little trouble to seek them out, and the half-page entry he devotes to Shakespeare in his *Worthies* is massively uninformative. He tells us correctly of his birth in Stratford but even the date of his death – for which he had only to glance at the monument in Holy Trinity church – is left a blank. In place of facts, he gives us generalities deriving from Jonson's eulogy about his natural genius and 'wood-notes wild'. Sketchy as it was, Fuller's account remained the primary source for subsequent biographical entries in the seventeenth century.

John Aubrey's random jottings, made around 1681, had to wait over two hundred years for publication as *Brief Lives*. They contain interesting scraps of information from various stages of Shakespeare's life but, though conscientiously recorded, they had come to him only at second or third hand and are not to be taken at their face value. For example, on a visit to Stratford he was told by one of the locals that Shakespeare was the son of a butcher and had occasionally taken a turn at his father's craft; 'when he killed a calf', his informant assured him, 'he would do it in high style and make a speech'. We know now that William's father, John Shakespeare, was in fact a glover by trade and in later life something of a general merchant in agricultural produce. That he was ever personally involved in the slaughter of cattle seems improbable, and that his young son was allowed to carry out the butchery himself (in whatever style) even less likely. Either Aubrey's informant was having him on, or had picked up and misunderstood a genuine tradition from an earlier time, in which the act of killing a calf was mimicked in pantomime, or shadow play behind a curtain, by travelling showmen; a trick that William may have seen at a fair and performed for the amusement of his family and neighbours. There is a record from 1521 in the household accounts of Princess Mary (then six years old) of a 'man of Windsor' being rewarded for 'killing of a calf before my Lady's grace behind a cloth'.[2] That the adult Shakespeare was familiar with it, we know from *Hamlet* where, in answer to Polonius' boast that at university he had acted Julius Caesar and been killed in the Capitol, he has Hamlet reply, 'It was a brute part of him to kill so capital a calf there' (III.ii.104) – an ironic anticipation of Polonius' death behind a cloth – the arras behind which he has hidden to overhear the scene between Hamlet and Gertrude and through which he is killed by Hamlet's rapier. Aubrey was seemingly unaware of this background to the story he tells: a testimony to his accuracy as a reporter but to nothing else. The anecdote contains a true statement but we have to put it back into its original context to know what it means.

To set the record straight, the slaughter of those animals whose skins were used in the glover's trade (mainly pigs and goats) was

the job of the butchers, whose shambles in Stratford was situated
in Middle Row. Schoenbaum suggests that it was in visiting his
uncle Henry's farm in Snitterfield that William may have
witnessed a scene that was to stay with him and return to his
mind in writing *Henry VI*.[3] Seeking an analogy to convey the
young king's distress at the arrest of 'good Duke Humphrey'
which has just taken place in his presence, and anticipating the
old man's fate, he has Henry say of him that,

> . . . as the butcher takes away the calf,
> And binds the wretch, and beats it when it strains,
> Bearing it to the bloody slaughter-house;
> Even so, remorseless, have they borne him hence;
> And as the dam runs lowing up and down,
> Looking the way her harmless young one went,
> And can do nought but wail her darling's loss;
> Even so myself bewails good Gloucester's case
> With sad unhelpful tears, and with dimm'd eyes
> Look after him, and cannot do him good . . .
>
> (2 *Henry VI*, III.i.210–19)

If, as I later suggest, he was to play the part of Henry himself,
these words would, at their first hearing, have come from his own
lips. A later speech in the same play takes us into the shambles
itself, for when Warwick is questioned about his suspicions as to
the identity of the murderers, he asks in reply,

> Who finds the heifer dead, and bleeding fresh,
> And sees fast by a butcher with an axe,
> But will suspect 'twas he that made the slaughter?

and goes on,

> Who finds the partridge in the puttock's nest,
> But may imagine how the bird was dead,
> Although the kite soar with unblooded beak?
>
> (III.ii.187–92)

It is recollections such as these from Shakespeare's upbringing in
a small country town, and observations from nature in the

countryside around it, that give life and substance to the more rhetorical passages in his early plays, and mark them as his own.

I need to say a little more at this point about William's father. Deriving from yeoman stock in the nearby village of Snitterfield, John Shakespeare had moved to Stratford in about 1550. As we have seen, he was a glover and wittawer (dresser of soft leather) by trade. In the town his business had prospered so well that in the course of a few years he had been able to buy land and property, including the house in Henley Street that William was later to inherit. In 1559 he had married Mary Arden, the daughter of a well-to-do local farmer with connections to a gentry family of the same name that could trace its Warwickshire roots to before the Norman conquest. William, their eldest son, had been born in April 1564; the day of the month is unknown, but he was baptised in the Stratford parish church of Holy Trinity on the 26th. By then, John had already recommended himself to the town elders as a suitable candidate for municipal office, and in 1557 was serving as ale-taster, the first of a series of minor posts that was to lead, in 1568, to his election as Bailiff or Mayor. Thereafter, he was always addressed as *Master* Shakespeare. Though he was Bailiff only for a year, and was not, like some of his fellow burgesses, re-elected to the office, he acted as Chamberlain (treasurer) in several years both before and after his mayoralty, and went on to serve the town as alderman for nearly two more decades.

We have no firm evidence relating to William's education. Biographers mainly assume that he attended the King's New School in Stratford, which occupied an upper chamber of the Guildhall (Plate 3). As tuition there was free to the sons of burgesses and it was not far from his home in Henley Street, it would have been the natural place for him to go. Contrary to anti-Stratfordian arguments, his schooling there would have been sufficient to provide at least an adequate basis for the classical learning he was later to exhibit in the plays. Ben Jonson, who is patronising in his eulogy about Shakespeare's 'small Latine and lesse Greek', is known to have completed a similar course at Westminster School. Though, exceptionally, Jonson may have stayed on at Westminster a year or two longer, the normal age at which boys destined to go into one of the crafts or professions

finished their grammar school education was fourteen or fifteen.
At this age, William would have found himself in Stratford
looking about for future employment. The year was 1578 or
1579.

Up to this time all had gone well with John Shakespeare and,
as late as 1575, we learn of his extending his property in Henley
Street by the purchase of an adjoining tenement with orchards
and gardens; but between September 1576 and January 1577
something occurred that was to throw the current of his life
completely off course. An application he had made to the College
of Heralds for a coat of arms as 'gentleman' – an honour to
which as former Bailiff of an incorporated town (one with a royal
charter) he was fully entitled – was unaccountably abandoned.
He was sued for debt, ceased to attend Council meetings, and
failed to respond to repeated demands for payment of various
dues and levies that were made upon him. Though treated with
exceptional leniency by his Council colleagues, their patience
finally ran out, and in 1586 two new aldermen were elected to
take his place and that of another defaulter, because they did not
'Come to the halles when they be warned nor hathe not done of
Longe tyme'.[4]

It would be tiresome to the reader to rehearse here the several
contradictory theories that have been advanced to account for
this dramatic change in John Shakespeare's fortunes. That they
were at least in part religious is suggested by his inclusion in a list
of those who failed to come monthly to church to receive
Communion as the law required, and more explicitly by the
discovery, after his death, of a 'spiritual testament' – a form of
Catholic devotion originally composed by St Charles Borromeo
of Milan – in the rafters of his Henley Street house. In this,
among other evidence of his attachment to proscribed beliefs and
forms of worship, he requests his friends and relations, 'lest by
reason of my sins I be to pass and stay a long while in Purgatory,
they will vouchsafe to assist and succour me with their holy
prayers and satisfactory works, especially with the holy sacrifice
of the Mass . . .'.[5] Printed copies of this document in English are
known to have been brought from Milan and distributed in
England by two Jesuit missionaries, Thomas Campion and
Robert Persons, and both men are known to have passed through
Warwickshire in 1580. Persons was entertained by Edward

Arden, then head of the Arden family, at Park Hall; Campion by Sir William Catesby at Lapworth, for which Catesby was arrested and imprisoned in the Fleet.

The Elizabethan era has often been depicted retrospectively in rosy hues, but the England in which William grew up was riven by deep divisions and uncertainties in which politics and religion had become disastrously entangled; a time of plots and rumours, fears of foreign invasion and mounting paranoia, in which the unprincipled prospered while men of conscience such as Edward Arden could end up with their head stuck on the end of a pike on Tower Bridge. If John Shakespeare was indeed sympathetic to the old religion of his youth, he was treading a dangerous path.

Traditional accounts of William's early life delay his entrance into the acting profession to as late as 1590, 'or a few years earlier', as one recent biographer vaguely puts it. But the craft of the player is not learnt in a day or even in a few years – a fact of which biographers in general and academics in particular appear blissfully unaware. In proposing that a mature young man in his middle twenties, with no previous training or experience, could come from the background I have indicated and, by 1592, advanced to a point where Henry Chettle (a man thoroughly versed in the ways of the theatre) could describe him in print as 'exelent in the qualitie he professes' (that of a player), and to have acquired a 'facetious grace in writting, that aprooves his Art',[6] is to assume the impossible. It betrays both a degree of contempt for the player's art and total disregard of theatrical conditions in the period, when the normal, if not invariable, routes of entry to the profession were either by patrimonial inheritance or apprenticeship at an early age (between ten and sixteen) to a senior member, usually a 'sharer', in one of the existing companies.

Richard Burbage followed his father into the Queen's men. Edward Alleyn is said by Fuller in his *Worthies* to have been 'bred a Stage-player'; his father was a London innkeeper and he may have begun his acting career playing minor roles with the companies that had used the inn for their performances. If we look at the list of 'Principall Actors in all these Playes' printed by Heminges and Condell at the front of their 1623 edition of Shakespeare's *Works* (shown in Plate 1), we find that all those named of whose beginnings we have any information were involved in the apprenticeship system in one way or another – as masters or apprentices. Nicholas Tooley was Burbage's apprentice. In his will of 1605, Augustine Phillips bequeathed a legacy to Samuel Gilburne, 'my late apprentice'. John Rice was John Heminges' boy when, in 1607, he performed for James I at a Merchant Taylors' dinner; Alexander Cooke also acknowledged Heminges as his master. Robert Gough is first recorded playing a female role in *The Seven Deadly Sins* in about 1590/1; Thomas Pope, who remembered Gough in his will of 1603, was probably his master. Robert Armin had begun as apprentice to a London goldsmith and is reputed to have been encouraged as a 'wag' by Queen Elizabeth's jester and player, Tarlton, who prophesied that he should 'enjoy my clownes sute after me', which in course of time he did. Of the twenty-six actors named, only William Ostler, Nathan Field, John Underwood and Richard Robinson are known to have entered the profession in any other way, and that was as singing boys in one of the royal chapels or children's companies.[7] Nor is there a single player in the whole period known to have been accepted into any of the companies in his early to middle twenties without previous training or experience, as is supposed of Shakespeare.

If apprenticeship was the normal pattern of recruitment for those boys and adolescents who had not been 'bred to the stage', as the evidence suggests, there is no reason to believe that Shakespeare, for all his later renown as poet and dramatist, would, as a player, have been treated any differently to other boys of his class and education, or would not have been obliged to climb the same arduous ladder to advancement.

The hoary legend of the young Shakespeare stealing a deer from the park of Sir Thomas Lucy and so arousing the enmity of its owner that he was 'oblig'd to leave his Business and Family in Warwickshire, for some time, and shelter himself in London', as propagated by Nicholas Rowe in 1709,[8] was demolished by Edmond Malone in his uncompleted *Life* published by Boswell in 1821;[9] that it survives at all in subsequent biographies may be due to its usefulness in absolving authors from the painful task of explaining how it came about that the gentle Shakespeare they like to depict could have brought himself to abandon his wife and young family without visible means of support in pursuance of his late-developing histrionic ambitions. But of course there is no real evidence that he did anything of the kind. The dates of his marriage to Anne Hathaway and births of their three children have no relevance to the time of his first departure from Stratford. 'All they prove', as John Dover Wilson pointed out, 'is that he must have been at home about August 1582, nine months before the birth of Susanna; in November of the same year for his marriage; and once again in the early summer of 1584, nine months before the birth of the twins', and, because it was in the summer that plays were normally suspended in London because of the plague, 'the dates referred to do not at all forbid us supposing Shakespeare to have been already a professional player at this period'.[10] Indeed, the fact of his marriage in 1582 gives added support to the hypothesis I am putting forward, for whereas it is easily understandable that an unencumbered boy of fifteen or sixteen should have entered the profession of his choice after completing his grammar school education a year or so earlier, as was normal in the period, it is far from easy to envisage circumstances that might have induced him to do so as a mature young man with family responsibilities.

Nor was there any lack of opportunity for him to have taken that step at the earlier age, for companies of players had been visiting Stratford from 1569 onwards, when he was five, and continued to come there throughout the whole period of his boyhood and adolescence. As troubles came upon him from 1576 onwards, John Shakespeare would have had good reason for wishing his son away from the town and, as alderman and justice, he was ideally placed to facilitate his engaging himself to one of their senior men. For we know that all such players' apprenticeships – whether effected by a simple contract of service or more formal indentures requiring the seal of some regulatory third party[11] – were concluded, not with the company as a constituent body, but with an individual 'sharer' by agreement of his fellows. For the sharers – those who had invested in the company's capital stock of costumes, props and playbooks – '*were* the company, and all the others in the troupe merely their employees'.[12] It is true that no record survives of William having been apprenticed in this way; nor are we given any later hint as to the company or player concerned, the payment of a premium, or the nature and term of his engagement. But neither are we afforded any other reliable information about him at the time and, if William's recruitment and subsequent life as an apprentice player remains a blank, the same is true of the vast majority of other boys of his age recruited into one or other of the numerous companies of players then on the road. By examining the Stratford records of those companies known to have visited the town in the period, it may however still be possible, by process of elimination, to arrive at a working hypothesis as to the one he had joined, and that in turn may lead us to the identity of the player whose responsibility it would have been to instruct him in the rudiments of his craft. Though based only in probabilities, such an investigation is unlikely to remain for long in the dark for, by following the footsteps of that company and player through their subsequent histories so far as these are known to us, we shall be able to test our conjectures by the destination to which they take us. If they bring us to a point where Shakespeare is known to have been when he first emerges from obscurity to public notice in the early 1590s, we shall have confirmation that we have been on the right track from the start. Even if it should later transpire that we have taken a wrong turning in the course of the journey, the attempt will still have been worth making if it suggests a more credible alternative – a more possible process of climbing – than the impossible leap to eminence with which we are usually presented.

THREE

The Apprentice

. . . when we find a man of thirty already near the top of his particular tree, we must assume some previous climbing.

John Dover Wilson[1]

The date at which troupes of travelling players first included Stratford in their itineraries is not precisely known but, interestingly, the first such visitors to be recorded came there in 1568/9,[2] the year in which John Shakespeare served as Bailiff. Was he instrumental in bringing them there?

The first to arrive were the Queen's players – not the more famous company brought together by Walsingham in 1583 of which Richard Tarlton, Elizabeth's jester, was the star attraction – but an earlier troupe she had inherited from Edward VI and Queen Mary of which little is known. That was in the summer of 1569. A month or so later came Worcester's men, who looked for protection as patron to William Somerset who had succeeded to his title as third earl of Worcester in 1548 and lived until 1589. Protection was needed from the vagrancy laws and within a few years was to become an absolute necessity with the passing of the Act for the Punishment of Vagabonds in 1572 which, among other things, laid down that 'all Fencers Bearewards Comon Players in Enterludes & Minstrels, not belonging to any Baron of this Realme or towards any other honorable Personage of greater Degree . . . shalbee taken adjudged and deemed Roges Vacabounds and Sturdy Beggers . . . to be grevously whipped'.[3]

The procedure followed by the players on their arrival in incorporated towns where they hoped to perform, is well set out by a man called Willis, written much later when he was aged seventy-five but relating back to the time of his boyhood in the late 1560s or early '70s in Gloucester.

> In the City of Gloucester the manner is (as I think it is in other like corporations) that when Players of Enterludes come to towne, they first attend the Mayor to enforme him what noblemans servants they are, and so to get licence for their publike playing; and if the Mayor like the Actors, or would shew respect to their Lord and Master, he appoints them to play their first play before himselfe and the Aldermen and common Counsell of the City; and that is called the Mayors play, where every one that will comes in without money, the Mayor giving the players a reward as hee thinks fit to shew respect unto them. At such a play, my father tooke me with him and made mee stand betweene his leggs, as he sate upon one of the benches, where wee saw and heard very well.[4]

Normally, as at both Gloucester and Stratford, the 'mayor's play' was given in the 'town house' or guildhall. As we shall discover later, admission to this first performance was not everywhere free to the public as Willis tells us it was in Gloucester, and in many towns even councillors were expected to contribute to the reward. If the play was approved and received a licence, further public performances followed – usually in the guildhall as before or, if that was not available, in a nearby inn. At these subsequent shows, attendance was charged in the form of a 'gathering' to which everyone present was expected to contribute.

At the tender age of five, the young Shakespeare may have been too young to stand between his father's legs as Willis had done; but as the Queen's and Worcester's men were succeeded by Leicester's in 1573 and Warwick's in 1575, we can be reasonably sure he was there in the Guildhall (with or without his father) to see and enjoy their plays.

From the point of view of William's joining one of these companies, the crucial period is between 1577 when he was thirteen and starting his last year or two of studies at the King's school, and 1580 when he was sixteen and had already left. Worcester's and Leicester's men were both to make return visits to the town in 1575/6, and Worcester's were there again at or around Christmas 1577 and at the same time of year in 1580.

Derby's came in 1578/9, and three other companies – those of Lord Strange, Lord Berkeley and the Countess of Essex – in that or the following year. Of these six, three can be eliminated fairly easily. The visit of Leicester's troupe (probably in October 1576) is a little too early as William would then have been only twelve, and it was not to return until 1586/7, which is far too late. Berkeley's makes only rare appearances in the records elsewhere and sinks from view altogether in the vital period between 1586/7 and 1597. The Countess of Essex had inherited a company of players on her husband's death as recently as September 1576, but this is unlikely to have survived for long after 1579 when her secret marriage to Leicester was revealed to the Queen.[5] At first sight, the related troupes of the Earl of Derby and that of his son and heir, Ferdinando Lord Strange, offer the most promising alternatives as William's choice of company because of the connection with Strange's that he is known to have had in the early 1590s at the Rose and elsewhere; but Derby's men were to go into limbo in the upheavals of 1583, and the Strange's company of 1590–2 had little, if any, connection (apart from its patron) with the one that had visited Stratford and, in the 1580s, appears to have specialised in acrobatic displays at court for the Queen.

This leaves only Worcester's men, which is usually dismissed as being merely a provincial company in the period, its first recorded London appearance being not until 1602. But this early provincial status accords very well with the fact of Shakespeare's obscurity during his apprentice years, and though we lack all knowledge of its repertoire of plays – a particular loss in that Shakespeare in the decade of the 1580s is likely to have contributed to it, if only by way of revisions – we know a good deal of its personnel and history in the years immediately ahead. Moreover, while the visits to the town of Essex's, Derby's and Strange's men recorded above were unique in the period, Worcester's were there on no fewer than six occasions between 1569 and 1584, so there was ample opportunity for John Shakespeare and his eldest son to have made the acquaintance and established personal relations with their leading men, including William's future 'master'.[6]

There is another important factor to be considered. Though, as Dover Wilson correctly discerned, the dates of Shakespeare's marriage and of the births of his children tell us nothing about the time of his *first* departure from Stratford, the fact that it was during the period of William's youth and early manhood that he met with, courted and finally married Anne Hathaway, giving her three children before 1586, does require that he remained in those years near enough to his home town to have paid fairly regular visits to it, and specifically to have been there in the summer of 1582 and again in 1584. Worcester's are the only one of the six troupes I have named whose movements would have enabled him to fulfil this requirement. The two Stanley companies of Derby and Lord Strange ranged particularly widely and spent much of their time in the north, especially the north-west, where the earl and his heir kept palatinate state in their manors of Lathom, Knowsley and New Park. Derby's men (as patronised by Henry Stanley, the fourth earl) disappear from the records in 1583, and Strange's (apart from their tumbling at court) were to make only intermittent visits to the south after that date until their amalgamation with the Admiral's in about 1590/1.

It is possible that William joined Worcester's men on their third visit to the town in 1577, but he was then only thirteen and we should allow him a little more time both to complete his education and get to know Anne. The company were performing in Coventry on 22 November 1580, and were in Stratford, probably for Christmas in that year, when William was sixteen. The most probable course of events is that he joined them then, having already paid court to Anne; that he consummated his betrothal to her in the summer of 1582, and returned to marry her later that year.

The impression of hurry and confusion that the records of their marriage produces – that the final date for posting the banns before the prohibited Christmas season was missed; that a special licence was thus required; that the application for it was made, not by the bridegroom as was usual, but by friends of the bride; and the clerk's mistake in confusing Anne Hathaway of Shottery with Anne Whately of Temple Grafton – is more readily explained by the simple circumstance of William's having been away from Stratford on tour when Anne's pregnancy became apparent, and his thus having to hurry home for the wedding ceremony as soon as he could, than by any of the more involved and romantic theories that have so far been advanced. We know that Worcester's men were in Coventry in 1582, though we are given no indication of the month.[7] As no evidence survives of where or exactly when the wedding took place, it is equally possible that Anne travelled to join him elsewhere in the diocese. (Stratford lay within the diocese of Worcester, whose bishop had granted the special licence.)

Moving forward, their first child was baptised in Holy Trinity church on 26 May 1583. William is unlikely to have been able to join in the celebrations, but we know that the company was at Stratford at some time in the following year, so he would have seen his daughter Susanna then, if not before. The company was recorded at Gloucester on 22 December 1583, at Leicester after 6 March 1584, and in Coventry also in 1584. If the players came from Leicester or Coventry to Stratford in April or May, that would be consistent with the birth of the twins in February 1585.[8] I am not intending to suggest that these were the *only* occasions when Shakespeare visited Stratford in the years immediately following his marriage to Anne – there were slack times in the company's year, as in Lent, and even apprentices were allowed occasional holidays – but simply to demonstrate that he was there (or could have been there) at those times when the subsequent births of his children require him to have been. Our conjectures having taken us thus far, let us now look a little more closely at Worcester's company in the period to discover who his fellows would have been and, if possible, the identity of the senior man among them to whom he was apprenticed.

At Southampton in June 1577, we are told that the company comprised ten men (sharers); and in the course of a contretemps with the Mayor of Leicester in March 1584, a licence was produced from the Earl of Worcester, dating from January of the previous year, in which they were named as Robert Browne, James Tunstall, Edward Alleyn, William Harryson, Thomas Cooke, Richard Johnes (Jones), Edward Browne and Rychard Andrewes. (Two others, not named in the licence – William Pateson and Thomas Powlton – are also mentioned and make up the complement of ten men referred to at Southampton.) As usual in such records, their apprentices and any hired men or other functionaries they had taken with them on tour were ignored.[9]

Of the ten sharers, two names immediately stand out: Robert Browne and Edward Alleyn. Browne, whose name is given first and may be taken therefore as the leader, was to achieve a European reputation as pioneer, from 1590 onwards, of the tours of English players to Germany and the Low Countries; Alleyn was soon to be recognised as the most accomplished player of his generation. Though some eighteen months younger than Shakespeare and only sixteen at the date of the 1583 patent, his listing in third place among the sharers is indicative of a remarkable and precocious talent. Richard Jones was later to accompany Browne to the continent, but little is known of the others. If Shakespeare was apprenticed to Browne as is probable, he is likely to have learnt as much, if not more, from the junior but already experienced Alleyn.

In the absence in the period of any other form of training, apprentices learnt on the job, playing minor roles in which they were coached by their masters, learning to fence, dance and play a variety of instruments, as well as making themselves generally useful on tour in the way that 'acting ASMs' were expected to do until comparatively recent times. Then, their duties would have included packing and unpacking the cart with props and costumes, setting out the benches for performances, providing refreshments for their masters and helping them with their changes. In Leicester, the players having defied a ban on their performing that night at their inn, 'went with their drum & trumppytts thorowe the Towne'.[10]

The young Shakespeare was to stay with Worcester's men for four or five years. And all that while he was learning the basics of his craft as a player – slowly and painfully as any such process of trial and error must be, but also, I am sure, with enthusiasm and a sense of joyful discovery. Like a present-day drama student thrown in at the deep end of a hectic repertory season or fit-up tour (but much less well equipped from a technical point of view), it would have been largely a matter of sink or swim. He might have had a similar experience in any number of companies, but could have chosen much worse than Worcester's, with the capable Browne as his mentor and Alleyn as model. Though sometimes today unjustly characterised as old-fashioned in his style of acting as contrasted with the later Burbage, Alleyn was no barnstormer and, among his many qualities as a player, the one that writers of his time picked out most often for comment was his exceptional grace of movement and speech.

We have no record whatever of the company's repertoire of plays at this time, though they would doubtless have included historical moralities of a similar kind to Tarlton's *Seven Deadly Sins* and the anonymous *Knack to Know a Knave*. We can be sure that William was already thinking he could do very much better and testing himself out in that way. At the same time, he was discovering England. I picture a sixteen-year-old lad on a cart, growing year by year into manhood, journeying out of the Arden of his childhood into ever more unfamiliar, distant regions, travelling ill-made roads in all weathers, sleeping in inns, hearing and memorising strange new dialects and forms of speech, meeting with every possible type and character of person; learning, most of all perhaps, from the audiences to which he played in guildhalls and inns: their varied responses, likes and dislikes, what 'held' and what did not, along with the more arcane mysteries of the player in holding successfully the mirror up to nature. From the very partial records that survive – and apart from its regular visits to the Midland towns of Stratford, Coventry, Gloucester and Leicester, as already noted – we find the company at Plymouth and Abingdon (Oxon) in 1580/1; Bridgwater (Somerset) on 19 September 1581 and 30 July 1582; Ipswich and Southampton in 1581/2; and Norwich, Doncaster and Hythe (Kent) in 1582/3.

It was no tired, cynical collection of old hacks that Shakespeare had joined, but a young, impetuous band of players with their future before them. Browne was still near the beginnings of his distinguished career; Ned Alleyn was only fourteen in 1580. Impatient no doubt of the ponderous deliberations of mayors and aldermen, their defiance of the Leicester mayor in 1584, when they had played at their inn in despite of his ban (for which they had later to apologise and eat humble pie), was not the first or only such brush they had with civic authority in the course of their travels. In spite of pleas to the mayors involved that their disputatious behaviour should not be reported to their patron, the earl of Worcester, word of it may eventually have reached him. For having visited Stratford again in 1584, Maidstone in 1584/5, and made the long journey to York in 1585, the company appears to have been disbanded, and nothing more is heard of it until 1589, when the third earl died and was succeeded by his son. In the meantime, at least five of its former sharers – Robert and Edward Browne, Ned Alleyn, Tunstall and Jones – were recruited by Lord Charles Howard of Effingham on his appointment by the Queen as Lord High Admiral in 1585, and from thenceforward were known as Admiral's men. As Shakespeare would still have had a year or two of his apprenticeship to serve (the normal term for a youth of his age was seven years), he would almost certainly have gone with them. He would thus have entered upon the most exciting and fruitful of his apprentice years that were to have a profound effect on his development as both player and playwright.

FOUR

Admiral's Man

It is extremely likely that he [Shakespeare] acted in
Marlowe's plays, and developed much of his own power
by learning Marlowe by heart.

Peter Levi[1]

We have only to look at the repertoire associated with the
Admiral's men in the years between 1585 and 1590 to
realise its significance for Shakespeare's biography; for among
many other less familiar titles, we find Kyd's *The Spanish Tragedy*
and three of Marlowe's plays: both parts of *Tamburlaine the Great*
and *The Jew of Malta*. As performances of all four plays are
believed to pre-date, and to have influenced the writing of
Shakespeare's early plays, and none was published before 1590
(*Tamburlaine* in that year, the *Spanish Tragedy* in 1592, and the
Jew of Malta not until 1633), it is axiomatic that he could only
have seen and heard them in the theatre.[2] But for them to have
impressed themselves on his mind in the way they did, how much
more probable it is that he had *acted* in them. And if he had acted
in them, he could only have done so as an Admiral's man. (I
return to this point, and to a consideration of the parts he played
in them, later in the chapter.)

In June 1585, the newly constituted company were in Dover,
Folkestone and Hythe, and on 6 January 1586 played at court for
the Queen. They then set out on a long tour that was to take
them, among other towns, to Ipswich (on 20 February),
Cambridge, Coventry, Leicester, Folkestone, Faversham and
Hythe.[3] In January 1587, the Admiral's were reported by an
agent of Secretary Walsingham, along with the Queen's,
Leicester's and Oxford's men, as posting their bills in the City of

London every day of the week, 'so that when the bells toll to the Lecturer, the trumpets sound to the stages to the Joy of the wicked faction of Rome'.[4] In May of that year they were back in Ipswich (a favourite port of call), Coventry and Leicester, as also at Norwich, York, Southampton, Exeter and Bath.[5]

In November 1587, a tragic accident occurred during a City performance of the second part of *Tamburlaine*, when a misfired pistol killed a pregnant woman and a child in the audience and 'hurt another man in the head very soore'. (The scene in question was identified by Chambers as the execution of the Governor of Babylon in *2 Tamburlaine*, V.i.)[6] This disaster may have resulted in a suspension of the company's activities. Needless to say, the Puritans made the most of it as a sign of God's displeasure and, apart from two court performances in the holiday season of 1588/9, there are no further records of the Admiral's men in London or on tour until November 1589, when they were to reappear at Ipswich. I believe it was during this long interval that Shakespeare – released from the pressures of daily performance and constant travel – began work on the first of his own acknowledged plays, and may have returned to Stratford in order to do so.

In his induction to *Bartholomew Fair* of 1614, Ben Jonson was to link *Titus Andronicus* with *Jeronimo* (an alternative title for Kyd's *Spanish Tragedy*) as, in the opinion of the type of playgoer who sticks to his own views come what may, 'the best plays yet', a judgement that 'hath stood still these five and twenty, or thirty years'.[7] If interpreted literally, this would take *Titus* back to between 1584 and 1589. And that it was written for the Admiral's men is indicated by the nature of its leading role, for if ever a role was tailor-made for Alleyn, it was Titus. He dominates the play in the same way that Hieronimo dominates the *Spanish Tragedy*, or Tamburlaine (another Alleyn role) the Marlowe plays. It is a part that demands of any actor who undertakes it a bravura performance, and Alleyn was then emerging as the finest actor of his day. But if Jonson's double-edged compliment to *Titus* and *Jeronimo* in *Bartholomew Fair* should suggest that the kind of dominance required was of the exaggerated, ranting style to be parodied by Hamlet as 'out-heroding Herod', it should be remembered that Jonson himself, in a later epigram addressed to Alleyn, compares him to the two men of classical times who, in the period, represented an ideal of excellence in acting, 'skilful Roscius and grave Aesop', and tells him he is one,

> Who both their graces in thy self hast more
> Out-stript than they did all that went before:
> And present worth in all dost so contract
> As others speak, but only thou dost act.[8]

The influence that Alleyn (Plate 7) had upon Elizabethan acting in general has yet to be fully acknowledged. He did more than anyone else to raise it to the level from which the acting of Shakespeare's great tragic heroes was later to become possible for Burbage.[9]

If *Titus Andronicus* was regarded by Jonson as between twenty-five and thirty years old in 1614, and was written by Shakespeare for Alleyn and the Admiral's men, a date for its composition of 1587/8 appears likely, though because of the temporary disgrace into which the company had fallen, and a consequent depletion in its ranks, it may not have been performed before 1589/90.[10]

The Taming of the *Shrew* was once thought to have been a revision by Shakespeare of an anonymous play published in 1594 as *The Taming of* **a** *Shrew*; but, since the 1920s, scholars have been gradually coming round to the opposite view: that Shakespeare's play was written first, and that the one with the indefinite article in its title was a pirated version of Shakespeare's original – a 'memorial reconstruction' put together by a group of players who had acted in it some time before. In a closely reasoned introduction to his Arden edition of 1981, Brian Morris has persuasively argued for a date prior to 1592, and proposes 1589, which would make it the first of Shakespeare's comedies. In line with the earlier date I have given for Shakespeare's departure from Stratford, I would take the play back a year or two more, and thus roughly contemporary with the writing of *Titus*.

For its main plot, the *Shrew* draws on traditional stories that would have been familiar to Shakespeare from an early age; and for its subplot, the wooing of Bianca by Lucentio, it is clear he made use of Ariosto's Italian comedy, *I Suppositi*, as translated by George Gascoigne in 1566. In the induction to the play, a tinker called Christopher Sly, who tells us he is 'old Sly's son of

Burton-heath' is discovered in a drunken stupor; Barton-on-the-Heath is an actual village some sixteen miles out of Stratford, where Shakespeare's aunt, Joan Lambert, lived. For a joke, Sly is put to bed in an inn and, when he wakes up, treated as if he were a lord who had dreamed what he believes to have been his former life as a tinker. Meantime, a band of players arrives and agrees to entertain Sly with a play – the *Taming of the Shrew* – the plot of which is itself driven by a whole series of pretended changes of identity.

It would have been wholly in the spirit of the comedy for Shakespeare to have taken the character's surname from the actor who played him, William Sly, a member of the combined Admiral's/Strange's company from about 1590, who was later to join the Chamberlain's men with Shakespeare and to feature (in ninth place) in the First Folio list of 'Principall Actors in all these Playes'. (See Plate 5: there were Slys in Stratford as well as in London, but William was probably a descendant of the John Slye who had led one of Henry VIII's companies of interluders in the 1520s.)[11] So, in the final analysis, Sly is neither Christopher the tinker nor the lord that everyone pretends him to be in the play, but William Sly the player, purporting to be both – a theme of confusions of identity to which Shakespeare would return and put to a variety of uses. That the Second Player in the Induction – who would have doubled a part, probably the Tailor, in the play-within-a-play – was acted by John Sincler is clearly established by the prefix 'Sinklo', his usual nickname, that Shakespeare gives to his solitary line. We are to meet with him again in *Henry VI*, and it is interesting to find that several other players can be identified by Shakespeare's use of their forenames or abbreviated surnames as having future connections with the Admiral's men.[12] There can be little doubt that Petruchio was written for Alleyn and first played by him, but we can only guess at the part that Shakespeare took for himself. In 1587 he was twenty-three. I give him Lucentio because he opens the play proper and is there at the end to speak the final line – something that he liked to do, as many later and surer instances will show.

We should not overlook that 1588 was the year of the Armada, or that in 1587 the company's patron, Lord Howard, had been appointed by the Queen as supreme commander of the country's naval defences. In the frenzy of preparations to repel the Spanish invaders – reaching inland even to Stratford with the mustering of the trained bands – theatrical activity generally came to a halt. It was in an atmosphere of patriotic fervour, engendered first by the threat of the Armada and then by the scale and completeness of its destruction, that Shakespeare conceived and put into execution his ambitious plan for a series of plays that were to focus, not on one heroic figure from ancient history, as *Tamburlaine* and his own *Titus* had done, but on a 'quasi-Biblical' story of England 'from the original sin of Henry IV to the grand redemption of the Tudors'.[13] Their theme – as dramatised from the chronicles he was reading, especially Hall's – would have struck home to his contemporaries as highly relevant to the turbulent times through which they were living; that 'as by discord great thynges decaie and fall to ruine, so the same by concord be revived and erected', and England 'by union and agrement releved pacified and enriched'.[14]

But when the London playhouses reopened and touring resumed in September 1588, the Admiral's – with exception of the two court performances already mentioned (in December 1588 and February 1589) – remained in the doldrums; and while Shakespeare may reasonably be conjectured as working on the three parts of his *Henry VI* – perhaps with financial support from Alleyn – his fellows would have had to look elsewhere for their bread. Only Alleyn at this time appears to have had access to a ready supply of money. In January 1589 he purchased from Richard Jones (one of Worcester's men who had transferred to the Admiral's) his share in the company's stock of costumes and playbooks, which up to that time had been held on an equal basis with John Alleyn and Robert Browne, and the transaction was witnessed by another former Worcester sharer, James Tunstall. John Alleyn was Edward's elder brother, and was not a player. He is described in the bill of sale as 'citizen and inholder of London', and is said elsewhere to have 'dwelt with my very good lord, Charles Heawarde'. Chambers suggests that it may have been through him that Edward and his fellows of Worcester's company had come to be Admiral's men in the first place. If so, he may well have continued to act as intermediary between his brother and Howard, and to have supplied the cash, either from his own pocket or Howard's, that enabled Edward to make the above and other purchases that followed. As no new sharers are named as having been admitted, he appears to have been taking advantage of a difficult period in the company's history to draw financial control of its capital resources (and thus of its future profits) into his own hands.[15]

We know that by late October or early November 1589, the company had resumed playing in the City; for when, on 5 November, an order went out from the Lord Mayor that all the companies then in the City should cease playing because of the Martin Marprelate controversy – a pamphlet war between pro- and anti-theatre factions – the Admiral's were named as one of the companies affected. Robert Browne may also have sold out to Alleyn at this time, and one or two others may have done the same. Browne was in Holland in 1590. When the company reappears in provincial records, they were at Ipswich, a port often used by players travelling to the Low Countries. Alleyn and the others may have accompanied their former leader so far and given two farewell performances with him to raise money for his travel expenses.[16] The company's subsequent appearances at court on 28 December, 'shewinge certen feates of activitie' (an acrobatic display by the apprentices), and on 3 March with a play, was probably a reward for their prompt compliance with the closure order of 5 November (which a newly reconstituted Strange's had defied), and marks a return to favour in which their patron Howard may have been instrumental.[17]

From 1590, however, we find them working ever more closely with Strange's, and this may reflect the loss of Browne, Jones, perhaps others. But the subsequent confusion in the records of both City and provincial appearances – where the company is sometimes named as Strange's, sometimes as the Admiral's or Alleyn's, and sometimes as a combination of the two – can only be explained if we assume (with Chambers) a virtual amalgamation of which Alleyn was leader and principal player.[18]

There was in these years a good deal of fluctuation in the personnel of the companies generally. The formerly prestigious Leicester's men had been dissolved on the death of their patron in 1588, a year which also saw the passing of Richard Tarlton and the start of a steady decline in the fortunes of the Queen's men. The alliance of the Admiral's and Strange's – the latter strengthened by a number of experienced recruits from Leicester's including George Bryan and Thomas Pope – was thus enabled by 1590 to take prime position as the most popular and successful of all the noblemen's companies then on the road, in the City, or at court.

It was to achieve its finest hour at the Rose in 1592; but, in the meantime, Shakespeare would have rejoined his fellows and brought with him completed manuscripts of an early version of *Titus* (with its splendid new role for Alleyn) and the three parts of *Henry VI* to add to the company's repertoire. By 1588, he would have reached his twenty-fourth year and attained his freedom as a player. As he is unlikely at that time to have had the means to buy himself into the privileged position of sharer (had Alleyn been willing to admit him, which is far from certain), he would then have been employed as a 'hired man' or journeyman player on a small but regular salary. But whatever his status, with some seven years' solid acting experience behind him, he is likely to have been cast in increasingly important parts.

I give my reasons in the following chapter for believing that among these roles was the young king of the title in *Henry VI*. There is no obvious part for Alleyn (unless it was Talbot in Part One), but with availability of the additional forces brought to the alliance from Strange's, there would be no shortage of experienced men to take the many other good parts that the plays offer. (With Titus, Tamburlaine and Hieronimo among his roles in the current repertoire, Alleyn would doubtless have welcomed an occasional 'play out' and a rest.)

Many of the Strange's men and their apprentices would have been new to Shakespeare in 1590, but that in writing the plays he had had in mind for the smaller parts some familiar fellows from the Admiral's is evident in his use of their first names or nicknames in the stage directions and speech prefixes of Parts Two and Three that eventually were to find their way into the First Folio.

'Bevis' of Part Two is otherwise unknown; but John Holland who plays a short scene with him as a fellow rebel in IV. ii is named in a 'plot' (a synopsis of scenes and characters posted backstage as an *aide-mémoire* for the actors) of Tarlton's *Seven Deadly Sins*, of which a single performance was to be given at the Rose on 6 March 1592.[19] In Part Three, the Messenger of I.ii.47 is assigned to 'Gabriel', and the Keepers of III.i to 'Sinklo' and 'Humfry'. 'Gabriel' was almost certainly Gabriel Spencer,

'Sinklo' a nickname for John Sincler (whom we have already encountered in the *Shrew*), and 'Humfry', a man called Humphrey Jeffes.[20] Like Holland, Sincler was to remain with the company, and went on to become the thin-faced actor of the Chamberlain's men, but there is no further trace of either Spencer or Jeffes in the English records between 1592 and 1597. We know, however, that Robert Browne, having returned from his first, exploratory trip to the continent in 1590, was to set out again with a full company of players for Germany in February 1592, for which he obtained a passport from the Admiral. The passport names Browne, Richard Jones, two others whose names are previously unknown (John Bradstreet and Thomas Sackville) '*avec leurs consortz*', and Howard refers to them collectively as '*mes Joueurs et serviteurs*' ('my players and servants').[21] The probability is that Spencer, Humphrey Jeffes and his brother Anthony (recorded in Germany in 1595) were included in the party as '*consortz*'. On their return to England in 1597, these three rejoined the Admiral's, and Spencer was to be killed in a duel with Ben Jonson in 1598.[22]

But in the meantime, the Admiral's company would have been left decidedly weak in numbers in relation to Strange's – especially as regards the proportion of senior men among them. By early 1593, when all the London theatres were closed by the plague and application was made to the Privy Council for a new licence for the company to travel, Alleyn was the only remaining Admiral's man to be so distinguished in a list of its sharers. At what precise point the combined company became, in effect, Strange's, and whether, or to what extent, Shakespeare transferred his allegiance from the Admiral to Strange is unknown. As his status was still that of a hired man, he may easily have come to feel somewhat out on a limb.

Having sketched the history of the Admiral's men so far, and indicated how Shakespeare's early plays may have come into being in the years between 1585 and 1590, it is time to look more closely at his contribution to the company's work as an actor, and to do this we shall need to retrace our steps a little. For if, as I suggested earlier, Shakespeare's identity as player is the key to a fuller understanding of him as a person and historical figure, the more we can learn of the parts that he played, both in other men's plays and his own, the more surely we can dispel those mists of invisibility that veil him from our view, and the nearer we can hope to get to the man himself.

One or two more or less reliable traditions of his later roles survive that we shall be examining in due course, and we have an important clue in some lines of John Davies of Hereford as to his playing 'Kingly parts'; but an actor, however talented, does not begin his career by playing kings or any other such leading roles. If he is to 'discover himself' in the sense of learning by trial and error the nature and limits of his particular gifts, and so attain that mastery of his craft we know that Shakespeare came to possess (for Aubrey tells us on good authority that he 'did act exceedingly well'),[23] he requires above all else the opportunity of essaying a large variety of roles in as many different plays.

I have said that Shakespeare's familiarity with Kyd's *Spanish Tragedy* and several of Marlowe's plays (evident in his recollections of them in *Titus*, the *Shrew*, and the *HenryVI/Richard III* tetralogy) is more likely to derive from his having acted in those plays than in any other way as, of them all, only *Tamburlaine* had been published before 1592. This being so, the possibility arises that, by a close study of the sources of his recollections, we may be able to arrive at some knowledge of the particular parts that he played in the course of his apprenticeship and early career.

Actors' powers of recall are of several kinds and operate at varying levels of efficiency. The actor with visual memory is able to memorise his lines with remarkable speed and accuracy, and may even be able to tell you on what page of his written text they occur and their position on the page. Aural memory is by far the more common. Performing in a play brings to the actor a general familiarity with the text as a whole – for even while changing or resting off-stage, he needs to give half an ear to what is being spoken on stage if he is not to miss his entrance cues, though he is unlikely to be able to reproduce it with any great accuracy.[24] However, the lines of the part he is playing, having been committed to memory by dint of constant, spoken repetition in private study and rehearsal and subjected to that process of mimetic identification whereby the actor seeks to make them his own, may become integral to his personal thought processes and imagining, and the longer he continues to perform the part, the deeper they reach. In the receptive mind of a young player-poet like Shakespeare, the more familiar they become, the more likely they are to resurface – often quite unconsciously and not necessarily in any instantly recognisable form – in his future writing.

They are rarely of the word-for-word, literal kind that might be regarded as plagiaristic. More often, a striking expression is re-phrased and adapted to another, perhaps analogous character or situation, but with the retention of certain key words which enable us to identify its source; or a visual image deriving from a certain dramatic situation or stage picture is recycled as metaphor in a contrasting context. Thus, Hieronimo's line in the *Spanish Tragedy*, 'Sweet lovely Rose, ill pluckt before thy time', becomes in *Henry VI, Part Three*, 'How sweet a plant have you untimely cropp'd', and an image of Tamburlaine's entrance in the second part of the Marlowe play, drawn in a chariot by two of the African kings he has defeated in battle, is applied with memorable effect in the opening scene of *Henry VI* to the coffin of Henry V carried in procession by his former comrades, 'like captives bound to a triumphant car'. Taken together with other, more superficial similarities of phrase or image that are of no great significance in themselves and might easily – perhaps a little *too* easily – be dismissed as commonplace or accidental, they have much to tell us of an otherwise unknown chapter in Shakespeare's life as a young actor, the plays in which he appeared, and some of the parts he played in them. (For line references to the above, and many other quoted examples, see Appendix A, where they are set out, play by play, in tabular form.)

There are forty-seven named roles in the two parts of Marlowe's *Tamburlaine*, and many other unnamed, smaller roles which – however large the combined company may have been – would have necessitated a lot of doubling. And by 'doubling', I mean that most of the actors would have been required to take, not just two, but sometimes three or more roles in the course of a performance. Since 1586/7, when the Admiral's first acquired them, Shakespeare is thus likely to have been cast in many different parts in the two plays, starting perhaps with unnamed messengers and soldiers and, as time went by and he became more experienced and skilled, progressing to larger and more important roles. This in itself would account for the exceptionally large number of his recollections of *Tamburlaine* in his own early writings (see Section 1 of Appendix A). As the text of the plays would also have been available to him in their published form from 1590, some later verbal echoes might derive (in theory at least) from his reading. He seems, however, to have had a particular familiarity with the speeches of Theridamus, one of the three young shepherds in whose company Tamburlaine is discovered in Scene 2 of Part One, and who accompanies him throughout most of the succeeding action. Many of Tamburlaine's recollected lines are spoken in the presence of Theridamus, and some are actually addressed to him. (It is as important for the actor to know his cues as it is to learn his own lines.) Shakespeare may also at some point have understudied Tamburlaine.

The impact of Marlowe's *Jew of Malta* on Shakespeare is more apparent in the influence that its machiavellian villain Barabas (as played by Alleyn) had on his conception of Aaron in *Titus* and of Richard III than in his recollections of its language (Section 2 of the Appendix). All three characters are outsiders; all three pursue their criminal careers with zestful energy and sardonic humour strongly reminiscent of the Vice of earlier morality plays. So far as they go, his memories of the play suggest that his own part was the kingly one of Ferneze, Governor of Malta, one of whose lines he echoes in the *Shrew*, and others in *Henry VI* and *Richard III*. This could only have been from memory as the text remained unpublished until after his death.

His recollections of the *Spanish Tragedy* (See section 3 of Appendix) go deeper and are more revealing. A speech in *Henry VI* and three in *Richard III* echo the Prologue to Kyd's tragedy, which is spoken by the Ghost of Andrea, a young courtier whose death in battle prior to the action of the play is seen to trigger a series of brutal murders by which he is finally avenged. The only other character on stage throughout the Prologue is the Spirit of Revenge, to whom Andrea describes his journey through the underworld, for which Kyd draws heavily on Virgil. Revenge tells him he has now arrived

> Where thou shalt see the author of thy death,
> Don Balthazar, the Prince of Portingale,
> Depriv'd of life by Bel-imperia –

who is Andrea's former lover. 'Heere sit we downe', Revenge continues,

> to see the misterie,
> And serve for Chorus in this Tragedie. (I.i.87–91)

Two further recollections from later scenes between Andrea's Ghost and Revenge in *Titus* and *Henry VI* leave little doubt that Andrea was Shakespeare's part. And in view of the character's presence on stage throughout the whole of the play, occasional echoes from other scenes and speeches to be found in his subsequent writing require no further explanation. (Interestingly, one of the few roles in his own plays that Shakespeare is said by his first biographer to have played was the Ghost which – like that of Andrea but in a more powerful and realised form as both 'perturbed spirit' and 'Spirit of Revenge' – motivates the action in *Hamlet*. His acting of that role was reported to have been the 'top of his Performance';[25] if it was, the basis for it may well have been laid here.)

Shakespeare's debt to the *Spanish Tragedy* goes far beyond his occasional recycling of image and phrase. More significant parallels in character and plot development between that play and *Titus* in particular have often been pointed out, including the play-within-a-play device that he was to use also in the *Shrew*, and again in *Hamlet*.[26] The play that Hieronimo stages to effect his revenge on the murderers of his son in Act 4 was based on a story that was given a separate, full-length dramatisation (probably by Kyd himself) as *Soliman and Perseda*, though whether this was already in existence when the *Spanish Tragedy* was written – in line with Hieronimo's claim that,

> When in Tolleda there I studied,
> It was my chance to write a Tragedie . . .
> Which, long forgot, I found this other day –
> (IV.i.76–7, 79)

or was later in date, remains uncertain.[27]

But that *Soliman and Perseda* existed by the late 1580s, and that Shakespeare had acted in it, is indicated by a further series of recollections in *Henry VI* (Section 4 of Appendix). It is apparent from these that his role was that of another unfortunate lover, Erastus, in love with and loved in return by Perseda, who falls victim to the jealous enmity of the tyrant Soliman. Perseda avenges Erastus, and at the same time brings about her own death, by challenging Soliman to a duel in the disguise of a man. When, in dying, her identity is revealed, she offers Soliman a notorious poisoned kiss: 'A kisse I graunt thee, though I hate thee deadlie', which was to find an echo on the lips of Queen Margaret to the dying York.

Unlike the *Spanish Tragedy, Soliman and Perseda* was not to be included in the Rose season of 1592, and a description of Erastus in the play as 'not twentie yeares of age,/Not tall, but well proportioned in his lims' (III.i.18–19) takes it back to an earlier time. If Erastus was one of the first of Shakespeare's juvenile roles, it is understandable that some of its more striking images and phrases (eagles gazing against the sun, 'a sunshine day', 'dazzle mine eyes') should have stayed in his mind.

Marlowe and Kyd were not the only contemporary dramatists to have provided material for Shakespeare's acting. Two other plays, one said to be anonymous and the other by Peele, remain to be discussed before we bring the chapter to a close; but in the case of the first, the question of the role or roles that he played is complicated by the possibility of his authorship or part-authorship.

The plot of *Arden of Faversham* derives from an actual murder, and many of its details, including the names of its incompetent hitmen, Black Will and Shakebag, come from Holinshed's account of the real event in the second, posthumous edition of his *Chronicle*, which appeared in 1586 – a year in which the Admiral's men are on record as having visited Faversham in Kent, the scene of the murder. (In Faversham records, Shakebag's name is given as Loosebag.) The dark humour of the play – which mainly consists in the bungling and frustrated attempts of Black Will and Shakebag to waylay and kill Arden at the behest of his wife and her lover – is suggestive of both Marlowe and Kyd, but also of Shakespeare; one thinks especially of the prison scenes in *Measure for Measure* and the shady underworld of Falstaff and his cronies in *Henry IV*. Black Will boasts of having robbed a man at Gad's Hill, and after the murder Shakebag takes refuge with a 'bonny northern lass,/The widow Chambley' in Southwark, but ends up pushing her downstairs and cutting 'her tapster's throat'. He is finally burnt for his crimes 'in Flushing on a stage'. As Peter Levi remarks, 'the connection with Shakespeare is at least as obvious as that of Sir Thomas Lucy with Shallow'.[28]

Informed that Arden is sleeping in a certain house, Shakebag approaches it with a speech that would not have seemed wholly out of place in a later play of Shakespeare's on the theme of another, yet more terrible murder.

> Black night hath hid the pleasures of the day
> And sheeting darkness overhangs the earth,
> And with the black fold of her cloudy robe
> Obscures us from the eyesight of the world,
> In which sweet silence, such as we triumph.
> The lazy minutes linger on their time,
> Loth to give due audit to the hour,
> Till in the watch our purpose be complete
> And Arden sent to everlasting night.[29]

When, however, he and Black Will try the door, they find it is locked. Tragedy descends into bathos.

'Sheeting darkness', 'the lazy minutes linger on their time' bear a Shakespearean stamp. In the realism with which the social situation of the characters is depicted (not so distant from Shakespeare's own bourgeois background), the truthfulness of its psychology and the generosity of its treatment of the smallest roles (another Shakespearean trait), it is, as Keith Sturgess has said, very much an actor's play.[30] I believe it was written by Shakespeare with some unknown collaborator for the Admiral's men, and performed by them in Faversham, if not in 1586, in 1591/2 when they were also to be there.[31] The play was published in 1592 anonymously – as were the quartos of all of Shakespeare's early plays.

His later recollections of its lines (Section 5 of the Appendix), though particularly striking, are of little help in determining the part that he played as he would here, as likely as not, have been unconsciously echoing himself, for *Titus*, as we have seen, was written at about the same time and *Henry VI* a year or two later. It was probably either Shakebag or the Franklin (an invented character who fulfils, among other functions in the play, a choric role) – perhaps, on different occasions, both.

According to the Victorian scholar F.G. Fleay, some lines of Queen Elinor in George Peele's *Edward I*, addressed to Baliol, whom Edward has just appointed King of the Scots, indicate that he had played the title role in that play.

> Now brave John Baliol Lord of Gallaway,
> And king of Scots shine with thy goulden head,
> *Shake thy speres* in honour of his name,
> Under whose roialtie thou wearst the same.[32]

Unsurprisingly, Chambers found the conjecture 'not very convincing',[33] but Peele was renowned for his puckish sense of humour and, if it is not to be interpreted in the way that Fleay suggested, it seems an odd thing for Elinor to say. Why – unless with ironic intent – should she tell the Scots to *shake* their spears?[34]

Little is known of the play. Fleay assigns its first performance to 1591, by which time Shakespeare would have been sufficiently advanced in his profession to play the title role, with Alleyn perhaps as Lluellen. If written as late as this, the lines quoted in Section 6 of the Appendix would derive from Peele's recollection of *Titus*, rather than Shakespeare's of Peele, and may have been intended as a graceful tribute to their author. It was licensed in October 1593 as 'an enterlude entituled the Chronicle of Kinge Edward the firste surnamed Longeshank . . .' and a corrupt text was published shortly afterwards. A play called *Longshank* (probably the same) was acted fourteen times by the Admiral's men at the Rose in 1595/6, by which time, however, Shakespeare had left the company, and in 1602 it was sold by Alleyn with another old play for £4. ('Long-shanckes sewte' – described in Peele's text as of translucent appearance – is in the Admiral's inventory of 10 March 1598.)[35]

Shakespeare is thus seen to have enjoyed an actor/author relationship with three of the leading playwrights of his early years: Marlowe, Kyd and (less certainly) Peele – ironically, two of whom Greene was shortly to warn of the 'upstart Crow' that was coming among them. By then, Shakespeare's talents as a player – if not his greater potential as poet and dramatist – would hardly have been news to them.

To summarise our findings, then, as to Shakespeare's roles in the course of his apprenticeship and early career as an Admiral's man, the indications are that in those plays that were familiar enough to him to be echoed in his own later writings he had played a variety of parts: probably including Theridamus in Marlowe's two *Tamburlaine* plays, Ferneze in *The Jew of Malta*, the Ghost of Andreas in Kyd's *Spanish Tragedy*, Erastus in *Soliman and Perseda*, and Shakebag or the Franklin (perhaps both) in *Arden of Faversham*, with the title role in Peele's *Edward I* as a possible late runner.

With a change of play usual every day and the large repertoire that the Admiral's would thus have needed to carry with them on tour, this could only be the merest sampling from all the parts that he would have been required to play over a period of seven years, though they are likely to have been among the more important. Even so, they represent a not-inadequate grounding in the versatility of skills in many types of role that he would then have been able to contribute to the performance of his own future plays. It is to these and, in the first place, his involvement as both player and dramatist in the climactic season at the Rose in 1592, that we now turn.

FIVE

The Rose, 1592

Shakespeare's memory has been fully vindicated from
the charge of writing the above play by the best critics.
Bishop Thomas Percy of Titus Andronicus *in 1794*[1]

that Drum and trumpet Thing
Maurice Morgann of Henry VI *in 1777*[2]

The occasion of Shakespeare's emergence from the obscurity of
his apprentice years was the season at the Rose beginning 19
February 1592 that was to mark a high point in the alliance of
Strange's and the Admiral's men; the several public acknowledge-
ments of it were to be in effect his first press notices. He was to
come to it – not as a 28-year-old tyro from the country, recently
advanced from such mundane tasks as holding horses' heads at
the playhouse door or call-boy, as has been seriously suggested –
but as an accomplished actor with a twelve-year apprenticeship
behind him, who was already becoming a little too old to play the
young lovers of Marlowe and Kyd.

The Rose, built and managed by an entrepreneur called Philip
Henslowe on the south (Surrey) bank of the Thames (Plate 4),
had only recently opened its doors after refurbishment when
Alleyn and the combined company moved in, following a row
between Alleyn and the Burbages (father and son) that had
effectively closed the company's normal London venue, the
Theatre in Shoreditch, to them. And the exceptionally full
information we have of this season all derives from a diary kept
by Henslowe for his own, mainly financial purposes, in which he
noted in idiosyncratic shorthand the title of each day's play and
his share of its takings.[3]

In determining the nature and extent of Shakespeare's involvement (both as author and actor), much depends on the interpretation we give to two particular sets of entries. The first is a record of 'harey the vi' on 3 March, repeated at varying intervals thirteen times in the succeeding period to 23 June, when the season was interrupted by a Privy Council interdict occasioned by riots in the City;[4] the other relates to a play described as 'titus & vespacia', first recorded on 11 April and repeated six times during the same period. The first mention of each play is glossed as 'ne' – Henslowe's shorthand for 'new'.[5] When, after an interval of six months, the season was resumed for a further month, two more showings of 'harey the vi' are noted and three of 'titus', with no further mention of 'vespacia'.

Much scholastic ink has been expended on the question of whether Henslowe's 'titus and vespacia' in the first part of the season referred to Shakespeare's *Titus Andronicus*. Some editors, not wishing to accept such an early date for Shakespeare's play (the earliest published edition of which dates only from 1594), have conjectured that it was the title of an otherwise unrecorded play on the subject of the conquest of Jerusalem by the Roman emperors Vespasian and his son Titus in AD 90. But would Shakespeare have named his own protagonist 'Titus' if a play including that name in its title was already in the company's repertoire? More probably, *Titus and Vespasian* was Shakespeare's original title, of which the second name was misheard or misread by Henslowe as 'Vespacia'; the former pawnbroker is unlikely to have been able to boast much classical learning. But who, then, was Vespasian if he was not the father of Titus?

The significant clues were provided (as so often) by Chambers. The first is that a play about Shakespeare's Titus was taken to Germany at an indeterminate date by a company of English players, translated into German, and belatedly published in a collection of *Englische Comedien und Tragedien* in 1620 under a title which (when translated back into English) reads, *A Very Lamentable Tragedy of Titus Andronicus and the Haughty Empress*.[6] Though stripped to the barest essentials and in prose, this follows the plot and sequence of scenes in Shakespeare's play fairly closely, but varies from it mainly in that all the characters bar Titus himself bear different names, and that of Titus's son (Lucius in the surviving English text) appears as Vespasian. We

have seen that Robert Browne led a break-away section of the
Admiral's company to Germany in February 1592 (at just the
same time that their remaining fellows were opening at the Rose
in combination with Strange's), and we know that they took with
them from the company's current repertoire several of Marlowe's
plays because they were recorded as performing these at
Frankfort Autumn Fair in September of that year.[7] The question
thus arises: did they also take with them an early version of
Shakespeare's *Titus* that was eventually to find its way into the
Englische Comedien und Tragedien of 1620? The part of Titus's son
in later, published texts of the play is too small to justify its
naming as co-hero in the title; but in the German translation
(and probably therefore in Shakespeare's original), it is of greater
importance, and it is he, not Marcus, who enters with the crown
in the opening scene to offer it to Titus. Also, Titus's quarrel
with his sons and the killing of Mutius are omitted in the
German version and there are signs in Shakespeare's published
text that these were later additions.[8] That Henslowe's 'titus and
vespacia' was indeed an equivalent title for Shakespeare's play in
its original form gains further support from Chambers' second
clue; for in a list of six play titles deriving from the Revels office
in 1619, of which at least four, and probably five, of the plays are
by Shakespeare, the sixth is given as 'Titus and Vespatian'.[9]

The interpretation is supported also by a re-examination of the
famous Peacham drawing (shown in Plate 16) – the only contemporary illustration to survive of a Shakespeare play in
performance. This shows seven characters strung out across the
stage, of which the two central figures have usually been
identified as Tamora, Queen of the Goths, pleading to Titus for
the lives of her sons who are kneeling behind her, and this
appears to be confirmed by the writing across the top of the
picture which reads, 'Tamora pleading, written by Henry
Peacham – author of the complete gentleman'. The difficulty is
that the action as shown in the sketch fails to match at all exactly
with the forty or so lines from *Titus* transcribed below it – or with
any other scene in the play. But, as June Schlueter has recently
pointed out,[10] it bears a much closer relation to an equivalent
scene in the German *Very Lamentable Tragedy* which, as argued
above, derives from Shakespeare's early version of *Titus*, named
by Henslowe in 1592 as 'titus and vespacia'. In Shakespeare's

revision, the stage is crowded with characters ('as many as can be'); in the *Lamentable Tragedy* there are only eight. In *Titus*, Tamora pleads for the life of one of her three sons; in the German play, there are two sons (as in the drawing) and neither is threatened. In the *Lamentable Tragedy*, Aetiopissa, the Queen, is not pleading for their lives but submitting herself and them to Titus, who is about to present them to the Emperor on his right. A stage direction reads, 'takes the Queen by the hand and leads her to the Emperor'; this, I suggest, is just about to happen. Somewhat differently to Dr Schlueter, I interpret the characters in the drawing as (from L to R) Vespasian; the Emperor (wearing German armour of an outdated kind); Titus with ceremonial spear and wearing a laurel wreath (as a stage direction stipulates); Queen Aetiopissa, described as 'lovely and of fair complexion'; her two sons (Helicates and Saphonus); and the Moor of the play (Morian), who is boasting of his valiant deeds in battle as he does in a soliloquy which immediately follows the scene I have described. Only a silent Andronica, Titus's daughter, is missing. All of which suggests that the play that Peacham saw, and sketched at a particular moment of performance, was not *Titus Andronicus* but the earlier *Titus and Vespasian* of which the *Lamentable Tragedy* is a translation, and that the quotations written below the drawing, as well as the reference above to 'Tamora pleading', were made by other and later hands.

The probable course of events was therefore as follows. The play was written by Shakespeare in 1587/8 as *Titus and Vespasian*, performed by the Admiral's/Strange's alliance under that title from 1590, and taken to the continent by Browne and his fellows in February 1592, where an abbreviated version was translated into German. During the six months' break in the Rose season from June to December 1592, Shakespeare revised his original text, reducing the part of Titus's son in size and importance and (to avoid confusion with the historical emperors, Vespasian and Titus) changing the character's name from Vespasian to Lucius. It was then performed at the Rose as *Titus Andronicus* (abbreviated by Henslowe to 'titus') for the remainder of the season, which came to an end in February 1593. (It seems that Henslowe himself was confused by the changes, for when, in January 1594, the play was revived by Sussex's men at the Rose, he refers to it nonsensically as 'titus & andronicus'.)[11]

That the play recorded by Henslowe as 'harey the vi' was not just *Henry VI, Part One*, as is usually assumed,[12] but comprised all three parts of the play in rotation is evidenced by the terms of Greene's bitter attack on Shakespeare which I shall quote in a moment: but is deducible also from the frequency of its performances and their financial returns. In the eighteen-week period from 19 February to 22 June, in which twenty-three plays were given one or more performances, *Henry VI* (in one or other of its parts) was acted on fourteen occasions – more often than any other, including Kyd's immensely popular *Spanish Tragedy* (with thirteen performances) and Marlowe's *Jew of Malta* (with ten).[13] By contrast, Greene's *Friar Bacon and Friar Bungay*, in spite of having opened the season, was thought to justify only three repeats in 1592, and his *Orlando Furiosa*, given two days later, none at all. (No wonder Greene was put out!) In financial terms, against an average return to Henslowe of £1 14s per performance, 'titus and vespacia', averaging £2 8s 6d over seven performances, was by far the most profitable, with the fourteen showings of 'harey the vi' achieving a more than respectable average of £2 0s 6d. (See Appendix B for a suggested breakdown of the way in which the three parts of the play were rotated to allow for five complete cycles of the trilogy to be given.)

When the season was interrupted in June 1592, the two companies (the Admiral's and Strange's) took to the road and toured independently.[14] When, after a six months' break, they came together again at the Rose, several new plays were added to their joint repertoire, including Marlowe's *Massacre at Paris* (described by Henslowe as 'the tragedy of the gvyes'). There was still no sign of *Richard III* though by then it would almost certainly have existed in manuscript, and may even have been in rehearsal when the season was interrupted once more; this time by the plague, and finally abandoned.[15] The last performance of the season – the *Jew of Malta* by the Admiral's – was on 1 February 1593, after which the London theatres were to remain closed for almost a year.

I have said that if ever a part was written for Alleyn, it was Titus. Though only twenty-one in 1587 (the year of the fatal shooting when *Tamburlaine* was in performance in the City), he would already have been playing the lead in that play, and Barabas in the *Jew of Malta*, for the actor/playwright Thomas Heywood was later to specify both these roles in praising him as 'the best of actors',

> Proteus for shapes, and Roscius for a tongue,
> So could he speake, so vary.[16]

By 1587, when Shakespeare was writing *Titus*, Alleyn was indisputably the Admiral's leading player and the part could only have been meant for him.

As we do not have an extant text for Shakespeare's original version of *Titus* (Henslowe's 'titus & vespacia'), it is impossible to say what part he himself played in it, or in its subsequent revision as *Titus Andronicus*. In view of his close relationship with Alleyn as companion, and perhaps role model, of his apprentice years, it may have been that of Titus's elder brother, the tribune Marcus, played as an older man, Titus's son Vespasian (renamed Lucius in the revised text) having gone to a younger apprentice. If Marcus, it was the first of his 'old man' parts – 'thou reverend man of Rome', as Emillius addresses him.[17]

But if Titus was, in a sense, Shakespeare's tribute to Alleyn and an acknowledgement of his debt to him, in writing *Henry VI* he is likely to have had in mind a more central and significant role for himself, and I have already suggested that this was the young king of the title. In his mid-twenties, he was at the optimum age to embody all stages in the character's development – from the 'sweet prince', as yet uncrowned, who makes his first entrance in Act 3 of Part One to the mourning father and doomed king of Act 5, Part Three. Though the part is small in terms of lines (it has less than 200 in the whole of Part One), Henry remains throughout the focal figure, and his presence on stage in so many scenes would have enabled Shakespeare to influence their staging and the performances of his fellows in line with his intentions as author. (In the absence from the Elizabethan stage of a director as such, and the equal status of the sharers, the contribution that he was to make in this way to the success of these and all his future plays in the theatre can hardly be overestimated; it is an aspect of his creativity to which I return.)

It was in response to these performances of four of his plays and his involvement as actor in the season as a whole – for he would still have been playing his usual roles in *Tamburlaine*, the *Spanish Tragedy* and other plays in the Admiral's repertoire – that the first published notices of Shakespeare as player and dramatist come to light. The earliest was by Thomas Nashe and appeared in his *Pierce Penilesse his Supplication to the Divell*, which was entered in the Stationers' Register in August 1592:

> How would it have joyed brave *Talbot* (the terror of the French) to thinke that after he had lyne two hundred yeares in his Tombe, hee should triumphe againe on the Stage, and have his bones newe embalmed with the teares of ten thousand spectators at least, (at severall times) who, in the Tragedian that represents his person, imagine they behold him fresh bleeding?[18]

– as clear a reference as one could hope to find to *Henry VI, Part One*, where Talbot is likewise described as 'the Terror of the French' (I.iv.41), enjoying a 'triumph' (III.iii.5), and with his son, fresh bleeding (IV.vii). The capacity of the Rose is thought to have been between 2000 and 2400. At something less than capacity, five repetitions of Part One ('at severall times') accords very well with Nashe's 'ten thousand'.

But the proof that Henslowe's 'harey the vi' was indeed Shakespeare's *Henry VI* and comprised all three parts of the trilogy was to come from the disappointed playwright Robert Greene, who, lying on his squalid deathbed in the late summer of that same year, launched a blast of vituperation against players in general and one in particular whose plays had so recently triumphed over his own at the Rose. Addressing himself to three of his fellow authors (probably Marlowe, Nashe and Peele) that 'spend their wits in making plaies', he tells them they are

> Base minded men all three of you, if by my miserie you be not warnd: for unto none of you (like mee) sought those burres to cleave: those Puppets (I meane) that spake from our mouths, those Anticks garnisht in our colours . . . trust them not: for there is an upstart Crow, beautified with our feathers, that with his *Tygers hart wrapt in a Players hyde*, supposes he is as well

able to bombast out a blanke verse as the best of you: and beeing an absolute *Johannes fac totum*, is in his owne conceit the onely Shake-scene in a countrey.[19]

'Tygers hart wrapt in a Players hyde' is a slight adaptation of York's line to Queen Margaret in *Henry VI, Part Three* (I.iv.137), 'O tiger's heart wrapp'd in a woman's hide!' As the play had not been published in any form at that date, and the London theatres had been closed from 22 June until after Greene's death on 3 September, the only possible way he could have heard Shakespeare's original line so recently as to have remembered it, and turned it in the way that he did against its author, was in a performance of Part Three of the play from the stage of the Rose.

Greene's gibe hurt – as doubtless he intended it should – and, in December of the same year, it was followed by a graceful and equally famous apology from Henry Chettle, himself a prolific writer and reviser of plays for Henslowe who had edited Green's posthumous confessions for the press.

About three moneths since died M. *Robert Greene*, leaving many papers in sundry Booke sellers hands, among other his Groatsworth of wit, in which a letter written to divers play-makers, is offensively by one or two of them taken; and because on the dead they cannot be avenged, they wilfully forge in their conceites a living Author: and after tossing it to and fro, no remedy, but it must light on me. How I have all the time of my conversing in printing hindered the bitter inveying against schollers, it hath been very well knowne; and how in that I dealt, I can sufficiently proove. With neither of them that take offence was I acquainted, and with one of them I care not if I never be: The other, whome at that time I did not so much spare, as since I wish I had, for that as I have moderated the heate of living writers, and might have usde my owne discretion (especially in such a case) the Author beeing dead, that I did not, I am as sory as if the originall fault had beene my fault, because my selfe have seene his demeanor no lesse civill than he exelent in the qualitie he professes: Besides, divers of worship have reported his uprightnes of dealing, which argues his honesty, and his facetious grace in writting, that aprooves his Art.[20]

If Marlowe was one of the two who had taken offence – the person with whom Chettle was not acquainted and 'care not if I never be' – the other whose demeanour he had seen as 'no lesse civill than he exelent in the qualitie he professes' was unquestionably Shakespeare. And it is interesting to find that the terms that Chettle used in expressing his regret for Greene's intemperate words tell us more of the high regard in which Shakespeare's acting had come to be held than of his standing as author, for 'exelent in the qualitie he professes' clearly refers to his worth as a player, of which the facility and grace of his writing and 'uprightness of dealing' are merely said to 'aproove' – or, as we might put it now, confirm.

Neither *Titus* nor the *Henry VI* plays have been much appreciated for their qualities as dramatic poetry (unjustly so, as it seems to me, for they contain some magical lines), and in all the complex discussions of their origins as published texts as between their quarto and folio editions – of which came first and how the differences between them are best accounted for – the scholars, primarily concerned as they are with *literary* values, are in danger of losing the wood for the trees. For it is only when these texts have been performed, and (in the case of the *Henry VI/Richard III* tetralogy) performed in sequence as they were intended to be, that they have commanded recognition for their exceptional qualities as *plays*. It is when the scholars have turned their attention from textual niceties to the plays' structure that they have begun to be appreciated at their true worth as the work of a master craftsman.

In defiance of Mere's listing of *Titus* among Shakespeare's tragedies in 1598, and its inclusion by Heminges and Condell in the First Folio, *Titus* has been dismissed by a majority of critics and editors from the seventeenth century onwards as unworthy of Shakespeare's pen, as more 'a heap of Rubbish than a structure'; and as late as 1947 Dover Wilson was able to describe it as 'like some broken-down cart, laden with bleeding corpses from an Elizabethan scaffold, and driven by an executioner from Bedlam dressed in cap and bells'.[21]

I had the privilege of holding a spear in the definitive Peter Brook production at Stratford in 1955 with Olivier as Titus, and was able to witness at first hand how a play that had previously been regarded as virtually unactable and, in its succession of horrors, even something of a joke, could be lifted by a great performance in the title role to the status of high art which, in its finer moments, critics of the time did not hesitate to compare with *King Lear*. As George Rylands once wrote, Shakespeare's plays require, not so much interpretation, as collaboration from the actors who perform them, and this is perhaps more true of the early plays than any of the others. It was collaboration of precisely the kind that Shakespeare demands that Olivier brought to Titus, and it was enough, in combination with Brook's stylistically sensitive direction, to trigger a radical revision in both popular and critical opinions of the play. (Angus McBean's posed photographs of this production, often reproduced, though excellent in their way, do less than justice to the stark austerity of the decor or the visceral power of Olivier's performance at Stratford.)

Likewise with *Henry VI*. As Andrew Cairncross explains,[22] 'It became part of the Shakespeare "mythos" that anything unworthy of his genius or repulsive to the sensibilities of the critic's time should be removed from the canon, and fathered on some alternative writer, or even a "symposium" of writers, with Shakespeare possibly adding a few scenes or revising the whole. In *1 Henry VI*, "the revolting treatment of Joan", and the "mean and prosaical" style were sufficient grounds, along with two or three shreds of contemporary evidence and some "echoes" and inconsistencies in the play, for an elaborate theory involving the part authorship of Greene, Marlowe, and Nashe, or some of them.' Though the 'revision' theory of the play's origins had been demolished by Alexander in 1929, it was mainly as a consequence of a series of pioneering productions of all three plays of the trilogy in sequence, for which first credit must go to an American company in 1903, and to more recent productions at Birmingham, Stratford and the Old Vic[23] that critical opinion, after centuries of disparagement, began to revert to Dr Johnson's refreshingly commonsense views, that 'the diction, the versification, and the figures, are *Shakespeare*'s', and (in a note to *2 Henry VI*) that 'this play begins where the former ends, and continues the series of transactions, of which it presupposes the first already known' so that 'the second and third parts were not written without dependance on the first'.[24]

What Shakespeare achieves in these plays, as H.T. Price pointed out in his seminal study of their structure, is to impose 'upon a body of historical data a controlling idea, an idea that constructs the play'.[25] And we have only to look at their opening scenes to see how that controlling idea is planted and followed through in such a way as to command the immediate attention of the audience, to hold it through the two or three hours' 'traffic of the stage', and to lead it on into the next play in the series. This could only have been done by someone with hard-won practical experience of the theatrical medium in which he was working. By someone who had stood on a stage, known and shared the excitement of an audience gripped by the action of the play and the lines he was speaking. Or, conversely and perhaps even more instructively, had come to recognise the unmistakable signals put out by an audience whose attention is slipping away by default of its author, and been powerless to arrest it.

Nor should it ever be forgotten that he was so present on stage in all the first productions of his plays. He was in those circumstances his own collaborator, able to give a lead to his fellows by example in the kind of acting that each of them demanded. For, in so far as each in its own way was innovatory in aims and achievement, they required something new in the style of acting appropriate to them. And he would have been able to give his fellows that lead – not, as he was later to imagine Hamlet as doing, from the condescending heights of an amateur patron – but in just such a way that professional actors in all periods most respect, as one of themselves.

The parts that he played remain open to debate; but the nature and quality of his acting is of far more than incidental importance in arriving at a true estimate of his achievement as poet and playwright, or to an adequate account of his life. It is at the heart of both.

I said in Chapter 2 that the test of the hypothesis I have been putting forward in the previous chapters as to Shakespeare's early adoption of the profession of player and the identity of the company he first joined would come at the point of his emergence into the public arena as player and playwright. We have now reached and encompassed that point, and it will be for the reader to judge of its credibility.

A course has been plotted for Shakespeare's career through the obscure and shifting sands of Elizabethan theatre history that has brought it into line with what we know of his fellows and prevailing theatrical conditions in the period, and that also explains how, by long process of assimilation and practice as apprentice, he attained that excellence in his profession as player attested by Chettle. The choice of Worcester's men as his first company has been shown as consistent with the Stratford records, the dates of his marriage and subsequent births of his children; it has been seen as leading him as active participant into that crucial period of dramatic renaissance associated with Marlowe and Kyd, and the alliance of Strange's and the Admiral's men at the Rose. It has brought him into intimate working relations with the greatest actor of his time, Edward Alleyn, and the patronage of one of the Queen's most influential and powerful ministers, Howard of Effingham. If accepted, such a course disposes once and for all of the problem of the 'lost years'. An undeniable gain. It has provided a credible context in which his early plays were written and performed and has gone some way to explaining the nature and extent of the debt he owed to his predecessors. The evidence for it remains circumstantial and may never be proven. I submit that it explains too much that is incomprehensible in other, more traditional accounts of his early life (which, let it be said, are in truth equally conjectural) to be wholly mistaken.

SIX

The Player Poet

With this key, Shakespeare unlocked his heart
Wordsworth on the Sonnets

Did he? If so, the less Shakespeare he!
Browning's reply[1]

In the Middle Ages, poets were primarily tellers of stories. We know less, much less, of the author of *Piers Plowman* than we do of Shakespeare: only his name (William Langland), his parentage, and the approximate year of his birth (1332). His identity is subsumed in the character of Piers and the story of his dream, and the dreamer is a 'dramatic *persona* whose function, as in other medieval dream-poems, is to provide a link between the reader and the visions'.[2]

Chaucer's *Canterbury Tales* (from 1386) is a collection of stories told by a wonderfully diverse cast of characters to entertain each other as they make their way on pilgrimage to St Thomas's shrine. Gower's *Confessio Amantis* (1390–3) follows a similar pattern of story-telling set within a single, unifying frame. Shakespeare, as well as drawing on classical and Renaissance sources familiar from his schooldays, inherited and remained closely in touch with this literary tradition of the English medieval poets. He knew and loved their writings. There are traces of Chaucer's *Knight's Tale* in *The Two Gentlemen of Verona* and its successor *The Two Noble Kinsmen* (written much later with Fletcher), and he was not only to take the plot of *Pericles* from Gower but also to include the poet himself in his cast as the play's presenter. As a writer, we think and speak of him now as much, perhaps more often, as playwright than we do as poet, but to his contemporaries he was simply a poet. That said it all. It was not just that he wrote largely in verse; poets were also understood to be tellers of stories and dreamers of dreams, and he was notably both.

'For God's sake', Richard II tells his followers in the hour of defeat,

> let us sit upon the ground
> And tell sad stories of the death of kings . . .

and the irony is, of course, that the play itself is another such story. In Macbeth's despairing vision, 'Life's but a walking shadow . . . a tale/Told by an idiot, full of sound and fury,/Signifying nothing'. The *Henry VI/Richard III* tetralogy is, as we have seen, a story of England and, like all the old stories and plays, ends with a moral and a prayer.

> England hath long been mad, and scarr'd herself . . .
> Now civil wounds are stopp'd; peace lives again.
> That she may long live here, God say Amen.[3]

The Comedy of Errors is set within the frame of Egeon's story of his life, with which it begins and ends. The imagery of dream and of dreaming pervades the plays at every stage of Shakespeare's writing. 'Am I a lord and have I such a lady', asks Christopher Sly, 'Or do I dream? Or have I dreamed till now?' 'Are you sure/That we are awake?' asks Demetrius. 'It seems to me/That yet we sleep, we dream.' And for Prospero, the world of reality is as insubstantial as the magical pageant he has conjured for the instruction of the play's lovers.

> We are such stuff
> As dreams are made on; and our little life
> Is rounded with a sleep.[4]

But if Shakespeare inherited a literary tradition of story-telling and dream poetry from the Middle Ages, he was also the bearer of another, more ancient and popular tradition: that of the minstrels and harper-poets who, like himself, were both author and performer of their songs and stories, and whose ancestry goes back to Homer.[5] It is to these, rather than to his own, more literary productions, that the revivified Gower of *Pericles* seems to refer.

> To sing a song that old was sung.
> From ashes ancient Gower is come,
> Assuming man's infirmities,
> To glad your ear, and please your eyes.
> It hath been sung at festivals,
> On ember-eves and holy-ales . . .   (I.i.1–6)

Like Shakespeare, the harper-poets had little interest in publication; books appeared to them more as a threat to their livelihood as performers than as a means of preserving their compositions for the enjoyment of future generations. It was for that very reason, and because they looked to near-illiterate magnates and the mass of the people for patronage and appreciation rather than to the learned, that they were despised by the literati of their time – just as Shakespeare's plays and those of his fellows were ignored or regarded as 'riff-raffs' by bookmen such as Sir Thomas Bodley. Their audience was as mixed as his own at the Rose or the Globe; typically comprising a lord or lady of the manor at table with family, steward and chaplain, one or two visiting neighbours, with a crowd of servants filling the benches and standing at the back of the hall – craftsmen, apprentices and labourers. The harper, with his tale of Sir Orfeo or Gawain, represented a popular oral tradition of performing poets, of which Shakespeare may be claimed as the greatest – possibly the last.

When the season at the Rose came to a premature end in February 1593 because of a serious outbreak of plague, there was an inevitable dispersal of the players who had been engaged in it. Some of them joined a new travelling company which, in the previous year, had succeeded in obtaining the patronage of Henry Herbert, earl of Pembroke: Pembroke's men. They had spent the final months of 1592 in the Midlands, but on Boxing Day of that year, and on 6 January 1593, performed at court for the Queen. The new recruits from the former alliance, including a certain George Bevis who had played a rebel in *Henry VI, Part*

Two, were to bring with them pirated versions of that play and its sequel, put together from memory with addition of some written parts they had collected of the longer speeches.[6] When their subsequent tour in the summer of 1593 proved unviable and the company went bust, these were sold to a publisher as *The First part of the Contention betwixt the two famous Houses of Yorke and Lancaster (Henry VI, Part 2)* and *The true Tragedie of Richard, Duke of Yorke (Henry VI, Part 3)*. (We know that Bevis was one of them because there is a jokey reference to him in Act 2, Scene 3 of the *Contention*.) Others, especially from the Admiral's, may have gone to join Browne and other of their former fellows in Germany.

The main part of Strange's, with Alleyn still at their head as leading man, hesitated for a while – hoping, perhaps, for a speedy lifting of the ban that had closed the London theatres to them – but finally gave up, and in April 1593 applied to the Privy Council for a new licence to travel. This was granted on 6 May 1593, naming Edward Alleyn ('servaunt to the right honorable the Lord Highe Admiral'), William Kempe, Thomas Pope, John Heminges, Augustine Phillips and George Bryan.[7] Significantly, Shakespeare's name is missing, and we have no further record of him until March 1595, when he appears in the accounts of the Queen's Treasurer as joint-payee with Kempe and Richard Burbage (all three 'servantes to the Lord Chamberleyne') for plays performed before the Queen at Greenwich the previous Christmas.[8] But he is likely to have been a sharer in the new company from June 1594, when it joined with a reconstituted Admiral's for a short season under Henslowe's management at Newington Butts; this closed after only ten performances, though not before Shakespeare's *Titus* and the *Shrew* had been given. What, then, had he been doing in the meantime?

Though we have no evidence of a quarrel between Shakespeare and Alleyn then or later, the most likely conjecture is that on the breaking of the alliance in February 1593 the two men had reached a natural parting of the ways. Alleyn, who in October 1592 had married Henslowe's step-daughter, Joan Woodward, and was already involved in business dealings with his father-in-law, was plainly set on a course of theatre ownership and management that was to lead within a few years to his amassing a large fortune and, in about 1603, to his retirement from the stage. Shakespeare would have had good reason to be grateful to him, and doubtless was, but his own immediate needs and ambitions were different. Not only was it essential for him, after his long apprenticeship, to find more adequate means of supporting his young family – Susanna would then have been nine and the twins just eight – he would have been seeking to accumulate sufficient capital to buy himself a share in one or other of the major companies that would guarantee a more stable income in the future and, at the same time, secure him a measure of aristic control over future productions of his plays – a position that Alleyn was either unable or unwilling to provide. The success he had had in the theatre with his early plays must have given him great confidence in his abilities, but the *Shrew* and Parts 2 and 3 of *Henry VI* were then in process of exploitation and deformation by pirates, and his manuscript of *Richard III* (which I believe had been written for Alleyn, and what a magnificent part it would have been for him) remained unperformed.

In the want of any other information, we must look to internal evidence presented by the poems and plays he wrote in the fifteen months that followed the closures of 1593 for clues to his situation in the period. In examining this, we shall find that in temporarily turning aside from active involvement with any of the surviving companies, he did not cease to be a player any more than he ceased to be a poet when he was acting. He was of that rare breed in his time (perhaps in any time), a player-poet.

Venus and Adonis was published in London by a former Stratford neighbour of Shakespeare's, Richard Field. As the book was registered at Stationers' Hall on 18 April 1593 and is known to have been on sale in the shops less than two months later, I find it hard to believe that it was wholly written in the seven-week interval between 1 February (when the Rose season was brought to an end) and 18 April. The poem is remarkable for the freshness and spontaneity of its verse, but the spontaneity is of the kind that conceals art and can only be achieved by hard and sustained labour. With Shakespeare, however – then in the springtime of his creativity – we can never be sure; we know that he could write very quickly ('without a blot') and usually did. If he had returned to his home in Stratford, at the heart of the Warwickshire countryside, in early February, and the poem was

written in a concentrated burst of creative energy, it might help to
account for the vivid observations of the life of nature that
transfuse its classical setting with a sense of down-to-earth reality,
expressed in 'true, plain words': the 'dive-dapper peering through
a wave', the milch-doe with 'swelling dugs', the 'angry chafing
boar', and Watt, the terrified 'purblind hare'.

That the poem was written by someone familiar with the
dramatic requirements of the theatre is apparent from the very
first stanza; for, with the minimum of introductory matter, he
plunges us straight into action.

> Even as the sun with purple-coloured face
> Had tane his last leave of the weeping morn,
> Rose-cheeked Adonis hied him to the chase;
> Hunting he loved, but love he laughed to scorn.
> > Sick-thoughted Venus makes amain unto him,
> > And like a bold-faced suitor gins to woo him.

Of the poem's 1194 lines, nearly half are of direct speech and
dialogue. That the poet was also a player is manifest in the extent
to which he is able to enter into and identify with the characters
in the story: the alluring goddess and the reluctant, embarrassed
youth. These are individual people who are speaking, not poetic
abstractions, and they are talking, not as in so many narrative
poems to the reader, but to each other. Adonis becomes present
to us in his first directly quoted speech – he is flat on his back
with Venus pinning him down:

> 'Fie, no more of love!
> The sun doth burn my face, I must remove.' (ll. 185–6)

But she stays where she is, and so does he. Goddess though she
is, Venus, in her embodiment of conflicting human qualities and
emotions – seductive beauty and self-willed determination,
playfulness and dignity, tenderness and anger – becomes as real
to us as Cleopatra.

Shakespeare's name is absent from the title page of the printed
book but, in an obvious bid for personal patronage, appears at
the end of a dedicatory letter addressed to Henry Wriothesley,
earl of Southampton.

Right Honourable, I know not how I shall offend in dedicating my unpolisht lines to your Lordship, nor how the worlde will censure mee for choosing so strong a proppe to support so weake a burthen, onelye if your Honour seeme but pleased, I account my selfe highly praised, and vowe to take advantage of all idle houres, till I have honoured you with some graver labour. But if the first heire of my invention prove deformed, I shall be sorie it had so noble a god-father: and never after eare so barren a land, for feare it yeeld me still so bad a harvest, I leave it to your Honourable survey, and your Honor to your hearts content which I wish may alwaies answere your owne wish, and the worlds hopefull expectation.

Your Honors in all dutie,
William Shakespeare[9]

It is more than possible that Southampton had visited the Rose and sat at the side of the stage during a performance of *Titus* or *Henry VI* in which Shakespeare had acted. The earl and the actor may thus have been known to each other by sight and even exchanged an occasional greeting. But in view of the social chasm that yawned in the period between members of the aristocracy and that lowest of life forms, the players, it is most unlikely (to put it no stronger) that their relationship was then, or ever, closer than that of master to servant, patron to client. Though the eighteen-year-old earl had the contemporary reputation of being well disposed towards poets and artists, it is doubtful, indeed, that Shakespeare would have cast his bread on the waters in his direction without some previous assurance that the dedicatee would regard his doing so with favour – or at least without taking offence – and preliminary soundings may have been made through Shakespeare's former patron as Admiral's man, Lord Howard. (Howard was intimate with Burghley, and Southampton was Burghley's ward.)

As Chambers pointed out, Elizabethan patrons were expected to put their hand in their pocket. That Southampton did so is indicated by the sequel; for when, in the following year, Shakespeare completed *The Rape of Lucrece* (that 'graver labour' he had promised), he was to dedicate that also to the earl in slightly warmer and more confident terms. But for all their flowery phrases and exaggerated expressions of devotion (quite normal and expected of literary dedications in the period), both of Shakespeare's published letters to Southampton end in due and proper form, 'Your Honors [Lordships] in all dutie'.

Whatever Shakespeare received for *Venus and Adonis* by way of donation ('The warrant I have of your Honourable disposition') would have gone some way, if not all the way, in providing the capital he needed to fulfil his ambition of purchasing a share in one of the companies.[10] The opportunity for that lay still in the future; through 1593, the theatre remained in disarray because of the plague. In the meantime he had other work to do. *The Rape of Lucrece* and the first of the Sonnets were already in hand, but his mind would also have been buzzing with the plays he would write for the company, as yet unknown, he was soon to join.

If we wanted to find an overall theme and title for Shakespeare's writing in 1593 and early 1594, it would have to be Love and Friendship. The narrative poems and Sonnets are often considered in isolation from the plays, which is a big mistake because the numerous similarities of thought and language that echo between them indicate that they were written in tandem and, when considered in that way, are mutually illuminating. (For some of the more obvious verbal correspondences, see Appendix C.)

If Shakespeare had looked to Kyd and his classical precursors for initial inspiration in the writing of *Titus*, and to the rough and rowdy tradition of the English interludes and Italian popular comedy for the *Shrew*, it was the near-contemporary prose dramas of John Lyly that provided his starting point for *The Two Gentlemen of Verona*. Like them, it is courtly in tone and draws on the ancient but currently fashionable Friendship Cult to demonstrate the way in which a Platonic relationship between two men (however sincere, even passionate) is liable to founder when subjected to the demands of Eros and exigencies of love and marriage.

The play begins with a parting of two such friends, Proteus and Valentine, who address each without inhibition as 'my loving Proteus', 'sweet Valentine'. Valentine is leaving to serve at the Emperor's court; Proteus stays behind to pursue his wooing of Julia. Valentine mocks at love,

> where scorn is bought with groans;
> Coy looks, with heart-sore sighs; one fading moment's mirth
> With twenty watchful, weary, tedious nights . . . (I.i.29–31)

but on arrival at court, soon becomes a victim himself by falling in love with the Emperor's daughter, Silvia. Despatched by his father to join Valentine at court, Proteus (forgetting Julia) is attracted to the same girl, and betrays his friend by revealing to the Emperor Valentine's plan to elope with her. The triangular situation between these three is not dissimilar to the dimly discernible plot at the heart of the Sonnets, where the 'dark lady' is the disruptive factor, though here treated in lighter, comedic vein. With the arrival of the abandoned Julia disguised as a boy (the first occasion on which Shakespeare makes use of what was to be a favourite device), the trio of lovers becomes a quartet.

One immediately striking feature of the play as compared with its predecessors is the smallness of the cast. Clearly the crisis year of 1593 was not a time for large, unwieldy epics that would be unviable on tour – as Pembroke's men discovered to their cost that same summer. Of its thirteen named roles, at least four could be doubled, and four others are written for boys, playing the girls' parts and a quick-witted page called Speed. It could thus have easily been acted by a company of seven actors, four boys – and a dog, of which more in a moment.

Unlike the *Shrew* and *Henry VI*, the text has no 'rogue' references to its first performers – which is not surprising if, as I believe, he had begun to write it 'on spec'. But the insertion in the cast of the clownish servant Launce, at what Clifford Leech has shown to be a late, probably final, stage of composition,[11] suggests that Shakespeare made this important addition to the play in the early part of 1594, when he learned that William Kempe was to be one of his fellows in the Chamberlain's men. The character is an obvious precursor of Costard and Launcelot Gobbo, and has the stage persona of Kempe written all over it. He and Kempe had worked together before of course at the Rose, and Shakespeare would have known very well what he could do with such a role. Launce's interventions in the play are, for the most part, independent of plot, and his speeches – especially the soliloquies in which he plays off his mongrel Crab in the same way that some music hall comedians of recent memory used an equally silent but expressive stooge – may have derived in part from one of Kempe's solo performances as clown, for which he was already famous. They provide the funniest moments in the play.

> When a man's servant shall play the cur with him, look you, it goes hard: one that I brought up of a puppy; one that I saved from drowning, when three or four of his blind brothers and sisters went to it . . . I was sent to deliver him as a present to Mistress Silvia, from my master; and I came no sooner into the dining chamber, but he steps me to her trencher, and steals her capon's leg. O, 'tis a foul thing, when a cur cannot keep himself in all companies . . . If I had not had more wit than he, to take a fault upon me that he did, I think verily he had been hanged for't. You shall judge: he thrusts me himself into the company of three or four gentleman-like dogs, under the Duke's table; he had not been there (bless the mark) a pissing while, but all the chamber smelt him. 'Out with the dog', says one; 'What cur is that?' says another; 'Whip him out', says the third; 'Hang him up', says the Duke. I, having been acquainted with the smell before, knew it was Crab; and goes me to the fellow that whips the dogs: 'Friend', quoth I, 'you mean to whip the dog?' 'Ay, marry do I', quoth he. 'You do him the more wrong', quoth I; ''twas I did the thing you wot of'. He makes me no more ado, but whips me out of the chamber. How many masters would do this for his servant?
>
> (IV.iv.1–30)

There could be no better illustration of the kind of collaboration that Shakespeare's fellow performers were able to offer, or the contribution they made to the richness and variety of his dramatic inventions. Apart from its obvious entertainment value, the particular service of Launce to the play is to anchor the romantic Arcadia which the other characters inhabit to the world of ordinary, everyday experience, thus providing a sub-text of affectionate mockery to which Crab contributes by simply remaining what he is: a dog.

At twenty-nine (a mature age in Elizabethan times) Shakespeare would have considered himself too old to play either of the two gentlemen. The role he had had in mind for himself, and probably did perform when the play eventually reached the stage, was that of the Emperor, or 'Duke' as he is invariably described in speech prefixes and stage directions; another of those 'kingly parts' that were to keep him in control at the centre of the action on stage without burdening himself with too many lines.

Shakespeare's 'dukes' are worthy of more detailed study than they usually receive. Often they are lumped together as among the least interesting of his characters and regarded as virtually indistinguishable. If approached with such preconceptions by the actor, they can indeed be very boring. But looked at more closely, they reveal important individual differences – not least in authority. Though described merely as 'duke', Silvia's father is in reality a monarch with absolute power, whose court is consistently referred to in the text as 'the Emperor's'.

We meet him first *en famille*. He enters (in II.iv) without fanfare as Silvia tells Valentine (as it might be the postman), 'Here comes my father'. In the scene that follows, Valentine addresses him as 'my lord', as today, in similarly informal circumstances, we might address a member of the royal family as 'ma'am' or 'sir'. His royalty is veiled by a manner of friendly courtesy, but it should nevertheless be apparent in Valentine's attitude towards him that this is the most powerful person in the play. The same is true of the subsequent scene (III.i) in which the Duke, by his assumption of the same urbane condescension (seeking advice as one gentleman to another) tricks Valentine into revealing his plan to elope with Silvia. Only then – and it should be as big a shock to the audience as it is to Valentine – does his true authority and power reveal itself in a splendid speech of barely controlled anger.

> Why, Phaeton, for thou are Merops' son
> Wilt thou aspire to guide the heavenly car?
> And with thy daring folly burn the world?
> Wilt thou reach stars, because they shine on thee?
> Go, base intruder, overweening slave,
> Bestow thy fawning smiles on equal mates,
> And think my patience (more than thy desert)
> Is privilege for thy departure hence . . .   (III.i.153–60)

This is far from being the most interesting or challenging of the kingly roles that Shakespeare was to write for himself, but no one can truly claim that it is either obvious or boring – or, for that matter, easy of performance.[12]

That the play was written quickly, and probably (as Leech argues) in a series of interrupted phases, in the intervals of which he was also working on other plays and poems, is suggested by its frequent inconsistencies in geography and loose ends in plot development of the kind that cause such worry to scholars but which audiences rarely notice. The play was not published till its inclusion in the First Folio of 1623 in a text deriving from Shakespeare's manuscript. There are no surviving performance records from the sixteenth or seventeenth centuries, but Meres' listing of it in first place among Shakespeare's comedies in 1598 tells us that it *had* been performed and was popular from an early date.

In *The Comedy of Errors*, the writing of which is thought to have followed that of the *Two Gentlemen* fairly closely, Shakespeare's intended role would again have been that of the 'Duke', and here also he uses the term in a generic sense to include a ruler or prince of royal blood; for as the Duke in question, named Solinus in the first line of the play, explains to Egeon,

> were it not against our laws,
> Against my crown, my oath, my dignity,
> Which princes, would they, may not disannul,
> My soul should sue as advocate for thee . . . (I.i.142–5)

The situation at the play's opening is that Egeon, a merchant of Syracuse, has fallen foul of the law of Ephesus, of which Solinus is ruler, by venturing into its territory in search of his wife and sons, from whom he was separated by a disaster at sea when the sons (identical twins) were still in their infancy. The law ordains that unless he can redeem himself by payment of a thousand crowns before the evening of the same day, his life is forfeit. It is Egeon's story of his misadventures as told to the Duke that frames the comedy within the play; and for the plot of the comedy, Shakespeare returned to his classical reading, adapting a Latin play by Plautus, the *Menaechmi*, to his own purposes. It was also a return to those confusions of identity he had mined so successfully in the *Taming of the Shrew*, but here the confusions take on a positively surreal quality.

Egeon's sons, Antipholus of Ephesus and his twin, Antipholus of Syracuse, separated from each other as well as from their parents by the accident at sea Egeon has already recounted, fortuitously find themselves in Ephesus at the same time, unbeknown to the other, each accompanied by a servant called Dromio, the two of whom are likewise identical twins. Antipholus and Dromio of Ephesus are resident in the city and known to its inhabitants; their twins of Syracuse are, like Egeon, visitors, and the people they meet are strangers to them. Once this latter pair have parted company, as happens very soon when Dromio is sent on an errand, we enter on a complex and beautifully constructed sequence of scenes in which servants mistake their masters, masters their servants, and the people they meet mistake both masters and servants for their twins, but in which (until the final scene) the two sets of twins are never confronted face to face with their respective doubles. The outcome is mounting disorder and panic as all involved try to understand the strange things that are happening to them, and are unable to do so.

An expert farceur, Ralph Lynn, once remarked that the essence of farce was *worry*. *The Comedy of Errors* is not a farce, but the elements of farce that it contains can only work their comedic effect if they are based in a real and credible uncertainty in the Antipholus twins as to their own identity. The visitor from Syracuse is not only threatened by the same law that has been seen to put his father in irons, so that he is obliged to adopt a false persona but, deprived of his parents and twin, feels himself to be

> like a drop of water
> That in the ocean seeks another drop,
> Who, falling there to find his fellow forth,
> (Unseen, inquisitive) confounds himself.
> So I, to find a mother and a brother,
> In quest of them, unhappy, lose myself.   (I.ii.35–40)

Failing to find them, and meeting instead a succession of strangers would be bad enough: for him to encounter people he does not know but who *seem to know him* induces superstitious dread and fear of madness, from which he is saved by his discovery of a dawning love for one of the strangers, Luciana, who later turns out to be his brother's sister-in-law. His twin of Ephesus – who we do not meet until Act 3 – is found to be subject to another form of disorientation resulting from the jealousy of his wife Adriana, Luciana's sister.

>   How comes it now, my husband,

she demands of him,

>   O, how comes it,
>   That thou art then estranged from thyself?–
>   Thyself I call it, being strange to me,
>   That undividable, incorporate,
>   Am better than thy dear self's better part.
>   Ah, do not tear away thyself from me . . .   (II.ii.119–24)

But unfortunately it is not her husband she is addressing with her reproaches, as she thinks, but his Syracusian twin, who is, of course, bewildered by them. (It is interesting to find that these and several other of Adriana's lines provide cues for Shakespeare's meditations on the complexities of human relationships in the Sonnets – see Section 2 of Appendix C.)

If this were all, the play would by now have ceased to be a comedy, but the brothers' crises of identity are judiciously balanced by the involvement of their servants, the Dromios who, in their indignant responses to the many undeserved beatings they receive in the course of the play, remain (like Crab in the *Two Gentlemen*) joyously, irrepressibly themselves. These two characters have no equivalent in Shakespeare's principal source; in creating them, I believe he was again anticipating the presence of Kempe in the cast, and that he intended Kempe to play both parts, as their masters, the Antipholus twins, were also meant to be doubled. To do so presents difficult but not insurmountable problems, but the effort and ingenuity required in overcoming these brings rich rewards in terms of the credibility of the action, and thus of the audience's enjoyment of it.[13] The only other character we can safely associate with a particular actor – if at this stage only in Shakespeare's imagination – is Dr Pinch, the quack-physician, whose description by Antipholus of Ephesus as a 'hungry lean-fac'd villain;/A mere anatomy', 'A living dead man', 'with no-face (as 'twere) out-facing me' (V.i.238–45) brings to mind the unmistakably skeletal form of John Sincler, who as 'Sinklo' we have already encountered in the *Shrew* and *Henry VI*, and will meet with again in similar roles as a Chamberlain's man.

But basic to the comedy of errors and confusions throughout the play is the essential seriousness and potential tragedy of its opening scene in which Egeon tells his sad story to the Duke. Apart from *The Tempest*, this is the only play of Shakespeare's to preserve the unities of time, place and action – that is, if we accept Ephesus as a single place. The Duke's sentence of death on Egeon, failing payment of a fine that we have been told far exceeds his resources, is to be carried out on the evening of the same day. The progress of the sun in the sky and the movements of a clock dominate the action, to the moment in the final scene when 'the dial points at five', and Egeon and the Duke re-enter

> to the melancholy vale,
> The place of death and sorry execution
> Behind the ditches of the abbey here.   (V.i.120–2)

(It is from the abbey that the person who is to set all their misunderstandings to rights will emerge.) Unless those first and final scenes are played with due conviction and, in spite of its considerable length and convoluted form, Egeon's story commands the credibility of the audience, the rest of the play is doomed to failure; that it should do so is necessary to give edge to the ensuing comedy, especially its farcical elements, but also to enable the play's deeper meanings to resonate as Shakespeare intended they should. If, as an easy way out, it is guyed, the rest can easily degenerate, as it sometimes does, into a pointless romp. We do not know who Shakespeare had in mind to play Egeon, or who did eventually play him in the first recorded performance at Grays Inn on 28 December (Innocents' Day) 1594 – which, as it happened, turned out to be a comedy of errors in quite another sense[14] – but we can readily understand why he should have wanted to be in charge as the Duke.

We have seen how some of the thought that lies behind the characters and their relationships in the *Two Gentlemen* and

Comedy of Errors points to the Sonnets. In our review of Shakespeare's writing in the period, we cannot fail to take these wonderful, if puzzling, poems into consideration, if only to bring out a little more clearly their connection with the plays.

Apart from his ostensibly successful marriage to Anne Hathaway, we know so little of Shakespeare's emotional life – of his loves and personal attachments – it is understandable that biographers have looked to the Sonnets to fill the gap. As the 154 poems that make up the completed series are unique among his works in featuring the authorial 'I' (or what is taken to be the authorial 'I'), they assume that he was here, to quote Wordsworth's phrase, 'unlocking his heart' for their inspection. The search is then on for the identity of the Fair Youth, the 'master-mistress' of his passion, to whom most are addressed. Of a long list of historical characters proposed, Henry Wriothesley, the young earl of Southampton to whom he had dedicated *Venus and Adonis* and was shortly to dedicate the *Rape of Lucrece*, has been and remains the front-runner. When they were first published sixteen years later, the Sonnets were also to carry a dedication:

TO . THE . ONLIE . BEGETTER . OF
THESE . INSUING . SONNETS.
Mr. W. H. ALL . HAPPINESSE.
AND . THAT. ETERNITIE.
PROMISED.
BY.
OUR . EVER-LIVING . POET.
WISHETH.
THE . WELL-WISHING.
ADVENTURER . IN.
SETTING.
FORTH.
T.T.

– about which the only certainty is that T.T. stands for Thomas Thorpe, the book's publisher. The dedication, then, was Thorpe's, not Shakespeare's, and the mysterious 'Mr W.H.' no more, perhaps, than a publisher's device to whip up speculation and increase his sales.

The riddles that remain have given rise to acres of print, and I do not mean to add to them. Those who make the assumptions on which they are based mostly forget, or do not want to accept, the simple fact of Shakespeare's occupation as a player and writer for the public theatres. The scrivener and versifier John Davies was not alone in believing that 'the stage doth staine pure gentle bloud'; it was, as we have seen, the common opinion of the time, an opinion of which Shakespeare could not fail to be aware and to have regretted.

> O, for my sake do you with Fortune chide,
> The guilty goddess of my harmful deeds,
> That did not better for my life provide
> Than public means which public manners breeds.
> Thence comes it that my name receives a brand,
> And almost thence my nature is subdued
> To what it works in, like the dyer's hand.   (111.1–7)

But we should take note that when read in context with the two preceding sonnets, 'harmful deeds' is seen to refer to the infidelities to which the poet has there confessed, and it is the brand his name has received, not the 'public means' in themselves, that have threatened to subdue his nature. Furthermore, though generally understood in an autobiographical sense as referring to the theatre, the 'public means which public manners breeds' is open to other interpretations, such as politics or the law; the deliberate ambiguity surrounding the poet's identity is thus preserved. His defiance of those who would drag him down by association should also be noticed:

> 'Tis better to be vile than vile esteemed
> When not to be receives reproach of being . . .
> No, I am that I am, and they that level
> At my abuses reckon up there own;
> I may be straight though they themselves be bevel.
> By their rank thoughts my deeds must not be shown,
>   Unless this general evil they maintain:
>   All men are bad and in their badness reign.
>   (121.1–2, 9–14)

But in view of the prevailing social prejudices, is it conceivable that such a branded individual could in any circumstances have formed an intimate friendship with Southampton or any other aristocratic nominee for the title of the Fair Youth to the extent of having shared a mistress with him? I think not. There is, perhaps, a kind of reverse snobbery at work in such claims. Because of their admiration for Shakespeare, the man and the poet, those who put them forward seek to exalt him by making him a familiar companion of the highest in the land; but in so doing, they not only contradict the known facts of his social situation, they deny the great and glorious thing that he was; of all the poets who ever lived, he is least in need of such promotion. Nor can we safely assume that in writing the poems in the first person he was simply engaged in a form of self-expression. John Kerrigan puts the truth of the matter best when he writes that 'The text is neither fictive nor confessional. Shakespeare stands behind the first person of his sequence as Sidney had stood behind Astrophil – sometimes near the poetic "I", sometimes farther off, but never without some degree of rhetorical projection. *The Sonnets are not autobiographical in a psychological mode.*'[15]

What seems to me most likely is that the first sixteen (perhaps nineteen) poems in the sequence were commissioned by the parents or guardians of a high-placed young man, probably unknown to Shakespeare except by repute, whom they wished to marry against his own inclinations, to be sent to him anonymously; that in fulfilling this demand, Shakespeare adopted the persona of a slightly older admirer of similar social status, and that both this assumed persona and that of the Fair Youth he had envisaged so took root in his imagination as to stimulate a continuation of the series, in which he was able to express (at one remove) his deep insights into love, friendship, the Friendship Cult and its betrayal. It was the way his creative imagination normally worked. The authorial 'I' was thus, like Langland's Piers, Sidney's Astrophil or Marlowe's Passionate Shepherd, in part an invented character in the story he was telling – along with the Fair Youth, the Dark Lady and the Rival Poet. This is not to deny that in writing the poems he drew on his own life experience and that of the people he had come into contact with in the theatre or elsewhere, though the characters in them are more likely to be amalgams of several such people than identifiable individuals. To try to pin them down in that way is thus a futile exercise that risks missing the point of what Shakespeare is really meaning to say. For the ambiguity in which both the poetic 'I' and his beloved are clothed – his withholding of their names and of any clue to their identity – is the secret of the unique appeal the Sonnets have always had to the reader who, whatever his or her own circumstances may be, is thereby enabled to respond directly to the poet's thoughts and feelings, and identify with them. He invites the collaboration of the reader in giving his lovers a face and an identity in the same way that he invites the actor to embody the characters of his plays, and his audience to 'piece out our imperfections with your thoughts'. He gives them room enough to put their imaginations to work, but never so much as to make them redundant.

There can be no question, then, of Shakespeare's sincerity. For all their technical brilliance and dexterity of word-play, the Sonnets are passionately sincere. But are they any more sincere than the heartfelt speeches he gives to the characters in his plays: to Romeo or Juliet, Hamlet or Lear? The tone of his poet's voice varies, occasionally falters but, as Muriel Bradbrook wrote, in all their variety of accomplishment, 'there is no variation in that capacity for a transfer of the whole centre of being into the life of another, which is the mark linking these sonnets to dramatic art'.[16]

To the Puritans of Shakespeare's time, plays were all lies, and the players who performed them retailers of lies, no better than deceiving whores – pretending to be what they were not, dissembling emotions they did not feel, and doing both for money. The prejudice survives in the common assumption that acting and sincerity are so mutually incompatible as to be, to all intents and purposes, opposites. But whatever may be said of the people in ordinary life who conceal or disguise their true identity or feelings in order to deceive and manipulate others, actors in their professional capacity make no such pretences, nor do they seek to deceive. Depending on their individual ability and command of their craft in holding the 'mirror up to nature', their acting may be true or false; but the actor *per se* is the most truthful person in existence for, whatever part he or she is playing, no one can be in any doubt as to who they are, or what they are doing on the stage. So it is with the poets and the stories they tell. So it was with Shakespeare. At the core of the Sonnets there is certainly the story of an intense, emotional attachment, but to interpret it as necessarily Shakespeare's is to confuse the story-teller with the story, the player with the play.

Curiously, the play that relates more closely to the Sonnets than any other belonging to this period of Shakespeare's 'resting' as a player is one that until recently has rarely been claimed as his, though his part-authorship has often been suspected: the anonymous *Edward III*.

It was entered in the Stationers' Register on 1 December 1595, and published in the following year, 'as it hath bin sundrie times plaied about the Citie of London'.[17] But no mention is made of its author or the company that played it; nor does any record survive of its performances in the City or elsewhere. Though no one claimed it as Shakespeare's before the second half of the seventeenth century, his familiarity with the play is evident, not only in the lines relating to the Sonnets quoted in Section 3 of Appendix C, but in numerous other less precise echoes or anticipations of image and language to be found in his recognised plays, both early and late.[18] Some of these correspondences might be accounted for by his having acted in the play, when the words he had spoken entered so deeply into his conscious or unconscious memory as to be later recycled in his writing in the same way that images and phrases from Marlowe and Kyd have been seen to resurface in *Titus* and *Henry VI*. But that could only have been prior to 1593 when the City theatres were closed, which is too early, and there would hardly have been time for him to have toured in the play any later than that. Moreover, the Edward/Countess scenes of Acts 1 and 2, which provide what has always been seen as the most persuasive evidence of his authorship, stand out from the rest in the quality and style of their verse to so large a degree as to make such an explanation untenable.

One scene in particular – that between the king and his secretary (Act 2, Scene 1) – supplies such clear echoes of lines from the Sonnets as to indicate that they were written very close to each other in time.[19] The scene has also what I take to be a nice example of Shakespeare's self-deflatory humour: a mocking glance at himself where he is being most earnest, as in the Sonnets. The secretary (Lodowick) is ordered by the king to compose a poem in praise of the Countess and, after several pages of detailed instruction as to what it should say, succeeds only in producing two comically inappropriate lines. But a serious point is also being made about the futility of poetical comparisons and flattery – a central theme of the Sonnets to which he was shortly to return in *Love's Labour's Lost*.

It is significant, however, that in all those features in which the earlier *Arden of Faversham* has been claimed to be strong – characterisation, social realism and treatment of its minor roles, to which I would add coherent structure – *Edward III* is notably weak. After what would have been for Shakespeare a uniquely feeble opening, in which Edward's claim to the throne of France is introduced, the remainder of the first two acts is occupied by his attempted seduction of the Countess, the wife of one of his nobles, and only when her honour and courage have been shown to triumph over his lust do we cross to France for a confused account of the battles of Sluys, Crécy and Poitiers. The two parts of the play (Acts 1 and 2, and 3 to 5) fail to hang together, and the character of the king remains an enigma. The Countess lacks the outraged dignity that Shakespeare would have given her, and the other characters are little more than ciphers.[20]

The most likely explanation for Shakespeare's undoubted connection with the play is that during the latter part of 1593 or early 1594, Henslowe, in anticipation of the combined season of the Admiral's and Chamberlain's men at Newington Butts in June of the latter year, offered Shakespeare the part of Lodowick (doubling, perhaps, with King John of France in Part 2), and that Shakespeare accepted on condition that he could revise those scenes of the play in which he appeared, mainly Act 2. But the season failed and came to a premature end while *Edward III* was still in rehearsal. On the renewed separation of the two companies, it would then have gone to the Admiral's, with which Henslowe (through Alleyn) retained a close connection, and was played by them in the City prior to its publication in 1596. (That it was not performed after 1603 is explained by the play's uncomplimentary references to the Scots that would certainly have been taken as gravely offensive to King James and thus have landed its authors in jail.)

— ★ —

> From the besieged Ardea all in post,
> Borne by the trustless wings of false desire,
> Lust-breathed Tarquin leaves the Roman host
> And to Collatium bears the lightless fire,
> Which in pale embers hid lurks to aspire
>   And girdle with embracing flames the waist
>   Of Collatine's fair love, Lucrece the chaste.

So begins the product of that 'graver labour' Shakespeare had promised Southampton. Again, we are plunged straight into action; but in contrast to the sunlit outdoors of *Venus and Adonis* with its frequent reminders of the vibrant life of nature in the background, here we are taken indoors at 'dead of night', where the tapestried walls of Lucrece's chamber are illuminated only by the 'lightless fire' of Tarquin's torch and the hellish embers of his lust.

The scene is more obviously theatrical, but in a mode of sombre tragedy to which Shakespeare would not return until, some ten years later, he came to write *Othello* and *Macbeth*. For the story of Lucrece, he drew on the Latin of Ovid and Livy; but in putting it into English he was following in the footsteps of his medieval predecessors – of Chaucer, Gower and Lydgate – who had already made of it a familiar tale and established the figure of Lucrece as an admired moral exemplar. It was the nearest Shakespeare ever came to writing a tragedy in the unalloyed classical manner, and he goes so far in that direction as to indicate the formalised gestures, as laid down by classical writers on oratory, its performance would require.[21] The prose 'Argument' that precedes the poem in the published text may draw some of its details from Painter's translation of Livy in his *Pallace of Pleasure* (1566) and reads almost like a theatrical 'Plot'. Of its 1,855 lines, again nearly half (as in *Venus and Adonis*) are of direct speech, and some of its rhetorical set pieces – especially Lucrece's invocation to the Night in the aftermath of her rape – cry out for a great classical actress (a Sybil Thorndike or a Diana Rigg) to deliver:

> O comfort-killing Night, image of hell,
> Dim register and notary of shame,
> Black stage for tragedies and murders fell,

> Vast sin-concealing chaos, nurse of blame,
> Blind muffled bawd, dark harbour for defame!
> Grim cave of death, whisp'ring conspirator
> With close-tongued treason and the ravisher!
>
> (ll. 764–70)

– and so on for a further thirty-eight tremendous stanzas of complaint. And this is followed by a beautifully sensitive scene between Lucrece and her maid – awe-struck by the intensity of her mistress' grief and not yet understanding its cause – that, without a word of alteration, might have graced a play for the stage if Shakespeare had chosen to write it.

The poem lacks the narrative flow and interplay of *Venus and Adonis*, and the unrelieved pain of its subject matter makes it the more difficult to read. It contains, as we might expect, a number of cross-references to *Venus* and the earlier Sonnets. Nothing could better illustrate Shakespeare's flexibility of mind and the many-sided nature of his creative imagination than that he was able to combine in so relatively short a period work on so many contrasting themes with such wide divergencies of mood.

The poem was published, again by Field, in May or June 1594, with another self-deprecatory dedication to Southampton.

To the Right Honourable, Henry Wriothesley, Earle of Southampton, and Baron of Titchfield.

The love I dedicate to your Lordship is without end: wherof this Pamphlet without beginning is but a superfluous Moity. The warrant I have of your Honourable disposition, not the worth of my untutored Lines makes it assured of acceptance. What I have done is yours, what I have to doe is yours, being part in all I have, devoted yours. Were my worth greater, my duety would shew greater, meane time, as it is, it is bound to your Lordship; To whom I wish long life still lengthned with all happinesse.

Though generally considered to be warmer in tone, the letter ends as before, 'Your Lordships in all duety, William Shakespeare'.[22]

Shakespeare was in exuberant mood when, probably in the early months of 1594, he came to write *Love's Labour's Lost* – the last of his plays belonging to the period. Like the *Two Gentlemen*, its ambience is courtly Arcadian. It tells a story of the King of Navarre and three of his young courtiers who vow to devote themselves to philosophy for three years in rural seclusion, and during that time to forgo the society of women; whereupon a Princess of France with her ladies promptly arrive on the scene with predictable results. The play fairly fizzles with word-play, and the popular element in it – represented not only by Kempe as Costard the clown, but also a supporting cast of richly comic characters for which Shakespeare clearly had other known actors in mind – is more pronounced than in the *Two Gentlemen*.

The high spirits of its author, which I attribute to his success in obtaining a share in the new company then in process of formation, the Lord Chamberlain's, overflow into good-humoured satire at the expense of figures in the literary-cum-political circles of the time, and their factional in-fighting. This has made of the play a happy hunting ground for scholars in search of hidden meanings; of a general theory that would throw light on Shakespeare's own allegiances in the period (an aim that no one yet has come near to achieving, if any such meaning is there to be found). Editions of the published text are thick with recondite notes in which every quibble and pun is subject to a learned essay. All this is doubtless necessary and valuable to the student, but should not be allowed to smother the spirit of uninhibited fun which, in an unimpeded reading or performance, is the play's dominant mood. We do not need to know that in the tortuously rhetorical speeches of the fantastical Spaniard Don Armado, Shakespeare may be satirising the prose style of some contemporary pedant to find them funny; or appreciate that Armado's page, Moth (a supercharged Speed from the *Two Gentlemen*), may relate to the personality of the mercurial Nashe to enjoy the comic interplay between them. The learned exhibitionism of the schoolmaster Holofernes, the simple folly of the parson Sir Nathaniel, and the honest stupidity of Dull may or may not reflect the failings of particular individuals among Shakespeare's contemporaries (if they do, no two scholars agree as to their identity), but they can just as easily be taken and enjoyed as representative of varieties of pomposity to be as commonly encountered now as they would have been then. Most of the textual obscurity that remains derives from the particularity of Shakespeare's references to traditional songs, proverbs and stories familiar to his audience but which have since been forgotten, and the apparent inability he betrays (here more than in any other of his plays) to refuse any and every opportunity for a pun, however far-fetched; both of which would have been especially enjoyed by the groundlings. In a modern production, they can be pruned to advantage.

Both in its mockery (more affectionate than savage) of the inconstancy of the king and his friends in having so easily abandoned their vows of celibacy on the appearance of the ladies, and (more broadly) those who, through self-conceit and a desire to impress, mangle the language, the message of the play (in so far as it has one) lies in its assertion of the superiority of common sense over misapplied learning, and the ways of nature over artificiality of behaviour and expression. 'The words of Mercury' may be 'harsh after the songs of Apollo', but are just as necessary and desirable. The same message pervades the Sonnets. I give a few of the more obvious parallels in Section 4 of the Appendix; but it should not be overlooked that the scene in which the hypocrisy of the king and his companions is revealed (IV.iii), the crux of the plot, turns upon their secret composition of Sonnets and other poems of love. The more recondite references that have been alleged to the Marprelate and other controversies of the time remain conjectural, and the mention of the 'school of night', of which so much has been made, may, as likely as not, result from a misprint.

On the supposition that the play would have been 'caviare to the general', it is said to have been written for private performance in some nobleman's house (possibly Southampton's), where the larger than usual number of boys required to play Moth and the five female roles would have been available from among the resident choirboys and pages. On the contrary, I find it much more probable that Shakespeare wrote it for court or City performance, drawing on the resources of an existing company of players, including Kempe and other skilled men who would have brought their trained apprentices with them to play the boys' parts,[23] and that the company in question was the newly formed Chamberlain's men. In such a company,

Shakespeare, at the age of twenty-nine or thirty, would have been ideally cast as Ferdinand, the king. The play was to remain generally popular. It was performed for the Queen at Christmas 1597 or 1598, and again for King James in 1605. According to the Second Quarto of 1631, it was also acted 'by his Majesties Servants at the Blacke-Friers and the Globe'.[24]

Shakespeare's period of inactivity as a player was over, and later in 1594 we find him with Kempe, Richard Burbage and others as a sharer-member of the Chamberlain's (ultimately King's) company, which he was to serve as poet and player for the rest of his career. He had used his enforced 'sabbatical' to write two lengthy narrative poems, a substantial number of sonnets, three plays, and found time to make important revisions to a fourth, not his own. As we embark in the following chapter on a survey of his future plays and the parts that he played in them, we must also take occasion to look more closely at the personalities of his fellow players and the theatrical conditions prevailing in the period that were to govern their collaboration. For though his own genius was to make by far the most significant and lasting contribution to the company's work, his fellows deserve more credit than they usually get for what was to be a unique theatrical enterprise; one that was to provide him with the ideal setting in which his outstanding abilities as dramatic poet were to grow to greatness.

SEVEN

Chamberlain's Man

However much we may think of him as a genius apart, to himself and to his age he appeared primarily as a busy actor associated with the leading stock-company of his time; . . . writing that his troupe might successfully compete with rival organizations; and, finally, as a theatrical proprietor, owning shares in two of the most flourishing playhouses in London. Thus his whole life was centred in the stage and his interests were essentially those of his 'friends and fellows', the actors, who affectionately called him 'our Shakespeare'.

J. Quincy Adams[1]

We do not know the exact circumstances surrounding the formation of the Chamberlain's men in 1594, or on what basis players were selected to become its original sharers. No doubt it was an honour to be asked, especially as the position was to carry with it the privileges of a Groom of the Chamber including protection from arrest; but a financial investment was also required in a capital fund from which costumes and props could be purchased as well as a repertoire of plays. To these last, Shakespeare would have been able to contribute in kind from the fruits of his labours in the preceding year which, as we have seen, included the *Two Gentlemen of Verona*, the *Comedy of Errors* and *Love's Labour's Lost*, along with the previously unperformed *Richard III*, over which he had presumably retained the rights. But others of his earlier plays that in course of time were to feature in the Chamberlain's programme would have had to be bought in from those who had first commissioned them: *Titus* (already in print) from Henslowe; the *Shrew* and *Henry VI* from Alleyn. It was, however, primarily as a player, rather than a dramatist, that he had been invited to join the new company, and for that reason he is unlikely to have been wholly exempt from the obligation to contribute to the considerable costs of setting it up; for it was on the basis of that initial stake in its capital that his subsequent share in the profits of the enterprise would, like those of his fellows, depend.

The Lord Chamberlain who had initiated the company by granting it his patronage was Henry Carey, Lord Hunsdon. It was not the first troupe of players to have looked to him for protection; a company known originally as Lord Hunsdon's men is recorded on tour and as giving occasional performances at court between 1564 and 1585 when, on Hunsdon's appointment to his high office, it became the Chamberlain's. But the last we hear of this earlier troupe is at Maidstone in 1590, and there is unlikely to have been any continuity between it and the one that Shakespeare joined in 1594.[2]

The decline of the Queen's players following the death of their chief attraction, Tarlton, in 1588, and the disbandment of Leicester's in the same year, had left a gap that needed to be filled: but more immediately the new company may have owed its inception to the breaking of the Admiral's/Strange's alliance in February 1593 because of the plague, and the dispersal of its players. It was one of the Chamberlain's responsibilities, exercised through the Master of the Revels, to provide court entertainment of a quality to satisfy the high demands of the Queen. In the best of times this was no easy task, but by the autumn of 1593 it had become an impossible one. The Pembroke company had collapsed on tour in the course of the summer. Even Henslowe of the Rose was feeling the pinch: 'comend me harteley to all the reast of youre fealowes in generall', he wrote to Alleyn in August, 'for I growe poore for lacke of them'.[3] There were none of the usual plays at court that Christmas, and the sudden death of Ferdinando, earl of Derby (formerly Lord Strange), in April of the new year can only have added to the general uncertainty. With the plague easing, and the London playhouses starting to reopen in the summer of 1594, there was both need and opportunity for a new beginning.

It is interesting to find that the company's first appearance was in conjunction with Alleyn and a remnant of the Admiral's under Henslowe's management, and that the venue was an out-of-the-way theatre at Newington Butts – well outside the City limits. This was in June 1594, and Shakespeare's personal involvement is suggested by the presence of his *Taming of the Shrew* and *Titus Andronicus* among the plays performed. The season lasted only ten days and is usually put down as a failure, but may have been primarily intended as a try-out for the new company. At all events, it was out of that short season that the shape of the future Chamberlain's emerged, and it will be seen that with the notable exception of Alleyn (who had other irons in the fire), it included the more senior and experienced men from all the previously existing companies.

Richard Burbage (Plate 6) had begun his career in the 1580s with his father James as a Queen's man, and in 1590 is found playing important parts in a revival of the second part of Tarlton's *Seven Deadly Sins* by the Admiral's/Strange's alliance – probably at the Theatre, which his father had built. But his connection with that company and its leading player, Edward Alleyn, is unlikely to have survived a bitter dispute that had broken out during the company's tenancy between the Burbages and Alleyns (Ned and his elder brother John, who was not a player) over division of the box office takings, in the course of which James had made slighting remarks about the Lord Admiral. This had resulted in Alleyn abandoning the Theatre for the Rose. It is equally unlikely then that Richard had played any part in the season at the Rose of 1592/3, when Shakespeare's *Henry VI* had attracted the praise of Nashe and the envy of Greene.[4]

Like his father, Richard was – in those young days at least – of a fiery temperament and, in the heat of another dispute involving James's business dealings, had wielded a 'broom staff' to see off an unwelcome visitor to the theatre yard and twisted another man's nose.[5] His date of birth is not recorded, but he was junior to his brother Cuthbert, born in 1566/7; at the time of the quarrel with Alleyn he would have been about twenty-two or twenty-three, and thus a mature twenty-six or seven when he found himself a fellow of Shakespeare's in the Chamberlain's. He was to succeed Alleyn as the leading player of his day, but in

1594 his great potential may not have been immediately apparent. Actors develop their individual powers in responding to the challenges that dramatists give them. As Alleyn had risen on the wings of Kyd's Hieronimo, Marlowe's Tamburlaine, Barabas and Faustus, Burbage was to reach even greater heights in essaying Shakespeare's Hamlet, Othello and Lear; in 1594 these roles were still some way in the future.

William Kempe, on the other hand, came to the company with an already established reputation as comedian and clown in the tradition of Tarlton, but he was also an experienced actor. He is first recorded as a Leicester's man in the Low Countries in 1586/7, from where he had made his way to Denmark, as attested by an Elsinore pay-roll. He was back in England by 1590, when Nashe dedicated his *Almond for a Parrat* to him, describing him as 'that Most Comicall and conceited Cavaleire Monsieur du Kempe, Jestmonger and Vice-gerent generall to the Ghost of Dicke Tarlton'.[6] After the death of Leicester, Kempe had joined the Admiral's, and had played one of the men of Goteham in the anonymous *A Knacke to know a Knave* at the Rose in 1592/3. When the play was published in 1594, it was described on its title page as 'Newlie set foorth, as it hath sundrie tymes bene played by ED. ALLEN and his Companie. With KEMPS applauded Merrimentes of the men of Goteham, in receiving the King into Goteham'. As the 'Merrimentes' occupy little more than a page of the printed text and read as only moderately amusing, the prominence of Kempe's name on the title page may be taken as a publishers' device (not entirely unknown today) to attract additional sales, and thus as an indication of Kempe's popular appeal at the time.[7] That Shakespeare knew him well, admired his skills, and anticipated working with him again in the not-so-distant future is strongly suggested by the roles of Launce, the Dromios and Costard that he had written for him in the previous year.

We cannot be sure of the exact number of founding sharers, but there were certainly eight and possibly ten. Along with Shakespeare, Burbage and Kempe, three others may be taken as certain as they are named at various times between 1594 and 1598 as receiving payment on behalf of the sharers as a whole for the company's court performances; these were George Bryan, Thomas Pope and John Heminges. Bryan and Pope were former

Leicester's men who (along with Kempe) had accompanied their patron to the Low Countries in 1585 and, after their return and the death of Leicester in 1588, had transferred to Strange's and from Strange's, to the Alleyn-led alliance. Heminges had probably begun his career as a Queen's man but had transferred to Strange's by May 1593. All three were senior to Shakespeare – certainly in professional status.

To these original sharers, we should probably add the names of Augustine Phillips, William Sly, Richard Cowley and Henry Condell who, with those already mentioned, occupy the first nine places after Shakespeare himself in the list of 'Principall Actors in all these Playes' printed by Heminges and Condell at the front of their First Folio of 1623, reproduced in Plate 1. All would have been familiar to Shakespeare as former colleagues from the Admiral's or the Admiral's alliance with Strange's. Phillips was another former Strange's man and, like Bryan and Pope, had been a sharer in that company. Sly we have already encountered playing the tinker 'Sly' in the *Shrew* back in 1587/8, and, so far as we know, had remained with the Admiral's ever since.[8] Of Condell and Cowley, I shall have more to say in a moment. Though our knowledge of all these fellows of Shakespeare, and of the roles that each of them played, is so limited, we should not underrate their abilities, or the significance of the contribution they made to the plays he wrote for them. They were all distinguished men in their day. Apart from Burbage and Kempe (of whom we know a good deal more than the others), Pope was famous for his playing of 'clowns' – in modern terms, as a character comedian – and, along with Phillips and Sly, was to receive valedictory praise from Thomas Heywood in his *Apology for Actors* of 1612, in that, though all three were then dead, 'their deserts yet live in the remembrance of many' – the best that can be said of any actor.[9]

Though the sharers, as we have seen, *were* the company in a legal and constitutional sense, they were not the *whole* of the company; rather, a nucleus of leading men who shared financial and managerial responsibility for its success or failure. They did not appear in every play; nor did they always play the leading roles.[10] In the operation of a repertoire system of the kind to which they and other companies in the period all adhered, with daily rotation of plays and limited time for rehearsal, that would have been impossibly exhausting, and it would often have fallen to them to take (and often to double) smaller, but nonetheless important, subsidiary roles. But in casting the plays – doubtless in consultation with his fellows – Shakespeare and other dramatists like Ben Jonson who wrote for the company were able to draw on a much larger body of players, comprising apprentices and 'hired men'. Of these, the apprentices were of prime importance, for not only did they play all the younger female parts, but these were often among the leads. (We have only to think of Kate in the *Shrew*, Portia in the *Merchant of Venice*, Helena in *All's Well that Ends Well*, Juliet, Cleopatra and Cressida for the point to be made.) Nor were they limited to female parts, for in addition to the numerous messengers and servants that would necessarily have gone to them, there is reason to believe (as argued below for Romeo) that they played many of the male juvenile leads also.

Much confusion has surrounded the question of the age at which boys were apprenticed and the length of their apprenticeships, and the only certain conclusion to be drawn from currently available evidence is that both were extremely variable. The age is found to vary between ten and sixteen, and the term between three and twelve years; nor can we assume that the younger the boy, the longer the term; indeed, the opposite may well have been true. In the children's companies, such as the Queen's Revels in 1606, boys were contracted for only three years – presumably until their voices broke. In the Chamberlain's, where the usual age of recruitment was probably thirteen or fourteen, the term appears to have been seven or eight years to take the boys to their majority at twenty-one, but in one late instance extended to twelve.[11] During the whole period of their training, the boys were maintained by their individual masters and instructors, who were, however, entitled to charge the common funds of the company with an agreed amount in return for their services.[12] On completion of whatever term he had agreed to serve, the apprentice was normally employed as a 'hired man' (journeyman player) before becoming a sharer himself – though the final step was not guaranteed; it would have depended on the talents he had to offer and, as for Shakespeare himself who did not achieve it until he was thirty, the availability of a vacant place, for which he might have to wait a considerable time and still be required to pay a hefty premium as the price of his admission. As a hired man, he received a weekly wage which, like the sharers' expenses in the maintenance of their apprentices, was charged to the company, along with other production expenses, before division of the profits (if any) among the sharers.

In the absence of complete, printed texts of the plays when they were first performed, the actors had to make do in rehearsal with individual, hand-written parts and cues. As they were often required to double or treble parts, it was usually necessary to post a notice backstage to remind them of the sequence of characters and scenes in which they appeared. These were known as 'plots' and, fortunately, several have survived. One for the second part of Tarlton's *Seven Deadly Sins*, found among Alleyn's papers at Dulwich and dated to about 1590 (before Alleyn's break with the Burbages and move to the Rose), is especially valuable as it gives the names of most of the actors who were members of the alliance at the time, including the apprentices, along with the parts that they played.

By comparing the names in the plot with those in the Folio list of principal actors, it may be possible to recover the identities of some of the Chamberlain's original apprentices, as these are likely to have accompanied their masters into the new company at the time of its foundation. As nearly all the 'principal actors' are known to have been, in fact, sharers in the Chamberlain's or King's at one time or another, we may also be able to determine how many of the apprentices did eventually obtain that final promotion. One difficulty, however, is that while the sharers in the plot (such as Bryan, Pope and Phillips) appear under their surnames graced by the prefix 'Mr', and the hired men under surname and initial, the apprentices are referred to only by first names or nicknames, so we cannot always be certain of their identity.

In the plot, Harry, Kit and Vincent are recorded as playing small male roles, and Saunder, Nick, Robert, Ned, Will and T. Belt, female roles. 'Harry' and 'Kit' were very probably Henry Condell and Christopher Beeston. Both were to be named by Jonson as 'principall Comedians' in the cast of his *Every Man In his Humour* as performed by the Chamberlain's in 1598, but only Condell became a sharer – perhaps as previously suggested from the start, but certainly by 1603; Beeston (who was to be named by Phillips in his will as his 'servant') had by the latter year transferred to a reconstituted Worcester's.[13] 'Vincent' is unusual among players in the period as either Christian or surname; he is likely to have been the Thomas Vincent we know to have occupied the important post of book-keeper and prompter at the Globe, and may even have done so from the company's beginnings.[14]

Of the younger apprentices who had played women's parts in the *Deadly Sins*, 'Saunder' or 'Sander' is an obvious abbreviation of Alexander that also appears as a speech prefix in the pirated version of Shakespeare's *Shrew* – the one with the indefinite article, performed by Pembroke's; almost certainly, it relates to Alexander Cooke, who was to become a sharer in the later King's company (he is thirteenth in the Folio list of principal actors). He may have gone to Pembroke's as a boy on the breaking of the Admiral's/Strange's alliance early in 1593 but, when Pembroke's collapsed in the summer of the same year, would then have been free to join the Chamberlain's as Heminges' apprentice. Heminges was a freeman of the London Grocers and had used his privileges as such to apprentice Cooke for, having served his time, Cooke was to be received into that company in 1608. This does not imply (as some scholars have suggested) that either Heminges or Cooke led 'double lives' as players and grocers. The full-time nature of their commitment as players makes that very improbable and there is no evidence for it. It was, in fact, quite possible for a boy to be apprenticed as a grocer *to learn the craft of a player* if that was his master's usual occupation, as evidenced by the case of William Trigg, apprenticed to Heminges in 1626 for a term of twelve years for 'la arte d'une Stage player'.[15] If Cooke had entered into his apprenticeship with Heminges on the formation of the company in 1594 or a year or two later, and was enfranchised in 1608, he would have served a similar term. He features under his full name in the cast-lists of all of Jonson's plays, and one by Beaumont and Fletcher, acted by the King's between 1603 and 1613, probably playing the more mature women's parts, as he may also have done in Shakespeare's plays during the same period, for he would then have been in his late twenties or early thirties. He was to die young in 1614, leaving a young family. In his will, he was to appoint Heminges and Condell as trustees for his children, and requests them to take charge of the money he had left for them and 'see it saflye put into grocers hall'. He also refers to a sum of £50, 'which is in the hand of my fellowes as my share of the stock'.[16] This, then, was the premium he had paid on becoming a sharer, which after his death would be returned to his estate.

Nick was quite a common name among players of the period, but the 'Nick' of the plot was probably Nicholas Tooley, born in 1575. He may have begun his career in the Admiral's, playing several small servant roles with the prefix 'Nicke' in the Folio text of the *Shrew* when he was aged twelve or thirteen, and a female role in the *Deadly Sins* when he was fifteen. If so, he would have been nineteen at the formation of the Chamberlain's. His first, fully named appearance with the company was in Jonson's *The Alchemist* in 1610, but he is likely to have been active in Shakespeare's plays from a much earlier date, if not from the beginning. He never married, and was to die in the house of Richard Burbage's brother Cuthbert, referring in his will to Richard (who had predeceased him) as his 'late master'; he is named in nineteenth place in the Folio list. The 'Ro. Go.' of the plot is plainly Robert Gough, who was a beneficiary of Pope's will in 1603, and probably his apprentice, along with John Edmans (later a Queen Anne's man); they were to divide their former master's 'wearing apparrell and armes' between them. In the same year, Gough was to marry Phillips' sister, Elizabeth, and to witness his brother-in-law's will in 1605. He had three children, one of whom, Alexander, followed him into the profession. He is known to have played male roles in the King's, and was a sharer by 1619 – twenty-third in the Folio list. We can only guess at the other boys named in the plot: 'Will' as perhaps William Eccleston, who was a King's man at various times between 1610 and 1622, like Gough a sharer by 1619, and (in twentieth place) a 'Principall Actor'; 'Ned' as just possibly Shakespeare's younger brother Edmund who is said to have followed him into the profession, though in 1590 he would have been only ten. 'T. Belt' wholly escapes us.

Though not distinguishable in the plot, several others are likely to have been apprentices in the Chamberlain's from an early date. Samuel Crosse, though listed twelfth among the principal actors, did not survive long enough to be named in any of the

Jacobean cast-lists, and may have been a victim of the plague which, though quiescent in the City in the late 1590s, rose to a new peak of virulence in 1603. Samuel Gilburne (in fourteenth place in the Folio list) is named in Phillips' will of 1605 as his 'late apprentice' and was bequeathed 40*s* in money, his master's velvet hose and white taffeta doublet, black taffeta suit, purple cloak, sword and dagger, and a bass viol. There is a fleeting reference to him as 'Gebon' (which is probably how his name was pronounced and known to Shakespeare) in a rogue stage direction in *Henry V*, and touchingly, his signature has been found in a copy of the First Folio.

James Sandes appears in Phillips' will as his current apprentice, and was to receive the same amount of money as Gilburne, plus a 'Citterne, a Bandore and a Lute', but only at 'thexpiracon of his yeares in his Indentur or Aprenticehood'. The management of Sandes' apprenticeship was to be taken over by Sly, one of Phillips' executors, who when he came to make his own will in 1608 left him a munificent £40.[17]

It is impossible to be exact, but Burbage, Pope and Heminges all appear to have brought apprentices with them from their previous companies, and others were recruited. At the company's formation, there could hardly have been fewer than seven or eight boys apprenticed to one or other of the sharers. And as these moved slowly up the ladder to become hired men and often sharers in their turn, there would have been no lack of applicants to replace them.[18] It was a royal road to advancement in their profession and few appear to have fallen by the way. Once they had joined, the majority were to remain with the company for the rest of their active careers – and usually that meant for the rest of their lives.

Of the hired men of the *Deadly Sins* plot – those whose surnames and initials are given without the distinguishing 'Mr' – only R. Burbage, W. Sly, R. Cowley, J. Duke and J. Sincler joined the Chamberlain's; Burbage, Sly, perhaps Cowley, from the start. Richard Cowley was to be named by Shakespeare in a 'rogue direction' as playing Verges to Kempe's Dogberry in *Much Ado About Nothing*. John Duke appears with Christopher Beeston in the cast of Jonson's *Every Man In his Humour* in 1598 but, like Beeston, he was to leave the Chamberlain's for Worcester's by 1603 and was never a sharer. But where in the plot, we may ask, were Mr Heminges and W. Shakespeare who, by 1590, would both have been well-established as members of the Alleyn-led alliance? And where for that matter is Alleyn himself? Presumably taking a play 'out'; but for Heminges and Shakespeare we must look to the play's presenters: John Lydgate the poet and King Henry VI who, because they never leave the stage and it would be impossible for them to double, need no reminding of the parts they are playing or the sequence of scenes in which they appear.[19]

These then were Shakespeare's fellows when he started out in 1594 as a Chamberlain's man: eight, possibly ten sharers with their apprentices, and four or five regularly employed hired men including one or two player-musicians.[20] I have spent some time in establishing their identities – in so far as that is now possible – because the company was to be of unique importance in theatrical history; not only because Shakespeare belonged to it and wrote for it, but for its unparalleled success as a co-operative enterprise, which was to survive the passing of both its original sharers and principal playwright, and take it to the eve of the civil wars and the closure of the playhouses by the Puritans in 1642. It was something much more than a group of actors brought together for a particular production or, at best, for a season of plays (as the term 'company' is understood today), but rather a living, self-perpetuating community. Professor Baldwin wrote of it as the 'Shakespeare clan'; it would be more accurate to describe it as a family: a body of players with their musicians, tiremen and stage keepers working together on a permanent basis and, in many instances, living in close proximity to each other in the same suburb of the City; self-perpetuating because it contained within its structure both a school of acting and a natural means of progression whereby its members could advance in their profession so far as their abilities were sufficient to take them from being apprentices to hired men, and from hired men to sharers.[21] And for evidence that the relations of its members with each other were far closer than merely professional, we have only to read their wills; the way in which masters remember their apprentices and former apprentices, apprentices their masters, and the sharers their fellows. To refer to it as the 'Shakespeare clan' or the 'Shakespeare company' is to mistake both Shakespeare's place in it – always one of partnership, never of dominance – and the nature of the company itself, founded as it was on the equality of its sharers and leading men under its successive patrons.

One consequence of the general neglect by biographers and scholars of Shakespeare's professional activity as performer and man of the theatre has been to separate him from his fellows; because of his concurrent role as dramatist, to see him as somehow detached from them; choosing themes and subjects to explore in accordance with his personal interests or moods of the moment with little, if any, regard for the men who would be called upon to perform the plays and carry responsibility for their success or failure, whereas all the evidence from the period as to the position of the dramatist in relation to the troupe he served indicates a collaborative process.[22] Every aspect of the plays and their production – initial choice of theme and title, intended performance venues, size of cast, casting of the principal and apprentice roles, hired men to be employed – would necessarily have been subject to the agreement of his fellows. It is no denial of Shakespeare's genius as poet and dramatist to state that the plays he wrote for the company, from *Romeo and Juliet* to *Henry VIII*, were shaped and brought to the form in which they have come down to us as the result of a co-operative effort by the company as a whole, to which the youngest apprentice and the most junior hired man would have had a contribution to make; it is rather to affirm it.

In 1594, there was only one thing that the Chamberlain's men lacked to ensure the company's success, and that was a permanent home – a theatre in the capital they could call their own and that would serve as a base for all their future activities. That was to come their way five years later. In the meantime, they did what the companies had always done: they took to the road.

In the late summer of 1594, we find them at Marlborough, and there were doubtless visits to other Wiltshire and Berkshire towns; but on 8 October they were back in London, as attested by a letter from Lord Hunsdon to the Lord Mayor, requesting him, 'the time beinge such as, thankes be to god, there is nowe no danger of the sicknes', to suffer his 'nowe companie of Players' to exercise their quality at the Cross Keys inn in Gracechurch Street in the City.[23] Requests from the Lord Chamberlain were not lightly refused, and the probability is that the company performed there throughout the winter of 1594/5. Its repertoire would almost certainly have included *Titus* and the *Shrew* as these had been given at Newington Butts in June and were already in the repertoire. The opening scenes of the *Shrew*, set in an inn, would have made good use of the Cross Key's galleries and yard, which by this date had probably been covered to protect the groundlings from the worst of the weather. *The Comedy of Errors* is another virtual certainty for inclusion in the Cross Keys season because we know that a special performance of it was given on Innocents' Day (28 December) at Grays Inn, where a stage had been built and scaffolds set up 'to the top of the house'. *The Two Gentlemen* and *Love's Labour's Lost* are also likely to have received their first City performances during the course of the winter. There were good parts in all of these plays for several of the players we have identified as present in the company, including Burbage, Sly, 'Sinklo', Shakespeare as their respective 'dukes', and not least Kempe, who would already have been one of the company's big attractions. Only Alleyn would have been missed.

I have said that in forming the company, Hunsdon is likely to have been motivated in part by the need to supply quality entertainment to the Queen and the court, who had been starved of it throughout the time of plague. In writing to the Lord Mayor on its behalf in October – an unusual, though doubtless welcome, step for a patron to take – he may have had the same consideration in mind, for by bringing his players to the capital and ensuring a winter venue for them there, they would also have been available for duty at court. This is borne out by the record already quoted of a payment of £20 to William Kempe, William Shakespeare and Richard Burbage for performances at Greenwich on 26 and 28 December.[24]

In the meantime, Shakespeare would have been hard at work on the two plays that most editors agree were next in the sequence of his writing: *Romeo and Juliet* and *A Midsummer Night's Dream*. With these, Shakespeare was to enter on a new, more confident and lyrical phase that was to produce some of his most magical and universally popular plays. For the first time, he had a large company comprising many of the finest acting talents of the day at his disposal, supported by a more than adequate supply of enthusiastic apprentices of various ages, and a position among them that ensured his voice would be heard. The five years that followed were also to see the creation of *King John*, *Richard II*, *The Merchant of Venice*, *Henry IV* (1 and 2), *Henry V*, *The Merry Wives of Windsor*, *Much Ado About Nothing*, *As You Like It*, and the second of the Roman plays, *Julius Caesar*. It was as though all the brakes and restrictions on his creativity he had suffered in the past were removed at a stroke. Though never exempt from those numerous hard choices and petty difficulties that theatrical conditions at all times impose on authors and players alike in bringing a new play to life on the stage, he now found himself with a straight path before him – one from which he was never to turn back.

Romeo and Juliet is the first of Shakespeare's undoubted masterpieces. The story was not new; orginating in folklore, it had gained wide currency in England through the publication of Arthur Brooke's poem, *Romeus*, in 1562. Its dramatic potential would have been obvious to Shakespeare's fellow sharers from the moment he first suggested it to them as a possible subject. Theatrically, the play has everything: 'a pair of star-crossed lovers', an Italian setting, sharply defined and believable characters, a nail-biting plot, and language ranging in tone from the grossly bawdy to the sublimely lyrical. In the frantic four days into which the plot is compressed, the whole life of a Renaissance city is brought before us in scenes of civil brawl, domestic turmoil, merriment, and sudden death. Nothing remotely like it had ever been put on the stage before.

It is a play of the summer, and is likely to have been first performed in James Burbage's Theatre, which lay across fields in the parish of St Leonard's, Shoreditch, just outside the Bishopsgate entrance to the City, in the summer of 1595. The Theatre's open thrust stage, closely encompassed by tiered galleries and a yard, accommodating some three thousand people all in intimate communication with the performers, offered an ideal venue for the expansive action of the play.

There were several doors at the back of the stage, one of them being used as a curtained entry point, from which, for example, Juliet could quickly appear to take the stage after the scene of the Romeo/Tybalt duel –

> Gallop apace, you fiery-footed steeds,
> Towards Phoebus' lodging. Such a waggoner
> As Phaeton would whip you to the west
> And bring in cloudy night immediately.　　(III.ii.1–4)

– one of the most astonishing moments in the whole of
Renaissance drama, which has the effect of changing the scene in
an instant of time from Verona's sun-baked, blood-stained piazza,
where the pronouncement of Romeo's banishment still hangs in
the air, to the shadowed intimacy of Juliet's chamber. For the
lovers, the time that keeps them apart cannot pass too quickly;
when they are together they seek to delay it; this relativity of time
is of the essence of the play. As audience, we are ahead of them
both. We know how the story is to end because Shakespeare tells
us in the Prologue, but nevertheless are kept in a state of
suspenseful anxiety as we watch it unfold. He makes us care very
much about the fate of all his characters.

The extreme youth of the lovers is vital to the play's
credibility. Juliet's age is reduced by Shakespeare from sixteen
in his immediate source to just short of fourteen, and was
necessarily played by a boy of similar age. Romeo is young
enough at the play's opening to be still in the thrall of calf-love;
'run through the ear with a love song', as Mercutio puts it,
'And is he a man to encounter Tybalt?' (II.iv.14–17). Plainly, he
is not. At twenty-seven or eight, Richard Burbage would have
been too mature a man to play the part convincingly or match
with a thirteen-year-old Juliet. It would have gone to one of the
older apprentices or younger sharers (Beeston, perhaps, or
Condell), with Burbage as Mercutio and the comedian Pope as
Capulet. That the small part of Peter, the Nurse's man, was
intended for Kempe, we know from a 'rogue' direction in the
Good Quarto text (at IV.v.99), 'Enter Will Kemp', copied no
doubt from Shakespeare's manuscript, and that the Apothecary
was written for his favourite thin man (John Sincler) is apparent
from Romeo's description of him as a 'caitiff wretch', 'meagre'
of looks, whose 'Sharp misery had worn him to the bones'
(V.i.40 ff).

I have little doubt that the Chorus who speaks the Prologue
and a linking narration after the masque (both in the form of a
sonnet) was taken by Shakespeare in his dual capacity as poet

and performer – a representative voice. It is a collective, not authorial, possessive he is using:

> Two households both alike in dignity
> (In fair Verona, where *we* lay *our* scene) . . .
>
> The fearful passage of their death-mark'd love . . .
> Is now the two hours' traffic of *our* stage;
> The which, if you with patient ears attend,
> What here shall miss, *our* toil shall strive to mend.

It was the first occasion on which he had begun a play with a prologue and spoken it himself, but it was not to be the last, and it did not preclude him – either here or later – from assuming other parts in the play that was to follow. The entrance of the Prince at an intermediate point between the two choruses (at I.i.78) makes it unlikely, however, that this admittedly 'kingly' role was one of them; it is too similar in diction and insufficiently distinctive in character to make a viable double.[25] The disappearance of the Chorus from the play after the opening of Act 2, and the absence of a formal Epilogue,[26] suggest to me a change of mind: that Shakespeare had originally intended entering as poet at intervals throughout the play, but in the course of writing, finding further Chorus interjections unnecessary, rejected his initial idea in favour of doubling his choric role in the first two acts with that of the Friar, whose first entrance is in Act 2, Scene 3.

Friar Laurence is sometimes misconceived as a loquacious old dodderer who has nothing better to offer the desperate lovers than conventionally pious sentiments and a dubious 'magical potion'. When played in that way, the effect on the energy levels and pace of the performance can be near fatal. It is true that he speaks of his 'ancient ears', and his 'old feet' stumbling at graves; but Lady Capulet likewise refers to her 'old age' and she can be little more than twenty-eight. Like the passage of time, age in the play is relative. If the lovers are played as young as they should be, there is no need for the Friar to be more than middle-aged. He is the voice of prudence and conventional wisdom in the play, but also of good sense, and his strictures to the banished Romeo (in III.iii), if delivered with the authority and force that the situation requires, are necessary and effective in restoring the demoralised and near-hysterical youth to a semblance of manhood. However dubious the potion he prescribes for Juliet may appear to us now, it is, as he explains, a desperate remedy for a desperate situation, and it does in fact work; it is not his fault that the timing goes so disastrously wrong. Nor can we altogether blame him when, at a moment of crisis in the tomb, he loses his nerve. He does not have a superfluous line in the play, and his long, expository speech in the final scene – so often butchered in recent productions – is essential to the audience's understanding of the play's conclusion.[27]

There is a further consideration that may have weighed with Shakespeare in choosing to play the part himself, and it is one that introduces the more general question of the extent to which he was involved in directing this and other of his plays. He would have realised that the scenes in which, first Romeo, and then Juliet, come to the Friar's cell, positioned in the play as they are (Romeo's after the magical balcony scene), are ones in which the impetus of the performance might easily be lost, and that the necessarily limited experience of his young actors, however talented and well instructed, needed the stiffening of a seasoned adult for them to play against. If so, who better than himself?

The play was to make heavy demands on the company's apprentices – as the conjectural doubling plot I give in Appendix D demonstrates; for not only does it draw on them for its two leads and all the female characters, but also for most of its numerous servants, and Paris. It is sometimes assumed that, in the absence of a designated director, Elizabethan actors were left to find their own way about the stage; but, whatever may have happened elsewhere, in relation to Shakespeare and the Chamberlain's there is no call for any such unlikely assumption. As author, Shakespeare would have been present at morning rehearsals of his plays as a matter of course to explain how he had conceived the action, to elucidate his text where elucidation was needed, and choreograph movement on and off the stage. And that this was the normal practice is attested by Richard Flecknoe in his *Short Discourse of the English Stage* of 1664, where, looking back to that golden age of Shakespeare, Jonson, Beaumont and Fletcher, he tells us, 'It was the happiness of the Actors of those Times to have such Poets as these to instruct them, and write for them; and no less of those Poets to have such docile and excellent Actors to Act their Playes as a *Field* and *Burbidge*.'[28] The practice is confirmed by the testimony of a German scholar, Johannes Rhenanus, who, on a visit to England in 1611, observed that the English actors were 'daily instructed, as it were in a school, so that even the most eminent actors have to allow themselves to be taught their places by the dramatists, and this gives life and ornament to a well-written play, so that it is no wonder that the English players (I speak of skilled ones) surpass others and have the advantage over them'.[29] If this was true of men such as Burbage and Kempe, there can be no question whatever that it was true of the more junior members of the company.

As an actor himself, and one who, on most occasions, was to take part in the performances that followed, Shakespeare could not have been better placed to fulfil the function of instructor. The adult roles in his plays had been written for specific actors of experience with whom he enjoyed a ready rapport and mutual respect. It is the apprentices – especially here his Romeo and Juliet – who would have occupied most of his time in rehearsal, and his presence on stage with them as the Friar at critical moments of the performance would have been a further encouragement to them to give of their best. We know how good that best could be and, in particular, that a well-trained boy playing a female role was capable of winning an audience's complete belief in the truth of his impersonation.[30]

Not all the present-day functions of a director would have fallen to him, for Kempe, a renowned dancer in his day as well as the most popular comedian, would have been on hand to choreograph the masque;[31] Augustine Phillips, a versatile musician who was to bequeath four different instruments to his apprentices in his will of 1605, to organise the music; and Richard Burbage to arrange the fights. The book-keeper was, of course, in charge of the all-important prompt-copy, and was responsible for calling rehearsals, writing out the actors' parts and the backstage 'plot' to remind them of their entrance cues. A stage-keeper was in charge of any furniture required on stage, while the tireman looked after costumes and the smaller props. All the sharers would have had individual contributions to make to the preparation and performance of the plays, quite apart from their acting roles, and we know that Heminges came in time to carry most of the managerial and financial responsibility. It was a co-operative enterprise throughout: 'our scene', 'our stage', 'our toil'.

I have suggested that *Romeo and Juliet* was first performed in the summer season of 1595 at James Burbage's Theatre, the precise location of which has recently been confirmed as at the junction of Curtain Road and New Inn Yard, close to the present site of Liverpool Street Station.[32] We are not to suppose, however, that it enjoyed a continuous run of the kind we are accustomed to today; instead, single performances would have been slotted into the current repertoire with whatever frequency its popularity was found to justify.

If Shakespeare was so fully engaged in rehearsal and performance as I have claimed, we may justifiably wonder how he found time to write two new plays in each of the years between 1595 and 1599 as he is known to have done. The company's London seasons were not of course continuous through the year; apart from other interruptions (touring commitments, eruptions of plague and civil disturbance), the lack of indoor venues in the winter would have prevented that. But clearly he must often have been under considerable pressure. A rare intimation of that pressure emerges from a stray note of John Aubrey's, deriving from Kit Beeston (who may have shared lodgings with him in the period) through his son William, who was contemporary with Aubrey. 'He was not a company keeper', we are told, 'lived in Shoreditch, wouldnt be debauched, & if invited to writ; he was in paine'.[33]

If Shakespeare's coaching of the company's apprentices had contributed to the success of *Romeo and Juliet*, it was to be a crucial factor in the staging of *A Midsummer Night's Dream* in the autumn and winter of the same year: for out of a cast of twenty-two named characters, at least ten including five of the major roles were to be played by the same apprentices – a remarkable tribute to their abilities and Shakespeare's confidence in them.

The *Dream* is by general consensus Shakespeare's most lyrical play; it is also the most magical. Unusually, the plot appears to have been largely of his own invention, and may in part have been inspired by a request from some highly placed courtier to provide entertainment for a family wedding celebration; and certainly, its theme of the consummation of love in marriage would have made it an ideal choice for such an occasion. Of the various court weddings known to have taken place in the period, the one most likely to have occasioned it is that of Sir George Carey's daughter Elizabeth to Thomas, son of Lord Berkeley, at Blackfriars on 19 February 1596; Elizabeth was the granddaughter of Lord Hunsdon, the company's patron, whom Sir George was to succeed as Lord Chamberlain in 1597. Much has been made of some complimentary references in the play to the Queen as suggesting she was present, and that this was its first performance. It is also said that Sir George maintained a musical *schola* at the time on which Shakespeare might have drawn for his fairies. But as we have seen in relation to *Romeo*, Shakespeare had a sufficiency of boys in the company without any need to draw on outside resources, and the title page to the Quarto text of 1600 specifically states that it had been 'sundry times *publickely* acted, by the Right honourable, the Lord Chamberlaine his servants'.[34] As Stanley Wells points out, 'If Shakespeare's company could at any time muster enough boys for public performance, we have no reason to doubt that it could have done so from the start'.[35] We know, moreover, that the company was paid for court performances at Richmond that Christmas, both before and shortly after the date of the Carey wedding (on 26, 27 and 28 December 1595, and 6 January and 22 February 1596) and, as the *Dream* was almost certainly one of the plays performed, the references to the Queen could just as easily have been inserted then.[36]

It is of course a midsummer play; the lovers sleep out in the wood, and Titania lies on a 'bank where the wild thyme blows,/Where oxlips and the nodding violet grows', but is unique in that seven or eight of its nine scenes take place at night or in the early dawn, lit by moonlight. The moon, indeed, is the presiding luminary planet in the play, as its opening lines establish:

> Now, fair Hippolyta, our nuptial hour
> Draws on apace; four happy days bring in
> Another moon: but O, methinks, how slow
> This old moon wanes!

Though many of the later plays intended for performance in public theatres open to the elements such as the Rose and the Theatre contain night scenes, and the convention was one readily accepted by Elizabethan audiences, there would have been little point in writing a play in which such scenes predominate unless it was intended for indoor performance where the artificial light of candles would have aided its mysterious effect. It is difficult to imagine its being played on the open stage of the Theatre on dank afternoons in the depths of an English winter, by all accounts an exceptionally severe one.

The play was probably rehearsed in the late summer of 1595, using boys who were then appearing in *Romeo*, and acted indoors (both publicly and privately) during the autumn and winter that followed, with performances in the Theatre withheld until the spring and early summer of 1596. In view of the situation in London, where inns such as the Cross Keys were in process of being closed to the players by City ordinance and where James Burbage's plans to open an indoor playhouse in one of the buildings of the former Blackfriars' Priory had yet to reach fulfilment, the *Dream* may, in fact, have opened out of town, where indoor performance was the norm. We know that the company was in Cambridge and Ipswich before 29 September 1595, and that in Ipswich the players received a record reward from the town's bailiffs of 40*s* for their initial performance in the Guildhall.[37]

The ancient Guildhall in Ipswich would have been familiar to Shakespeare from his earlier visits to the town with Worcester's and the Admiral's men, and though space was limited there, the bailiffs' play was followed by others for the public at large to attend – probably in the same venue (see Plate 23).

Accumulating indications from what has been said already of Shakespeare's roles in the plays suggest that he liked to be on stage at their opening (if not to open them himself), and that he usually contrived to be there again for their final scenes – leaving himself both time and opportunity to work with his fellows on other parts of the plays.[38] We have seen him doing just this in *Titus*, the *Comedy of Errors*, *Love's Labour's Lost*, and *Romeo*. And so, I believe, he did in the *Dream*, playing Theseus, to whom, though widely acknowledged King of Athens, he gives the lesser title of Duke, as with three of his previous 'kingly' roles.

With so many parts being played by the company's apprentices, the casting would have made only modest demands on the sharers. All we know of the boys who played the girls' parts is that Hermia was short in stature and Helena tall, and we find the same contrast between Hero and Beatrice in *Much Ado About Nothing*, Celia and Rosalind in *As You Like It*, and Maria and Viola in *Twelfth Night*. The two male lovers Lysander and Demetrius would have been drawn from the older apprentices (Romeo and Paris?), with Pope or Bryan as the pompous father, Egeus, and Heminges perhaps as Philostrate, the Master of Revels at Theseus' court. We can be more confident of three of the mechanicals: Cowley and Kempe as Quince and Bottom, and Sincler as Starveling; for Cowley and Kempe were to play in similar relation to each other as Verges and Dogberry in *Much Ado*, where Shakespeare records the actors' names, and 'Sinklo' as Starveling is in line with his casting in thin-man roles in all the plays in which we know him to have featured. This was not so much a matter of type-casting as that Shakespeare wrote these parts especially for him, as he wrote for other members of the company who are not so clearly distinguishable because we know too little about them as individuals; it is only by virtue of Sinklo's unusual physique that we are able to identify him in some of the parts that he played. In writing his plays, Shakespeare was engaged in creating roles for particular actors to inhabit, not character types to which they might be fitted. That is why, when embodied by sensitive performers, they come over still as human beings rather than as puppets of the dramatist's imagination.[39]

William Kempe is often dismissed or patronised as one of the blabbing clowns condemned by Hamlet as speaking 'more than is set down for them'; but we should take note of the progressively more complex roles that Shakespeare writes for him, from that of Launce in the *Two Gentlemen* with his simple but hilarious monologues, through the Dromios – a *tour de force* of doubling requiring extraordinary acting skills – to Bottom, who proves in the play to draw on surprising philosophical depths. And there were greater challenges for him ahead! Among the fairies, only Oberon requires more authority than a skilled apprentice could be expected to supply, and calls out for the experience and *élan* of Burbage; in the magical world of the wood, the disparity of age between Titania and himself would not have been a problem.

As the unashamedly lowbrow humour of Launce and Crab had done in the *Two Gentlemen*, the play of Pyramus and Thisbe, which the mechanicals are shown as rehearsing at intervals throughout the *Dream*, serves to anchor the courtly intrigues of the lovers in the plebeian realities of life as experienced by the artisans of Athens, and more immediately those of the groundlings who, in the summer of 1596, would have crowded the yard of the Theatre in Shoreditch. And there is surely here, on Shakespeare's part, an element of self-parody that would have delighted his fellows. For Peter Quince is not just the book-keeper for the play but also, it appears, the poet; receiving the idiotic objections to his text and suggestions for its improvement put forward by Bottom and the others with judicious gravity and, in the performance before the Duke that brings the comedy of the play to a glorious climax, speaking his own Prologue and making such a hash of it!

In this most fruitful and prolific period of his creativity, Shakespeare was now to switch the focus of his attention back to history. The date of *King John* is uncertain, but as I find it hard to believe that having once embarked on his second great history cycle beginning with *Richard II*, he would have wished to return to the much earlier reign of John before going on to continue the series with the two parts of *Henry IV*, I incline to date *John* the earlier: to the winter of 1595/6 (following closely on the *Dream*), with *Richard* in the summer of 1596, and *Henry IV* in the winter that followed. I am referring here to their *production* dates.[40] As these plays were to provide him with some of the largest and most significant roles of his acting career, and in writing and performing them he was to pursue an intense and abiding interest in the nature and limits of kingship, I defer consideration of them to the following chapter, where I shall be looking at other of his 'kingly' parts and can relate them to each other. In what remains of the present chapter, I confine myself to the two remaining comedies of the period: *The Merchant of Venice* and *Much Ado About Nothing*.

A date sometime in the autumn of 1596 for the *Merchant*, proposed by Chambers, is supported by the later discovery that Antonio's 'wealthy Andrew dock'd in sand/Vailing her high top lower than her ribs/To kiss her burial' (I.i.27–9) derives her name from that of a Spanish galleon captured at Cadiz in 1596, the news of which reached England in July of that year. The historical *Andrew* had been captured when it ran aground in the approaches to Cadiz, and when brought to England narrowly escaped a similar fate on sands in the King's Channel off Chatham, suggesting to Shakespeare the fate of Antonio's *Andrew*.[41]

The play brings together two quite different stories – neither of Shakespeare's invention but deriving from ancient tradition. One concerns the wooing of Portia by Bassanio and the love-test of the caskets; the other that of a rapacious usurer (Shylock) who seeks the death of a rival merchant (Antonio) by imposing the forfeit of a pound of his flesh as penalty for failure to repay a loan he has made him by the due date. Nor was Shakespeare the first to bring the stories together. His immediate source is disputed and need not concern us. For all its fairy-tale improbabilities, his masterly handling of this material ensures that the play in performance carries its audience with it in ready suspension of disbelief. There is much true Shakespearean magic in the play that in later times has often been dimmed by miscast or routine productions, or over-familiarity on the part of jaded theatre critics.

As an exemplar of unstinting generosity to his friend, Antonio – the merchant of the title – is the central figure, and the indications are that Shakespeare played it. He is there at the play's beginning to speak its opening lines and initiate the plot, returns for the pivotal scene with Shylock to negotiate the loan, and again for the trial, but otherwise remains largely on the margins of the action; a characteristic procedure that allowed him time (with a minimum of lines to learn) to guide the players in rehearsal and also to be with them on stage at critical moments of performance. When, in the final scene, he appears once more to receive the unexpected but welcome news of the safe return of three of his ships, he gives himself one of the shortest lines in the play, 'I am dumb!', and has only three more lines to add to it before the close.

Shakespeare would have been thirty-two in 1596; again, as for the lovers in *Romeo* and the *Dream*, it is essential for Bassanio and Portia to be appreciably younger, and the same is true for Bassanio's companions, who would all have been drawn from the company's apprentices and younger sharers.

Portia especially (Plate 9) needs to be played as she describes herself in the scene of Bassanio's choosing of the caskets, as

> . . . an unlesson'd girl, unschool'd, unpractised,
> Happy in this, she is not yet so old
> But she may learn: happier than this,
> She is not bred so dull but she can learn . . .   (III.ii.159–62)

She does, and gains in experience and authority through the play; but from her opening scene with Nerissa, through all of the casket scenes to this one and beyond, we need to see that she has still some way to go in that learning process.

The play would have been performed in repertoire with *Romeo* and the *Dream*, and the first performances of all three plays are near enough together in time for the same pair of boys to have played consecutively, on the one side, as the mute Rosalind of *Romeo*, Helena and Portia (tall and fair), and on the other, as Juliet, Hermia and Nerissa (small and dark in colouring). Older sharers would have taken the Duke, Morocco, Tubal, and Portia's stately servant Balthazar: 'Madam, I go with all convenient speed' (III.iv.56) – one of the biggest laughs in the play if his exit is taken with due deliberation.[42] There is obvious scope for doubling. Perhaps Shakespeare wrote another role for his favourite thin man (Sinklo) in the proud, ridiculous figure of Arragon, confronting a jester's head on a stick. 'Did I deserve no more than a fool's head?', he asks into a resounding silence, 'Is that my prize? are my deserts no better?' (II.ix.59–60). That Kempe was Launcelot Gobbo is a near certainty, and represents a return to his original stage persona as rustic clown. If we were right to cast him and Cowley as Bottom and Verges in the *Dream*, the partnership may well have extended to what is here little more than a double-act for young and old Gobbo.

Shylock may equally well have gone to the veteran Bryan as to Burbage; neither would have been inhibited from playing him as the villain that Shakespeare intended – motivated by envy and malice throughout, caring more for his money than he does for his daughter. That he is a villain conceived in human terms, who even in the frustration of his evil purpose in the trial commands our pity in face of the cruel baiting he receives, is testimony (if one were needed) to Shakespeare's largeness of vision. Though a

Jew, he is not represented as typical of his race or religion; on the contrary, he is described as a devil 'in the *likeness* of a Jew' (III.i.20).[43]

If, as proposed, its composition was completed in the late summer of 1596 – though naturally Shakespeare would have begun work on it some months earlier – the play would have fitted well into the company's autumn and winter seasons of that year, and would have been equally effective in both indoor and open-air venues. The play begins in daylight and the text is suggestive of exterior settings. Towards the end of Act 2, there is talk of evening and dinner. Jessica, Shylock's daughter, is stolen away in darkness, and it is nine o'clock when Antonio interrupts preparations for a masque to hurry Gratiano away to join Bassanio for his voyage to Belmont. For the Belmont scenes we are in daylight until the final act which, like that of the *Dream*, is set wholly outdoors and at night, lit by a fitful moon. On the open stages of the Theatre or its neighbour the Curtain, the natural light of the afternoon would by then have been drawing in, and the introduction of candles and torches on stage, with perhaps Portia and Nerissa approaching through a darkening yard, would have had a magical effect.[44]

> *Portia*: That light we see is burning in my hall:
> How far that little candle throws his beams!
> So shines a good deed in a naughty world.
> *Nerissa*: When the moon shone we did not see the candle.
> *Portia*: So doth the greater glory dim the less . . .
>
> (V.i.89–93)

Here music sounds 'much sweeter than by day', differences between the lovers are resolved, and Antonio's and Lorenzo's fortunes are repaired. Only Shylock remains disturbingly outside the circle of love and reconciliation.

We cannot be sure of the theatre in which the *Merchant* was first performed. Though James Burbage had completed his purchase of a building in Blackfriars, he was prevented from opening it as an indoor theatre by an objecting petition from important residents of the estate – including, oddly enough, Sir George Carey who, in July of that year, was to succeed his father as Lord Hunsdon and the company's patron. To be patron of a highly regarded band of players was one thing; to have them as near neighbours in a public playhouse was quite another and not to be endured! As the City inns were also now closed to them, Shakespeare may again have taken the cast of his new play out of town for their final rehearsals and an opening in the Market Hall of Faversham in Kent, where we find them 'aboute Lamas' (1 August) receiving 16*s* from Mr Saker, the Mayor.[45]

If, as was usual elsewhere, the Mayor's performance at Faversham was followed by public shows in the same venue or, if that was not available, one of the town's inns, the company may still have been there or in the vicinity when Shakespeare received the dreadful news of the death of his eleven-year-old son Hamnet in Stratford. He would have hurried home to comfort Anne and Hamnet's surviving twin sister Judith, though it is hardly possible that he was in time for the funeral on 11 August.[46] The first London performance of the *Merchant*, then, was probably one of those given at Whitehall for the Queen and court at Christmas or New Year 1596/7, for which Thomas Pope and John Heminges received the Queen's reward on behalf of their fellows.[47]

If Shakespeare had wished to express his grief at the death of Hamnet, it is hidden away in *Richard II* or *Henry IV*, which he went on to write in the year that followed; but I doubt that he allowed events in his personal life, whether distressful or joyful, to impinge in that immediate way on his writing. The actor goes on stage and fulfils his professional commitment to the play and his fellows whatever his state of mind or the nature of his role, and so, I believe, did Shakespeare in his work as a dramatist. If events of that kind were to find an echo in the plays, it would be very much later: perhaps this particular grief lingers in the haunting epitaph that Cymbeline's sons were to speak over Fidele:

> Fear no more the heat o' the sun,
>   Nor the furious winter's rages,
> Thou thy worldly task has done,
>   Home art gone and ta'en thy wages.
> Golden lads and girls all must,
> As chimney-sweepers, come to dust . . .
>
> (IV. ii. 258–63)

Four histories in a row would have been too much of a good thing even for an Elizabethan audience, and between the second part of *Henry IV* and its sequel, *Henry V*, belongs one of the three most perfect comedies Shakespeare was ever to write: *Much Ado About Nothing*. It was not included in Meres' listing of his plays in *Palladis Tamia*, entered in the Stationers' Register on 7 September 1598, and we know that William Kempe, who is mentioned in Shakespeare's text as playing Dogberry, left the company early in 1599, which makes *Much Ado* a play for the autumn and winter of 1598/9, acted perhaps more often indoors than out. Again, there are several notable night scenes, including, of course, the setting of the watch; and when, in the penultimate scene of Act 5, Claudio and the Prince visit what they believe to be Hero's tomb they are followed by 'three or four with tapers'.

Though it would have gone down very well with that section of the public who are more attracted by easy laughs than subtleties of meaning, there is more in the title than first appears; certainly, 'much ado', but it is only late in the action that we discover it is all 'about nothing'. Like the *Merchant*, the play combines two separate stories of ancient origin: the attempted sabotage of a marriage that is due to take place between Hero and Claudio by means of a slander against Hero's reputation, involving impersonation of her by one of her gentlewomen, and the contrivance of a marriage between two notorious mockers against love and marriage (Beatrice and Benedick) by the spreading of false reports that each is secretly in love with the other. There is a satisfying symmetry here: a marriage threatened and a marriage achieved, and both by reports that are false; the first eventually revealed to be so, the second found after all to be true. The author of the second, more fortunate invention is the Prince of the play, Don Pedro, and all he intends is a mischievous joke against Benedick; the prime mover in the attempt to blacken Hero's name is the Prince's bastard brother, Don John, who is resentful of his brother's friendship with Claudio. The masterly way in which Shakespeare integrates the two stories and brings them to simultaneous climax in the church scene of the play must be left to the theatre-goer to enjoy.

Shakespeare's role is Leonato, the father of Hero, the slandered bride. He speaks the opening line of the play and is there at its close; if, at thirty-four, he was young for the part it was not by much, for Hero can be little more in age than fifteen, as was his own daughter, Susanna. The emotional drive of Leonato's speeches in the latter part of the play herald a new kind of dramatic utterance – new in his own work and that of any other – that was to find fuller expression in the great tragedies that lay ahead. This to Leonato's elder brother, Antonio, who had attempted to comfort him in his grief and anger on Hero's behalf:

> I pray thee cease thy counsel
> Which falls into mine ears as profitless
> As water in a sieve. Give not me counsel,
> Nor let no comforter delight mine ear
> But such a one whose wrongs do suit with mine.
> Bring me a father that so lov'd his child,
> Whose joy of her is overwhelm'd like mine,
> And bid him speak of patience;
> Measure his woe the length and breadth of mine,
> And let it answer every strain for strain,
> As thus for thus, and such a grief for such,
> In every lineament, branch, shape, and form.
> If such a one will smile and stroke his beard,
> Bid sorrow wag, cry 'Hem!' when he should groan,
> Patch grief with proverbs, make misfortune drunk
> With candle-wasters, bring him yet to me,
> And I of him will gather patience . . .   (V.i.3–19)

If Shakespeare can be said anywhere in his writing to have 'unlocked his heart', it was in speeches like this.

The part is of medium size (334 lines as against Benedick's 430, and the Prince's 320). While Benedick's wit and skill with words call out for Burbage, I give Shakespeare the smaller role the more confidently in the belief that the kingly part of Don Pedro, the Prince, should be played by an actor much younger than himself – one more of an age with Claudio, who is in his late teens or early twenties.[48] When Leonato and Antonio confront the two young men after the church scene in which Claudio has rejected Hero at the altar with the Prince's support, the normal deference they give to the Prince is overborne by indignation at his and Claudio's acceptance of Hero's guilt, and Antonio goes so far as to address them as 'Boys, apes, braggarts, Jacks, milksops!', and again as 'Scambling, outfacing, fashion-monging boys'. Leonato, who up to this point has tried to restrain his brother, answers a further refusal by the Prince to hear him with a curt 'No? Come, brother, away! I will be heard' and exits in anger.

The master-stroke by which Hero is finally vindicated is Shakespeare's invention of the incomparable Dogberry and his band of idiot watchmen, who are supposed to be guarding Leonato's house from intruders. By sheer chance, they overhear an incriminating conversation between the two rogues whom Don John had employed to stage the scene, witnessed by Claudio and the Prince, which has persuaded them of her unworthiness; but will they have the sense to make known their discovery of the plot, and do it in time? Anxiety remains.

The character of Dogberry, a pompous and very stupid local official who is nevertheless convinced of his own sagacity and importance, is one of the joys of the play. Here, there can be no doubt whatever that it was played by Kempe for Shakespeare prefaces some of his lines in his manuscript with the actor's name rather than that of the character, and these have found their way into the Quarto and Folio texts. And nothing could be more conclusive of Kempe's ability, for the part is not one for a 'clown' but for a true actor, in which the slightest hint of awareness in the performance that what he is saying may be considered funny – or indeed is anything less than the epitome of wisdom – kills the humour stone dead. I said earlier that Shakespeare was engaged in creating roles for actors, not character types to which they might be fitted. This is exemplified in Dogberry who, apart perhaps from sharing Bottom's self-conceit, has little in common with any of the previous characters that Kempe has played, and yet was specifically written for him.

Shakespeare was not much interested in the psychology of his characters, in their motivations or the 'whys' of their behaviour. There is no attempt to explain or justify Don John's 'discontent' – or, for that matter, why Iago hates Othello or Lear gives away his kingdom. Nor can they explain it themselves. Don John tells us, 'I am a plain-dealing villain . . . let me be that I am'. This, Shakespeare appears to be saying, is how things are; they are given to us as *data* we must accept if the story that follows is to make any sense. But these are just starting points. It is in the relations his characters are seen to have with each other, and the way these develop in response to changing circumstances and events, that the interest lies; and it is in the interchange of language between them – to be fully appreciated only when we hear it in performance – that the characters emerge in all their complexity of being. We know very well, of course, that they are not real – only characters in a play – but in watching the play we are persuaded to suspend that disbelief. Part of the illusion lies in their embodiment by the actors who inhabit them, but the more significant factor is the way in which they imitate life in their responses to each other and, in so doing, gain in awareness of themselves. 'All the world's a stage,/And all the men and women merely players', acting a series of roles; but conversely in Shakespeare's art, the players assume in their role-play with each other an uncanny resemblance to real men and women. Here also, *Much Ado* exemplifies the process, for as Claudio remains the rather shallow young man we suspect him to be from the beginning, and Dogberry as invincible in his ignorance and inviolable in his self-esteem, Beatrice and Benedick are transformed. As for Don John, Benedick has the last word;

> Think not on him till tomorrow; I'll devise thee brave
> punishments for him. Strike up, pipers!

EIGHT

He that Plays the King

To our English Terence Mr. Will: Shake-speare

> Some say good *Will* (which I, in sport, do sing)
>   Had'st thou not plaid some Kingly parts in sport,
> Thou hadst bin a companion for a *King*;
> And, beene a King among the meaner sort.
> Some others raile; but raile as they thinke fit,
> Thou hast no rayling, but, a raigning Wit:
>   *And* honesty *thou sow'st, which they do reape;*
>   *So, to increase their Stocke which they do keepe.*
>   *John Davies of Hereford, c. 1611*[1]

> He that plays the king shall be welcome; his Majesty
> shall have tribute of me . . .
>   *Hamlet, II.ii.318–19*

While the old idea that each player in the Chamberlain's men had a characteristic 'line of parts' that was consistently adhered to in the casting of the plays is no longer accepted, we must allow that certain of the players came to be regarded as specialists in a certain broad category of role. The obvious examples are of Kempe and his successor Armin in 'clown' parts, and Sincler in 'thin-man' roles – though that, perhaps, was more of a physical limitation than a specialism. Was Shakespeare another in his playing of 'Kingly parts'? The first of the quotations above – from John Davies' *Scourge of Folly* – would seem to suggest so. 'If only you hadn't acted those kingly parts in plays', he is saying, 'you might have been a fit companion for kings, and have come to be regarded as something of a king yourself among ordinary people.' To judge of the reliability of Davies' evidence, we need to know a little more about him.

Born a year or two earlier than Shakespeare, he was the most renowned penman and writing master of his day, when the art of calligraphy was more valued than it is today, and a prolific versifier whose extant works fill two sizeable volumes. As a teacher of calligraphy, he numbered among his pupils the Earl of Northumberland and the Countess of Derby with their families, the Earl of Pembroke and, most exalted of all, King James's son and intended heir, Prince Henry. He is said by one of his pupils to have been a recusant Catholic. Apart from the epigram to Shakespeare, there are others in the same collection dedicated to Ben Jonson, Marston and Fletcher. He seems to have enjoyed a wide acquaintance with poets and other writers of the time including Nashe, Gabriel Harvey and Dekker, to all of whom he refers in his works. His attitude to the players – like most of his contemporaries – was ambivalent. He castigates them for their pride:

> But that which grates my *Galle*, and mads my *Muse*,
> Is (ah that ever such just cause should *Bee*)
> To see a *Player* at the put-downe *stewes**
> Put up his *Peacocke's* Taile for al to see,
> And for his hellish voice, as prowde as *hee*;
> What *Peacocke* art thou prowd? Wherefore? because
> Thou *Parrat*-like canst speake what is taught thee.
> A *Poet* must teach thee from clause to clause,
> Or thou wilt breake *Pronunciation's* Lawes.

– but praises them warmly in other respects, '*Players*, I love yee and your Qualitie', he tells us a few lines later,

> As ye are Men, *that* pass-time not abus'd:
> And some I love for *painting, poesie*,
> And say fell *Fortune* cannot be excus'd,
> That hath for better *uses* you refus'd:
> *Wit, Courage, good-shape, good partes*, and all *good*,
> As long as al these *goods* are no *worse* us'd,
> And though the *stage* doth staine pure gentle *bloud*,
> Yet generous yee are in minde and *moode*.[2]

---

* As Davies explains in a note, 'stewes' (brothels) 'once stoode where now Play-houses stand'.

And in the margin against the second line, 'And some I love for painting, poesie', Davies glosses the initials, 'W.S.R.B.': William Shakespeare and Richard Burbage, the latter known to have been a competent painter.

These are not Davies' only references to Shakespeare. In *Speculum Proditori* of 1616, he tells us, 'I knew a *Man*' – and by 'man' in this context was commonly meant an actor, as in 'Chamberlain's man' –

> I knew a *Man*, unworthy as I am,
> And yet too worthie for a *counterfeit*,
> Made once a *king*; who though it were in *game*,
> Yet was it there where *Lords* and *Ladyes* met;
> Who honor'd him, as hee had been the same,
> And no subjective *dutie* did forget;
>   When to him-selfe he smil'd, and said, lo here
>   I have for noght, what *Kings* doe buy so deere.
>
> No odds there was in shew (and but in show,
> Kings are too often honour'd) save that *he*
> Was but twelve gamesome *daies* to *king* it so:
> And *kings*, more *yeares* of soveraigne misery.
> His *raigne* was *short* and *sweet*, theirs *long* in *wo*.
> He after liv'd: they, with or for *theirs*, die.
>   He had a tast of *raigne*, with powre to leave;
>   They cannot tast, but life must *take* or *give*.[3]

Grosart, his Victorian editor, interprets this as referring to 'private theatricals' in which Shakespeare had been invited to participate, but the place is more likely to have been the tiring house of one of the public theatres, and the 'twelve gamesome daies' a series of performances (not necessarily consecutive) in which he had played the part of a king. (We have seen that fourteen performances of *Henry VI* were given at the Rose in 1592.) That the players were accustomed to receive distinguished patrons in the tiring house appears from another quotation from the *Scourge of Folly*:

> I came to English Aesop (on a tide)
>   As he lay tirde (as tirde) before to play:

– meaning presumably 'attired', ready in costume –

> I came unto him in his flood of pride;
> He then was King, and thought I should obay.
> And so I did, for with all reverence, I
> As to my Soveraigne (though to him unknowne)
> Did him approach; but loe, he casts his Eye,
> As if therein I had presumption showne:
> I, like a Subject (with submisse regard)
> Did him salute, yet he re-greeted mee
> But with a Nod, because his speech he spar'd
> For Lords and Knights that came his Grace to see.

Davies is greatly put out by Aesop's unceremonious nod, and takes it as cue for another attack on the players' pride. He blames himself for approaching Aesop in the way that he did when 'I well knew him (though he knew not me)'

> *To be a player, and for some new Crownes*
> *Spent on a Supper, any man may bee*
> *Acquainted with them, from their Kings to Clownes.*[4]

Again the ambivalence of his attitude comes to the fore – though in truth Aesop's casual acknowledgement of him may have been indicative of that state of mind that most actors experience in the half-hour or so before performance, in which (often quite unconsciously) they assume the manner of the character they are about to play, rather than intended as a deliberate snub. As to the identity of 'Aesop', he could just as well have been Burbage (who also played some notable kings including Richard III and Lear), but there can be little doubt of Davies' more intimate knowledge of Shakespeare, and genuine admiration for him in spite of what he saw as the unworthiness of his profession. It was with Shakespeare that he mainly associated 'kingly parts' and, as an almost exact contemporary, he was in a good position to know. With this in mind, let us briefly review Shakespeare's history plays up to 1599 and see what other indications we can find of the roles that he played in them.

In *Henry VI*, as I have already suggested, Shakespeare's part was almost certainly that of the young king, and in reading the play we find the character bears a curious stamp of detachment. From the opening scene of Part One, in which his presence is imagined off-stage as an infant, Henry is presented as at once the fulcrum of events and, by reason initially of his tender years and later of his personal deficiencies of character, powerless to influence them. In the bearpit of conflicting interests and self-seeking ambitions into which the body politic has descended, his Christian virtues of piety and desire for peace and reconciliation appear only as weakness, and the few assertions of authority that he brings himself to make as more disastrous in their effects than his more usual passivity.

His first entrance is in Act 3 of Part One, and his initial attempts to reconcile his feuding uncles fall on deaf ears. In Part Two he watches horrorstruck the innocent Humphrey arrested and taken away, 'as the butcher takes away the calf . . . Bearing it to the bloody slaughter-house', and is powerless to prevent it. When, in Part Three at the culmination of his tragedy – which is also the tragedy of England, with France lost and the country divided in internecine strife – he is confronted by the murderous York, the poet gives himself these lines:

> So flies the reckless shepherd from the wolf;
> So first the harmless sheep doth yield his fleece,
> And next his throat unto the butcher's knife.   (V.vi.7–9)

The image of the slaughter-house returns in force as an immediate threat, and Henry goes on to ask – of York? the audience? perhaps mainly himself –

> What scene of death hath Roscius now to act?

Roscius was, of course, the great Roman actor, cited by Elizabethans as an ideal representative of the acting profession. The actor on stage, performing the part of the deposed and threatened king, becomes at this moment, in a deliberate confusion of identities, both victim and observer in the scene of his own murder.

The play metaphor by which 'All the world's a stage,/And all the men and women merely players' was not, of course, unique to Shakespeare. It derived from the classical drama of Greece and Rome, and had been employed before him by Kyd, Marlowe and many lesser writers. Indeed, by the 1590s, it may already have become something of a cliché. But no other dramatist had ever used it with more subtle, discreet or telling effect than Shakespeare was to do. We shall be considering his recourse to it more fully in the following chapter, but the sense of disjunction it here provides between actor and role – the sudden shock of self-awareness in the character as to who he is and what he is doing in relation to those around him – is not confined to Henry VI; we shall come to recognise it also in others of his characters and plays, notably in *Richard II* and *Hamlet*. It will be seen to have a particular relevance to Shakespeare's dual occupations as poet and performer.

Richard III had probably been written for Edward Alleyn, and when performed by the Chamberlain's men in its due place as sequel to the three *Henry VI* plays was to provide Burbage with one of his most famous roles. He is the joker in Shakespeare's pack of kings. A monstrous creation of unalloyed, unblushing villainy, whose demonic energy and black humour recall the Vice of the old interludes and moralities, he is a character with whom Richard explicitly associates himself in an aside:

> Thus, like the formal Vice, Iniquity,
> I moralize two meanings in one word.   (III.i.82–3)

In the opening speech of the play, he buttonholes the audience into complicity by telling them plainly what he is about, for

> . . . since I cannot prove a lover
> To entertain these fair well-spoken days,
> I am determined to prove a villain,
> And hate the idle pleasures of these days.
> Plots have I laid, inductions dangerous,
> By drunken prophecies, libels, and dreams,
> To set my brother Clarence and the King
> In deadly hate, the one against the other . . .   (I.i.28–35)

I have said that Shakespeare created roles for actors rather than character types; but with Richard he goes a step further, for Richard is himself an inveterate role-player, a man who invents a whole series of characters to play in the deception of others and achievement of his ultimate purpose to be King: to Clarence, the sympathetic brother; to Lady Anne, the impassioned lover; to the citizens of Act 3, the saintly recluse. He even takes it upon himself to prompt others in the art, and finds an equally adept performer in Buckingham.

Richard:	Come, cousin, canst thou quake and change thy colour,
	Murder thy breath in middle of a word,
	And then again begin, and stop again,
	As if thou were distraught and mad with terror?
Buckingham:	Tut, I can counterfeit the deep tragedian,
	Speak, and look back, and pry on every side,
	Tremble and start at wagging of a straw,
	Intending deep suspicion. Ghastly looks
	Are at my service like enforced smiles,
	And both are ready in their offices
	At any time to grace my stratagems. (III.v.1–11)

The theatre imagery continues into Act 4, in which Richard's mother, the old Duchess of York, joins with the widows of Henry VI and Edward IV (Margaret and Elizabeth) in lamenting Richard's innocent victims, who now include Margaret's husband and son, Elizabeth's young sons, and Clarence. It is an extraordinary scene, and we must assume there were present in the company older apprentices or hired men who were capable of playing these three embittered women, in their passionate reproaches to each other and imprecations on Richard, in such a way as to compel belief in the truth of their performances. Margaret describes the events she has witnessed as a 'dire induction' (prologue) to the tragedy that is still to unfold; the Duchess speaks of 'Woe's scene, world's shame, grave's due by life usurp'd;/Brief abstract and record of tedious days' (IV.iv.27–8); and Margaret of 'this frantic play'; addressing her successor, Elizabeth, as

> ... poor shadow, painted queen,
> The presentation of but what I was;
> The flattering index of a direful pageant ...
> A queen in jest, only to fill the scene.   (IV.iv.83–5, 91)

It is in Act 4 that Richard attains the crown, and in this final role he is not so impressive; he makes mistakes, forgets his lines. When, on the eve of Bosworth, he is assailed by a long procession of ghosts of those he has murdered, his former confidence in his identity as villain is fractured by stirrings of conscience and, in the course of a tragi-comic sequence of questions and answers, incongruously recalling Launcelot Gobbo's debate with himself in the *Merchant* ('"Budge", says the fiend, – "Budge not!" says my conscience'), he is brought to the edge of despair.

> O coward conscience, how dost thou afflict me!
> The lights burn blue; it is now dead midnight.
> Cold fearful drops stand on my trembling flesh.
> What do I fear? Myself? There's none else by;
> Richard loves Richard, that is, I and I.
> Is there a murderer here? No. Yes, I am!
> Then fly. What, from myself? Great reason why,
> Lest I revenge? What, myself upon myself?
> Alack, I love myself. Wherefore? For any good
> That I myself have done unto myself?
> O no, alas, I rather hate myself
> For hateful deeds committed by myself.
> I am a villain – yet I lie, I am not! ...   (V.iii.180–92)

The play has the longest cast-list of any in the canon and names some fifty-two speaking roles. Even when we have subtracted the female characters and boys who would have been played by apprentices (doubling as necessary with unnamed messengers and other minor roles as well as with each other), it could not have been played by less than a full complement of sharers with the addition of several hired men, and the only one of them who would not have been required to double was Burbage as Richard. This is true even of the shorter Quarto versions, in which several characters are combined and others excised altogether.[5] There is no part in the play for a clown other than Richard himself, who contains in his role as Vice both villain and joker. But this does not mean that Kempe would have had the day off! He was too versatile and useful an actor to be left aside in that way. He could have played the First Murderer (who is 'strong-framed' as Costard was said to be of 'great limb or joint') with Cowley or Sincler as his reluctant assistant in Act 1, Scene 4, and the nervously compliant Mayor of Act 3, Scene 7. A touch of humour in the playing of both would not have come amiss (nor would it today) in a play that has so much the character of a latter-day morality.

Shakespeare would not have been exempt from the general necessity for doubling, and I give him Clarence in Act 1 and Richmond in Act 5: Clarence because, though relatively small, the exceptional demands that the part makes of the actor in the handling of its verse are of the kind that, as author, he was ideally equipped to supply, and Richmond because it qualifies in every respect as one of those kingly roles with which he was especially associated, and which by now he would have acquired a practised skill in performing. The accuracy with which both parts are recollected in the reconstituted Quarto text of 1597 supports the view that he had played them.[6] Richmond is presented as quietly confident in the justice of his cause and the constancy of his supporters, whereas Richard is shown (with good reason) as distrustful of his. While Richmond commits his cause to God and contemplates the possibility of defeat with resignation, Richard can appeal only to the pride of his soldiers, and recommends that 'Our strong arms be our conscience, swords our law'. 'March on', he tells them in a last defiant throw,

> Let us to it pell-mell –
> If not to Heaven, then hand in hand to Hell!

From this time on, Shakespeare and Burbage were to divide the kingly parts between them, with Burbage taking the larger, more extrovert roles (Henry V, Antony and Lear) and Shakespeare most, if not all, of the others – Alonso, Duncan and John, as well as previously, the king or duke of the comedies.

King John, as we have seen, probably belongs to the winter of 1595/6, along with the *Dream* – though it could not be more different in feeling. If not in the first division of Shakespeare's plays, it must be placed near the top of the second. Written wholly in verse of a strikingly direct and muscular kind, its first two acts sweep through with only a single change of scene – from England to France at the end of Act 1.

The opening lines set the businesslike tone.

John:	Now say, Chatillon, what would France with us?
Chatillon:	Thus, after greeting, speaks the King of France,
	In my behaviour, to the majesty,
	The borrowed majesty, of England here.
Q. Eleanor:	A strange beginning – 'borrowed majesty'?
John:	Silence, good mother; hear the embassy.
Chatillon:	Philip of France, in right and true behalf
	Of thy deceased brother Geoffrey's son,
	Arthur Plantagenet, lays most lawful claim
	To this fair island . . .

The dubiety of John's claim to the English throne is signalled as clearly as Shakespeare dared in the political climate of the 1590s by the strange little scene with the Faulconbridge brothers that follows, in which the elder brother's title to his dead father's estate is preferred to that of the younger, to whom it had been bequeathed by the father's will; for by the same token, on King Richard's death, the crown should properly have gone to Geoffrey's son Arthur, and not to him. The elder brother, Philip, is recognised by Queen Eleanor and John, moreover, as the illegitimate son of Richard (the Lionheart), and is named thereafter as the Bastard.

In Act 2, set beneath the walls of Angers, the action takes the form of a series of formal exchanges between the opposing kings, enlivened by a slanging match in which Eleanor and Constance, Arthur's mother, trade insults, with ironic asides from the Bastard. To his disgust, Hubert, who first appears as spokesman for the citizens of Angers, brokers a marriage alliance between the two sides by which Arthur is granted nominal title to Brittany, and all John's territories in France are ceded to the French Dauphin.

> Mad world, mad kings, mad composition!

– the Bastard comments in his role as informal Chorus to the play.

Act 3 brings the intervention of the Pope's emissary, Cardinal Pandulph, who, in response to John's refusal to admit Stephen Langton to the see of Canterbury, imposes excommunication on him, the effect of which is to rekindle conflict between England and France and leads to John's imprisonment of Arthur.

Shakespeare, who would have been at this time under pressure to produce more plays for the still under-provided company, drew largely for his structure and sequence of scenes on the anonymous *Troublesome Reign of King John* (1591), which in turn looked back to John Bale's interlude of *King Johan*, a piece of blatant anti-papal propaganda, performed before Cranmer. But Shakespeare's treatment of John is very different to theirs. In Bale, he is a proto-Protestant martyr, poisoned by a monk; in the *Troublesome Reign*, a repentant sinner and, in his dying speech, a prophet;

> I am not he shall buyld the Lord a house,
> Or roote these Locusts from the face of earth:
> But if my dying heart deceave me not,
> From out these loynes shall spring a Kingly braunch
> Whose armes shall reach unto the gates of *Rome*,
> And with his feete treade downe the Strumpets pride,
> That sits upon the chaire of *Babylon*.[7]

Shakespeare is having none of this. His John is a usurper and a cold-blooded murderer – an unrepentant one at that. (When he changes his mind about Arthur, it is not through any moral considerations.) On the controversial question of relations with Rome, Shakespeare is careful to maintain a neutral position. The points at issue are clearly stated but not in such a way as to give offence to either party. The ludicrous scene in the *Troublesome Reign* in which the Bastard, in search of monastic gold, discovers a nun hiding in a chest and a friar in the nun's cupboard, is thankfully omitted, and Pandulph puts the case for the Pope in Act 3 fairly and with impressive authority.[8]

At the opening of Act 4, the action of the play, which up to this point has required a large, open stage and daylight for its performance, narrows in focus to Orford Castle and its surroundings.

It is in the dungeons of Orford – of which historically Hubert de Burgh was Keeper – that the play's most famous scene of Hubert's attempted blinding of Arthur is set.[9] The voice of the angel ('an angel spake') that heralds Pandulph's approach to the invading French in Scene 2 of Act 5 is, I suggest, a rumble of thunder, and the final scenes take place in gathering gloom, lit by lanterns. As John dies miserably in the orchard of Swineshead Abbey, Pandulph negotiates a peace, and the English nobles, who have deserted John for the French on the death of Arthur, return to their allegiance.

The play offers three magnificent roles – John, the Bastard and Hubert – as well as a number of meaty supporting parts including Pandulph, King Philip and Louis of France, and for the older apprentices, Eleanor and Constance. There is an obvious cameo for Sincler in the 'half-faced' Robert Faulconbridge, the Bastard's younger brother. Again, there is no part for a 'clown', but there is a small but fitting one for Kempe in the lion-clad Duke of Austria.

As the bluff and extrovert Bastard would surely have gone to Burbage, with Sly perhaps as Hubert, we cannot deny John to Shakespeare. (Again, he speaks the opening line and is there, though dead, at the close.) As in *Henry VI*, he is the focus of the action but in responding to events rather than initiating them; unsure of himself, dependent for the strength that he lacks on the support of others, notably Eleanor, Hubert and the Bastard. Deprived of that support – Eleanor disappears from the play after Act 3, and Hubert is disabled by his pity for Arthur – he flounders. Only the Bastard remains quixotically loyal to the end. There is no separation here between the man and his role, and little apparent interior life. He is given less than a dozen lines of soliloquy – and they are of the bleakest. This, an aside:

> Withhold thy speed, dreadful Occasion!
> O, make a league with me till I have pleased
> My discontented peers. What? Mother dead?
> How wildly then walks my estate in France! (IV.ii.125–8)

And later in the scene, when he is left alone, he repeats despairingly, 'My mother dead!' For a title role, the part is small, barely 400 lines against the Bastard's 520. Though present on stage for much of the action, John is laconic in his responses or uncomfortably silent; he has no more than three or four lengthy speeches. The part is all in the acting: a fearful, haunted presence at the play's centre.

In his last, dying speeches, he compels our compassion.

> Poisoned, ill fare; dead, forsook, cast off,
> And none of you will bid the winter come
> To thrust his icy fingers in my maw,
> Nor let my kingdom's rivers take their course
> Through my burned bosom, nor entreat the north
> To make his bleak winds kiss my parched lips
> And comfort me with cold. I do not ask you much;
> I beg cold comfort. And you are so strait
> And so ungrateful, you deny me that.   (V.vii.35–43)

It is left to the Bastard to deliver the patriotic moral – a much-quoted plea for national unity.

> O, let us pay the time but needful woe,
> Since it hath been beforehand with our griefs.
> This England never did, nor never shall,
> Lie at the proud foot of a conquerer
> But when it first did help to wound itself.
> Now these her princes are come home again,
> Come the three corners of the world in arms
> And we shall shock them! Naught shall make us rue,
> If England to itself do rest but true.

Though popular in the Victorian period – largely, it would seem, for the opportunities it provided for spectacular scenic effects and antiquarian costuming – the play is not a fashionable choice among present-day directors. Its politics are perhaps too distant and its patriotism too overt. It awaits a contemporary interpretation that would do adequate justice to its considerable merits.

— ★ —

In the sequence of Shakespeare's plays, *Richard II* follows directly on *King John*, and was probably staged at the Theatre in the summer of 1596. It is a summer play and again requires an open stage for its performance. It initiates the second of Shakespeare's great historical cycles (the 'Henriad') that was to take the story of England and its kings from the fall of Richard through the 'unquiet' reign of Henry IV to the triumphs of Henry V. And as the first three plays in the series (the second *Richard* and the two parts of *Henry IV*) were to appear within a period of little more than eighteen months, with *Henry V* joining them a year or two later, and as all four plays are likely to have been performed in repertoire thereafter in close proximity to each other, a continuity in the casting of its leading roles would have been highly desirable, if not essential. The Bolinbroke of *Richard*, for example, must surely have been played by the actor who was to be Henry IV, and whoever played Prince Hal in *Henry IV*, the title role in *Henry V*. Anything else would have been confusing to the public, and have resulted in one of the great bonuses enjoyed by the Chamberlain's men – the near-permanent status of its players – being needlessly thrown away. Given that Shakespeare and Burbage divided the kingly roles between them, the consequences are obvious and inescapable. If Burbage played the more showy part of Richard, Shakespeare would have taken Bolinbroke in the first of the plays. Shakespeare goes on to play the King, and Burbage Prince Hal, in Parts One and Two of *Henry IV*, with Shakespeare as Chorus and Burbage as King in *Henry V*. The fact that Hal, though mentioned as present off-stage as Bolinbroke's dissolute son, never appears in *Richard* may be taken, perhaps, as confirmation of this particular division, and that it was planned from the start.

Pre-eminently, Richard II is the Player King. Like Richard III, he is a role-player but, unlike him, is limited to a single role and believes in it with all his heart. Nevertheless, it remains a role; deprived of this assumed identity by the fact of Bolinbroke's usurpation, he is lost in uncertainty as to who or what he is.

In the opening scene of the play, surrounded by his court and all the panoply of royalty, he is superb. Heralded by trumpets, he takes the chair of state upstage-centre and plays the impartial judge, epitome of kingly grace and power, to perfection.

> Old John of Gaunt, time-honoured Lancaster,
> Hast though according to thy oath and band
> Brought hither Henry Herford, thy bold son,
> Here to make good the boisterous late appeal,
> Which then our leisure would not let us hear,
> Against the Duke of Norfolk, Thomas Mowbray?

Bolinbroke (titled at the time as Hereford), who is Richard's cousin, has accused Mowbray of the murder of their uncle, Gloucester. Each announces his name and states his case as in a court of law. The hatred between them is palpable. Addressing Richard as 'gracious sovereign', 'most loving liege', 'dear, dear lord', they nevertheless reject his pleas for reconciliation and insist on their right to submit their quarrel to trial by combat. Reluctantly, the king agrees. The scene shifts to Coventry where, after elaborate, chivalric preliminaries have been completed, Richard suddenly announces that to prevent the spilling of his 'kindred's blood' he has decided to banish them both, Bolinbroke for six years, Mowbray for life. It is in the short scene that follows between Richard and his cronies that the façade of impartial royalty cracks. His fear and suspicion of Bolinbroke now emerge, and when news is brought of the mortal illness of 'time-honoured Lancaster', Bolinbroke's father, the falsity of his kingly performance in the earlier scenes of the play is shockingly revealed:

> Now put it, God, in the physician's mind
> To help him to his grave immediately.
> The lining of his coffers shall make coats
> To deck our soldiers for these Irish wars.
> Come, gentlemen, let's all go visit him.
> Pray God we make haste and come too late.   (I.iv.58–63)

The trial has been a sham, and Richard's impartiality as judge a lie; not only is Mowbray guilty of Gloucester's death, but Richard knows that he is for it was he who ordered it.

In *Henry VI*, Bolinbroke's usurpation of the throne was presented as the original sin whereby the seed of future factional strife that was to bring the country to its knees in the Wars of the Roses was planted. In stepping back in time to that historical moment in *Richard*, Shakespeare sees it very differently. The fault

now lies in the king; in his unwillingness or incapacity to assume
the responsibilities of the role he has inherited. He plays the part
convincingly, knows his lines and delivers them with practised
skill, but they are only words – eloquent but false.

The disparities and confusions that arise between man and his
office, reality and image, actor and role, are a recurring preoccu-
pation in Shakespeare's writing, and his life as a player (especially
perhaps a player of kings) would have kept it in his thoughts. We
find it in *Hamlet* –

> The time is out of joint; O cursed spite
> That ever I was born to set it right!

– and in *Lear* who, in giving away his kingdom, loses both his role
and his reason. The last two acts of *Richard* are a sustained
meditation on this theme in which the metaphor of the stage as
microcosm of the world is variously employed.

The identity of king and kingdom – the belief that the king *was*
England in a metaphysical sense, and that the well-being of the
nation depended in a very real way on the moral worth of its
ruler – was still current in the Elizabethan period as it had been
dominant throughout the Middle Ages. Here, both king and
kingdom are in deep trouble. Gaunt is dying, but sees that
Richard also is mortally ill, and that

> Thy deathbed is no lesser than thy land,
> Wherein thou liest in reputation sick,
> And thou, too careless patient as thou art,
> Commit'st thy anointed body to the cure
> Of those physicians that first wounded thee.
> A thousand flatterers sit within thy crown
> Whose compass is no bigger than thy head,
> And yet encaged in so small a verge
> The waste is no whit lesser than thy land. (II.i.95–103)

Richard angrily dismisses Gaunt's diagnosis, but a new, more
pragmatic view of kingship is gaining ground that he will be
unable to ignore. Just as the actor's success in the part he is
playing is not simply dependent on the imaginative power and
self-belief that he is able to bring to it, but also on the degree to

which he is able to carry his audience along with him in that belief, so the king, playing what he believes is his divinely ordained role on the stage of the world, is likewise dependent on its acceptance by his subjects, and that in turn on the worldly power he has at his command.

On returning from Ireland to find Bolinbroke's invading army already landed, Richard is full of confidence in the sacred nature of his office and the nominal power of his kingly title. When he is told that twelve thousand of his Welsh soldiers have deserted, dispersed or fled, it is only momentarily that his confidence and courage fail. 'Am I not king?' he asks,

> Awake, thou coward! Majesty, thou sleepest.
> Is not the king's name twenty thousand names?
> Arm, arm, my name! A puny subject strikes
> At thy great glory. Look not to the ground.
> Ye favourites of a king, are we not high?
> High be our thoughts.   (III.ii.83–9)

But with news of further defections arriving every moment, he is forced to face the reality of the situation, and ends by placing both his crown and his person meekly into Bolinbroke's hands.

Though the self-absorption and role-playing continue, it is in the humiliation of his fall that Richard discovers a new voice and a more truthful eloquence that arouses our compassion.

> Cover your heads, and mock not flesh and blood
> With solemn reverence. Throw away respect,
> Tradition, form and ceremonious duty,
> For you have but mistook me all this while.
> I live with bread like you, feel want,
> Taste grief, need friends. Subjected thus,
> How can you say to me I am a king?   (III.ii.171–7)

His degradation is to go much further. Through York's tear-filled eyes, we are given a picture of the royal cousins riding together into London; Bolinbroke,

> Mounted upon a hot and fiery steed
> Which his aspiring rider seemed to know,

> With slow but stately pace kept on his course,
> Whilst all tongues cried 'God save thee, Bolinbroke!'

Richard following behind; and,

> As in a theatre the eyes of men
> After a well-graced actor leaves the stage
> Are idly bent on him that follows next,
> Thinking his prattle to be tedious,
> Even so or with much more contempt men's eyes
> Did scowl on Richard. No man cried 'God save him',
> No joyful tongue gave him his welcome home,
> But dust was thrown upon his sacred head . . .   (V.ii.8–30)

In all this, Bolinbroke is presented as the opposite pole to Richard; he is the man of action as against the self-regarding poet. He is at his most eloquent in his accusations of Mowbray in the opening scene. He returns in arms from banishment, not as usurper, but as Duke of Lancaster to reclaim his father's lands, which Richard has unjustly sequestered. At his first meeting with the humbled king, he kneels to him and treats him with respect. Thereafter, his attitude is wholly pragmatic. When Richard offers him the crown, he accepts it. In speech, he is increasingly taciturn. He has little more than 400 lines to Richard's 750. In the Deposition scene, Richard addresses him as 'silent king'. While Richard commands the stage with speeches of eloquent self-pity, Bolinbroke commands Richard in saying very little. It is a battle royal between the intoxicating spell of words and the unspoken realities of military and political power. One of Richard's few remaining supporters describes it later as a 'woeful pageant'. (The scene was cut from the first published text in deference to the Queen, who is reported to have said, 'I am Richard'. Though one may doubt the truth of the comparison, it would have made uncomfortable reading for her.) As Richard is effectively deposed by the desertion of his subjects, Bolinbroke is enthroned by their need to fill the consequent vacuum. He ascends the throne to the acclamations of his supporters with the flattest of lines: 'In God's name I'll ascend the regal throne.' In the end, he wishes Richard dead – and the sycophantic Exton is on hand to oblige. The sin is acknowledged by Henry as his, and will haunt him through the next two plays in the cycle. It is interesting and significant that Shakespeare chose to play this role. And it was not because he thought it was easy, because it is not.

Of the two old men of the play, Gaunt, with the marvellous speech in which he describes his dying vision of England, would probably have gone to Bryan or Heminges, and the somewhat comical York (the 'mad-cap Duke', as Hotspur later calls him) to Pope. The part of the senior Gardener may well have been Kempe's. The various lords and other subsidiary characters require careful casting and are easily distinguishable in performance, though they lack in the writing (no doubt deliberately so) the sharper edge that Shakespeare normally gives to his supporting roles as well as to many smaller ones.

Though Henry is the stronger of the two kings, and emerges as the victor in the struggle between them, the play and the tragedy are Richard's. Alone in prison, he searches for his lost identity.

> . . . play I in one person many people,
> And none contented. Sometimes am I king,
> Then treasons make me wish myself a beggar,
> And so I am. Then crushing penury
> Persuades me I was better when a king,
> Then am I kinged again, and by and by
> Think that I am unkinged by Bolinbroke,
> And straight am nothing. But whate'er I be
> Nor I nor any man that but man is
> With nothing shall be pleased till he be eased
> With being nothing.   (V.v.31–41)

— ★ —

I have proposed that *Richard II* was performed in the summer of 1596, and the *Merchant of Venice* in the autumn of that year. The twelve months that followed were to be an eventful and difficult period in the history of the company. As already recounted, the company's first patron, Lord Hunsdon, had died in July 1596, and was succeeded as Chamberlain by Sir William Brooke, Lord Cobham, and as patron by Sir George Carey, Hunsdon's son and heir. Early versions of the two parts of *Henry IV* under the title of

Sir John Oldcastle were staged in the winter of 1596/7, but were objected to by Cobham on the grounds that the historical Oldcastle, whose name Shakespeare had borrowed for his principal buffoon, was an ancestor of his and highly regarded by the Puritan party as an early Protestant martyr. The plays were withdrawn for revision. But in March 1597, Cobham died and was succeeded as Chamberlain by Carey, the second Lord Hunsdon (whereupon the company reverted to their previous title, having been known as Hunsdon's in the interim). At the same time, Shakespeare was commissioned to produce an entertainment to celebrate their new patron's appointment as Knight of the Garter, and an early version of *The Merry Wives of Windsor*, probably comprising little more than the final masque of the play as we have it now, is thought to have been staged at Windsor for Carey's installation in May.[10]

Then, in July, all the London playhouses were closed by the Privy Council in reaction to the staging by Pembroke's men (probably at the Swan) of an allegedly seditious play by Jonson and Nashe, *The Isle of Dogs*, that landed its authors in gaol. The Chamberlain's took to the road, visiting Rye and Dover, Marlborough, Bath and Bristol, and the first authorised publication of any of Shakespeare's plays – the 'good' Quarto of *Richard II* and the reconstituted text of *Richard III*, sold to the printer Andrew Wise in August and October of the same year – may well have been occasioned by a cash-flow crisis resulting from the July closures and a need for extra funds to finance the tour.

One other important change in the company's fortunes in 1597 should be mentioned. In February, James Burbage (Richard's father) died, leaving a financial muddle behind him, with the ground lease of the now ageing Shoreditch Theatre nearing its end, and his projected indoor playhouse at Blackfriars still in limbo. Consequently, when, in October, the London theatres were allowed to reopen, the company moved its operations in London from the Theatre to the Curtain, which stood nearby and in which the Burbage brothers had inherited an interest. It was probably there that the first London performances of the revised and renamed *Henry IV* plays were given.[11] It is quite possible, therefore, that like the *Dream* and the *Merchant*, they were premiered and brought to a high state of finish in the course of the company's autumn tour.[12] However that may have been, the necessity for revision resulting from the Oldcastle/Falstaff controversy ensured an exceptionally long gestation period for the plays, and this shows. They are among Shakespeare's greatest achievements; superbly crafted and breaking wholly new ground.

The lyricism of *Richard II* now gives place to a more realistic treatment of character; poetry to an alternation of strongly dramatic verse and rhythmical prose. At the same time, the focus widens from Richard's self-absorption and the verge of the court to the whole of England, in which every class and section of society is represented. The small scene between the carriers that opens Act 2 of Part One, set in the yard of a Rochester inn with its early morning bustle, lanterns and occupational jargon, is a good example of Shakespeare's widening vision in the plays, and comes straight from his own experience as a player on the road; it has little relation to plot, but contributes to the general impression we get of a continuum of energetic life at the ordinary, humdrum level enveloping the big events of the play and its significant relationships, which are those between the King and his son, Hal and Falstaff. The Boar's Head scenes in both parts, though dominated by Falstaff, Shakespeare's greatest comic creation, are models of accurate observation and reporting in which the meanest of the tavern servants, Francis the drawer, with his catch-phrase of 'Anon, anon, sir', is given his moment.

Prince:	How old art thou, Francis?
Francis:	Let me see, about Michaelmas next I shall be –
Poins:	[*Within*] Francis!
Francis:	Anon, sir – pray stay a little, my lord.
Prince:	Nay but hark you, Francis, for the sugar thou gavest me, 'twas a pennyworth, was't not?
Francis:	O Lord, I would it had been two!
Prince:	I will give thee for it a thousand pound – ask me when thou wilt, and thou shalt have it.
Poins:	[*Within*] Francis!
Francis:	Anon, anon.
Prince:	Anon, Francis? No, Francis, but tomorrow, Francis; or, Francis a-Thursday; or indeed, Francis, when thou wilt . . . (1H4: II.iv.53–66)

(The Boar's Head and Rochester scenes would have found a perfect venue in inns along the roads to Dover and Bristol.)

In view of the number of named roles (42 in Part Two), he would be a brave person who attempted a doubling plot. Hotspur is a part that the best of actors have been glad to play, and in Glendower we have the first of a series of Welshmen of whom I shall have more to say in the following chapter. All we can say for sure of the smaller roles is that Sincler doubled Simon Shadow and the First Beadle in Part Two, where he is named in a stage direction as 'Sinklo' and addressed by Doll and the Hostess as 'paper-faced villain', 'starved bloodhound' and 'goodman bones' (V.iv). He would also have made an excellent Rumour. It is a 'company play' if ever there was one and would have been a joy to perform – as it still is!

Though he has no more than six out of nineteen scenes in Part One, and only three in Part Two, Shakespeare's role as the King is the hub around which the plays turn; and the tug-of-war between himself and Falstaff for the soul of Hal, their central and cohesive theme.

Historically, only two years have elapsed between the end of *Richard II* and the beginning of *Henry IV*, but in that time Henry's character has appreciably soured. We now find him testy, worried and ill. The burdens of office, his role as king, have taken their toll. The patience and courtesy of the man as shown in *Richard* – his kneeling to his defeated opponent, his treatment of the common people,

> How he did seem to dive into their hearts
> With humble and familiar courtesy

is revealed as having been a calculated strategy, as Richard had suspected. 'By being seldom seen', Henry now confides to Hal,

> I could not stir
> But like a comet I was wonder'd at,
> That men would tell their children, 'This is he!'
>   (1H4: III.ii.46–8)

And in lines that follow, Richard is characterised as 'the skipping King', who

> ambled up and down
> With shallow jesters, and rash bavin wits,
> Soon kindled and soon burnt, carded his state,
> Mingled his royalty with cap'ring fools,
> Had his great name profaned with their scorns,
> And gave his countenance against his name
> To laugh at gibing boys . . .   (III.ii.60–6)

Henry's nightmare is that Hal is following the same path that led Richard to his ruin.

> . . . in that very line, Harry, standest thou,
> For thou hast lost thy princely privilege
> With vile participation. Not an eye
> But is a-weary of thy common sight,
> Save mine, which hath desir'd to see thee more . . .
> For all the world
> As thou art to this hour was Richard then . . .
> (III.ii.85–9, 93–4)

In Henry's apprehensive vision, Hal *is* Richard, and the fact that the actor playing Hal (Burbage), now standing before him, had been Richard in the earlier play would have made the point more effectively than any other casting could have done.

In effective opposition to the king in his struggle to retain the allegiance of his son stands Falstaff, and as Henry dominates the court scenes, which are wholly in verse, Falstaff dominates the world of the tavern, wholly in prose – prose of a quality that Shakespeare was never to surpass.

Falstaff has been described in many ways: as buffoon, vice, wit, liar, coward, toper, parasite, scoundrel, con-man and clown; he is all of these, and more. He contains, as has been said, multitudes, and yet remains irredeemably and consistently himself. So much has been written about him – not always in context – that he is in danger of being mythologised out of existence. The plain fact is, of course, that he is neither real nor fictional, but a role in a series of plays written for a particular actor who would have brought to his performance of the part his own unifying personality and presence that now we can only guess at. Though not as yet generally acknowledged, I believe that John Dover Wilson was right in assigning it to Kempe.[13]

There is no doubt that Kempe was the principal fool of the company, and one who had, through his playing of Dogberry and Peter – and probably also the Dromios, Launce and Bottom – demonstrated exceptional ability as a versatile character actor who kept to the lines his author gave him. Being large in limb, the part would have been (with the aid of padding) within his physical range. The self-defining function of the fool is to evoke laughter, and this is precisely Falstaff's function in the play.

> Men of all sorts take a pride to gird at me. The brain of this foolish-compounded clay, man, is not able to invent anything that intends to laughter more than I invent, or is invented on me; I am not only witty in myself, but the cause that wit is in other men.   (2H4:I.ii.5–9)

To see him as the central figure is understandable but mistaken. For his humour, though spreading around him like a benign penumbra to everyone he meets, whether receptive or not, has a specific purpose and is directed to a particular person: it is to make Hal laugh, and so educate and humanise him. We see him storing up material to this end – observing people's behaviour, listening to their chatter, drawing them out as he does with Shallow, and making mental notes of the future use he can make of the results. 'I will devise matter enough out of this Shallow', he tells us in soliloquy,

> to keep Prince Harry in continual laughter the wearing out of six fashions . . . O, you shall see him laugh till his face be like a wet cloak ill laid up!   (2H4:V.i.75–7, 81–2)

There is calculation here – just as there is calculation in Hal's relation to Falstaff. For however much they enjoy their double-act together, the relationship between them is more one of mutual self-interest than affection. Both are playing a role. Hal's role is as prodigal son, sowing his wild oats. He loves Falstaff's humour, participates in it, feeds and grows on it as a human being. It is necessary to him as an escape from the repressive expectations of his father; but there is always a reservation in his performance of it, an awareness that when the moment comes he must and will reject it to assume his destiny as king. He makes no promises to Falstaff, but means to provide for him, and does. Falstaff's role is as buffoon to the Prince;[14] but he lacks the simplicity of the fool, for he too has a further objective in view: to provide for his future prosperity and comfort. He has misjudged his man. In rejecting Falstaff, Hal is also rejecting his *alter ego* as Richard. 'Master Shallow', Falstaff wryly observes when the penny finally drops, 'I owe you a thousand pound.'

There is a textual indication of Kempe's casting in the role. In the 'good' Quarto edition of Part Two, we find a rogue stage direction, 'Enter Will', after II.iv.18 – some 14 lines in advance of Falstaff's marked appearance, singing. The prompter would have been stationed at stage level. If, as is probable, Falstaff was intended to enter at the upper level, he would have needed an early signal to climb the backstage steps to be ready on cue for his entrance on the gallery; the song would have covered his descent to the stage.

But the clearest pointer to Kempe as Falstaff's original performer is in the Epilogue of Part Two. Though some recent editors like to divide this and apportion its several sections to different occasions and various speakers, it is included in full (with only slight variations) in both Quarto and Folio versions of the play, and hangs together very well. From Pope onwards, early editors attributed the whole to a 'Dancer'; they were right, for Kempe was famous for his dancing as well as for his fooling, and was the author of published jigs. As the play ends and all the characters left on stage exit, Falstaff hurriedly returns from the opposite side, having escaped from the guards who are escorting him to prison.

> First, my fear; then, my curtsy;

– he takes a bow to tumultuous applause –

> last, my speech. My fear, is your displeasure; my curtsy, my duty; and my speech, to beg your pardons. If you look for a good speech now, you undo me, for what I have to say is of my own making; and what indeed I should say will, I doubt, prove mine own marring.

This tells us plainly enough that it is not the play's author who is speaking, but one of the other actors and, from the terms of the apology he goes on to make, it is equally clear that it has to do with his previous performance as Sir John Oldcastle, and the 'displeasing play', the play of that name that Shakespeare has now revised and retitled.

> Be it known to you, as it is very well, I was lately here in the end of a displeasing play, to pray your patience for it, and to promise you a better. I meant indeed to pay you with this; which if like an ill venture it come unluckily home, I break, and you, my gentle creditors, lose. Here I promised you I would be, and here I commit my body to your mercies . . .

In the final part of the speech, Kempe is part in, part out of character. He would still, of course, have been wearing his costume and padding as Falstaff. Though we are not told whether Falstaff is much of a dancer, Kempe is, and speaks as such. When he tells us that 'Oldcastle died martyr, and this is not the man', the identity of the speaker is put beyond doubt.

> If my tongue cannot entreat you to acquit me, will you command me to use my legs? And yet that were but light payment, to dance out of your debt . . . One word more, I beseech you. If you be not too cloyed with fat meat, our humble author will continue the story, with Sir John in it, and make you merry with fair Katharine of France; where, for anything I know, Falstaff shall die of a sweat, unless already a be killed with your hard opinions; for Oldcastle died martyr, and this is not the man. My tongue is weary; when my legs are too, I will bid you good night.

The last line is cue for a jig and, as the musicians strike up, Kempe is joined on stage by the rest of the company, including Shakespeare, who take a dancing call. The play, as originally performed, thus ends on a much lighter note than the text may at first suggest; and if the audience are still upset by Falstaff's rejection (as so many critics have been), they are comforted in the knowledge that he is to be given a further lease of life in the play's sequel.

That, as we know now, was not to be, for he does not appear in *Henry V*, and the Falstaff of the *Merry Wives*, a few years later, has somehow lost the true flavour and bite of Shakespeare's original creation. The reasons for this have been much debated, but the most obvious one is that the player who had first acted the role, and become associated with it through its several incarnations, was no longer of the company, and that Shakespeare baulked at the necessity to introduce another actor in the part while the memory of its first performer was fresh in the public's mind. Here again, Kempe – and only Kempe of the senior sharers – fits the bill, for we know that he left the company in mysterious circumstances in 1599 to embark on his dancing journey to Norwich; as shown in Plate 20. (He is in the actor-list of Jonson's *Every Man in his Humour* of 1598 but not in that of his *Every Man out of his Humour* of 1599, and sold his share in the Globe shortly after the lease of 21 February 1599 was signed.)[15] It is not, however, true (as often stated) that he claimed to have danced himself out of the world, meaning the Globe. The claim was made by some unauthorised hack of a ballad-singer, the truth of which Kempe only half allows ('others guess righter'), for he had probably never been in the Globe. He had danced, as Falstaff, out of the Curtain.[16]

Enough has been said to indicate that stylistically the two *Henry IV* plays are very different to their immediate predecessor, and yet they retain a unity within the cycle of the Henriad. And as *Richard II* and *Henry IV* belong together, so *Henry V* will be found to belong with *Henry IV*. The shift in style and mood from *Richard* to its sequels is thus less a matter of Shakespeare's leaving behind a lyrical phase in his writing for one that is more prosaic and realistic than a deliberate shift in perspective – an adaptation of manner both to the varying events that history presented to him and the changing demands of the public. In the difficult conditions of 1596/7, the company badly needed a hit, Shakespeare pulled out all the stops to provide it and, having courted disaster with his first attempt, ended by writing a masterpiece. 'Uneasy lies the head that wears a crown.' In his role as Bolinbroke, the 'silent king' of *Richard II*, he had given the stage to Richard; as Henry IV he moves to its centre. The reconciliation scene between himself and Hal in Act 4 of Part Two is both the true dramatic crux of the whole and a perfect induction to the play that is to follow.

NINE

The Globe, 1599–1601

> The Globe Theatre was a magical theatre, a cosmic
> theatre, a religious theatre, an actor's theatre, designed to
> give fullest support to the voices and the gestures of the
> players as they enacted the drama of the life of man
> within the Theatre of the World . . . His theatre would
> have been for Shakespeare the pattern of the universe,
> the idea of the Macrocosm, the world stage on which the
> Microcosm acted his parts. All the world's a stage. The
> words are in a real sense the clue to the Globe Theatre.
>
> *Frances A. Yates[1]*

When, in October 1597, the London playhouses were allowed
to reopen after the *Isle of Dogs* controversy, by which time
the ground lease of the Shoreditch Theatre had run out, the
company moved into its near neighbour, the Curtain. We know
very little about the Curtain except that it was of the same age
and had been used as an 'easer' to the Theatre, which suggests
that it was a good deal smaller. Nevertheless, it provided a
metropolitan base for the Chamberlain's company in the two
years that followed, where Shakespeare's plays written in the
period, including both parts of *Henry IV* and *Much Ado About
Nothing*, received their first London performances. But whatever
merits the Curtain possessed by reason of its intimacy were
outweighed by its practical disadvantages, for like the Theatre it
would now have been showing its age, and its more limited
capacity would have greatly restricted the company's share of box
office takings, on which the players largely depended.

The degree of frustration they were feeling in this situation is
apparent in what happened next. For under cover of darkness,

one night near the end of December 1598 or early in January 1599, a group of them, assisted by a dozen or so labourers under the supervision of a builder called Peter Street, entered Burbage's original building, the old Theatre, and proceeded to demolish its timbers. These they transported, presumably by barge, to a new site on the opposite, Surrey, side of the Thames, not far from the Rose in the parish of St Saviour's, Southwark, where they were to set about building the Globe. Though the owners of the land on which the Theatre had stood subsequently launched a writ of trespass against Richard and Cuthbert Burbage, who had inherited ownership of the theatre's structure from their father, the brothers had right on their side and, after several years of legal wrangling, were finally exonerated.

They were not, however, able to meet more than half the cost of the rebuilding from their own resources, so five others of the company's senior men – Heminges, Kempe, Phillips, Pope and Shakespeare – contributed 10 per cent each and so became, not only sharers in the company's profits as they had been from the beginning, but also co-owners ('housekeepers', as they were termed) of its theatre, and entitled to an additional share in half the gallery takings. (General admittance to the theatre was charged at a penny a head, which went to the company; for further admittance to one or other of the galleries an extra penny or twopence was charged, and traditionally this was divided equally between company and owners.) Such joint ownership by a company of players of the building in which they performed was unique in the period and has rarely, if ever, been repeated. It also placed them in the enviable position of exercising a controlling influence on the design of the new theatre. As plans of neither Theatre nor Globe have survived and we have only a few exterior sketches (one is shown in Plate 19), we can only guess at the nature and extent of the changes they effected, but in view of the rapid developments that had taken place in the drama since the earlier building – the first of its kind – had been erected back in 1576, they are likely to have been significant, especially as regards the internal architecture of the stage and proscenium in relation to the yard and galleries. We may take it as certain that, as a senior sharer and the company's resident author, Shakespeare's views in the matter would have carried considerable weight. Though I have earlier objected to the expression 'Shakespeare's company' as sometimes used of the Chamberlain's men, it would be difficult to dispute Miss Yates' claim that the Globe was in large measure Shakespeare's theatre, reflecting his personal view of its function. This is borne out, I suggest, by the plays that he wrote specifically for it.

Most scholars who have studied *Henry V* agree that Shakespeare's reference in his Act 5 Chorus to the Earl of Essex as 'General of our gracious Empress' who is expected on his return from Ireland to bring out the sort of crowds on the streets of the City that welcomed Henry on his triumphant return from France, dates the composition of the play to between 27 March 1599, when Essex left on his pacifying mission to Ireland, and his far from triumphant return on 28 September of the same year, which corresponds with the period when the Globe would have been under construction. As the company would have been eager to obtain use of their new playhouse as soon as possible, and we know that the builder, Street, later contracted to erect a similar structure (the Fortune) within a period of four months, the Globe would almost certainly have been ready for occupation by June or July 1599.

In *The Life of Henry the Fift*, as the play is entitled in the First Folio, Shakespeare reverted to the role of story-teller he had adopted and then abandoned half-way through in *Romeo and Juliet*. He enters as poet, invoking inspiration:

> O for a muse of fire, that would ascend
> The brightest heaven of invention,
> A kingdom for a stage, princes to act,
> And monarchs to behold the swelling scene!

But this was not to be. If all the world's a stage, the stage is here conversely an unworthy scaffold and a mere cockpit. 'Can this cockpit hold/The vasty fields of France?' he asks.

> Or may we cram
> Within this wooden O the very casques
> That did affright the air at Agincourt?

Given the 'flat unraised spirits' who have dared 'bring forth/So great an object', and the poverty of means at their disposal, they can only succeed with the active co-operation of the audience. But an apology for the players' presumption is followed by a series of uncompromising imperatives –

> Suppose within the girdle of these walls . . .
> Piece out our imperfections with your thoughts.
> Into a thousand parts divide one man . . .
> Think, when we talk of horses that you see them . . .

– that are to continue through the play in the choruses that precede each of the acts. Having played out his previous role in *Henry IV*, Shakespeare is freed to act as Chorus in its sequel, but he is more than Chorus in the traditional mode; rather, a magician, a Prospero-to-be, whose vision of the play's hero and his victories is to work directly on the audience's imagination in bringing him and them to immediate life on the stage. That is the kind of theatre the Globe is to be: a theatre of the imagination, an actor's theatre, a magical theatre.

I said earlier that *Henry V* belongs together with *Henry IV* as *Henry IV* explains and clarifies *Richard II*, for the 'warlike Harry' of *Henry V* is identical to the reformed Hal who makes his first appearance in Act 5 of *Henry IV, Part 2*:

> . . . Princes all, believe me, I beseech you,
> My father has gone wild into his grave,
> For in his tomb lie my affections;
> And with his spirits sadly I survive
> To mock the expectation of the world,
> To frustrate prophecies, and to raze out
> Rotten opinion, who hath writ me down
> After my seeming.   (V.ii.122–9)

Hal has rejected Falstaff as the Christian is exhorted to expel the old Adam and, as Henry in the present play, he allows Bardolph to go to his death for stealing a pyx without a flicker of recognition that he had ever known him. In that, he is his father's son and fulfils his promises to him in full measure; but if his wildness now lies in his father's grave, the same cannot be said of his humanity. He is presented in *Henry V* as the ideal king, the ideal military commander, but if Shakespeare can be accused with some justification of idealising the Henry V of history – by most accounts a somewhat humourless fanatic – it was by making him more, rather than less, human. The common touch he has acquired as Hal – the ability to communicate with all classes and conditions of men and relate to them at their own level – never deserts him, and only in one confessed moment of anger ('I was not angry since I came to France/ Until this instant') does he lose a sense of proportion. He assumes the role of king he has inherited and it fits him like a glove, but it remains a role; he is not obsessed by its accidentals, as was Richard, nor reduced by its burdens like his father.

For all its interconnections with its predecessors in the Henriad, stylistically the play again breaks the mould. Deriving the main lines of its plot from Holinshed with hints from an earlier, cruder dramatisation (the anonymous *Famous Victories*), it is epical and episodic in form; but in its alternation between three contrasting worlds, each with its own distinctive set of characters – the English court, that of the opposing French, and the English army in the field – the play is unlike any other in the canon.

The thirteen nobles who comprise the English court are given only a fitful, shadowy presence in the play. They come and go, appear and disappear as required by the exigencies of doubling and, with the exception perhaps of Exeter and Erpingham, have little opportunity of establishing themselves as individuals. The bishops who open the play after the first chorus are, more often than not, ruthlessly pruned in performance, and sometimes guyed (as in Olivier's classic film), but what they have to say is important in establishing the nature of Henry's reformation for those in the audience who have missed out on earlier performances of *Henry IV*. Of the six nobles who are named as appearing in the court scene that follows, only Westmorland and Exeter speak, and they have less than thirty lines between them. They provide an appropriately grave and distinguished audience for the bishops' justification of Henry's proposed invasion of France and the entrance of the French ambassadors, but do little more than dress the stage. We must imagine them as grouped about the throne that is raised at centre back of the stage.

The French court is more strongly individualised, and functions in the play as a reverse image to the English. The figure of the French King (Charles VI), often misconceived as either mad or senile, requires an especially strong performance as Henry's principal opponent. Whatever the historical record may say, in Shakespeare's text he is an awe-inspiring, fearful ghost from the past, reliving terrible memories of the time

> When Cressy battle fatally was struck,
> And all our princes captived, by the hand
> Of that black name, Edward, Black Prince of Wales;

whose warning to his feckless and over-confident nobles that the English king is 'a stem'

> Of that victorious stock, and let us fear
> The native mightiness and fate of him   (II.iv.54–64)

falls on deaf ears to their ultimate cost.

It is from the third category of subsidiary characters – those belonging to the English army – that most of the comedy derives. There can be little doubt that Shakespeare had originally intended to bring Falstaff into this part of the play (as he had announced that he would in the Epilogue to *Henry IV*), but was forestalled by Kempe's sudden withdrawal from the company.[2] Pistol, whose popularity with the Elizabethan public must have been second only to that of Falstaff to judge by his naming on the title page of the pirated Quarto of 1600,[3] appears nonetheless, along with Bardolph of the fiery nose and a new character, Nym. The three of them are shown as setting out for France, having heard from Mistress Quickly the news of Falstaff's untimely death, which they attribute to a broken heart at his rejection by Hal.[4] But amusing as Pistol's antics in France prove to be, he and his companions are essentially satellites of Falstaff, and the introduction of the delightfully loquacious Welshman Fluellen and his fellow captains never quite succeeds in filling the gap left by the missing knight.

The Folio text of the play is thought by scholars to derive in the main from Shakespeare's authorial papers. Given the thousand-and-one unforeseen eventualities that arise in the course of production, it may never have reached the stage in the complete form in which it has come down to us; but provides nevertheless a valuable insight into the working of his mind in constructing a play in which his fellows are so used as to exploit their individual strengths to the full in the achievement of his dramatic purposes.

George Bryan, one of the more senior sharers, having left the company in 1597 to take up a full-time post as Ordinary Groom of the Chamber, and Kempe having also departed, Shakespeare would have had available to him in casting the play only eight of the original sharers, but an increasing number of former apprentices would by now have been swelling the number of hired men as they matured into young manhood, and there would have been much for them to do, along with the younger recruits. Though any attempt to assign with any exactness the fifty speaking parts and 'double' them effectively is inevitably doomed to failure, I have made a conjectural doubling plot, shown in Appendix D, which I hope will be of interest.

As Chorus, Shakespeare would have been in a position to double any number of the smaller parts. I have given him Bedford and Burgundy for the reasons given in my notes to the plot. In suggesting other doubles, I have borne in mind throughout the principle enunciated earlier that it is always easier and more effective to combine contrasting roles than those that are similar. At least one of these – the doubling of the French King and Montjoy the herald, which I have given to Condell – is, I believe, integral to Shakespeare's dramatic intentions.

A further word should be said at this point about an important new recruit to the company, Robert Armin. He was to take over some of Kempe's 'clown' parts, including Dogberry, but was a versatile character actor in his own right, as well as a published author, and the roles that Shakespeare was to write for him were significantly different from those he had created for Kempe.

He would almost certainly have played Fluellen. Originally a member of Lord Chandos' men, Armin's first known London performance was in an early version of his own play, the *Two Maids of More-clacke* in 1596, when he had demonstrated his versatility by quadrupling four roles: that of a natural fool called Blue John (a real person whom he had known in London and was to write about in his whimsical study of such innocents, *Foole upon Foole*), Tutch, a clever household fool, Tutch in the disguise of

Blue John, and Tutch again in his impersonation of a Welsh knight. It has often been noted that Shakespeare's series of Welsh characters begins with a Welsh captain in *Richard II*, proceeds to Glendower in Part One of *Henry IV*, and thence to Fluellen. The likelihood is that Armin was spotted by Shakespeare in the *Two Maids*, joined the company immediately afterwards to play the Welsh captain and other minor roles in *Richard*, went with the company on tour and to the Curtain, playing Glendower, and from thence to the Globe as Fluellen.[5] If he was already a Chamberlain's man in 1596/7, there could be no question of his being brought in to fill the vacancy left by Kempe early in 1599, as is usually supposed; by then he would already have been an established member of the company, though not yet a sharer. I have assumed that Shakespeare would have made full use of his versatility in *Henry V*.

The play bears all the marks of a dual celebration. It celebrates and gives theatrical life to the memory of a remarkable king and his victories; but it is also a celebration of theatre, an opportunity for the players to demonstrate both their individual talents and their cohesion as an ensemble in an exciting new arena, the Globe. From the point of view of the scholar and the literary critic, it may not be among the more profound of Shakespeare's plays, but in the power of its language and richness of its characterisation it remains one of the most enjoyable and rewarding in performance.

That in writing *Henry V* Shakespeare was already thinking of Rome, and rereading his Plutarch, is suggested by the incidental references it contains to Roman history,[6] and the first performance of *Henry* at the Globe was soon to be followed by *Julius Caesar*, the second of his Roman plays and the first of his great tragedies.

The time of its production can be dated with exceptional precision by the report of a visit to London by a Swiss doctor from Basle, Thomas Platter, who was in England between 18 September and 20 October 1599:

> On the 21st of September, after dinner, at about two o'clock, I went with my party across the water; in the straw-thatched house we saw the tragedy of the first Emperor Julius Caesar,

very pleasingly performed, with approximately fifteen characters; at the end of the play they danced together admirably and exceedingly gracefully, according to their custom, two in each group dressed in men's and two [in] women's apparel.[7]

The performance he saw is unlikely to have been the first. If, as suggested, *Henry V* had appeared in June or July, *Caesar* is likely to have followed a few weeks later in July or August. (I return to his report of the dance.)

The language of the play has a classical austerity and directness with few rhetorical flourishes, which contributes to making it one of the most frequently quoted of Shakespeare's plays if *Hamlet* is excepted. The text is among the best and least polluted in the Folio, and there are no quartos (authorised or otherwise) to muddy the record. The familiar plot of friendship and its betrayal through allegiance to an abstract ideal of honour and freedom, and the terrible consequences of that betrayal, drives through with unparalleled urgency and power from the first scene to the last. It admits of no intervals or pauses for the shifting of scenery or extraneous 'business'.

If mute extras are omitted from the count, Platter's 'approximately fifteen characters' (by which I take him to mean actors) corresponds well enough with the size of the Globe company as previously estimated. With some forty speaking roles, doubling would have been as extensive as in *Henry V* but, because of the marked shift of direction and location that occurs in Act 3 – from concentration on the plot to assassinate Caesar to its effects, and from Rome to Sardis and Philippi – far less complex in its demands. The conspirators of the earlier part become in the main soldiers in the later, and of the twenty-one named characters in the first, only five survive into the second: Brutus, Cassius, Antony, Caesar (briefly as ghost), and the boy Lucius.

It is commonly assumed that Burbage played all the leading parts in Shakespeare's plays, by which is usually meant the largest, though the only ones we can be sure of from near-contemporary sources are Richard III, Hamlet, Lear and Othello. These are indisputably leads, but they do not entitle us to assume that he invariably took the lead; nor is the leading role invariably the largest.[8] Though Brutus is generally recognised as the first of Shakespeare's tragic heroes in that his fall can be attributed to a basic flaw of character and an interior conflict manifest in his Hamlet-like soliloquies, I believe the part would have gone to one of the younger men (perhaps Condell), and Burbage's skills reserved for the more extrovert Antony, whose long and subtly constructed oration in the Forum over the corpse of Caesar is the turning point of the play. Though briefly introduced with Caesar in Act 1, he has only seven lines prior to Caesar's death in Act 3, and only the third largest part with some 300 lines in all.

Age differences between the characters are important. Historically, Caesar was fifty-five at the time of his death and Antony about forty. Brutus is young enough to have been rumoured Caesar's bastard son. When Cicero is under discussion as a possible recruit to the conspiracy, Metellus suggests to Brutus and the others that his

> silver hairs
> Will purchase us a good opinion . . .
> Our youths and wildness shall no whit appear,
> But all be buried in his gravity.   (II.i.143–4, 147–8

Though 'wildness' is hardly applicable to Brutus, he is of the same generation as his fellow conspirators, while Antony is appreciably older. (In 1599, Burbage was thirty-two or thirty-three.) In that respect, the play is a conflict between youth and age, idealism and experience. With the entrance of Octavius in Act 4, the balance shifts. If Brutus is played young, as Shakespeare intended, even greater poignancy attaches to Caesar's dying words as Brutus advances to the kill, 'Et tu, Brute?', and as he strikes home, 'Then fall, Caesar'. In that moment, Brutus realises the true horror of what he is doing, and his character deteriorates rapidly to the washing of hands in Caesar's blood and the forced and mistimed rhetoric of the lines that follow:

Cassius: How many ages hence
Shall this our lofty scene be acted over
In states unborn and accents yet unknown?

Brutus: How many times shall Caesar bleed in sport
That now on Pompey's basis lies along,
No worthier than the dust?   (III.i.111–16)

– that have the double-mirror effect of making the performance on stage appear more real than the ghastly actuality it reflects.

Shakespeare's portrait of Caesar has been criticised for its emphasis on the character's pride and arrogance, though in that he is merely following Plutarch. At this point in his life, Caesar's military triumphs, on which his reputation rests, are behind him. He is old, ill, prone to superstition, and tetchy; but as Brutus admits, 'I know no personal cause to spurn at him', and 'to speak truth of Caesar/I have not known when his affections swayed/More than his reason' (II.i.11, 19–21). He is to be killed, not because he has given offence, but may do so in the future; not because any of his present words or actions can be faulted, but because the power that he enjoys renders him a potential threat to all that Brutus (the quintessential Roman) holds most dear. He is the serpent's egg that must be crushed before it hatches. Brutus' intentions are indeed honourable, but those of his fellows are less so, and their actions are to lead both him and Rome into evil and the destruction of all he had hoped to preserve. This is the core of the tragedy.

Shakespeare's problem with Caesar is that he has really nothing to do or say in the play except in responding to the weaknesses and deliberate provocations of others. He is, as Hazlitt noticed, like the man in the coffin at a funeral – an essential but passive character in the proceedings. The importunate warnings of the Soothsayer and Artemidorus are brushed aside with superb aplomb, and his proudest speeches are in contemptuous dismissal of the egregious flattery he encounters:

> I must prevent thee, Cimber:
> These couchings and these lowly courtesies
> Might fire the blood of ordinary men,
> And turn pre-ordinance and first decree
> Into the lane of children. Be not fond
> To think that Caesar bears such rebel blood
> That will be thawed from the true quality
> With that which melteth fools – I mean sweet words
> Low-crooked curtsies and base spaniel fawning.
>
> (III.i.35–43)

The negative impression of Caesar is more apparent in reading than in the theatre. The true note of offended dignity and patrician hauteur, as opposed to arrogant boasting, can only be found in performance. For all its passivity – indeed the more compellingly for it – the role requires the charismatic presence of a great actor. And that, I believe, is what Shakespeare would have brought to it when the play was first staged, for there can be little doubt that he played it himself. Both in its 'kingliness' and curious blend of centrality and detachment, it is a characteristic Shakespeare role.

Platter's report of the dance that concluded the Globe performance – executed, we are told, with extreme grace by two men in women's clothes and two in men's – calls for a further comment. Technically, this was known as a 'jig', and sometimes incorporated elements of characterisation and song, but we need to disassociate the term from the vigorous Irish jig of today. The meaning of its occurrence here is to be found in the very special feeling that Shakespeare had for music, especially in alliance with dance, which to him was the ultimate expression of harmony among human beings, reflecting the movements of the planets and the music of the spheres. Frances Yates (in the quotation at the top of the chapter) was right to speak of the Globe as a 'cosmic theatre, a religious theatre', and the ceiling of the canopy that overhung the stage is said to have been painted blue and dotted with stars.[9] In the course of the play, we have witnessed an assassination that was also a betrayal of friendship (the worst of sins in Shakespeare's moral code), a poet being torn to pieces by the mob, the suicides of Cassius and Brutus, the disruption of social coherence in the internecine clash of two Roman armies, and a near-total breakdown in human relations. The dance that brought the Globe performance to an end was an elegant coda to send the audience away in a calmer state of mind than they would otherwise have known; but more significantly also, a restoration of harmony to audience, players, and the theatre itself: that microcosm of the universe that the Globe represented.

After three consecutive histories and a tragedy, the company would have been pressing Shakespeare for a new comedy to take into the Globe and, if the traditional story is believed, the Queen was demanding another play about Falstaff – 'Falstaff in love' –

and hers was a voice not to be denied. But if *The Merry Wives of Windsor* belongs to the winter of 1599, *As You Like It* is a play for all seasons but especially summer, and so we shall glance at that first.

Dr Johnson describes it with his usual exactness as a fable 'wild and pleasing'.[10] It is justly one of the three most popular comedies that Shakespeare wrote, and contains in Rosalind, its leading role, one of his most delightful female characters.

The play begins in fraternal strife in two separate households; that of a royal duke, where the place of the elder brother (Duke Senior) has been usurped by the younger (Duke Frederick), and the legitimate ruler expelled to take refuge in the Forest of Arden; the other, that of the sons of Sir Rowland de Boys, where the elder, Sir Oliver, is tyrannising over a younger, Orlando, for whom he has conceived an unreasoning hatred. At the ducal court, we find also two unhappy cousins and friends, Celia, the daughter of Duke Frederick, the usurper, and Rosalind, the daughter of his exiled brother. The plot – which Shakespeare derived in the main from a popular prose romance by Thomas Lodge – brings Orlando and Rosalind together at court on the occasion of a wrestling match in which Orlando has challenged a professional fighter, Charles, who has been secretly bribed by Sir Oliver to kill him; but Orlando, though young, is no weakling and, having been brought up among peasants and their rural sports, triumphs in the contest to the obvious admiration of Rosalind. Returning home, Orlando is warned by Adam, an old and sympathetic family retainer, of the murderous intentions of his brother towards him, and the two of them take flight in the direction of the Forest. Concurrently, Duke Frederick, resentful of Rosalind's friendship with his daughter, banishes her, and the two girls likewise depart towards Arden. Act 2 follows them there, where we meet Duke Senior, and find that not only has he accepted the fact of his exile with remarkable stoicism, but has come to appreciate the virtues of the simpler, rustic way of life that he and his loyal courtiers have of necessity adopted. 'Hath not old custom made this life more sweet', he asks them, 'Than that of painted pomp?'

> Are not these woods
> More free from peril than the envious court? . . .
> Sweet are the uses of adversity

> Which like the toad, ugly and venomous,
> Wears yet a precious jewel in his head;
> And this our life, exempt from public haunt,
> Finds tongues in trees, books in the running brooks,
> Sermons in stones, and good in everything.
>
> (II.i.2–4, 12–17)

The events that follow, and the course of Rosalind's courtship of Orlando (who improbably fails to see through her male disguise), must be left to Shakespeare to reveal in his own good time in the theatre. I shall focus here on the play's characters, and what I conjecture to have been their original casting – in particular, the role that Shakespeare chose for himself.

A tradition originating with an eighteenth-century antiquarian, William Oldys, and first published by Steevens in 1778, suggests that Shakespeare's part in the play was that of Sir Oliver's old retainer, Adam.

> One of Shakespeare's younger brothers, who lived to a good old age, even some years, as I compute, after the restoration of *K. Charles II*, would in his younger days come to London to visit his brother *Will*, as he called him, and be a spectator of him as an actor in some of his own plays.

Questioned in extreme old age by some Restoration actors, 'greedily inquisitive into every little circumstance' which the old man could relate of his brother, all that he could recollect was the 'faint, general, and almost lost ideas he had of having once seen him act a part in one of his own comedies, wherein being to personate a decrepit old man, he wore a long beard, and appeared so weak and drooping and unable to walk, that he was forced to be supported and carried by another person to a table, at which he was seated among some company, who were eating, and one of them sung a song'[11] – which fits, of course (perhaps a little too neatly), with the situation in Act 2, Scene 7 of *As You Like It*, where Orlando carries the exhausted Adam to the Duke's table in the forest, and Amiens sings 'Blow, blow, thou winter wind' (ll. 167ff.). Though Shakespeare had no younger brother who survived later than 1613 (when Richard was buried), Oldys' anecdote makes a good story and has been generally adopted (with suitable reservations) for want of anything better in the way of evidence, and even made the basis for a belief that Shakespeare the player specialised in 'old man' parts.

As Schoenbaum points out in a similar context, 'the wish is father to many a tradition', and on the face of it, this one is just as dubious as most other of the personal anecdotes of Shakespeare that Oldys relates. But it is just possible that it preserves in a roundabout, multi-handed way a substratum of truth. And though there is a tenable alternative in the beneficent duke of the play, whose kindly spirit is the presiding genius in the green, healing world of Arden, the role of Adam commends itself as more likely by its own innate qualities, its uniqueness among Shakespeare's many servant characters, and position in the play. He is present on stage at the opening in a scene with Orlando, and though he disappears from the action very early (after II.vii), as Caesar had done, there is opportunity for his return at the close – as we shall see in a moment. As previously, he gives himself time to work with his cast in rehearsal, and a small but important role in performance that will have a significant impact at critical stages. There is no doubt that, as Peter Levi remarks, 'Shakespeare's heart is in Adam'.[12]

With less than half the number of named characters than in the histories, the casting would have been well within the compass of the existing company. Orlando is young, handsome, athletic, warm-hearted, shy with girls, and not over-bright. If I was right in saying that Burbage at twenty-eight was too old for Romeo in 1595, he would certainly have been out of the running for Orlando at thirty-two. The part would have gone to one of the older apprentices, perhaps Kit Beeston, or Nick Tooley who would then have been twenty-four. For his female roles – Rosalind and Celia, a pert shepherdess called Phoebe, and the feisty goatherd Audrey – he would have drawn on the company's more recent recruits. The age of the boy-actor playing Rosalind presents something of a puzzle. He would have needed to be young enough to represent the charms of Rosalind as a girl convincingly, but sufficiently tall and assured in her male disguise as Ganymede to act as confidant and instructor in the arts of love to Orlando. With some 700 lines, the part is by far the longest and most complex of Shakespeare's heroines who disguise themselves as men, and would have required exceptional ability and experience.[13] He would have had a particular boy in mind when he wrote it.

Jaques is one of two 'odd men out' in the play; he looks at life aslant, a true eccentric. Though he inhabits the ducal court, respects the Duke, and is regarded by him with affectionate amusement, he never quite belongs in his world. I assign it to Burbage in a possible double with Duke Frederick.[14]

It is Duke Senior (as played perhaps by Phillips) who gives the cue for the most famous speech in the play – if not in the whole of Shakespeare –

> Thou seest, we are not alone unhappy:
> This wide and universal theatre
> Presents more woeful pageants than the scene
> Wherein we play in.

Jaques:　　　　　　All the world's a stage . . .　　　(II.vii.136ff.)

The speech has been criticised by certain scholars as no more than a series of trite commonplaces, coloured by Jaques' melancholy view of man's end; but in that context – the late summer of the company's opening season at the Globe – it is superbly right and effective and, despite its present over-familiarity, can still send a shiver of pleasurable anticipation down the spine when we hear its opening line. Though from the point of view of plot construction, it is merely filling-in time to allow Orlando to fetch Adam to the feast, it is a perfectly judged restatement of the message that had already gone out strongly from *Henry V*, and was to remain at the back of Shakespeare's mind in writing all his subsequent plays: that the theatre – the particular theatre in which the play is presently being performed – is a figure in miniature of that 'universal theatre' in which we all play a part, that by the power of imagination aims to bring the whole of life within its walls. *Totus mundus agit histrionem*, as the Globe's motto put it. We are all actors to one degree or another.

The other outsider in the forest is of course Touchstone, who no one seriously doubts would have gone to Armin as the first of a series of clever fools that Shakespeare was to write especially for him; like Jaques, the character has no precedent in Shakespeare's sources for the play. But the debt he owed to Armin – or, more accurately perhaps, the extent to which he was able to mould the actor's talents and personality to his own purposes in this new creation – has not been fully acknowledged. For not only does the character's name combine that of Armin's Tutch from his *Two Maids of More-clacke* with a contemporary court fool called Stone, but the style of his wit, in its blending of whimsical humour and word-play with scraps of learning (verse 'as well blancke as crancke', prose that passes for 'currant', as Armin describes it himself), is anticipated in his *Two Maids*, and echoed in his *Foole upon Foole* and *Quips for Questions* of the following year.[15] The combination in Touchstone of cleverness and folly would have been new to Shakespeare's audience, as it is unexpected by Jaques on first meeting him:

> A fool, a fool! I met a fool i' th' forest . . .
> Who laid him down and bask'd him in the sun,
> And rail'd on Lady Fortune in good terms,
> In good set terms, and yet a motley fool.   (II.vii.12, 15–17)

Kempe's fools had been either comic servants like Launce, the Dromios and Gobbo, or characters such as Bottom and Dogberry who remain blissfully unaware of their own foolishness. Touchstone is the first of the professional fools to appear in the plays.[16] He is 'motley' in two senses: in his conscious assumption of folly and the costume he wears; not the 'idiot's robe' Armin is seen to be wearing for his impersonation of the natural, Blue John, as illustrated in Plate 21, but in its motley combination of colours.[17]

I doubt that Shakespeare intends us to take very seriously Rosalind's claims to magical knowledge; they are part of her ingenious device for bringing about a suitable occasion on which she can reveal herself to Orlando in her true gender – as the girl he loves and his prospective bride. The masque that ends the play is thus not, as sometimes presented, a true theophany comparable to that of Jupiter in *Cymbeline* or Diana in *Pericles*, but a theatrical event, a play-within-the-play that she has put together and rehearsed with the aid of her country friends. Realistically, the part of the god Hymen should most probably go to Corin (Heminges?), the wise old shepherd who met with her and Celia on their first arrival in the forest and found them a cottage in which to live, who is otherwise absent from the final scene; but the early disappearance of Adam from the play at the end of Act 2, when he is taken off by Duke Senior to recuperate in his cave, somehow requires that he should return before the end, and there is no other role in which he can do so more appropriately than as Hymen – especially as acted by Shakespeare. There are more songs in *As You Like It* than in any other of the plays, and music pervades it. As in Caesar – but this time as an integral part of the play – harmony is generally restored and celebrated in a stately dance in which not just two, but four, couples move about the stage in admirable and graceful combination with each other.

The Merry Wives of Windsor is a play of the winter and, though a variety of dates have been proposed, I think it most probable that the Folio text as we have it now was written in the summer of 1599, and first produced at the Globe in the winter of that year.

I mentioned earlier that it may owe its genesis to a previous event in the life of the company's patron, the second Lord Hunsdon, who in April 1597 was appointed Knight of the Garter, having recently succeeded Cobham as Lord Chamberlain. A tradition that the play was written by command of the Queen, 'who was so eager to see it Acted, that she commanded it to be finished in fourteen days' – first recorded by an unsuccessful playwright, John Dennis, in 1702 – is likely to have originated with a request from Hunsdon himself, who may perhaps have backed it with some hint of the pleasure it would give to the Queen.[18]

According to Leslie Hotson,[19] the play was first performed at a Garter feast in the presence of the Queen on St George's Day, 23 April 1597. The installation of the new knights (there were four others in addition to Hunsdon) was to take place as customary in St George's Chapel, Windsor, a month later, which fits with Mistress Quickly's instructions to the fairies in Act 5 of the play, to

> Search Windsor Castle, elves, within and out.
> Strew good luck, ouphes, on every sacred room,
> That it may stand till the perpetual doom
> In state as wholesome as in state 'tis fit,
> Worthy the owner and the owner it.

> The several chairs of order look you scour
> With juice of balm and every precious flower.
> Each fair instalment, coat, and several crest,
> With loyal blazon, evermore be blest!
> And nightly, meadow-fairies, look you sing,
> Like to the Garter's compass, in a ring . . .   (V.v.56–66)

But it is impossible to believe that the play as printed in the Folio could have been written and rehearsed in a fortnight – let alone ten days, as Dennis was later to assert. And there are problems in this early date for the play. As Chambers pointed out, the inclusion of Nym among Falstaff's cronies, and his naming as 'Corporal', would have made little sense if he had not previously been seen on the battlefield in *Henry V*,[20] which we can date rather precisely to the early summer of 1599. Nor does the play as a whole suggest that it was written for a courtly rather than a popular audience.

The most likely explanation for these incompatibilities in the evidence is that put forward by G.R. Hibbard: that Shakespeare was indeed comissioned to provide an after-dinner entertainment for the Garter feast of 1597, but that it consisted in a masque of the kind that Elizabeth is known to have enjoyed, featuring the legendary Herne the Hunter, a Fairy Queen and satyrs, which he could have put together rather quickly, and this was later utilised by him with his usual economy to form the final act of the play he was to write for the Globe in 1599.[21]

However that was, the play as we have it now is unique in the canon in drawing on the bourgeois life of a small country town that must have been close to Shakespeare's own experience of Stratford. There are links with the court as represented by the nearby Castle, and the character of Fenton who is said to have kept company with the 'wild prince and Poins' of *Henry IV*; but the main focus of the play is on the wives of the title in their humbling of Falstaff. In their combination of all the wifely virtues with wit, resourcefulness and an unfailing *joie de vivre*, they are set from the start to win hands down in their contest with the fat knight. They are depicted with such affectionate realism as to suggest they were based on real women very close to Shakespeare. They are matched in truth of observation and credibility by their husbands: George Page, the solid, well-to-do townsman, whose prejudices are tempered by toleration and love of fair play; and Frank Ford, who is not so consumed by his jealousy as to learn from his mistakes and, in the end, to beg pardon for them. Page's daughter, Anne, demonstrates in her reply to the proposition that she should marry the ludicrous French physician Caius – 'I had rather be set quick i' th' earth/And bowled to death with turnips' – that she has inherited much of her mother's spirit and wit. The other inhabitants of this small world are comic eccentrics. Bardolph, Nym and Pistol come in the wake of Falstaff from *Henry V*. They bring their familiar humours with them, but are given little scope for further development. Justice Shallow and his nincompoop nephew Slender – whose courtship of Anne Page is one of the joys of the play – are visitors from the Gloucestershire of *Henry IV*. In the persons of Mistress Quickly (another importation from the Henriad) and Dr Caius, much typical Shakespeare humour is made of their mistreatment of the language. The facetious host of the Garter inn is a still-recognisable portrait of his occupational kind. The play is written largely in prose and bowls along at exemplary pace with hardly a dull moment and many incidental delights, such as Sir Hugh's Latin lesson for the Pages' small son William (IV.i), and Caius' servant Rugby, whose only fault in Quickly's estimation is that he is 'given to prayer; he is somewhat peevish that way' (I.iv.12–13).

Scholarly criticism has been largely taken up with matters of dating and Shakespeare's treatment of Falstaff, which some nineteenth-century critics considered to be a degradation of his original conception of the character in *Henry IV*. Recent editors have rightly pointed out that it is not so much Falstaff who has changed as the context in which he appears, and his function in the play.[22] I do think, however, that though much of his spirit and wit remain, Shakespeare was missing Kempe in the role.

Otherwise, the casting of the play, with its relatively modest number of characters (twenty-two named roles with three or four additional children) would have presented little difficulty. Kempe's immediate replacement is unknown. Burbage would have brought real passion to his playing of Ford, and thus have provided a necessary ballast to the play's more farcical situations and scenes. Sir Hugh Evans, the parson, would almost certainly have gone to Armin as the last in a series of Welsh parts that had begun with his Welsh Captain in *Richard II* (see note 21 above). From Simple's description of him as having 'but a little wee face, with a little yellow beard', there cannot be much doubt that Slender was Sincler's part, with Pope, Sly and Cowley as Pistol, Bardolph and Nym (as in *Henry V*), and Cowley in a possible double of Nym and Shallow. The two wives, Anne, Quickly, Fenton and the servants would all have gone to apprentices of various ages, and there appears to have been an infusion of very young boys to play Robin, William and any extra fairies that were required.[23]

Shakespeare's part in the play could only, I think, have been Page. Though small in terms of lines (some 150), he makes an appearance in half the twenty-two scenes, and the fact of the character's normality among so many eccentrics gives it a special position; he is a yardstick of good sense against which we can measure the others' follies and self-deceptions. He might easily have been dull or sententious but is not allowed to become so. The reader may find this over-fanciful, but just as I have suggested that Shakespeare drew on the important women in his life for the wives, I think he may have drawn on his father for Page. John Shakespeare would now have been in his sixties. It will be remembered that back in 1568 he had made an approach to the College of Arms for a grant of arms that would have entitled him to the status and name of gentleman, but that as troubles engulfed him it had been allowed to lapse. In 1596, when William had begun to enjoy the first fruits of his success, he had renewed the application on behalf of his father and himself, and been successful in obtaining it; in 1599 John had less than two more years to live. (The names were common enough, but is it only coincidence that the Pages' children are named as Anne and William?) The background of the play is so close to what we know of Shakespeare's early life in Stratford that I feel sure there was for him a personal, nostalgic interest in the writing of it that lends a warmth to the whole, and makes it something much more attractive and appealing than it would otherwise have been. His participation as Page would have been at one with that.

The play has been most often presented as a midsummer romp, but a careful reading of the text reveals that the action was originally conceived as taking place in winter. As reward for his watching, Mistress Quickly promises Rugby a companionable, bedtime 'posset' (a milk-drink curdled with wine or ale) 'at the latter end of a sea-coal fire' (I.iv.8); Page queries Sir Hugh's appearance at Frogmore for his duel with Caius, 'youthful still – in your doublet and hose this raw rheumatic day?' (III.i.44); and at the conclusion of the play, his wife proposes,

> Good husband, let us every one go home,
> And laugh this sport o'er by a country fire;
> Sir John and all.

In recent theatrical history, Glen Byam Shaw was the first to return to a midwinter interpretation in his definitive Stratford production of 1955, with Angela Baddeley and Joyce Redman as the wives and Christmas-card settings and costumes by Motley, in which the company sweated through a hot Stratford summer (see Plate 11). Though there have been good productions since, it gave both room to the warmth at the heart of the play and a crispness to the comedy that I doubt has been surpassed.

Hamlet belongs to 1600 and *Twelfth Night* to 1600/1, and these two plays were to bring the present period of Shakespeare's writing to a close.[24] In their different ways, they bring him near to the peak of his achievement as a dramatic poet, and provide him also with two of his finest and most challenging acting roles.

Hamlet is the second of his great tragedies, but in the degree to which it has entered the mainstream of European thought and literature, and its language and imagery become part of the mindset and expression of English speakers everywhere, it is of course unique. The influence it has had, and continues to have, makes it all the more difficult for us to see it, as we must try to do here, in its original context as a theatrical event – a play among others, written for a specific group of actors to perform in a particular theatre (the Globe) at a given moment of Shakespeare's and the Chamberlain's history.

It has been described as the most problematic of his plays. Many of the supposed problems as seen from the study are found to disappear when we put it back where it primarily belongs – on the stage; but there is one problem at least that need never arise: the identity of the role he wrote for himself. For here tradition, and consideration of those other factors I have proposed as affecting his choice of parts, point in the same direction; it was that of the Ghost, the ghost of Hamlet's father, the former king.

Nicholas Rowe tells us in 1709 that

> His Name is Printed, as the Custom was in those Times, amongst those of the other Players, before some old Plays, but without any particular Account of what sort of Parts he us'd to play; and tho' I have inquir'd, I could never meet with any further Account of him this way, than that the top of his Performance was the Ghost in his own *Hamlet*.[25]

The information, along with most of the other anecdotes Rowe retails of Shakespeare's life, had come to him through the great Restoration actor, Thomas Betterton (*c.* 1635–1710), as he himself acknowledged, and though many of these stories, apparently gathered in the course of a visit by the actor to Stratford early in the Restoration period, are found to be little better than gossip – dubious at best, some demonstrably false – the probability of this one being true is strengthened by the indications we have already uncovered of Shakespeare having played similar spectral roles in Kyd's *Spanish Tragedy* and, more recently, *Julius Caesar*. The opening scene on the battlements of Elsinore in *Hamlet* has been justly praised for its imaginative power in creating an atmosphere of impending doom and fear among the watchers, into which the Ghost enters with awe-inspiring effect. One has only to compare it with the equivalent scene in Kyd, featuring the Ghost of Andrea, to realise how much Shakespeare as poet would have learnt from his playing of that role, and that the secret of his greater success with the Ghost in *Hamlet* lies in its economy of means; for while Kyd's Ghost immediately embarks on a long, detailed account of his journey through the underworld, Shakespeare's is initially silent, and it is not until Scene 5 of Act 1, when he finds himself alone with his son, that he confides:

> But that I am forbid
> To tell the secrets of my prison-house,
> I could a tale unfold whose lightest word
> Would harrow up thy soul, freeze thy young blood,
> Make thy two eyes like stars start from their spheres,

Thy knotted and combined locks to part,
And each particular hair to stand an end
Like quills upon the fretful porpentine.
But this eternal blazon must not be
To ears of flesh and blood . . .   (I.v.13–22)

– which, in its reticence, is all the more chilling.

To watch these scenes in rehearsal (as I have had the privilege of doing on several occasions) is to realise something else about the Ghost, related to this economy of description, that Shakespeare the player would have understood very well; that much of the effectiveness of the performance depends on its economy of movement; the extent to which the actor can bring to it a preternatural stillness, an immobility of posture in repose in contrast to the progressively more fevered reactions of the watchers. As indicated in Shakespeare's text and stage directions, it goes 'slow and stately' by them; it 'spreads its arms', it lifts its head,

> and did address
> Itself to motion like as it would speak.
> But even then the morning cock crew loud,
> And at the sound it shrunk in haste away
> And vanished from our sight.   (I.ii. 216–20)

When it does find a voice, we are often treated to sonorous, actorly tones, but the voice should surely be similarly detached from life and human emotion, unpractised, hollow of tone. (The curious thing is that the more these scenes with the Ghost are subjected, in later stages of the rehearsal process, to technological resources of the modern stage in the way of ghostly lighting, dry ice and electronic sound effects, the more the excitement engendered by Shakespeare's words and imaginative acting tends to be lost, and what was initially – and may remain in essence – thrillingly real is reduced in performance to mere spectacle and incoherence.)

If Shakespeare played the Ghost, it is unlikely to have been his only part in the play. There are eighteen named roles to be filled, along with at least five unnamed Players, the Grave-digger and his mate, a Captain, a Lord, a Priest or Minister, English Ambassadors, sailors and messengers – some thirty speaking parts in all, of which at least ten would have been doubled. The Ghost, who disappears from the action after the Closet scene (III.iv), is one of them.

The clue to the identity of Shakespeare's second role is to be found in the basic dramatic and moral structure of the play, which, reduced to its simplest terms, is the story of a king murdered by his brother and avenged by his son. It is the closely entwined triangular situation, deriving from Shakespeare's sources (including the lost *Ur-Hamlet* that once had a place in the company's repertoire) that dictates the 'idea' of the play and also its casting. The moral disparity between the brother-kings is stressed from the start. 'So excellent a king', says Hamlet of his father in the first of his soliloquies, 'that was to this/Hyperion to a satyr'; but Claudius' real offence in Hamlet's eyes lies not in his difference from his father but in his likeness; in the inescapable fact that they are brothers; that the marriage of Claudius with Hamlet's mother (Gertrude) is not just over-hasty but *incestuous*, and the murder of his father, *fratricidal*. Failing the unlikely presence in the company of two brothers of the right approximate age, the simplest and most effective way in which this blood relationship between the two can be realised on stage is for the parts to be doubled and, if we look in detail at the text and sequence of scenes, we find that Shakespeare has gone to some trouble to make that possible. If, then, he played the Ghost, as generally accepted, it is highly likely that he played Claudius also. Too often, *Hamlet* has been seen as a 'one-man tragedy, one vast part meant for a great actor'.[26] We need perhaps to stand the play on its head to see it afresh; not as one vast part for a great actor, but three parts of varied length for *two* great actors – Burbage and Shakespeare.

That Hamlet was indeed Burbage's part is attested to by an anonymous elegy following the actor's death in 1619:

> Hee's gone & with him what a world are dead . . .
> No more young Hamlett, ould Heironymoe.
> Kind Leer, the greved Moore, and more beside,
> That lived in him, have now for ever dy'de.[27]

All the world's a stage. We never lose sight of that theme for very long in the plays, and *Hamlet* brings it back to our attention in the most insistent manner possible, for not only does Shakespeare introduce a play-within-the-play (as Kyd had done before him in the *Spanish Tragedy*) and uses it to test the truth of the Ghost's accusation against Claudius, but daringly brings in a troupe of travelling players to perform it under Hamlet's direction. But there is more to it than that, for as Anne Righter points out,

> *Hamlet* is a tragedy dominated by the idea of the play. In the course of its development the play metaphor appears in a number of forms. It describes the dissembler, the Player King, the difference between appearance and reality, falsehood and truth, and the theatrical nature of certain moments of time. The relationship of world and stage is reciprocal: the actor holds a mirror up to nature, but the latter in its turn reflects the features of the play.[28]

The speech of the First Player, whom Hamlet greets as his 'old friend' and invites to give a taste of his quality on the players' arrival, has been sadly misunderstood and misplayed as parody. But its significant theme – the slaughter of Priam by one of his sons – is Hamlet's choice, not the Player's. And though abused by literary critics as 'bombast', 'bad verse' and similar terms, Hamlet is clearly of a different opinion for the speech is one that he 'chiefly loved' – to the extent that he has committed it to memory, and is able to quote a dozen of its opening lines in giving the Player his cue, which he takes up thus:

> Anon he finds him,
> Striking too short at Greeks. His antique sword,
> Rebellious to his arm, lies where it falls,
> Repugnant to command. Unequal match'd,
> Pyrrhus at Priam drives, in rage strikes wide;
> But with the whiff and wind of his fell sword
> Th'unnerved father falls . . .   (II.ii.464–70)

If this is bombast, it is very good bombast – the kind of bombast that Shakespeare might have written if he had set himself to do it. If the speech is elevated in style it is because, as Harold Jenkins explains, it 'has to stand out from the drama which surrounds it and which is already removed from ordinary life; and this . . . demands a style which rises above normal theatrical elevation as the latter does above natural speech'.[29] But it is not the style or content of the speech, with which he is already familiar, but the commitment and depth of feeling that the Player brings to it that astounds Hamlet, and acts as a spur to his future actions.[30] To guy the speech in the manner of an old-fashioned 'ham' for cheap laughs, as has regrettably been done, is not just artistically inept, but loses the main point of the scene, which is to bring Hamlet to the point of resolution.

As Brutus enjoins the conspirators in *Caesar* –

> Let not our looks put on our purposes,
> But bear it as our Roman actors do,
> With untir'd spirits and formal constancy   (II.i.224–6)

– so Hamlet takes strength from the Player's commitment to his role. The mirror throws back a reverse image: the world reflects the stage.

> O what a rogue and peasant slave am I!
> Is it not monstrous that this player here,
> But in a fiction, in a dream of passion,
> Could force his soul so to his own conceit
> That from her working all his visage wann'd,
> Tears in his eyes, distraction in his aspect,
> A broken voice, and his whole function suiting
> With forms to his conceit? And all for nothing!
> For Hecuba!
> What's Hecuba to him, or he to her,
> That he should weep for her? . . .
> Yet I,
> A dull and muddy-mettled rascal, peak
> Like John-a-dreams, unpregnant of my cause,
> And can say nothing – no, not for a king,
> Upon whose property and most dear life
> A damn'd defeat was made . . .   (II.ii.544–54, 561–6)

In admitting the centrality of the play metaphor in *Hamlet*, we must beware however of confusing two quite different levels of

The Workes of William Shakespeare,

containing all his Comedies, Histories, and
Tragedies : Truely set forth, according to their first
ORIGINALL.

The Names of the Principall Actors
in all these Playes.

William Shakespeare.	*Samuel Gilburne.*
Richard Burbadge.	*Robert Armin.*
John Hemmings.	*William Ostler.*
Augustine Phillips.	*Nathan Field.*
William Kempt.	*John Underwood.*
Thomas Poope.	*Nicholas Tooley.*
George Bryan.	*William Ecclestone.*
Henry Condell.	*Joseph Taylor.*
William Slye.	*Robert Benfield.*
Richard Cowly.	*Robert Goughe.*
John Lowine.	*Richard Robinson.*
Samuell Crosse.	*Iohn Shancke.*
Alexander Cooke.	*Iohn Rice.*

1 Shakespeare's principal fellows from the First Folio of 1623 (Shakespeare Folger Library, Washington, D.C.)

2 The memorial bust in Holy Trinity Church (courtesy of Shakespeare Centre Library, Stratford-upon-Avon)

3 Stratford Guildhall, upper chamber, as it was about 1900. From the 1560s this had been used by the King's School which Shakespeare attended, and probably also by the companies of players who visited the town from 1569 onwards. The desks shown in the photograph are a later addition. In Shakespeare's time, the pupils would have sat on benches, and the same benches might also have been used by those attending the plays (Shakespeare Birthplace Trust, Stratford-upon-Avon)

4 Reconstructed view of London south of the Thames in about 1600, showing location of the Rose and the Globe (from a painting by C. Walter Hodges by permission of the artist and the Museum of London)

5 William Sly by an unknown artist (by permission of the Trustees of Dulwich Picture Gallery)

6 Richard Burbage. Burbage was a painter as well as an actor and this is said to be a self-portrait (by permission of the Trustees of Dulwich Picture Gallery)

7 Anonymous portrait of Edward Alleyn (by permission of the Trustees of Dulwich Picture Gallery)

8 The Tomb of John Gower in Southwark Cathedral (formerly, from 1539, the parish church of St Saviour) where Shakespeare's younger brother Edmund was buried in 1607. In the following year, Gower was to feature as presenter in *Pericles* (courtesy of the Dean and Chapter of Southwark Cathedral)

9 An 18-year-old Portia, Jill Showell, in Glen Byam Shaw's production of *The Merchant of Venice* for the Young Vic in 1950/51 (author's archive)

10 A seventeenth-century depiction of 'Wee Three Logerheads', probably featuring (left) Tom Derry, an innocent in the keeping of Anne of Denmark, and Muckle John, a fool at the court of Charles I, with marotte (courtesy of the Shakespeare Birthplace Trust, Stratford-upon-Avon)

11 'What, the sword and the word? Do you study them both, Master Parson?' (Shallow). *The Merry Wives of Windsor*, Act 3, Scene 1, Stratford-upon-Avon, 1955. L to R: the author as Rugby, Michael Denison (Caius), Edward Atienza (Shallow), Patrick Wymark (Host), William Devlin (Sir Hugh), Ralph Michael (Page), Geoffrey Sassé (Simple), Geoffrey Bayldon (Slender). (Photograph by Angus McBean, author's collection)

12 The Moot Hall in Maldon as it was *c.* 1890. It was built as a private house and acquired by the town in 1576. The classical-style portico is much later in date and replaced a gallery from which proclamations were read (photograph by courtesy of the Maldon Society)

13 John Lowin in 1640. He lived until 1659, and in 1604 would still have been in early manhood. He is said by a Restoration writer to have played Henry VIII, and to have been instructed in the part by 'Mr Shakespeare himself'. (Ashmolean Museum, Oxford)

14 'When thou dost ask me blessing, I'll kneel down/And ask of thee forgiveness' (*King Lear*, V.iii.10–11). Sally Knyvette as Cordelia and the author as Lear in a production by Giles Block at Ipswich Arts Theatre in 1974 (photograph by Paul Levitton)

15 'When shall we three meet again?' (*Macbeth*, I.i). The Weird Sisters in a production by the author at Ipswich Arts Theatre in 1978, as played by John Dallimore, Pat Wainwright and John Matshikiza.

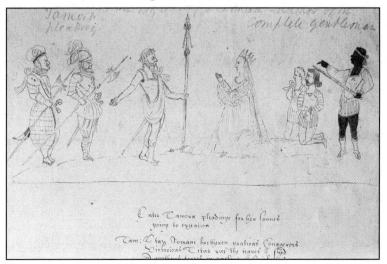

16 The Peacham drawing of 1595(?) (from the Portland Papers at Longleat by permission of the Marquess of Bath)

17 Nathan Field was the son of a clergyman. According to Cuthbert Burbage (Richard's brother), he came to the King's company from the Children of the Chapel in 1608/9. He later joined Lady Elizabeth's men but returned to the King's in 1615. Ben Jonson claimed him as 'his schollar'. He is seventeenth in the Folio list of Principal Actors after William Ostler (from an anonymous portrait in Dulwich Picture Gallery, by permission of the Trustees).

18 The Old Moot Hall in Cross Street, Sudbury, dates from the fourteenth century. This postcard view shows what it looked like before restoration in the 1940s (reproduced from Barry L. Wall, *Sudbury through the Ages*, Ipswich, n.d.)

The Globe

19 Detail from Claes Janzs Visscher's engraving of London in 1616 showing the Globe Theatre – presumably as rebuilt in 1614 (Folger Shakespeare Library, Washington, DC)

20 William Kempe with his taborer on a dancing journey to Norwich, from his *Nine Daies Wonder* of 1600 (Folger Shakespeare Library, Washington, DC)

21 Robert Armin as 'Blue John' from the title page of his play, *History of the two Maids of More-clacke*, as published in 1609 (British Library)

22 St Mary's Guildhall, Coventry, as it appeared after the restoration of 1824 (reproduced from Benjamin Poole's *Coventry: its history and antiquities*, 1870, by courtesy of Coventry City Archives)

23 The Gild or Moot Hall in Ipswich. In the fifteenth century, a Dutch carver had been paid to wainscot the interior of the upper floor, and a painter employed to decorate a cloth with the arms of the king, St George, and the Borough to cover the end wall behind a dais. It was demolished in 1812 (from a nineteenth-century print)

24 Possible portrait of Shakespeare in the role of Gower in *Pericles* from the title-page of Wilkins' 'Painfull Adventures of Pericles Prince of Tyre'. Note Gower's square-cut beard and medieval costume. He is carrying a bunch of fragrant herbs in his left hand. Does the lectern with an open book on it suggest that his speeches in the play were read?

reality which may, as Anne Righter has said, touch at certain points but should not be confused. For though the actors on stage who represent the Players are players themselves, they are nevertheless assuming roles in a play; and while the company of which they are members has points of similarity with the Chamberlain's men – such as the occasional need to travel and competition from 'little eyases' – it is *not* the Chamberlain's men, and the city from which it is said to have come could hardly have been London. There are indications that in the admittedly jocular terms in which Hamlet greets them –

> He that plays the king shall be welcome – his Majesty shall have tribute of me, the adventurous knight shall use his foil and target, the lover shall not sigh gratis, the humorous man shall end his part in peace, the clown shall make those laugh whose lungs are tickle a th' sear, and the lady shall say her mind freely – or the blank verse shall halt for't.   (II.ii.318–24)

– Shakespeare has in mind, not his own or any other contemporary troupe, but earlier interluders of the 'half-dozen men and a boy' tradition, in which it was accepted that each actor would specialise in a particular type of role (the King, the Knight, etc.) and rarely depart from it except in doubling.

Nor should we assume that in Hamlet's instructions to the Players, and his admonitions to them to avoid over-acting on the one hand and tameness on the other, Shakespeare was addressing his fellows of the Chamberlain's, as is commonly supposed, rather than making a generally applicable statement of principle;[31] or that the tone of patronising superiority adopted by Hamlet represents in the slightest degree one that Shakespeare in his own person would ever have used to his fellows. On the contrary, his intention throughout the scene is one of disassociation – of the 'double mirror' effect. For if, as Hamlet tells us, 'the purpose of playing . . . both at the first and now, was and is to hold as 'twere the mirror up to nature', it is by putting the Players *as players* on stage, so that they and their play become part of the picture the mirror reflects, that Shakespeare achieves the illusion of making the larger action appear more real than it would otherwise have done. The more he can strip away illusion from the play-within-the-play and from those who perform it, the more readily the audience will accept the play as a whole and those who carry it forward as a true reflection of reality. Here is magic of a high order, in which the players themselves are complicit. Illusion within illusion.

> The play's the thing
> Wherein I'll catch the conscience of the King.

— ★ —

The play that was to bring this extraordinary series of variations on the theme of reality and illusion to a joyful conclusion is one that has continued to delight audiences ever since, and has established itself (with *Much Ado* and *As You Like It*) as one of Shakespeare's three most popular comedies: *Twelfth Night, or What You Will*.

It has to be said that for the most part the scholars have made heavy weather of it, beginning in the eighteenth century with Dr Johnson. Though he found the play 'in the graver part elegant and easy, and in some of the lighter scenes exquisitely humorous', he considered the 'natural fatuity' of Sir Andrew (though 'drawn with great propriety') as 'not the proper prey of a satirist', and the 'marriage of Olivia and the succeeding perplexity, though well enough contrived to divert on the stage' as wanting credibility and failing to 'produce the proper instruction required in the drama, as it exhibits no just picture of life'.[32] Academics and scholarly editors generally continue to look for 'instruction' in the plays, and are disabled in their appreciation of comedy by a predisposition to interpret it as satire. *Twelfth Night* is comedy in its purest form, with an underlay of wistful romance, that requires no other justification for its existence than the pleasure it gives.

The circumstances in which Shakespeare came to write it and the occasion of its first performance point us in the right direction. Late in December 1600, it was announced by the Lord Chamberlain, Hunsdon (also the company's patron), that a visit was shortly to be made to the now-ageing Queen by a young and admired Italian nobleman, Don Virginio Orsino, duke of Bracciano, and the search was on for a play to entertain him that 'shalbe best furnished with rich apparell, have great variety and change of Musicke and daunces, and of a Subject that may be most pleasing to her Majestie'. The date proposed for the performance was 6 January 1601, the feast of Epiphany, the last of the twelve days of Christmas, a period when the court gave itself over to hectic enjoyment, and a Lord of Misrule was appointed to oversee the festivities, along with the Master of Revels. Clearly at such short notice (less than two weeks), there was no opportunity for Shakespeare or anyone else to write and rehearse a new play especially for the occasion; it was a question of choosing from what the principal companies already had on offer or could bring up to scratch in the time available. Was it merely coincidence that Shakespeare's new comedy (probably with the original title of *What You Will*) was already in rehearsal? It is difficult to think of any other contemporary comedy that might have been thought a more appropriate choice. Doubtless after a discreet enquiry as to whether the gesture would be acceptable to the Queen and her guest, the Duke of the play was named Orsino in the visitor's honour and, with the addition of one or two dances, which it otherwise lacks, the play was duly performed at Whitehall on the day appointed. It has been known ever since as *Twelfth Night*.[33]

As befits its festive occasion, the play is filled with music and song. It begins with music, and the now familiar, hauntingly beautiful lines –

> If music be the food of love, play on,
> Give me excess of it, that, surfeiting,
> The appetite may sicken, and so die.
> That strain again, it had a dying fall:
> O, it came o'er my ear like the sweet sound
> That breathes upon a bank of violets,
> Stealing and giving odour.

That Shakespeare spoke them in the character of Orsino admits of little doubt; the part would have been for him a return to the kingly dukes of his earlier comedies and, at thirty-six, he was at the optimum age to play it. Orsino is seriously in love with a young and beautiful neighbour, Olivia, who, in her mourning for a beloved brother, is unresponsive. Complications arise with the appearance of Viola, whom we first meet as survivor of a shipwreck in which she too has lost a beloved brother (or so she believes). Having made her way to Orsino's court disguised as a boy (Cesario), she is promptly recruited by Orsino as intermediary in his courtship of Olivia. It is the tangles of love between these three – Orsino for Olivia, Viola for Orsino, Olivia for Cesario – that take up most of the action. But a secondary plot, in which Olivia's bucolic and troublesome kinsman Sir Toby Belch and her gentlewoman Maria take the lead in a conspiracy to humble the pompous household steward, Malvolio, is important also in providing the play's broader, more uninhibited humour. Sir Toby is the self-appointed Lord of Misrule in Olivia's household in direct opposition to its puritanical steward, and Feste the clown is his jester. Along with Sir Andrew Aguecheek, a simple-minded knight whom Sir Toby is gulling for his money, these three constitute (as Feste points out) a personification of the then popular image of 'We three' – comprising two fools and an ass, or (as illustrated in Plate 10) a marotte.

The later arrival on the scene of Viola's supposedly drowned brother, Sebastian, who in appearance is identical to her in her disguise as Cesario and of Sebastian's friend Antonio, and the further confusions of identity that follow on their various meetings with each other, are wonderfully managed to bring the comedy of the play to an uproarious climax. Malvolio, who has been tricked into a belief that Olivia is in love with *him*, exits promising revenge on 'the whole pack of you'.

Orsino is a typical Shakespeare role. He opens the play, initiates the basic plot situation as between himself, Olivia and Viola, and contrives an early exit in Act 2 to return only for the play's resolution, and to speak the final lines. Malvolio, in his combining of self-love and gullibility, is a unique invention. He dominates the comedy – and to some extent the play. The part is not one for a clown or recognised comedian, whom we expect to be funny, but for a leading actor of 'straight' or tragic roles; it would surely have gone to Burbage. Sir Toby is again a fresh creation, and more than a surrogate Falstaff. Though buffoon in the sense of dependant, he lacks both Falstaff's massive bulk and his wit, but compensates with his sense of fun and unfailing belief in his own dignity. Though an inveterate toper, there is no compelling reason for him to be fat at all, and he has been played

with success as a trim, soldierly figure; it was a part for Pope or
for Cowley. He and Sir Andrew make a splendid double-act. Sir
Andrew, thin of face, a bloodless 'clodpole' with hair that hangs
'like flax on a distaff', is a close relation of Slender in the *Merry
Wives*; the latest in that long series of thin-man parts that we have
traced from as far back as the *Shrew* and *Henry VI* in having been
played by John Sincler.[34] If there had been any doubt that Armin
was of the company to play Touchstone in *As You Like It*, there
can be none at all about his participation here as Feste, for the
peculiar style of his wit is reproduced in full measure, and the
character bears the same marks of independence and freedom of
spirit as Touchstone. Both are professional jesters, dependent on
no one but themselves, without emotional ties. Nor are they
confined to any one place for, as Feste explains, 'Foolery, sir,
does walk about the orb like the sun, it shines everywhere'
(III.i.39–40). Here, too, in his impersonation of Sir Topas, is
more evidence of Armin's versatility, and of his skill as a singer
which, though strangely missing from *As You Like It*, he had
previously demonstrated as Tutch in the *Two Maids of More-
clacke*. I forbear even to guess at the names of the boys who
played Olivia, Viola and Maria; but they would doubtless have
been drawn from that same exceptionally gifted group who had
previously been cast (and were still performing) as Kate in *Henry
V*, Portia in *Caesar*, Rosalind and Celia in *As You Like It*, Ophelia
in *Hamlet*, and as the 'merry wives'. Shakespeare would have
spent much of his rehearsal time with them. For all its boisterous
Twelfth-night humour, there is, as I have said, an underlay of
wistful romance in the play, of which Orsino in his opening lines
sets the tone, and we hear it again from Viola, which must stand
with Rosalind, Helena and Imogen as one of the most beautiful
parts he wrote for his boys. Even Sir Andrew is given his moment
of nostalgic sadness: 'I was adored once too'.

We have seen that *Twelfth Night* was written for performance in
the winter, and there is at least a possibility that, like the *Merry
Wives*, its action was conceived as taking place in that season, and
specifically at Christmas. The indications of this are ambiguous;
the song of 'the wind and the rain', with which Feste brings the
play to an end, is perhaps more suggestive of an English summer
than an Illyrian winter, and the orchard location of the central
'letter scene' may likewise point in another direction.

Nevertheless, the midnight carousal of Act 2, Scene 3, with its burning of sack, singing of catches and 'On the twelfth day of December' (a version or concealed reference to the well-known carol, 'The Twelve Days of Christmas') give the impression of a traditional Christmas festivity. If played in that way and (where possible) in that season, the play gains an added dimension of enjoyment and a consistency entirely at one with its title.[35]

TEN

Travelling Man

> By far the most popular place for performances outside London was the Townhall, and a surprising amount of detailed evidence survives concerning the conditions in which performances were given in this favourite building.
>
> *Glynne Wickham*[1]

For a variety of reasons largely outside its control, the period 1601 to 1604 was a difficult one for the company. It was to see a first significant slackening in Shakespeare's production of new plays, and a return by him and his fellows to an earlier pattern of performance in which appearances at court (wherever the court happened to be at the time) alternated with extensive provincial tours; one in which their seasons at the Globe were frequently disrupted – often for months at a time – by political events and, most of all, by the plague.

The first such interruption to their playing in London was occasioned by the abortive Essex rebellion of 1601, which followed closely on the company's performance of *Twelfth Night* at court on 6 January. Having failed miserably in Ireland, and incurred Elizabeth's grave displeasure by his early, unauthorised return in the previous September, the arrogant and headstrong earl now planned to recover the situation by taking forcible possession of the person of the Queen, and occupying Whitehall. As cover and justification for this desperate adventure, he hoped to provoke the London mob into riot, and to that end the Chamberlain's men were commissioned to give a special performance of the 'deposing and killing of Richard II' (presumably Shakespeare's play) at the Globe on the eve of the intended rising. In ignorance of what was afoot, but somewhat naively perhaps, the company agreed to this proposal on the promise of a larger than normal fee, as the play was not in their current repertoire and would have needed fresh rehearsal. But when, on the day following the performance (8 February), the earl and his supporters took to the streets with the cry, 'For the Queen! For the Queen! The crown of England is sold to the Spaniard. A plot is laid for my life', the Londoners were more bewildered than alarmed and failed to respond. Whereupon, the earl and his men returned lamely to Essex House, where they were quickly surrounded by the Queen's guards and arrested. The players were left with some explaining to do, which Augustine Phillips as their spokesman did so effectively, when called before a commission of enquiry ten days later, that they escaped without apparent penalty, and we find them performing again at court within a few days. It is hardly to be supposed, however, that their public performances at the Globe were allowed to continue uninterrupted – at least until after the earl's execution on the twenty-fourth of the month. Having completed their season at court, the sharers may well have decided to travel for a while. There is a record of rewards to three unnamed companies at Oxford (the town, not the university) in 1600/1, and the Chamberlain's may have been one of them – perhaps with *Hamlet*.[2]

Though she reacted to it with her customary courage, and had to be discouraged at the age of sixty-eight from going out into the street to see whether any rebel dared fire a shot at her, the whole episode was a shock to the Queen, and the relevance of Richard's deposition to her own situation, if lost on the Londoners, was not lost upon her. When, in August of the same year, William Lambarde, her Keeper of the Records, presented her with an account of the historical documents in his care and she happened on some pages relating to Richard's reign, she remarked to him, 'I am Richard II, know you not that?'; and when Lambarde in reply spoke of Essex and his 'wicked imagination', she went on to say, 'He that will forget God, will also forget his benefactors; this tragedy was played forty times in open streets and houses'.[3] A reminder of the thin ice on which Shakespeare was often walking in his history plays.

If the company's unwitting involvement in the Essex affair left any shadow of doubt over the players' loyalty in Elizabeth's mind, it was soon dispelled. For by the end of the year there are records of the company's court appearances on Boxing Day and 27 December; a performance attended by the Queen, with her *candidae auditrices* (maids of honour, dressed always in white), at Lord Hunsdon's house in Blackfriars on the 29th and others at Whitehall on New Year's Day and 14 February 1602. Unfortunately, no mention was made of the plays presented, but they would probably have included a repeat performance of *Twelfth Night* as this was also given at the Middle Temple for its fellows' annual feast on 2 February, as noted by John Manningham in his *Diary*.[4]

The year that followed (1602) was to be the last full year of Elizabeth's reign – a time of increasing anxiety in the life of the nation. Though sound in health and with a mind as clear as ever, the Queen was now showing the inevitable signs of advancing age in an uncertain temper and sense of loneliness as so many of her loyal servants were passing, or had passed away, most affectingly Burghley in 1598. She was now given to pacing her privy chamber with a rusty old sword in her hand, which occasionally she would 'thrust into the arras in great rage'. An era was felt by all to be coming to an end.

Only two plays by Shakespeare can be assigned to this and the following year (1602/3) – *Troilus and Cressida* and *All's Well that Ends Well*[5] – and, for reasons that will appear later, it is doubtful whether either would have been deemed appropriate for performance at the Globe or at court until very much later – if at all.

The company were performing as usual at Whitehall on Boxing Day 1602. On 14 January 1603 the Queen and her court made a final journey in pouring rain to Richmond, which she spoke of as the 'warm box' to which she could 'best trust her sickly old age', and it was there the company travelled on 2 February to give what would be their last performance for her – if she was well enough to see it. She was suffering from a bad cold and was severely depressed. As the weeks passed she became no better. Refusing medicine, she lay for four days on cushions in her privy chamber until, too weak to protest, she was finally carried to her bed, where she died in the early hours of 24 March.

The playhouses were closed in respect and were to remain dark until after her funeral at the end of April. Within a week, James VI of Scotland was on his way south to enter on his inheritance as James I of Great Britain but, as he paused at the border town of Berwick on 8 April, the shadow of an old enemy was starting to fall across London with news of a recurrence of bubonic plague in the borough of Stepney, down by the docks. On 5 May, Henslowe at the Rose noted in his diary that 'we leafte of playe now at the Kynges cominge', and when, on the 19th of the month, the new king graciously took the former Lord Chamberlain's servants into his own service, the letters patent effecting their change of status contained an ominous qualification: that those named were 'freely to use and exercise the Arte and faculty of playinge . . . *when the infection of the plague shall decrease . . .*'.[6] Almost a year was to go by before any such decrease occurred. In the meantime, the infection intensified and spread; from 18 deaths in the City in the week prior to 12 May, to a weekly total of 158 in June, 917 in July, rising to an appalling peak of 3,035 (including outlying parishes) in the final week of August.[7] Not only was the plague to close the London playhouses and cast a blight on the life of the City throughout 1603, as it had done ten years earlier in 1593, but it was to throw a lengthening shadow forwards over much of the country during the remainder of Shakespeare's life and career. As we have seen, the company had never altogether ceased to travel during part of each year, and the royal patent of 1603 was to give them a renewed licence and authority for continuing to do so. For not only did it authorise them to exercise their art for the king's 'Solace and pleasure when wee shall thincke good to see them', but 'aswell within theire nowe usual howse called the Globe within our County of Surrey, *as alsoe within anie towne halls or Moute halls or other conveniente places within the liberties and freedome of anie other Cittie, universitie, towne, or Boroughe whatsoever within our said Realmes and domynions*'.[8] While continuing to make regular use of the Globe whenever plague restrictions allowed, they were to take full advantage of this larger freedom in the years ahead.

Before we move on to consider a further chapter in the history of the company, it is time to focus more especially on that portion of Shakespeare's professional life that lay outside the capital. For, contrary to the impression that is usually given by his biographers and editors, the fact is that a substantial part of his career as player and poet from 1580 (as previously proposed) or, more traditionally, from the middle or late 1580s – at a conservative estimate between ten and sixteen years in total – was spent 'on the road'.

He was, to begin with, a Warwickshire man; it was in Stratford that he maintained a permanent home and, until his purchase of an apartment in the Blackfriars Gatehouse in 1613 (within three years of his death), was never more than a lodger in London; nor, in contrast to most of his fellow dramatists in the period, did he ever write a 'London play'. Throughout most of his active years as a player, the guildhalls of such provincial centres as Coventry, Gloucester, Ipswich and Dover would have been almost as familiar to him as the Rose, the Curtain or the Globe itself. If we want to arrive at a balanced view of the theatre scene in which he spent his career, we need to give more careful attention to those alternative indoor venues than is generally afforded by traditional accounts.[9] Nor should we underestimate the importance of Shakespeare's position in relation to his patrons. Though we speak loosely of the Chamberlain's/King's men as 'London companies', the actual status of the players was invariably recorded in official documents as that of 'Servants to the Lord Chamberlain' or 'Servants to the King'. When the monarch moved away from London as Elizabeth and James frequently did – either to one of the outlying palaces or further afield – and the players were summoned to perform at court, they were expected to follow them there as a matter of course. Their position as members of the royal household defined their identity.[10]

From 1599, Shakespeare's company was of course unique in that it possessed a venue in the capital to which it alone had access, and which, from that time forward, naturally served as a base for its subsequent travels; but this does not imply that the company was ever resident there for more than a few months at a time, or – irrespective of the exigencies brought about by the plague and other exceptional circumstances prevailing in London – that it ever ceased to be what it had been from its beginnings: a company of travelling players.

Because no records of the company's performances at the Globe, such as those that Henslowe made in his diary for the Admiral's men at the Rose, have survived, and only a very partial record of their performances elsewhere, it is difficult, perhaps impossible, to establish a seasonal pattern. It has been claimed that, apart from those years in which recurrences of the plague prevented it, the players acted in London between mid-September and late June, and toured in the summer months of July and August when the state of the roads was more favourable to travel.[11] Against this is the fact that – until the opening of the Blackfriars indoor playhouse (which became available to them only in 1609) – their public performances in the capital were limited to the Globe, where audiences were in part exposed to the vagaries of the weather, and which in the depths of the English winter must often have been freezingly cold, impossible to heat, and difficult of access across the Thames. Would it not have been odd, to say the least, if the players had chosen to abandon their own purpose-built theatre at that very time of the year – the summer months of July and August – when it was likely to provide the most favourable conditions for enjoyment of the plays by a majority of London playgoers, and when, therefore, such performances were likely to have been most profitable to them?[12] If there was ever a normal pattern, which has yet to be established, it is likely to have been more complex than that suggested by the Oxford editors, and (allowing for variations from year to year) probably comprised Christmas at court, a Lenten break, Easter and high summer seasons at the Globe, with provincial tours in both early summer and autumn.[13]

A recent, detailed study of the plague years in relation to Shakespeare's output of plays in the period has shown that during the eight years between 1603 and 1611 the London playhouses, including the Globe, are likely to have been closed to the players for at least 68 months in total – that is, for two-thirds of the time.[14] Whatever the pattern of London residence and touring in the years prior to 1603, and from 1611, may have been, it would clearly have been disrupted throughout the whole of that period of recurrent plague, and to have resulted in more touring than was normal. It is significant, however, that between Easter 1611 and June 1613 – during which time the Blackfriars indoor theatre was available in addition to the Globe, and the plague was no longer a problem – the company continued to tour; in 1611 they were at Shrewsbury; in 1612 at New Romney (on 21 April) and Winchester; and in 1612/13 at Folkestone, Oxford, Stafford and Shrewsbury.[15]

Contrary, then, to the common assumption that from 1599 the Chamberlain's/King's men travelled out from their base in London into the provinces only when obliged to do so by the plague, the evidence suggests that such touring was always conceived – both by the players themselves and those who policed them – as a normal component in the annual round of their activities. And the more one studies in detail the varying pattern of the company's movements in each succeeding year, the more impressed one becomes by the evident flexibility and resourcefulness of the players in keeping their enterprise afloat in the face of so many difficulties. To maintain an ongoing establishment of some twenty men and boys, to meet the essential expenses of play production, weekly wages for the hired men, accommodation on tour, and still apparently make a profit for its sharers throughout so long a period (as their continuing prosperity attests) was an extraordinary achievement in itself. Bearing in mind Shakespeare's involvement as player and sharer in every aspect of the company's activity – travelling long distances on horseback or perched on a wagon over ill-made roads in all seasons – it is hardly surprising to find that his production of plays slackens. Prior to 1604, he had written twenty-six plays, including *Measure for Measure*; in the final twelve years of his life, he was to produce only eleven more if we include *Pericles* and *Henry VIII*, which may not all have been his. Do we need to seek any other explanation?

The belief that the Chamberlain's/King's men travelled only by force of necessity imposed by the plague is not the only unwarranted assumption to have distorted our understanding of the company's touring, and the estimate we make of its artistic and financial importance. Though in the absence of performance records from the Globe, we are ready enough to assume that, when not recorded as performing elsewhere, they were in occupation of their London base, the notices of their provincial visits are read as one-off events – as their only stopping places on each particular tour. Similarly, the rewards they received from local Chamberlains, as recorded in their accounts, are interpreted as the sum total of their receipts in each town. Given the economic realities of touring (then as now), which require that to reduce the heavy expenses of travel and accommodation, the legs between stops be kept as short as possible, and that whatever demand that exists in towns along the way is exploited to the full, such a narrow interpretation of the sparse records to have survived appears very unlikely. (Would the players really have travelled so far for so little?) If we look more closely at the records for 1603 in relation to the mass of evidence of other provincial touring in the period, we shall find that all such assumptions are equally open to question.

Apart from the possibility of a few days' playing at the Globe and elsewhere between the Queen's funeral on 28 April and the suspension of 5 May in anticipation of James's arrival in the capital, the London playhouses were to remain closed throughout the whole of 1603, and until May 1604.

With the exception of Kent, to which the plague had already spread, much of the rest of the country was still open to the players, but the further they travelled from the capital the more likely they were to find a welcome. Unfortunately, the Chamberlains' records of the companies' visits to their towns are, for the most part, not precisely dated, but merely group them together (sometimes in chronological order, sometimes not) as occurring within their annual accounting period which normally, but not invariably, ran from Michaelmas (29 September) to Michaelmas, or its octave (6 October). All we can say for certain, therefore, of the 1603 tour on the basis of those records that survive is that in the period between 19 May, when they were appointed 'Servants to the King', and the first few weeks of the new fiscal year in early October, the company was at various times at Bath, Shrewsbury, Coventry, Ipswich, Maldon and Oxford.[16] It takes no great knowledge of geography to realise that these places are widely spread over much of southern and middle England, but a glance at a map is enough to suggest a probable route. Starting from the nearest point to London, the little port of Maldon on the Blackwater estuary in Essex (where exceptionally the fiscal year began on 6 January, and their visit is thus recorded in 1603/4, rather than 1602/3 as elsewhere), they are likely to have travelled north to Ipswich, then in a rotary movement north-west through Coventry to Shrewsbury, from Shrewsbury southwards to Bath, and from Bath to Oxford, where they arrived early in the new fiscal year, beginning there at Michaelmas. We have thus both a probable starting point and terminus for the players' tour in this year. But were these the *only* towns with a suitable venue in which they could perform in the course of such a long and circuitous journey? Of course they were not.

The counties of Essex and Suffolk were curiously detached from London in the Elizabethan and Jacobean periods, and the roads through Chelmsford and Colchester to Maldon and Ipswich notoriously bad.[17] The first leg of their journey, therefore, is more likely to have been accomplished by sea on one of the small coastal vessels that plied between the east coast ports and London, bringing supplies of food to the capital and returning with whatever cargo they could find. On its return journey, there would have been room enough in one of these boats for the twenty or so players with costumes and props for the three or four plays they would have taken with them. (At Plymouth in 1618/19, Lady Elizabeth's men were to number twenty; the King's in 1603 could hardly have managed with less.)[18]

Their first performance in Maldon would have been at the Moot Hall, acquired in 1576, which survives in part (Plate 12).[19] This first performance was known as the 'mayor's play', and was attended, not only by the mayor in person, but also by his councillors, the town's principal officers and justices. It was rewarded by the Maldon Chamberlains with 15*s*. That the players should submit themselves to the mayors of the towns they visited for their approval in this way was not just a matter of custom but a legally binding obligation, imposed on them by a royal proclamation of Elizabeth's in 1559.[20] The Chamberlains' reward was a tangible sign of that approval, and normally carried with it a licence to give further public performances in the town. But the official reward for this 'mayor's play' was not the only income the players might expect to receive from it. In some towns, admittance to the mayor's play for ordinary members of the public who were able to find a place when the mayor and his men had taken their seats was free (as at Gloucester)[21] but in many others an additional charge was made by the players in the form of a 'gathering', the proceeds of which often exceeded the amount of the reward. At Bath (which the company was to visit later this year), the Queen's men in 1586/7 had received a civic reward of 19*s* 4*d* and also, to 'make it up', 26*s* 8*d* 'that was gathered at the benche', making a total return of £2 6*s*.[22] At

Leicester, the phrase 'more than was gathered' occurs regularly against a whole series of rewards from the 1550s onward. That these extra gatherings are rarely mentioned, however, should not surprise us, as whatever was gathered directly from the public in that way would have gone straight to the players, and was thus of little interest to the Chamberlains, who were only accountable for payments from the town chest. Similarly, receipts from gatherings at the subsequent public performances that, in all but the smallest towns, followed the mayor's play – more often than not in the same venue – are ignored in the official accounts, and for the same reason. If they are mentioned at all it is only by way of restriction. At Gloucester, for example, by a civic ordinance of 1580, the total number of performances permitted to a company was ruled to depend on the status of its patron: the Queen's players were allowed three performances in three days; those of a baron or noble of greater rank, two plays in two days; and players whose patron was of lesser rank, only one.[23] At Norwich from the 1580s, licences are variously given for two, three or four days – and, more rarely, for as long as a week or eight days.[24] In these respects, the recorded rewards for players on tour are generally deceptive, for when gatherings at the mayor's play and subsequent performances are taken into account, the sum of what the players received in the course of each visit to a town is likely to have been two or more times as much as the stated reward – depending on the number of performances given – and thus far less 'paltry' than is often suggested.[25]

The small size of Maldon may only have justified one or two public shows, after which the company travelled on – probably again by sea – to Ipswich. Here, Shakespeare (along with most of his fellows) would have been on familiar ground, for if my account of his apprentice years is accepted, he had visited it with various companies on at least seven prior occasions.[26] They would have played, as previously, in the ancient Moot Hall on the Cornhill, and if the building shown in Plate 23 looks small to have housed a production of *Hamlet*, or even of *All's Well* (which by now may also have been in the company's repertoire), together with the large audience that either play would have attracted, we should remember that before the fairly recent introduction of fire regulations, theatre managers generally were able to pack a surprising number of people, sitting on benches or standing, into the most confined of spaces, and that the mayor's play would have been followed by as many others as the demand for places warranted. And having arranged the seating to their liking and set up their props in the largest chamber the hall had to offer – in Ipswich, presumably the Council Chamber on the upper floor – they would have been reluctant to uproot themselves and move elsewhere.[27] The town's reward for the mayor's play was the sizeable sum of 26s 8d, and this is likely to have been matched several times over by gatherings at this and subsequent performances which here might easily have extended to a week.[28]

There were a number of other Suffolk boroughs, as well as manor houses, to the east and north of Ipswich likely to have welcomed a visit from the newly appointed King's men when their Ipswich run had come to an end, but whose records for the period have not survived.[29] The players, it is true, would have been in no hurry to return to plague-stricken London, but they had a long journey before them, and on this occasion may have decided to stay with a predetermined route that was to take them in a north-westerly direction to their next recorded venue in Coventry. From this point on, they would, of course, have required horses and a covered wagon to transport them with their precious costumes and other belongings across country. Unless they had been able to ship horses and a wagon from London, they would have purchased these in Ipswich. (When, in March 1615, Lady Elizabeth's players, comprising seven sharers and seven boys, arrived in Coventry, they had five horses between them.[30] The King's men would have needed more. Wagons are mentioned in other accounts.[31])

Setting out from Ipswich, then, a likely route to Coventry would have taken them through Hadleigh, Sudbury, Boxford, Haverhill and Cambridge; but until Cambridge, only Hadleigh and Sudbury preserve records, as well as buildings from the period in which they might have performed. At Hadleigh, they would have played in the fifteenth-century Guildhall which stands to this day in a remarkable state of preservation, and perhaps even more remarkably, retains many of its original functions as both centre of local administration and communal meeting place.

The Guildhall is actually a complex of small to medium-sized buildings of varying date, joined together. When I visited it (as it happens on a Sunday), its offices were closed but a wedding anniversary celebration was in full swing in the original hall on the ground floor. What I take to have been used as a communal hall in the early seventeenth century is a handsome upper chamber, some 80 feet in length by 22½ feet wide, with an open king-post roof, which, allowing for an unraised acting area of about 20 by 15 feet, might have accommodated an audience of some 250 people sitting on benches, with standing room at the back. Timber beams in the side walls still show scorch marks made by the candles that had once been affixed to them. Though no mention is made in the town's surviving records of payments to visiting players, an agreement made with a shoemaker called John Allen on his appointment as 'overseer of the poor' in January 1599 indicates that the hall was then being used for performances by them, albeit on certain conditions, for Allen is instructed

> that he shall not suffer any playes to be made within the guildhall without consent of syx of the Cheife Inhabitants of the towne under ther handwriting/and further that all such playes as shall be made there may be ended in the daye time and also that if any hurte or dammage be made by the saide playes or weddings kept there, that then the saide John Allen shall repaire & make the saide houses in as good sorte as they are nowe at his owne costs and charges.[32]

– the fulfilment of which conditions should not have proved too difficult for the King's own servants, with their leading poet. There was no mayor's reward because at this date in its history the town had no mayor, so Shakespeare and his fellows would have been dependent on whatever was 'gathered at the benche'.

That companies of players visited Sudbury and were rewarded by its mayor is attested by the town's records. Lord Oxford's men were there on 17 April 1585, Leicester's on 2 June of the same year, and Strange's in 1592, receiving rewards of 5*s*, 6*s* 8*d*, and 3*s* 4*d* respectively. The King's men are known to have performed in the town six years later (in 1609/10) when, oddly enough, they were given only 5*s* as against Leicester's reward of 6*s* 8*d* twenty-four years earlier, but unfortunately the relevant accounts for the years 1593 to 1606 are missing.[33] In 1603, they would have played either in the Old Moot Hall in Cross Street of fourteenth-century origin (Plate 18) – or its sixteenth-century replacement on Market Hill, which has since been demolished. For while most of the hall's official functions were transferred from Cross Street to Market Hill when the new hall was built in the reign of Queen Mary, the original building continued to be used by the town for feasts and plays well into the seventeenth century, as attested by a mural depicting the arms of James I over a chimney breast in the lower chamber of the fifteenth-century building shown on the left of the illustration.[34]

In theory at least, the absolute terms of the company's royal patent, so recently received – to exercise their art 'within the liberties and freedome of anie other Cittie, universitie, towne, or Boroughe whatsoever' – should have overridden long-standing Cambridge University statutes barring professional players from performing within five miles of the town centre, which had resulted in even the Queen's men having been turned away on more than one occasion; but, if it did, the surviving Town Treasurers' books have nothing to say of any reward. So in spite of the claim made by the pirated quarto of *Hamlet* (Q1), dated 1603, that the play had been acted by 'his Highnesse servants . . . in the two Universities of Cambridge and Oxford', a question mark remains over Cambridge. If the company did succeed in playing there at this time, it would not have been in any of the colleges but in the town's Guildhall. For while the undergraduates were encouraged to act in both Latin and English plays in their college halls (with consequent large expenditure on the replacement of window glass), the university authorities were steadfast in their opposition to any exposure of the students to the corrupting influence of professional players, Shakespeare not excepted. When, in 1605/6, Worcester's men were given permission by the Mayor to perform in the Guildhall, entrusted with the key, and order given to 'buyld theire Stage & take downe the glass windowes there' (a sensible precaution), he was overruled by the Vice Chancellor, and the players sent on their way under threat of a hefty fine.[35] Nevertheless, we know that the Chamberlain's men had performed there in 1594/5, receiving 40s, and that one or two other companies had also managed to do so at various times, so we cannot altogether exclude the possibility of an unrecorded visit by the King's. As the Guildhall measured only 22 by 17½ feet, however, and would hardly have afforded room for more than the Mayor and his guests, the mayor's play would have been followed by other performances – perhaps at Chesterton or elsewhere in the town.[36] When, in 1580, the great Lord Burghley, the university's Chancellor, wrote to John Hatcher, the Vice-Chancellor, to put in a good word for Lord Oxford's players (and was politely refused), he mentioned that they intended a stay of four or five days.[37] Perhaps the King's men escaped opposition and notice by arriving in the long vacation?

Moving on through Northamptonshire (doubtless stopping more than once on the way) the company arrived in Coventry in what by now would have been late summer. And here we find our next firm record: a Chamberlain's reward of 40*s* – the most generous they were to receive anywhere on this particular tour, but which undoubtedly would again have been greatly increased by gatherings. Though not specifically mentioned, there can be little doubt of the venue – the magnificent St Mary's Guildhall[38] – which, despite subsequent 'restorations' and the terrible blitz suffered by the city in the Second World War, has retained much of its original glory to the present.

The Victorian print reproduced in Plate 22 may act as a salutary corrective to those who write in a derogatory way of the company's out-of-town performance venues as necessarily 'makeshift'. This is not to deny that in the smaller guildhalls the players would have been hard-pressed to make the best of the limited space at their disposal, but here, as in other cities, they encountered conditions which, in terms of spaciousness, comfort and splendour, rivalled any of the London playhouses including the Globe; to which, indeed (if conjectural reconstructions of their stages are to be trusted), the Coventry hall bears some resemblance – as in the disposition of doors at the upper end, and the gallery above. With this advantage: that in Coventry neither actors nor audience would have been at the mercy of the elements.

Dating from the late fourteenth and early fifteenth centuries, the hall is some 76 feet long by 30 feet wide. In some respects the appearance of the hall in 1603 would have differed from that shown. In 1581, for a visit by the Earl of Leicester, a substantial screen (partly of stone) was erected to conceal the three arched doorways at the south end of the hall, of which the centre one led to the kitchen and those on each side to enclosed chambers (originally buttery and pantry) which might have been used by the players as changing rooms. The screen, which would have facilitated entrances and exits for the players, had gone by 1824 and has not been replaced. The original hall also featured an extensive dais at the north and opposite end of the hall, occupying almost a third of the total floor space, which disappeared in 1755 when the rest of the floor was boarded over and raised to the level of the dais. Here the more important guests would have sat at the front, with doubtless the Mayor and Master of the Trinity Guild sitting together at centre on the Guild chair which, in the illustration, stands against the west wall. The rest of the audience sat on benches (which, when not in use in the hall, were stored in the Undercroft) or stood at the back. The floor has since been lowered and the dais restored.

After over 100 miles of travel – mainly by horse and wagon – the players would have been in need of a rest. From Coventry, it is only 17 miles to Stratford, and Shakespeare would not have come so far without paying a visit to Anne and his daughters. Susanna would then have been twenty, and Judith eighteen. He may well have taken some of the company with him – especially the younger boys. New Place, which he had bought in 1597, was the second largest house in the town and could have accommodated most of them.

Setting out from Stratford to their next recorded stop at Shrewsbury, there are several routes they might have taken; the most likely being along what is now the A34 through Henley-in-Arden. There they would have played – not at the Guildhall which, like many other of the smaller halls of religious origin had been sequestered by the crown early in Edward VI's reign, and in 1603 was in private hands – but at the Market House or Townhall, demolished in 1793.

Like the Guildhall that still stands in Thaxted, Essex, it rested on wooden beams, and was open at ground level to give shelter to traders. The hall proper was, as usual, on the upper floor, and was described in the eighteenth century as extensive. In 1609, it was laid down by the Court Leet, which met there, that 'neither Master Bailiff nor any other inhabitant shall licence or give leave to any players to play within the Towenhale upon pain to forfeit

40s.'; which tells us that it had been visited by players *prior* to 1609, and we know that despite the prohibition they continued to come, because players are reported there again in 1615.[39]

From Henley, the company would have gone on through the Forest of Arden, the heart of England, to Bromsgrove, perhaps, and Bewdley, across the Severn at Bridgnorth, and so to Shrewsbury; a journey of some 60 miles as the crow flies, but at the pace of a horse-drawn wagon on country roads – stopping several times to perform and spend the night – must have taken them not less than a week. (Was *As You Like It* one of the plays they had brought with them? There is an indication later that it may have been; if so, it would of course have been especially appropriate on this leg of their journey.)

Performances at Shrewsbury were in the Booth Hall, which had been rebuilt in 1512 but has since disappeared. We know from the town's records that the major companies were accustomed to stay for several days, and that the mayor's play – for which, on this occasion, the company received a reward of 20*s* – was normally followed by a run of public shows, probably in the same hall and at night.[40]

The next stage of their journey to Bath (over 100 miles to the south) would necessarily have taken them through Ludlow and Gloucester, at both of which it was usual for travelling companies to stop and perform (as they probably did), but where the Chamberlains' accounts have since been lost so we cannot confirm it. The Gloucester accounts are entirely missing between 1596 and 1629, but the procedure by which visiting players were required to obtain a licence from the mayor has already been quoted from a contemporary witness (see p. 23), and is confirmed by a civic ordinance of 1580.[41]

It soon becomes apparent from the surviving records that the companies' hosts in the towns they visited were prepared to spend both time and money in meeting the players' needs. In the first place, the hall where they were to play would have had to be cleared of its usual furniture and fittings. At nearby Bristol (which the King's men are also likely to have visited on this tour, but where again the relevant accounts are missing), 20*d* was expended in 1573/4 for a visit by Leicester's men in 'taking down the table in the mayers courte and setting yt up agayne after the said players were gonne'.[42] Having cleared the space, it was often necessary in the larger halls to erect a platform stage at one end, as at Gloucester in 1567/8, where a man called Batty was paid 8*s* for '103 quarters of elme bourdes for a skaffold for playors to playe one', and 2*s* for a 'peece of tymber to sett under the bourdes'.[43] Many of the performances, here as elsewhere, took place in the evening. At Bristol where the Mayor's Audits that survive are unusually detailed, a sum of 22*s* was paid in 1577/8 to 'my Lord of Leycesters Players at the end of their Play in the yeld [guild] hall before master mayer and the Aldremen and for lyngkes to geve light in the evenyng',[44] which I read as a matinee for the Mayor and aldermen, and an evening show for the public on the same day. Links were torches of pitch and tow, more often used to give light in the streets; at Gloucester in 1561/2, 3*d* was paid for a pound of candles.[45] In the winter fires were lit in the chamber, as for Leicester's men at Ipswich on 21 February 1565.[46] At Bristol, in 1576, we hear of a need to strengthen the Guildhall door, and for 'mending the cramp of Iren which shuttyth the barre, which cramp was stretchid with the presse of people at the play of my lord Chamberleyns Servauntes in the yeld hall before master mayer and thaldremen'.[47] The crush of spectators in confined spaces inevitably resulted in other damage. At Bristol again, in 1581, after a performance by Strange's men, the 'mending of 2 fowrmes which were taken owt of St Georges Chapple and set in the yeld hall at the play, and by the disordre of the people were broken', cost 2*s* 5*d*.[48] At Leicester in 1608, 2*s* was paid for 'mending the glasse Wyndowes att the towne hall more then was given by the playors who broake the same', and at Barnstaple in 1592/3 there was even damage to a ceiling.[49]

That the mayors and their aldermen were not generally resentful of all this extra expense and inconvenience, but took it in their stride as an acceptable price to be paid for the rare pleasures that the players brought to their towns, is attested by frequent references to drinks with the players after the show: at Coventry in 1608, Lord Compton's men were entertained in the parlour with wine, sugar and bread; at Gloucester in 1559/60, the Queen's were given a 'banket' costing 5*s* 7*d*, and in 1565/6 the same company was treated to 'wine and chirries' at 'Mr Swordbearers'.[50]

For Shakespeare and the King's in 1603, Gloucester's Mayor is unlikely to have been any less hospitable. And so fortified, perhaps, they would have journeyed to Bath, and from there to their last recorded venue at Oxford, stopping several more times on the way to perform. At Bath, they received a generous mayor's reward of 30*s*, and at Oxford, 20*s*. In both cities, the fiscal year began and ended at Michaelmas or a week or two later. It appears from the dating of the Chamberlains' accounts that the company was at Bath towards the end of the fiscal year 1602/3 (probably in late September), and arrived in Oxford early in the next, 1603/4 – about the middle of October.[51] We have seen that in Bath in 1587, a reward of 19*s* 4*d* to the Queen's men had been supplemented by 26*s* 8*d* 'gathered at the bench', making a sizeable total of 46*s*. For the King's in 1603, it could hardly have been less and, if we add the gatherings at subsequent performances, the company's receipts from the visit as a whole are likely to have reached a most useful sum. They would almost certainly have played at the old Guildhall, which continued to be used as such until the 1620s when it was converted into a shambles (for the slaughter of cattle), the external dimensions of which were 56 by 24 feet.[52]

The Editor of the Oxford city records has it that the players stayed there at the King's Head in Cornmarket and that the plays were acted in its yard, but the once common belief that players at this time normally performed in inn yards has since been largely exploded.[53] Efforts by the university authorities to bar professional players from the city had proved, if anything, rather less successful here than in Cambridge, and in 1586 exemption had been made by the Mayor ('onlie at this tyme') for Essex's men to perform in the 'Guylde Hall courte'.[54] The likelihood is that the King's, armed with their new patent, were similarly treated, and that by the 'courte' was meant – not, as Salter thought, an outside yard – but a large chamber in the Guildhall normally used by magistrates or visiting judges. (Many guildhalls in the period were alternatively named as 'Court' halls and chiefly used for that purpose.) Was this the occasion when *Hamlet* was acted at Oxford – as claimed in the quarto of 1603? Another possibility, as we shall find in a moment, is *Troilus and Cressida*.

On 21 October of this year, Joan Alleyn, wife of the player Edward Alleyn, who was then on a visit to Sussex, wrote as follows to her husband:

My entire and well-beloved sweetheart, still it joys me – and long, I pray God, may I joy – to hear of your welfare, as you of ours. Almighty God be thanked, my own self (yourself) and my mother and whole house are in good health, and about us the sickness doth cease. . . . All the companies be come home, and well, for aught we know, but that Brown of the Boar's Head is dead, and died very poor. . . . All of your own company [the Admiral's] are well at their own houses.[55]

Similarly optimistic news of an easing of the plague in London (where, in fact, deaths, though falling, were still occurring at the rate of several hundred a week) may have reached the players in Oxford, along with a report that the court was intending to return to Hampton Court for Christmas. As it happened, court and players had earlier crossed paths. After his coronation on 25 July, the King had set out on a progress to the West Country, which had taken him to Woodstock, near Oxford, in September; but plague having by then already reached Oxford, he and the court proceeded to Winchester, and in late October to Wilton, near Salisbury – home of the young Earl of Pembroke. Anticipating, along with other companies, an early lifting of the closure order on the London playhouses as the severity of the plague diminished with the approach of winter, and also perhaps in expectation of a royal summons to perform at Hampton Court during the Christmas season, the players left Oxford to return to the capital. On arrival, however, discovering that the infection was still rampant in Southwark, they took refuge in the pleasant suburb of Mortlake on the river, where Augustine Phillips had a house. It was there apparently that the summons eventually reached them – not for Hampton Court but for Wilton. And so they were obliged to retrace their steps in double-quick time the way they had come. It was in Wilton on 2 December that they were to give their first performance for King James, and where Heminges, as payee for his fellows, was justly compensated with an exceptional reward of £30, 'for the paynes and expences of himself and the rest of the company in coming from Mortelake in the countie of Surrie unto the courte aforsaid and there presenting before his Majestie one playe'.[56] A later unconfirmed but reliable report, deriving from Wilton, has it that the play was *As You Like It*, and confirms (if confirmation were needed) that 'we have the man Shakespeare with us'.[57]

But no sooner had the company arrived at Wilton and given this, and perhaps one or two other performances, than there was yet another change of plan. It was decided that the King and the court should spend Christmas at Hampton Court after all, and Queen Anne was to leave for the capital only five days later,[58] followed by the King, the now weary players, and the rest of the court. There are varying estimates of the importance of the players' new, high-sounding status as 'servants of the King'. One thing is clear: it was no sinecure.

At Hampton Court, Heminges was again the payee for performances on Boxing Day, 27, 28 and 30 December 1603, and on New Year's Day (two plays) and 2 February 1604, with an eighth at Whitehall on 19 February. Though no titles are recorded, a letter from Dudley Carleton to John Chamberlain describes one as 'a play of Robin goode-fellow' (almost certainly, *A Midsummer Night's Dream*),[59] and Jonson's tragedy *Sejanus*, in which both Burbage and Shakespeare had leading roles, was probably another. For the plays between 26 December and 1 January, the company's reward had been £53, and for those on 2 and 19 February, a further £20.[60] (£10 per play was to be the normal payment for court performances throughout the whole of the reign.)

During the previous eight months, the company had travelled over 600 miles. Against a meagre total of six visits recorded in surviving accounts, the actual number of places in which they stopped to perform is more likely to have been (at a conservative estimate) in the region of twenty (one every ten days), and the number of performances given (averaging three in each town) about sixty. Similarly, when additional gatherings at the mayor's play and subsequent shows are taken into account (generally amounting to at least twice the stated reward), the sum of their recorded rewards (£7 11*s* 8*d*, averaging about 22*s* a visit) needs to be doubled, and then multiplied by a factor of sixty, to arrive at an approximate estimate of their total receipts from the tour: £132. Compared to the £10 per play they received for their court performances, this is still a relatively modest amount, but it would at least have met their expenses and kept the company solvent, which £7 11*s* 8*d* would certainly not have done.

What cannot be calculated is the pleasure and enrichment the players brought to the thousands of people who packed their guildhalls throughout a large swathe of the country to see and hear their performances; nor the satisfaction that Shakespeare and his fellows would have derived from that.[61] As King's men, this was the first of a series of extensive tours they were to undertake; in 1605, they were in Oxford again, at Saffron Walden in Essex, and Barnstaple, Devon; in 1606, at Marlborough and Oxford, in the Midlands as far as Leicester, and Maidstone and Dover in Kent; in 1607, at Oxford, Barnstaple, and Dunwich in Suffolk; and so on in almost every year to the end of Shakespeare's career.

In attempting to follow in Shakespeare's footsteps on this first of his tours as a King's man, and describing some of the venues in which he performed and the conditions he is likely to have found in them, we have come to grips with the concrete realities that surrounded his life as a travelling player which, as we have seen, occupied a substantial part of his career both before and after 1603. In doing so, we have hopefully come a little nearer to understanding the colour and texture of what his real life would have been as opposed to the myths of the popularisers and the 'cloud-capp'd towers' of literary theory erected by some academics. As poet, dramatist and player, the audience he served lay across the whole of the country, and not just in London. Though the Globe was important to him – both as symbol and, in a practical way, as an ideal venue for the performance of his plays – it had no exclusive claim on him. He remained at heart a 'travelling man'. But this, of course, is only half the story. It is time to return to the plays.

I said earlier that only two plays can with any reasonable assurance of probability be dated to the period 1602/3: *Troilus and Cressida* and *All's Well that Ends Well*. For the reasons advanced by G.K. Hunter and others, *All's Well* cannot be later than 1604, and I think that Chambers was right in putting it a little earlier into 1602/3.[62] I find it hard to believe that Shakespeare would have written a play that begins with a dying king after the accession of James I. Its composition belongs, with *Troilus*, to the last year of Elizabeth's reign and, if so, it would have been an obvious choice for the 1603 tour. With only fifteen named characters, including at least five boys' roles, and with little necessity for doubling, it would easily have been within the compass of a travelling troupe, and makes no demands in its staging that the smallest guildhall would not have been able to supply. It may even have been written for touring. Many of its more intimate scenes – if not exactly lost – would have been in peril of being so on the larger, more exposed stage of the Globe, while they are likely to have been most effective in the smaller, more enclosed setting of a guildhall. Then again, Shakespeare's use of cornets, a softer wind instrument than the more usual trumpets, to greet the entrance of the King at I.ii and II.i indicate an indoor venue, though the play is too early in date for Blackfriars.[63]

To scholars, it is the first of what have become known as the 'problem plays', but its sole intractable problem, as I see it, lies in its combination of a fairy-tale plot (Helena's near-magical cure for the King's illness, and the 'bed-trick' whereby she substitutes herself for Bertram's intended bed-mate, Diana) with the depth and realism of its character-drawing and rich complexity of language. In both, it represents an advance for Shakespeare: in its use of folk elements, it is a first, perhaps hesitant, approach to that sublimation of human conflict and suffering through faith in an ultimate, providential reordering to be found more fully realised in his later romances; in its observation of character and individuality of speech, it leaves all the earlier comedies behind it. It belongs to its time, the last troubled days of Elizabeth's reign and the approach of a still-unknown Jacobean era, but it does not succumb to those uncertainties; rather, it rises above them. To be part of it – to see it from the inside, as it were, as I have had the privilege of doing on two long-separated occasions – is to become increasingly aware of its distinctive qualities and beauty.

Helena is the heart of the play, and unique among Shakespeare's lovers in that all that happens turns upon her. The play tells a love story, but the love is all hers; the object of her love – the callow, immature, insufferable Bertram – is everything to her but very little in the play. It is one of those data that Shakespeare gives for our necessary acceptance that perhaps in some earlier phase of his boyhood (for he and Helena have grown up together), and perhaps again in the person who starts to emerge in the final scene, there is something in Bertram, someone who is worth loving. We have to take that on trust if the play is to make sense. The plot follows Helena's rise from humble beginnings as an orphaned physician's daughter in the Countess's household, where she occupies the position of serving woman, to one high in the King's favour through the esoteric knowledge of the healer's art which her father has bequeathed to her, and her own determination; and its sole motivation is love – to put herself on the same plane as the young count so that he is able to see her as the person she really is, not as she appears, and to return her love. In that respect, the play is as much about class and the nature of kingship as the true fount of honour and rank, as it is about sexual fulfilment and marriage – a theme that could not have been all that distant from Shakespeare's awareness of his own situation as a not very much more than menial servant of the King's, for so he was regarded by most of his contemporaries. Hence his invisibility to them, as Helen to Bertram. And the bed-trick, which Victorian moralists found so shocking, and which is not exactly in accord with feminist principles either, should be seen, not as a young Chambers among others saw it – as the ignoble means by which a young girl should get a handsome young man in her bed – or not predominantly that, but as a necessary sealing through consummation of the rite of marriage which Bertram has obstinately withheld from her.[64] She is perhaps the toughest and most determined of Shakespeare's heroines.

One of the reasons why so many actors find that acting in Shakespeare brings them more fulfilment than in plays by any other author, alive or dead, is that he always gives them, along with marvellous lines and formidable challenges, room to contribute something of themselves. This seems especially true of the parts he wrote for himself – and the King of France in this play is surely one of them. In writing such parts, he knew in advance exactly what he as a player could and would bring to them: a natural distinction of manner and personality, great authority, a total absence of self-pity in his early scenes, and a quirky sense of humour.

Both Helena and Bertram (like nearly all of Shakespeare's lovers) need to be played very young, and would have gone to apprentices: Helena by necessity, Bertram in order to match with her. Helena is seen to be emerging from girlhood into womanhood. 'I have those hopes of her good', the Countess tells us, 'that her education promises her dispositions'; she is still in process of achieving her goodness (I.i.36ff.). Like Portia, we see her mature and grow in confidence as the play proceeds. Bertram is described by his mother as an 'unseason'd courtier', and by the King as a 'proud, scornful boy'. When Lafew, the old lord to whose immediate charge the Countess has entrusted him, says of him in an aside, 'I am sure thy father drank wine; but if thou be'st not an ass, I am a youth of fourteen' (II.iii.99), he may be glancing at Bertram's actual age. (In modern terms, he might be played as a cocky sixteen- or seventeen-year-old; he too must be seen to develop – if only by way of humiliation.)

Parolles, Bertram's unworthy but self-appraising buffoon, is the second largest part in the play (after Helena) and carries the comic sub-plot of his own unmasking. It would probably have gone to Burbage who, like all the really great tragedians, was also an accomplished comedy actor. Both he and the crusty, good-hearted Lafew, who at last takes Parolles into his service, are new, joyful creations in Shakespeare's gallery of living portraits. Heminges would have been disappointed if he had not been given Lafew. Lavatch, the clown of the play, is one of the saddest of Shakespeare's household fools. 'A shrewd knave and an unhappy', Lafew remarks of him (IV.v.60); but he has his moments, and Armin would have made the most of them. The speeches of the First and Second Lords in Paris – to be identified with the Dumaine brothers of Florence – are somewhat confusedly distinguished in Shakespeare's text by the letters E and G, which probably refer to two of the company's older apprentices, Ecclestone and Gough.

The citizens of Ipswich and Shrewsbury would have thronged to see the play, and rewarded the players generously with their applause and contributions to the 'gatherings'. As the Epilogue (doubtless spoken by Shakespeare as the King) says in bringing the play to its end,

> Ours be your patience then and yours our parts;
> Your gentle hands lend us and take our hearts.

There is no mention of *All's Well* in performance records, or of a published version in the Stationers' Register, until its appearance in the First Folio of 1623, and yet, as recent productions have shown, it is eminently actable. One can only suppose, as suggested above, that in the early years of James I, its opening theme of a sickening king would have made its London production untactful to say the least. So far as the capital was concerned, it had missed its moment.

The same may also be true of *Troilus and Cressida* – but for different reasons. Here, however, we are given some clues. The play was first registered for publication on 7 February 1603 by a Master Roberts: 'to print when he hath gotten sufficient aucthority for yt, The booke of Troilus and Cresseda as yt is acted by my lord Chamberlens Men, 6*d*.'[65] Clearly, he had not at that time received the permission he needed, though the play was already in performance; we are not told where, but in February or March of that year, when the Queen lay mortally ill at Richmond, there is only one realistic possibility, and that is the Globe.

Contrary to recent scholarly opinion, which has it that the play is of a sophisticated kind, 'highly satirical at times, experimental in genre and attuned to an avant-garde idiom . . . rather like the play that Hamlet describes to the First Player as "caviar to the general"; it "pleased not the million"',[66] I make no doubt that it was written for a popular audience at the Globe and would have been a roaring success with the groundlings in particular. It has everything we know that they liked: a railing fool in Thersites supplying scatalogical humour, a compelling plot of love betrayed, chivalric display and processions, scenes of combat and murder, with drums and trumpets a-plenty. Nor would its basis in Greek history and legend have been at all likely to put them off. A lost play with the title of *Troy* had been acted at the Rose in 1596, and Chettle and Dekker's *Troilus and Cressida* (of which only a fragment survives) had been given by the Admiral's men in 1599. They would have been keen to see what Shakespeare and the Chamberlain's were to make of it. True, there are some long speeches with serious intent from Nestor and Ulysses (some of the longest in the canon), but even here we are on a knife-edge of parody, where eloquence teeters on the brink of a merely comic loquacity.

The immense potential that the play has for popular entertainment has been demonstrated beyond all possible doubt by the success of recent revivals. Were the mixed audiences at the Globe any more sophisticated in their tastes than an average audience at Stratford or the National? I take leave to doubt it. Is the play any more select in its appeal than *Hamlet*? But no sooner had it received its first few performances than the London playhouses were closed by the death of the Queen, then again by the imminent coming of James, and finally by the plague – all within a matter of weeks. When, in May, the players received their royal mandate as the King's servants and took to the road, would they not have taken their latest popular success with them? Though its cast has been described as too large for public performance, the conjectural doubling plot I give in Appendix D demonstrates that it was well within the resources of fifteen men, four boys, and one mute player-musician – no more than was required for *Hamlet* or *Henry V*. Though we should take note that, despite its epic structure, a surprising number of its scenes require no more than two or three people to be on stage together, and that the silent procession of warriors in Act 1, Scene 2 could have passed through the body of the hall, viewed (or merely imagined) by Cressida and Pandarus on stage, it may still have been too large in its demands for the smaller guildhalls; it would, however, have come into its own in Coventry. And if, as Professor Alexander conjectured, it found an ideal audience in one of the Inns of Court, it is likely to have received an equally enthusiastic reception from the undergraduates of Oxford and Cambridge, if the company was allowed to perform for them on its visits in 1603. Roberts' qualification of his Stationers' entry, that he intended to print the play only when 'he hath gotten sufficient aucthority for it', may have resulted from the players' reluctance to release a play for publication while it was still enjoying a successful run at the Globe or was intended for revival; but when, for the Christmas season of 1603/4, the company was at last able to return to London, the atmosphere at court and in the City was found to have changed and become more repressive. (It was in 1604/5 that Ben Jonson was clapped in gaol, in imminent danger of losing his ears, for his contribution to *Eastword Ho!* on account of some mildly satirical humour it contained at the expense of the Scots.) In short, the play was suppressed.[67] In 1609, it was to be re-entered in the Register and published by another printer, but its description on the title page, as 'acted by the Kings Majesties servants at the Globe', was rapidly expunged in a second, revised impression, to which was added a publisher's blurb claiming it as a 'new play, never stal'd with the Stage, never clapper-clawd with the palmes of the vulger, and yet passing full of the palme comicall'. Having been banned from the stage, it received the dubious puff of an appeal to a minority of allegedly enlightened readers, who were urged to buy it because 'when hee [Shakespeare] is gone, and his Commedies out of sale, you will scramble for them, and set up a new English Inquisition'.[68] The writer need not have worried.

Because of their innate need to categorise, the play has been troublesome to scholars and literary critics. It has been variously described as comedy, tragedy, tragi-comedy, history, satire or, more judiciously, as a unique blend of elements from all the more admitted genres. 'There is no one of Shakespeare's plays harder to characterize', Coleridge confessed; one scarcely knows 'what to say of it'.[69] Even Hemings and Condell found it difficult to place, eventually describing it as a tragedy and putting it in the First Folio between the histories and tragedies. Only the imperturbable Dr Johnson was to keep his critical cool:

> This play is more correctly written than most of *Shakespeare's* compositions, but it is not one of those in which either the extent of his views or elevation of his fancy is fully displayed. As the story abounded with materials, he has exerted little invention; but he has diversified his characters with great variety, and preserved them with great exactness. His vicious characters sometimes disgust, but cannot corrupt, for both *Cressida* and *Pandarus* are detested and contemned. The comick characters seem to have been the favourites of the writer, they are of the superficial kind, and exhibit more of manners than nature, but they are copiously filled and powerfully impressed.[70]

He is unduly hard, I think, on Cressida and Pandarus. Though presented as flawed, Cressida evokes more pity than condemnation, and Pandarus is too funny to have been detested by his creator. Though an out-and-out reprobate (as his Epilogue makes clear), he is a likeable one and, as one of the 'favourites of the writer', fully deserves the billing he is given on the revised title page of the 1609 quarto: 'The Famous Historie of Troylus and Cresseid. Excellently expressing the beginning of their loves, with the conceited wooing of Pandarus Prince of Licia', which strongly suggests (in contradiction of the statement in the blurb) that the play *had* been performed, and that Pandarus had proved a notable success. I see him as one of those middle-aged men of indeterminate sexuality that one used to meet with in theatrical boarding houses, taking an inordinate interest in the love affairs of the younger lodgers. His love-song for Helen and Paris, in which he accompanies himself on the lute, is a delight.

> Love, love, nothing but love, still love, still more!
> > For, O, love's bow
> > Shoots buck and doe.
> > The shaft confounds
> > Not that it wounds,
> But tickles still the sore.
>
> These lovers cry, 'O! O!', they die!
> > Yet that which seems the wound to kill
> Doth turn 'O! O!' to 'Ha, ha, he!'
> > So dying love lives still.
> 'O! O!' a while, but 'Ha, ha, ha!'
> > 'O! O!' groans out for 'Ha, ha, ha! –
> Heigh ho!   (III.i.109–21)

When, just before this, Helen remarks on his 'fine forehead', perhaps (as Bevington suggests) caressing it, I am reminded of Dr Rowe's enthusiastic comment on the Droeshout portrait of Shakespeare: 'What a powerful impression it gives . . . what a forehead, what a brain!'[71] And indeed, I think it probable that Shakespeare played the part. With a little under 400 lines, it is just the size of role that he preferred, and (as with the Friar in *Romeo*), nearly all of his scenes are with the company's apprentices – here with Troilus and Cressida, Helen and Paris – to whom he would have been able to give his support. After the pseudo-heroic Prologue, with its echoes of *Henry V*, he opens the play with Troilus, brings the lovers together, watches helpless as Cressida is taken away, but is absent from all of the action in the Greek camp, returning only for the Epilogue. (For some further suggestions on casting, see my doubling plot in Appendix D.)

Though the play is sometimes read as expressive of a mood of world-weary cynicism on Shakespeare's part, or (more reasonably) as an attempt to rival the recently devised genre of comical satire for which Jonson and Marston had set the fashion,[72] I see it rather as a case of Shakespeare stretching his wings; as a final anarchic fling in a number of different directions before settling himself to the more profound and integrated themes that he was to address in the years ahead. *Troilus* needs to be played with a light touch, with due weight given to its more lyrical and serious passages. To the literary scholar, it may present an impossibly intransigent medley of contradictory styles, tendencies and moods; in the theatre, it is rarely less than entertaining, and at best a triumphant success.

ELEVEN

King's Man

Shakespeare was not stung into tragedy by any Dark Lady. He was not depressed into tragedy by the fall of Essex, who threatened revolution and chaos in England, to Shakespeare's horror and alarm; the cruelty of anarchy was a thought that haunted the poet like a nightmare. He did not degenerate into tragedy in a semi-delirium of cynicism and melancholy, ending in a religious crisis. Shakespeare *rose* to tragedy in the very height and peak of his powers, nowhere else so splendidly displayed, and maintained throughout his robust and transcendent faith in God and his creature Man.

C.J. Sisson[1]

When Shakespeare and his fellows returned to London in the footsteps of Queen Anne in December 1603, they found themselves in an atmosphere very different from the one they had left in May to embark on their countrywide tour. To begin with, London – especially that part of it about the Globe with which they were most familiar – had been ravaged by the plague. The fact that no one famous in history or literature had succumbed (the court and those wealthy enough to own country estates where they could take refuge would naturally have escaped) has led historians and literary scholars to underestimate its effects, but Stowe's estimate of a death toll within the city and liberties of over 38,000 in a population of some 200,000 faces us with the stark reality. And among the humbler citizens of Bankside – those among whom the players customarily lived and moved, travelling from their lodgings to the theatre every day for rehearsals and shows – there must have been many a once-familiar face that would then have been missing. In the Christmas season of 1603/4 the crisis was not by any means over. Hampton Court may have been relatively safe, but in the city the death rate was still running at 74 per week at the end of December, and it was not until February that it fell below 30.[2] Nor can we safely assume that the company itself was altogether free of loss in the period, especially among the younger apprentices and hired men. John Sincler may have been one such victim. He is mentioned (as appearing under his nickname of Sinklo) in the prologue to Marston's *The Malcontent*, which was probably one of the plays acted at court that Christmas, but from this time on his name is absent from the records, and the thin-man parts that Shakespeare had written for him and of which he had made a speciality, disappear from the plays. Given the family feeling we have seen to have existed among the players, and the close personal relationships they enjoyed with each other, such losses would have been felt very deeply – not least by Shakespeare himself.

But the most far-reaching change that confronted them on their return to the capital was the presence of their new patron and principal employer in the person of James. In character and tastes, he could hardly have been more different to the old Queen, whose partialities they had come to know so well and to cater for so expertly, whereas in James they were dealing with a largely unknown quantity. By any standard, Elizabeth was a well-educated woman who liked to show off her knowledge of Latin and other languages, but whose tastes in humour inclined to the low-brow and whose favourite fools had been Tarlton and Kempe. All that the players would have known of James at this time is that he was a recognised scholar whose particular interest and expertise lay in the realm of theology, and who was given to instructing his subjects in lengthy treatises as to their moral behaviour.

The King's attitude to the players and to the theatre in general is a subject of continuing controversy. He had demonstrated an intention to retain, even to enhance, the existing system of court patronage of the drama by his speedy appointment of the former Chamberlain's men as his personal servants, and by the exceptionally broad patent he had given them. The summons to Wilton in November 1603, and the eight further performances he had commissioned on his return to Hampton Court in

December, provide additional evidence of that intention, while the reward of £30 to them at Wilton as compensation for the long journey they had made and, even more remarkably, of a further donation of £30 via Richard Burbage in January 1604, 'for the mayntenaunce and releife of himselfe and the rest of his company being prohibited to presente any playes publiquelie in or neere London' because of the plague, were unprecedented.[3] There is no question either that the number of performances given at court by the company between 1603 and Shakespeare's death in 1616 was to far exceed that of the previous reign: according to Chambers' reckoning, 177 by the King's men in thirteen years as against 31 by the Chamberlain's in nine, though this may in part by accounted for by the enhanced status of the company under James. But the actual pleasure he took in the performances was not always evident to his contemporaries, and remains in doubt; nor was he always personally present at them, being represented on occasion by the Queen or young Prince Henry. These other members of the royal family may, indeed, have been more enthusiastic playgoers – and behind the scenes more friendly to the players – than he was. By 1604, two of the company's principal competitors at court and elsewhere, the Admiral's men and Worcester's, had also been raised in nominal status to the position of royal servants: the Admiral's being named thereafter as the Prince's players, and Worcester's as the Queen's.

If 1603 had been a difficult year for the company, 1604 was to be, if anything, worse. The theatres remained closed throughout Lent, and though the Privy Council authorised their reopening for Easter (Easter Day this year was 8 April), by May deaths from the plague were again on the rise, and the probability is that the Globe was only intermittently open through much of the summer. But if in London the plague lingered on – rising to a weekly peak of 34 in June – in the rest of the country it was to spread more widely and increase in virulence so that the possibility of another lengthy provincial tour was no longer an option.

In March, ten of the company's leading players, along with a similar number from the Queen's and Prince's companies, had each been issued with 4½ yards of red cloth to take part in the King's long-deferred coronation procession through London. It has been pointed out that the King's men were not at this time grooms of the chamber, but only became so five months later, and that the cloth they received was of the lowest grade awarded to crown servants to wear on such occasions.[4] In August, Phillips and Heminges with ten of their fellows were appointed grooms, and roped in to attend on the Spanish Ambassador for eighteen days at the Queen's palace, Somerset House, which had been placed at the Ambassador's disposal during negotiations for an important new peace treaty with Spain. There is no suggestion that they were required to perform; their duties appear to have been merely those of liveried attendants. They were each paid two shillings a day for this service, which, though no more than the guards received, would have helped to eke out their dwindling resources.

The appointment of twelve of the players as grooms represents an increase of three to the nine who were named in the patent of the previous year, and indicates the advancement of three former hired men or apprentices to the position of sharers. The chosen three were probably John Lowin, Samuel Crosse and Alexander Cooke, listed in eleventh, twelfth and thirteenth places in the Folio list of 'Principall Actors'. As we have seen (pp. 91–3), Crosse and Cooke had been with the company, initially as apprentices, since its inception as the Chamberlain's in 1594, but if Crosse was indeed one of the three, he must have died fairly soon afterwards (another victim, perhaps, of the plague) for there is no subsequent record of him; he would have been replaced by another long-serving apprentice, Nicholas Tooley – then about thirty years old.

Lowin (Plate 13) had joined the company from Worcester's in 1603 and, as suggested in my doubling plot for *Troilus* (Appendix D), may already have toured with the play in that year. Both he and Cooke are named as principal tragedians in Jonson's *Sejanus*, performed for the court at Christmas, and Lowin went on to replace Kempe as Falstaff and to play Henry VIII.[5]

With the approach of colder weather and a general easing of the plague throughout the country in September and October 1604, the players set out on their customary autumn tour. Only a few provincial records survive from this year, but we know them to have been at Barnstaple (probably for the Michaelmas Fair), and they would hardly have gone so far without playing also in Exeter, Bristol, and towns along the way.[6]

But by the end of October they were back in the capital, receiving a summons to perform at court, and from the Revels accounts of that holiday season, we discover that Shakespeare had occupied his time in the previous year in writing two new plays.

Othello and *Measure for Measure* are of special interest as being the first of Shakespeare's Jacobean plays; and though in writing them he would have kept in mind the likes and dislikes of his regular public at the Globe and elsewhere, he would also have felt a pressing need to please the company's new, still unpredictable patron. All the speculation about the possibility of Shakespeare having experienced some form of emotional crisis or romantic disappointment in the previous period that turned him away from light-hearted comedy towards darker and more tragic themes in the years that followed can be dismissed as so much moonshine, based in a fundamental misunderstanding of his writing as motivated primarily by a need for self-expression, rather than by a combination of theatrical demands with a creative urge to understand and explore human nature in all its many aspects. One of the first of his plays had been an historical tragedy, *Titus*, whose protagonist is a figure of heroic dimensions. My own view is that he had always intended to return to such themes, and that in writing the more complex comedies and the tragedies that date from this time, he was rising to the best and finest potentialities that he knew to be in him, rather than sinking in a mood of despondency and disillusion to a more pessimistic view of the world. Not that he would have been unaware of or unaffected by the changes around him. The swashbuckling Elizabethan era (if it was ever truly that) had predeceased the Queen. This was a new, more challenging world in which he found himself. But the accession of James, with his moral preoccupations, arrogant interpretation of his kingly role, and (as time would reveal) increasingly inept performance of it, is more likely to have been a spur to his creativity than a discouragement of it.

For all their obvious differences, *Othello* and *Measure for Measure* possess these characteristics in common: both have relatively small casts and both appear to have been written for indoor performance, in which the intimacy and intensity of their best scenes would have found a more appropriate setting than in the daylit, open spaces of the Globe. The first recorded performance of *Othello* was for the King and the court at Whitehall on 1 November 1604. The choice of day (Hallowmas or All Saints, the eve of All Souls) was perhaps no more than coincidental, but could not have been more apt; for *Othello* is a play of contrasting light and darkness and the struggle between them, in which the love of Othello for Desdemona is poisoned at source through the malign, driving ambition of Iago. I suggested earlier that in writing *Troilus* and *All's Well*, Shakespeare was already preparing for a drastic shift in the focus of his artistic and spiritual vision. At some point along the long road he had come since he and his fellows set out on their 1603 tour, he had found the story he had been looking for that was to release a new flood of creative energy that was to take him to greater heights of dramatic achievement than any he had attained before. The sense of urgency is palpable in the opening scene. There is no question here of the play being plot-driven or character-driven. From the moment that Iago and his stooge Roderigo burst upon the scene in mid-flow, we are in the vice-like grip of a plot that *is* the play –

Roderigo: Tush, never tell me, I take it much unkindly
                That thou, Iago, who hast had my purse,
                As if the strings were thine, shouldst know of this.

Iago: 'Sblood, but you will not hear me.
                If ever I did dream of such a matter,
                Abhor me –

And there we remain – however painful the experience may be in repetition – until the play's exhausted and terrible end.

It is a commonplace to say that *Othello* – though not the greatest of Shakespeare's tragedies – is the best of them in terms of the total credibility of its characters and assured skill of its construction. In these respects, it is not only foremost among the tragedies but also perhaps the most technically accomplished of all his plays. My impression is that he wrote it quickly, but only after a long period of gestation for which the previous two years of travel and restricted London activity had provided space. Sometimes in the plays, we sense that he was feeling his way in the creation of his characters and the casting of them; in *Othello*, they enter fully formed and assigned from the start.

There was no longer any doubt about Burbage – as there may have been initially in *Hamlet*. His ability to throw himself into a role, and to identify with it wholly throughout the length of each performance, is well attested. 'Oft have I seene him' – an obituarist was to write –

> leap into the grave,
> Suiting the person which he seem'd to have
> Of a sadd lover with soe true an eye,
> That theer I would have sworne, he meant to dye.
> Oft have I seene him play this part in jeast,
> Soe lively, that spectators, and the rest
> Of his sad crew, whilst he but seem'd to bleed,
> Amazed, thought even then hee dyed in deed.[7]

Othello demands this kind of totally committed acting. It is a great tragic role in the tradition of Titus, Kyd's Hieronimo, Marlowe's Tamburlaine and Faustus as played by Alleyn; but with this difference, for here the burden of dominance is shared. There are *two* great parts in *Othello*; the other of course is Iago, and it is only when both are acted with equal weight and conviction that the play achieves the full effect in performance that Shakespeare intended.

Unusually, Shakespeare gives us Iago's exact age – twenty-eight; but rather than narrowing the field of possibility to Condell or Cooke as the actor for whom it was written – both men being now of that approximate age – I take it as a signal that the player concerned was somewhat older (as Burbage had been for Hamlet). Why else should Shakespeare have felt a need to state it so precisely? Shakespeare himself was at this time only forty, and who else could have brought to it the same degree of understanding and authority? The part is larger than any other I have given him – larger, indeed, than Othello; nor does it conform to any of the previous categories he had made his own, such as his kingly or presenter roles. But if ever there was an occasion for breaking the mould of what had been done before, it was this. Iago opens the play and is there at the end, though stubbornly silent. It has all the marks of detachment – though here of the most chilling and inhuman kind – that distinguish many of the parts to which Shakespeare was drawn. I give Brabantio to Heminges, his brother Gratiano to Sly, and the Duke to Phillips – if he was well enough at this time to take it, for he was to die in the following May – with Condell, perhaps, as Cassio, Armin as the Clown, and Cowley as Roderigo. Emilia may have gone to Cooke or to Tooley, and Desdemona to a more recent recruit – possibly (as suggested below) to William Ostler.

The first court performance of *Othello* – which could hardly have failed to be sensational – took place, as I have said, on 1 November. Going from one extreme to another of Shakespeare's dramatic range, it was followed a few days later by a revival of the *Merry Wives*, and the ready availability of both plays so soon after the company's return from travel suggests that they were drawn from its current repertoire, and that *Othello* had been premiered on tour, if not at the Globe in the previous summer. But nearly two months were to pass before the players were to make their next appearance at court with *Measure for Measure*, and as this was to be followed by a whole series of revivals extending to the eve of Lent, involving a good deal of recasting to take account of changes in the company that had occurred in the interim, much of this time would have been spent in rehearsal.

The first thing to say about *Measure for Measure* is that for all its serious concerns and darker moments, it remains from first to last a comedy, and was meant to be played as such. The day of its first court performance – which is likely to have been its premiere – may be significant in this respect: it was acted before the King in the banqueting hall at Whitehall on St Stephen's day – the start of the Christmas holiday season. Again, Shakespeare was to play a leading part, but one that was more familiar to him; that of Vincentio, the Duke of the play who, like his previous dukes, is plainly a ruler with regal authority. Was this Shakespeare's device for shielding himself from accusations of *lèse-majesté*? Nevertheless, when, in the opening moments of the play, King James, seated in a position of honour in his palace of Whitehall, was confronted by Shakespeare in this kingly role, a frisson of anxiety may have gone through the audience of courtiers as to how he might react. Shakespeare anticipates this, and plays on it in the scene that follows. Any obvious relation between the spectator King and the fictional Duke is avoided by

Shakespeare's setting of the story in Vienna, from which, it appears, the Duke is about to depart on urgent, undisclosed business elsewhere, leaving his deputy Angelo to rule in his place; but teasingly, he invites the comparison a few moments later when he has the Duke inform Angelo that he wishes to leave the city privately and unattended because, although he 'loves the people', he does not 'like to stage me to their eyes', which, as everyone in the audience would have known, was exactly James's reaction to the crowds who had thronged to see him on his journey south. Thereafter, however, reality and drama part company, for it shortly transpires that the Duke has not departed the city at all, but has remained behind to keep a hidden eye on Angelo, whom he intends to put to the test with the suspicion that he is not the man he appears, or believes himself to be.

This opening scene sets the key. Like *All's Well*, the play draws on a traditional story, and though Shakespeare improvises brilliantly to retain our credibility and keep us in suspense, there is a playfulness in his treatment of it that is often missed in performance. This is especially true of the Duke, and the way the part is played determines the whole. We may accept the impenetrability of his disguise as a friar as a not uncommon stage convention, and there can be no doubt of his serious purpose, but why does he complicate matters by concealing for so long Angelo's fall from grace in attempting to blackmail the beautiful Isabella into sleeping with him by threatening the life of her brother? And why, having saved the brother (Claudio), does he go to such lengths to hide the fact that he has done so – if not simply to maintain suspense and contrive a more effective ending? For if the play is plot-driven, there can be no question as to who is driving the plot. It is the Duke himself in the person of Shakespeare in his dual capacity of Player King at his most quixotic and Player Poet, controlling it all. Much of the comedy is what we might now describe as black, but it is comedy nonetheless, and however truly the other players act their parts – and I am not suggesting they should be acted for anything less than their full dramatic value – the audience knows that all will be well because the Duke is in charge.

Isabella is the latest in Shakespeare's series of young, strong-minded heroines, whose beauty and shining sincerity bring out the best and the worst of the various men she encounters – depending on their predispositions.[8]

With Condell as Angelo, I conjecture Heminges to have been cast as Escalus, and Burbage as Lucio, a 'fantastic'. The smaller comic characters fulfil an equivalent function in the play to the mechanicals in the *Dream* or Dogberry's watch in *Much Ado* (if, that is, they are not too drastically cut); by their inane incursions into the action, they keep the play on an appropriately comedic level. I see Lowin as Elbow, Cowley as Froth, Armin as Pompey the clown, and Sly as Barnardine. In recent times, the play has often been plunged in Stygian gloom, with undue emphasis given to its darker elements and a repressive 'Jacobean atmosphere'. There could be no surer way of killing the comedy, or of obscuring Shakespeare's meaning. For though the play draws its title from an Old Testament source, implying 'measure for measure' in the sense of an eye for an eye and a tooth for a tooth, the Duke stands the old harsh maxim on its head by exemplifying Christian charity in fullest, overflowing measure by forgiving all who have sinned – the penitent and impenitent alike. Even Barnardine, the condemned criminal who obstinately refuses to yield his head when one is required to substitute for that of the redeemed Claudio, is finally let off the hook.

— ⋆ —

It is apparent from the series of revivals of the company's earlier successes that followed the first performance of *Measure for Measure* that the players were pulling out all the stops in their effort to reinforce the favourable impression they had made on their new patron with *As You Like It*, the *Dream* and *Othello*. *Measure* on Boxing Day was succeeded two days later (in its usual slot on Innocents' Day) by the *Comedy of Errors*. In the New Year came *Love's Labour's Lost*, *Henry V* on 7 January, and on the next day, Jonson's comedy, *Every Man Out of his Humour*. Three weeks later (by special request?) the last play's precursor, *Every Man In his Humour*, was given with Shakespeare in a principal role, and on 10 February (a Sunday) the *Merchant of Venice*. An interesting pointer to King James's personal tastes is provided by his choice of the *Merchant* for a repeat performance on Shrove Tuesday – the eve of Lent.[9]

After a Lenten break, during which (one hopes) Shakespeare may have been able to manage a week or two's rest with his family in Stratford, the Globe reopened for an Easter season in April, when *Measure for Measure* and *Othello* would have received public performance along with the recent revivals of Jonson's and Shakespeare's comedies.

But the plague was still present in London. In July, there was already talk of a prorogation of the session of Parliament due to meet in September, and by the first week of October, when the weekly death toll had risen again to 30, another closure order went out from the Privy Council, and the theatres were to remain shut for the rest of the year. This was, however, a usual time for the company to travel, and an autumn tour may already have been planned, if not begun. Fortunately, an exact date for the players' visit to Oxford in this year is recorded as 9 October so we know that by then they were well on their way.[10] It was probably on this occasion that Jonson's *Volpone* was performed in the university city, as claimed on the dedication page of the play's 1607 edition, along with *Othello* and *Measure*. The players appear not to have travelled further west at this time, but to have returned on a roundabout route taking in possibly Cambridge, where Jonson also claimed *Volpone* to have received 'love and acceptance', and certainly Saffron Walden in Essex on the final leg of their journey.[11]

National events were now to play a part in keeping the London theatres closed, for on 5 November 1605 the Gunpowder Plot was uncovered, and it was not until 15 December that permission was given for their reopening. Ten plays were acted at court during the Christmas season of 1605/6, though we have no record of their titles. Nor do we have any direct information as to Shakespeare's personal reactions to the current political turmoil. Or to the witchhunt and ruthless purge of Catholics (some guilty but mostly innocent) that followed. That some of the victims would have been known to him personally – especially in and around Stratford, where a jury of citizens was summoned to root out alleged sympathisers – seems very likely. All we have to go on – and it is surely enough – are the plays that he wrote in the period: *King Lear* and *Macbeth*.

Though the stories they tell are completely different, the two plays have much in common. They both feature great but flawed heroes whose downfall is primarily brought about through self-indulgence of their moral failings: ambition in the one, pride and its concomitant vice, self-absorption, in the other. They continue Shakespeare's return, begun in *Othello*, to a more classical type of drama in which one or two characters dominate the whole. Macbeth has a partner in evil; Lear stands alone. They may not be the best of Shakespeare's plays but they are undoubtedly among the very greatest, and more profoundly disturbing. In them, Shakespeare confronts head-on the mystery of evil, and though Lear is finally destroyed by it, he achieves true majesty in the course of his struggle, whereas Macbeth follows an opposite curve; starting from a position of nobility and honour, his progression is all downhill. If the fatalism of *Macbeth* is redeemed by the poetic splendour of its language, *Lear* is the more terrible of the plays but also, in a paradoxical way, the more life-enhancing.

Much scholarly argument has turned on the question of when they were written and which of the two came first. It is more than possible, however, that in the 24 weeks between 5 November 1605 and a reopening of the Globe after the Lenten break on 21 April 1606, Shakespeare – working at white heat – had been able to complete them both, and that both were premiered at the Globe in the course of that Easter season.[12]

That Burbage played Lear is a matter of record – and who could refuse him Macbeth? But what of the other roles, and especially Shakespeare's? In *Lear*, I give him Gloucester – mainly because I cannot conceive of his entrusting the part to anyone else, or that any other actor in the company could have played it so well; especially with Burbage in the heart-stopping scene with the mad Lear, when he has been blinded.

Gloucester:	The trick of that voice I do well remember:
	Is't not the King?
Lear:	Ay, every inch a king:
	When I do stare, see how the subject quakes . . .
Gloucester:	O! let me kiss that hand.
Lear:	Let me wipe it first; it smells of mortality.
Gloucester:	O ruin'd piece of Nature! This great world
	Shall so wear out to naught. Dost thou know me?

Lear.   I remember thine eyes well enough. Dost thou
            squiny at me?
            No, do thy worst, blind Cupid; I'll not love . . .
                                    (IV.vi.106–8, 131–6)

In modern productions, the Fool – in spite of being addressed
by Lear as 'pretty knave', 'lad' and 'boy' – often goes to an older
actor. This may lend the role a certain added pathos, but is not, I
think, Shakespeare's intention. Historically, it is usually assigned
to Armin, but Armin at this date would have been too mature a
man to play it. It would have been given to one of the company's
younger apprentices (perhaps Armin's apprentice) as a double
with Cordelia – one of those doubles that transcends economic
necessity to fulfil an important dramatic function in the play.
Armin's versatility and expert knowledge of contemporary fools
would have been more valuably employed as Edgar – especially in
his assumed identity as Poor Tom.[13] It is, of course, Cordelia's
genuine love for her father, which shines out in the later scenes of
their reconciliation (Plate 14), that makes it impossible for her to
take any part in the phoney love-test of the first act, which sets
the tragedy in motion.

Regan and Goneril are parts for those older apprentices or
former apprentices (Cooke and Tooley?) who appear to have
gone on playing the more mature women's roles well into their
thirties. I see Condell as Kent, Cowley and Sly as Cornwall and
Albany, Gough or Gilburne perhaps as Edmund, Lowin as
Oswald, and Heminges as the Old Man of Act IV, Scene 1. With
over twenty speaking roles to be covered, a fair amount of
doubling was required.

All of that small minority of scholars who have given serious
consideration to the parts that Shakespeare took in his own plays
agree that King Duncan in *Macbeth* was one of them – doubling,
perhaps, with the Doctor attending on Lady Macbeth in Act 5.[14]
It is a nice example of the 'Kingly parts' he played 'in sport' and,
with only 69 lines, would have afforded welcome respite from the
other, much larger roles he was playing in the period. Small as it
is, it requires an actor of gentle, charismatic presence.

Macbeth is the only play of Shakespeare's in which the powers
of darkness are given material form, and their appearance at the
start must have sent a shiver of very real dread through the play's

early audiences. Since then the figure of the witch has been conventionalised, and so often guyed as to become merely risible, and present-day directors must find an alternative way of evoking the same effect (Plate 15). It is, however, only in stage directions and speech prefixes that they are described as 'witches'; to Banquo they 'look not like th'inhabitants o'th'earth,/And yet are on't' (I.iii.41–2), and Macbeth refers to them as 'weird sisters', meaning 'weyard', sisters of fate. In Jacobean English, 'hag' or 'witch' could mean, not only what it does today, but also a demon *disguised* as a witch. Though they have no power in the play to take Macbeth further along the path to treason and murder than he consents in his heart to go, they lead him on to damnation and death with half-truths and deceitful prophecies. But of course it is Lady Macbeth who pushes him over the edge into absolute evil, for if Macbeth is practised on by demons, his remorseless wife is possessed by them at her own invitation. We do not know who played the role in the first production – I suspect Tooley or Cooke – but it requires a strong performance from a very good actor. We may no longer believe in the powers of demons but the play can still convince us they are real. It is the nearest that Shakespeare came to writing a morality play. Good triumphs in the end but at fearful cost.

There are some thirty speaking parts in all, requiring extensive doubling. Nevertheless, with apprentices doubling the smaller women's roles with boys and servants, and the Weird Sisters appearing also as the murderers, Seyton and the drunken Porter, it would still have been possible to stage the play with a dozen actors, three or four apprentices and a few additional soldiers. Even today, the tighter the ensemble and the more completely the company is involved from start to finish, the greater the total effect is likely to be.

On 4 May 1605, Augustine Phillips had made his will, and died a few days later. He was one of the senior men of the company, a skilled musician and composer of jigs, a family man whose younger sister had married Robert Gough, and a respected figure in and beyond his profession whose advocacy with the authorities had saved the company from possible disgrace at the time of the Essex affair. His bequests to his fellows give a picture in little of the company's personnel and rankings – probably as it had been a few years earlier when the will was originally drafted, as two of the beneficiaries (Beeston and Fletcher) were no longer active in the company in 1605. Five pounds in gold were to be divided among the hired men; with thirty shillings each in gold to Shakespeare, Condell and 'to my servaunte' Christopher Beeston; and twenty shillings each to Lawrence Fletcher, Armin, Cowley, Cooke and Tooley (in that order). His late apprentice, Samuel Gilburne, was to receive forty shillings and items from his wardrobe including 'my purple Cloke, sword and dagger', and his present apprentice, James Sandes, forty shillings with his musical instruments, comprising a bass viol, cittern, bandore and lute – but only 'at thexpiracon of his yeares in his Indentur or Apprenticehood'. Heminges, Burbage and Sly were appointed 'overseers' of the will, each to receive for their pains a 'boule of silver of the valew of ffyve poundes apeece'. Gough is named as one of two witnesses to Phillips' signature.[15] He would have been much missed by all of his fellows.

During the early months of 1606, concurrent with the trial of the Jesuit Provincial, Fr Garnet, and further rumours of treason and plots, the plague in London continued to cause anxiety as the weekly total of deaths veered between single numbers and the twenties. Then, in the middle of July, there was a leap to 50, and by the end of that month to 66. Again, the Globe and other playhouses were closed, and probably remained so for eight or nine months until Easter 1607.

In 1606 the company was recorded at Oxford, Marlborough, and in Kent, and in the summer, Heminges was rewarded on behalf of his fellows for 'three playes before his Majestie and the kinge of Denmarke at Greenwich and Hampton Court'.

The Danish king was in England between 15 July and 11 August to visit his sister, Queen Anne, but during the first two weeks of his stay, the queen was still recuperating from childbirth at Greenwich. The players were at Oxford between 28 and 31 July, having travelled perhaps by way of Marlborough. The queen having been churched on 3 August, they were summoned to Greenwich for two performances there between the 3rd and the 5th. They would then have accompanied the royal entourage to Hampton Court, where a third performance was given and Heminges was paid.[16] As the plague in London was still on an upward curve, rising to a weekly death toll of 85 in August, 116 in early September, to reach a peak of 141 at the beginning of October, the company would have gone from Hampton Court as directly as possible into Kent.

Again we have only a partial record of the towns in which they played: Maidstone, Faversham, and finally Dover, which they reached on 30 August.[17] At Maidstone, an unusual entry in the Chamberlains' accounts reads, 'payd to the kinges players by mr maior & to the trompettors, £2 5s' – more than twice the usual reward. Though the Royal Corps of Trumpets and Drums is often found on tour independently, and their combining with the players here may only have been coincidental, the fact that Maidstone would probably have been the company's first stop after leaving Hampton Court on 8 August suggests that a section of the royal band accompanied them at least so far, and that the play was *Lear*, in which, apart from stipulated sennets, flourishes and drums, two trumpeters are required to appear and play on stage in Act 5. Their participation would have added an authentic touch of royal pageantry to the performance.

The writing of *Antony and Cleopatra* and *Coriolanus* belongs in all probability to the latter part of this year during which the Globe remained closed. Nine plays were given at court during the Christmas season of 1606/7 which extended from 26 December to 27 February in the second week of Lent, and *Antony* may well have been one of them.[18] We know that *Lear* was performed on St Stephen's day (26 December) before the King; not the most obvious choice of play for such a festive occasion, and, if the choice was that of James, one that would indicate that his taste in such matters was more discerning than he has usually been given credit for.

The Globe and other metropolitan theatres may have opened briefly at Easter 1607, for Easter and the early summer of 1608, and for one or two months in the early part of 1610; otherwise the whole of that three-year period was a blank so far as London was concerned. It is true that from the middle of December 1607 to May 1608, the weekly totals of plague deaths remained in single figures, but as the plague eased, Londoners had the Great Freeze to contend with, when the Thames froze over and conditions in the exposed theatres would have been impossibly cold both for the players and those who may have struggled across the ice in the hope of seeing them. Then in June 1608, the plague toll returned to double figures, rose steadily to a further peak of 147 in September, and remained at a prohibitively high level for the rest of that year and throughout the whole of 1609.

In 1608/9, Thomas Dekker was to describe the situation in London as one in which:

> Pleasure itself finds now no pleasure but in sighing and bewailing the miseries of the time . . . Play-houses stand (like taverns that have cast out their masters) the doors locked up, the flags (like their bushes) taken down; or rather like houses lately infected, from whence the affrighted dwellers are fled, in hope to live better in the country. . . . Playing vacations are diseases now as common and as hurtful to them as the Foul Evil to a Northern Man or the Pox to a Frenchman. . . . To walk every day into the fields is wearisome; to drink up the day and night in a tavern, loathsome, to be ever riding upon that beast with two heads (lechery) most damnable, and yet to be ever idle is detestable.

Only, he tells us, across the river in the Bear Garden, is any diversion to be found. 'The company of the Bears hold together still; they play their tragicomedies as lively as ever they did: the pied bull here keeps atossing and a roaring when the Red Bull [a theatre in Clerkenwell] dares not stir.'[19]

How would Shakespeare have reacted to this bleak situation? It is not a question that biographers often ask – let alone attempt to answer. At this point in their narratives they usually take refuge in generalities, or write in vague terms of Shakespeare distancing himself from his profession as player and from the company he served. I shall be looking more closely at the question of Shakespeare's alleged retirement, and the various dates that have been advanced for it in the following chapter; but it can be said here that if Shakespeare ever did withdraw from acting and his close involvement in the day-to-day activities of the company, which I doubt, we can be sure that it would not have been *now*; not (if my estimate of his character is anywhere near the mark) at this moment of crisis when, to all those involved, the very survival of the company and all that he and his fellows had worked to achieve and to build in the preceding fourteen years must have seemed under imminent threat of extinction.

One important advantage that Shakespeare enjoyed in the period in contrast to a free-lance playwright like Dekker – who, in consequence of the London closures, had been reduced to the necessity of pamphleteering in order to scrape a living – lay in his permanent attachment to a single company, the King's, and the continuing demand that was made upon it throughout the plague years for court entertainment, especially the provision of new plays which, as its principal author, he was expected to supply. We find the company at Whitehall on eleven occasions in the winter of 1607/8 – sometimes performing twice on the same day; giving twelve plays for the King, Queen, Prince Henry and the Duke of York (again at Whitehall) in 1608/9; and thirteen more in 1609/10. These 36 performances – not all of them of plays by Shakespeare, of course, though a good many were – produced £380 in rewards, along with two grants-in-aid totalling a further £70; the second of which (on 10 March 1610) was paid to Heminges 'for himselfe and the reste of his companie beinge restrayned from publique playinge within the citie of London in the tyme of infeccon duringe the space of sixe weekes in which tyme they practised pryvately for his majesties service'.[20] Nor did the company cease to travel. On 6 September 1607 we find them at Oxford again, and in the same year at Barnstaple, and receiving a modest reward of 6s 8d from the Chamberlains of the lost city of Dunwich on the Suffolk coast (now under the encroaching sea); in 1608 at Marlborough and Coventry; and in 1609 at Ipswich, and Hythe and New Romney in Kent. Though on all these extensive tours they would have been dodging the plague – and, as they moved from place to place, may sometimes have been paid *not* to perform – the few records that have survived the passing of four hundred years can represent (as in 1603) only a small proportion of the number of towns which they actually visited and in which they played, and the official rewards they received (rarely more than a pound in each) the merest fraction of their total receipts when additional gatherings at these and subsequent performances are taken into account. When compared with their usual takings at the Globe, their income from such visits would not have been large but, in conjunction with payments for their court performances, sufficient to keep the company together and operational on the proverbial shoe-string with the hope of better times to come; a not unfamiliar state of being to professional companies in this country, now as then.

If, as I have conjectured, *Antony and Cleopatra* was premiered in London in a court performance during the Christmas season of 1606 and featured in a brief season at the Globe at Easter 1607, it would almost certainly have gone with the company on the series of tours to Oxfordshire, Suffolk and Devon that occupied the rest of that year. Though clearly belonging to the sequence of tragedies of unparalleled power and invention on which Shakespeare was then embarked, it is different in both structure and aims from its immediate predecessors. Structurally, it represents a return to the looser, chronicle pattern of story-telling he had previously employed in his English history plays; in subject, it continues his account of the Roman world as reflected by Plutarch, and picks up the story of Antony where he had left it in *Julius Caesar*. He shows us, in a succession of vividly realised episodes, what some twenty years of power, political intrigue, and hard drinking had done to him; more importantly he shows him in love, for *Antony and Cleopatra* is as much a tragedy of love as was *Romeo and Juliet*.

For all its epic dimensions, this is a very personal, even intimate, play that is not helped by overblown, grandiose production. Its scenes are many and for the most part short, and there is rarely need for more than half a dozen characters to be on stage together. That is why it is perfectly valid for us to envisage it as equally (if not more) effective in the restricted surroundings of the Dunwich guildhall as on the open stage of the Globe.

It goes without saying that Antony would have been for Burbage; it is also apparent that Shakespeare had at his disposal at the time a boy player of remarkable ability for whom Cleopatra was written. Peter Levi has suggested that this was William Ostler, who had begun his career with the Chapel company (a children's troupe) with which he had taken a part in Jonson's *Poetaster* in 1601.[21] He is first recorded as a King's man in 1610 but is likely to have joined the company earlier. (He is given sixteenth place, after Robert Armin, in the Folio list of principal actors.) He was later to marry Thomasine,

Heminges' daughter, but died still relatively young in 1614. In an epigram in his *Scourge of Folly* of *c.* 1611, our old acquaintance, John Davies of Hereford, describes him as 'the Roscius of These Times' and a 'King of Actors', who

> . . . if thou plaist thy dying part as well
> As thy stage parts, thou hast no part in hell[22]

– which, of course, is where he assumes the majority of players to be headed!

If, as is quite possible, Ostler had already played Desdemona, he would have been well practised in the art of dying. But whether it was he or another recent recruit who played Cleopatra in the original production, he would have been in command of the bewildering mood changes, tricks and shifting strategies, as also the depths of true feeling, of which the character shows herself to be capable, and that makes her one of the two or three most complex and fascinating female roles that Shakespeare ever wrote.

I believe that his own part in the play was Enobarbus. It has the distinctive characteristic of detachment and is of the medium size (some 350 lines) that he preferred. Present on the sidelines in all the more significant scenes and situations, his chief function in the play is that of a witty, intelligent and perceptive observer of the action throughout; it is one of Shakespeare's presenter roles. Alone among the characters, he is able to give clear, objective expression to Cleopatra's motives and, on occasion, to put Antony right about them. When Antony speaks of her as 'cunning', he corrects him:

> Alack, sir, no, her passions are made of nothing but the finest
> part of pure love. We cannot call her winds and waters sighs
> and tears; they are greater storms and tempests than almanacs
> can report. This cannot be cunning in her; if it be, she makes a
> shower of rain as well as Jove. (I.ii.144–9)

His retrospective descriptions of her more spectacular self-dramatisations are so graphic as to bring them on stage, and make us feel we were there.

> The barge she sat in, like a burnish'd throne
> Burn'd on the water: the poop was beaten gold;
> Purple the sails, and so perfumed that
> The winds were love-sick with them; the oars were silver,
> Which to the tune of lutes kept stroke, and made
> The water which they beat to follow faster,
> As amorous of their strokes. . . .　　　　　　(II.ii.191–7)

In character, Enobarbus is another of Shakespeare's originals – combining the soldierly virtues of courage, honour and good humour with an intensely personal devotion to Antony. When, at the end of Act 3, he takes the sensible decision to desert his cause, realising it is doomed to failure, he is so unforgiving of himself as to die of grief. As with Mercutio in *Romeo*, it becomes dramatically necessary to remove him from the play at this point if the denouement – in its concentration on the two lovers – is to achieve its fullest tragic and poetic dimensions. Which it does. The apparent simplicity of the play's first four acts is deceptive; its cumulative effect is superb.

If *Antony and Cleopatra* is a tragedy of love, *Coriolanus* is a tragedy of honour; the story of a man who, by reason of an austere Roman upbringing by his formidable mother Volumnia, places an ideal of soldierly pride above all other virtues, even patriotism, to his own ultimate destruction. It is a powerful, intense drama, closely based, like *Antony*, on Lord North's translation of Plutarch. But it has contemporary relevance also. The corn riots in Rome reported by Plutarch are paralleled by food shortages and civil disorder in England throughout the Elizabethan and Jacobean periods, resulting from the replacement of tillage by pasture and enclosures of common land. Prices generally were rising; there was a dearth of corn in 1607 and 1608, and the former year saw a popular insurrection in the Midlands. Though the causes of the future civil war between King and Parliament were more constitutional and religious than social in origin, it is difficult not to see in the picture of civil unrest and class warfare that Shakespeare gives us in the play's opening scene an awful prognostication of what was to come. It is in the context of a divided and fractious population that the personal tragedy of Coriolanus is framed.

A reference in the first scene to the 'coal of fire upon the ice'

(l. 172) suggests that the play was written in the hard winter of 1607/8 when, as we have seen, the Thames froze – for the first time in over forty years – and there are reports of fires having been lit on the ice. And this fits with stylistic and other slight indications of date, as well as an entry in the Stationers' Register in May 1608.[23] It may have been premiered at court in February 1608, and staged at the Globe at Easter or early summer of that year. It is a play of violent action. It begins, like *Julius Caesar*, with a mob of mutinous citizens 'over the stage', and proceeds to some of the most blood-bespattered battle scenes that Shakespeare ever devised. It is clear from the stage directions, which make good claim to derive from his original manuscript, that it was written for the Globe, and demands all the space that the Globe's open stage – possibly also its yard – could provide. He was not to know that the company's London venue was to be available to it only for a few weeks, and that further performances there would be inhibited by the plague for a year and a half. It is doubtful whether more than a handful of the guildhalls that he and his fellows were to visit in the months that followed would have been able to accommodate it.

Shakespeare is careful to preserve a balance of sympathies as between the opposing parties: between the riotous citizens and their arrogant rulers, and later between Coriolanus and his fellow patricians. The plebs are more realistically drawn than in *Caesar*, and though they are just as fickle and bloody-minded, they are given more justification for being so. Coriolanus is seen at his worst in his relations with them but, in his natural environment of war, wins respect for his courage, his modesty – based as this appears to be in an egocentric disdain for publicity – and occasional bursts of generosity towards his defeated foes. The role would have gone by a now well-founded right to Burbage. Volumnia is the strongest of Shakespeare's older women and would have been a gift to one of the former apprentices who specialised in such parts. She has created in her son a monster of self-willed fanaticism, and the scene (V.iii) in which she turns aside his determination to destroy Rome out of revenge for what he sees as its ingratitude to him by an appeal to the filial debt that he owes her, is the best in the play. She succeeds, but only at the cost of Coriolanus' own death at the hands of the Volscians who, in sparing Rome, he has betrayed. 'Kill, kill, kill, kill, kill him!', they cry (echoing the mad Lear), in a final horrific scene as they cut him down and trample him under foot.

There is not much human warmth or humour in the play, and most of the little that Shakespeare allows in his stark retelling of the story is given to Menenius Agrippa. This elderly patrician, despite his loyalty to Coriolanus and admiration for him, is the voice of moderation and humanity in the play. I have little doubt that it was Shakespeare's role, and that his performance of it would have done much to ameliorate the play's otherwise chilling effect.

This, however, was not quite the end of the road in Shakespeare's exploration of the darker, more destructive sides of human nature on which he had first embarked in *Othello*. That was to come with *Timon of Athens*, which exists only in an imperfect, disjointed text which Chambers was probably correct in characterising as a first, unrevised draft. As such, I shall not do Shakespeare the injustice of discussing it as if it were anything more – though tidied-up versions have been staged with success in recent years. One thing that may be said of it with reasonable certainty – arising from its locales, use of space and stage directions – is that, like *Coriolanus*, it was intended for the open stage of the Globe. In a rare indulgence in conjecture, Chambers went on to suggest that the reason for its being unfinished is that Shakespeare 'dealt with it under conditions of mental and perhaps physical stress, which led to a breakdown'.[24] But as we have no grounds for doubting that during this whole period Shakespeare continued his normal activities, travelling with the company on its more than usually lengthy travels, playing his usual roles in its now rich repertoire of earlier plays including comedies, I think it more likely that the play was left unfinished because, by 1609, it would have become apparent to him that production at the Globe was no longer a viable option in the foreseeable future, and by the time of the Globe's reopening, he had found other, more promising themes to explore. Like *Troilus and Cressida*, it had missed its moment.

It can be admitted, however, that this is unlikely to have been a happy time in Shakespeare's personal life. Not only would he have lost friends and fellows to the plague but, towards the end of December 1607, his younger brother Edmund who had followed him to London to become a player, died when only twenty-eight years old. We know nothing of the circumstances, whether Edmund was, or ever had been, a member of the company, or how close the brothers were. All we really know about him is that earlier in 1607 an illegitimate son of his named Edward had been buried at St Giles, Cripplegate; and that when his own death followed four months later, someone (it was almost certainly William) arranged and paid for an expensive funeral in St Saviour's, Southwark, with burial in the church and a 'forenoon knell of the great bell'.[25] Nor was this to be the last of his griefs in the year that followed.

There is one other play belonging to the period 1607/8 still to be mentioned: *Pericles*. But this too only survives in an imperfect text – one so unsatisfactory to Heminges and Condell, who would have played in it, that they omitted it from the First Folio altogether. As it represents the beginnings of another of those sea changes in Shakespeare's shifting perspectives on the world of his time, it will be best to defer consideration of it to the following chapter.

TWELVE

Blackfriars

The latter part of his Life was spent, as all Men of good Sense will wish theirs may be, in Ease, Retirement, and the Conversation of his Friends. He had the good Fortune to gather an Estate equal to his Occasion . . . and is said to have spent some Years before his Death at his native Stratford.

Nicholas Rowe, 1709[1]

He . . . waited until 1613 before acquiring his first London property. It is sometimes said that he had already retired, and that he purchased the Blackfriars gatehouse purely as an investment . . . We think otherwise: in 1613 he was still in his forties, the gatehouse was conveniently close to the Blackfriars theatre, and had he not pledged to pay his share of this theatre's rent for twenty-one years? . . . He could not foresee in 1613 that he had only three more years to live; he might reasonably hope to continue his London career.

E.A.J. Honigmann and Susan Brock[2]

On the basis of the vague statement quoted above from Shakespeare's first biographer Rowe in the eighteenth century – qualified as it is by that notorious let-out, 'is said' – it has been almost universally accepted that Shakespeare retired from active involvement in the theatre to his home in Stratford at some time between 1610 and 1613. Chambers points out that his name does not appear in any of Jonson's cast lists after *Sejanus* in 1603 but, as he is named in only one other before that date (*Every Man in his Humour* in 1598), and as the lists are retrospectively compiled and far from complete, this tells us very little. In 1610 Shakespeare was only forty-six. Actors, then as now, do not retire in their forties (or ever) if there is still work for them to do. As indeed there was for Shakespeare. In 1610 there were definite signs that the plague was at last releasing its hold on London, and that the Globe might become available to the company again on a more regular basis, requiring new plays with which it might hope to recoup the losses of the previous seven years. In 1608 Burbage had finally succeeded in gaining access for the company to the Blackfriars indoor playhouse in which he and his brother had inherited an interest from their father, and which in the meantime they had been able to extend to take in some adjacent property. In 1600, following objections by wealthy neighbours to its use by the then Chamberlain's men, it had been leased to 'little eyases' – the Children of the Chapel Royal; but in 1608 that company had been closed down by the authorities and, previous objections to the adult company having meanwhile evaporated or been overridden, the King's were invited to take over the lease. A syndicate was formed by seven of the company's sharers, including Shakespeare, each committing himself to pay his share of the rent for twenty-one years. Though no longer exempt from City ordinances as once it had been, and the plague was to deny the use of it to them for a further eighteen months, the company now had a prestigious indoor playhouse north of the river that would provide a haven from the severities of winter weather. Shakespeare's plays of the period 1608 to 1613 show no signs of any withdrawal on his part from the hurly-burly of production, and continue to throw up parts for him to act.

Throughout the whole of his active career as a player, he had lived as a lodger in London. In 1597 he was recorded as resident in Bishopsgate ward, a short distance from the Theatre and Curtain, but by 1599 had crossed the river to the Liberty of the Clink in Southwark, near the Globe. In 1604, and for some time before and after that year, he 'lay in the house' of Christopher Mountjoy, a French milliner, in Cripplegate, not far from St Paul's – as we know from a court case that arose in 1612 concerning a disputed will, in which he was called and gave testimony as a witness. It was not until March 1613 that he purchased a house of his own, and unsurprisingly it was in Blackfriars itself, a short walk away from the company's new playhouse, and from a ferry at Puddle Wharf that would have taken him across the Thames to the Globe. Those biographers who by this time have packed him off to Stratford, as nearly all of them have, to enjoy its 'open fields and cool water meadows' (as Chambers puts it), are at a loss to account for this London purchase, and describe it as 'an investment pure and simple'. But why here, and why now? True, the purchase was hedged about with peculiarities which have not as yet been fully explained; for though, with the help of a short-term mortgage, he was the sole buyer, legal ownership was shared with three others: his fellow, John Heminges, William Johnson, perhaps the former Admiral's man who was landlord of the nearby Mermaid tavern in Bread street, and a certain John Jackson, who may have been the Hull shipowner of that name who frequented the Mermaid when he was in London. What was going on here? Shakespeare's gatehouse, which lay by, and in part over, a 'great gate' that in pre-Reformation times had led to the Prior's house of the Dominican friary, had previously been occupied by a succession of Catholic recusants, and in 1598 had been searched for hidden priests on a report of its containing 'many places of secret conveyance'.[3] Was Shakespeare taking a leaf out of his father's book in deliberately muddying the legal waters to circumvent a possible confiscation of the property? One would like to know more about the John Robinson, who was later to be mentioned in Shakespeare's will as 'dwelling' in the house, and may have rented from him one or more of its rooms.

Shakespeare was present in the Globe (he was probably on stage) when, three months later, on 29 June 1613 during a performance of *Henry VIII*, a cannon fired from an upper gallery set fire to the straw thatching of the roof and rapidly spread to consume the whole building. As one of the theatre's original 'householders', he contributed his share to the cost of its reconstruction; it was open again by 30 June 1614 – exactly a year later. Also in 1613, he collaborated with Richard Burbage in the making of an *impresa*, a painted chivalric device with appropriate motto, for the Earl of Rutland to bear in a tourney at court in celebration of the King's accession. And though there are indications during these years of visits to Stratford of the kind he had been accustomed to make throughout his career, there is no evidence of any protracted stay. According to one account, it was in London that he caught the fever from which he was to die. When, in 1709, Rowe claimed that Shakespeare's last years were spent at Stratford in 'Ease, Retirement, and the Conversation of his Friends . . . as all Men of good Sense will wish theirs may be', he was simply transposing into Shakespeare's biography what he and similarly placed men of his time regarded as a desirable close to a lifetime of literary endeavour. He had no conception or understanding of Shakespeare as a player who, however fulfilled as poet and dramatist he may then have been, would still have been committed to the continuing life of his plays on the stage.

During the long shut-down of the London theatres, lasting from July 1608 to 1610, the company would necessarily have been solely occupied in court entertainment and travel. *Pericles* had first been performed at the Globe in the early summer of 1608. When, at the end of July, the weekly death toll from plague rose to 50 and proceeded inexorably upwards, the players would have lost no time in preparing to tour – if they were not already planning to do so. But the horrors of the plague are likely to have been brought home to them in a more personal way by the passing of their old comrade, William Sly. Latterly, Sly had lived in Cripplegate as a lodger in the family home of Robert Browne of German fame, from where he was buried at St Leonard's, Shoreditch, on 14 August. That his death was sudden and unexpected we know from the fact that only five days earlier he had joined with his fellows in purchasing a share in the new Blackfriars playhouse, and that his will was nuncupative (declared orally) and signed only with a mark. (There were 79 plague deaths in the City that week.)

News of his mother's decline would have reached Shakespeare by early August when he and his fellows were planning their autumn tour; it may well have been instrumental in taking them in the direction of Stratford. Mary Shakespeare – now in her late sixties or early seventies – is a shadowy figure in the background of Shakespeare's life. Is there perhaps a trace of her character in the Countess of *All's Well* or Volumnia? In creating these strong but compassionate women, he clearly had a model in mind, and it is more than likely to have been his mother. Whether he was able to be at her bedside when she died in the first week of September, or to accompany her coffin to Stratford churchyard for burial on the

9th, we do not know; but that the company was in Warwickshire about this time is documented. Provincial records for the period are as usual sparse and mostly uncertain. The only exact date we have is for Coventry on 29 October, where, in the great St Mary's Guildhall, *Pericles* would have found an ideally spacious, medieval setting. A visit to Marlborough in Wiltshire (dated in an accounting period ending 9 December 1608) must also belong to this year.[4]

Twelve plays, almost certainly including *Pericles*, were given at court in the Christmas season of 1608/9. In 1609, while plague continued to rage unabated in London, the company were at Ipswich on 9 May, receiving their customary reward of 26*s* 8*d*; and that despite a civic ordinance of the previous year that 'Noe freeman or their servants or apprentises shall resort to any Playes to be holden within this Town under perill of fforfaiture for every offence, 12*d*.' Evidently, the King's men were made an exception, and from this time forward only companies with royal patrons were allowed, and in some years none at all.[5] The Protestant Puritan party which, in the course of the coming decades, was to close all the English provincial guildhalls to the players, and by 1642 the London playhouses also, was already gaining power in the towns and starting to exert its baleful influence. From Ipswich, the players would have travelled by boat around the coast to the port of Hythe in Kent, where they performed on 16 May, and at New Romney on the following day.[6] Further visits, dated only by fiscal year, which may thus refer either to the latter part of 1609 (from Michaelmas) or to the first nine months of 1610, are recorded in indeterminate order at Oxford, Shrewsbury, Stafford and the little town of Sudbury in Suffolk. They were back in London, however, for Christmas 1609/10, giving thirteen plays for the King and royal family 'in the tyme of the holidayes and afterwardes'.[7] It is probable that *Cymbeline* was one of them.

We know that the Globe was open again in the spring of 1610 because the visiting Prince Lewis Frederick of Württemberg saw a performance of *Othello* there on 30 April.[8] Plague deaths in that year remained about or below 20 a week until the beginning of July when, to general dismay, they rose to 38, and upwards thereafter to a peak of 99 in the final week of August. Once more the theatres closed, and the company resumed their travels until Christmas 1610/11, when they were back at Whitehall performing fifteen plays. By then, though they were not to know it at the time, the worst of the plague was over, and it was not to return in any significant way during the remainder of Shakespeare's life.

For 1611 we are fortunate to have two more detailed reports from London: one made by a quack doctor named Simon Forman of his visits to the Globe in the early summer, and a Revels account of the plays at court between 1 November 1611 and 23 February 1612.[9] From these we learn that after the usual Lenten closure, the Globe reopened for an Easter season in late March or early April, during which *Macbeth* and *Cymbeline* were performed, and that, by the following Christmas, *The Winter's Tale*, *The Tempest*, and *The Two Noble Kinsmen* (to which Shakespeare may have contributed scenes) had been added to the company's repertoire. From Easter 1610, the Blackfriars playhouse would also have been available to the players, though that too would have been closed by the plague during the latter part of the year until Easter 1611. As noted already, between April 1611 and June 1613, when the players had two London theatres at their disposal – one indoors, one outdoors, for all kinds of weather – and the threat of the plague had finally receded, they continued to embark on extensive, countrywide tours, which puts paid to the myth that the company only travelled out of London when driven by the plague. In 1611, they are included in a general entry as having visited Shrewsbury. In 1612, they were back at New Romney (on 21 April) and at Winchester, and between Michaelmas 1612 and Michaelmas 1613, at Oxford, Folkestone, Stafford and Shrewsbury – we do not know in what order.[10]

— ★ —

The transition between the tragedies and Shakespeare's last romances is, as Chambers puts it, 'not an evolution but a revolution'.[11] It is a near total change of emphasis from the negative aspects of human nature to the positive; from the deadly sins of pride, self-absorption, ruthless ambition, envy, false conceptions of honour and of bounty – leading to death and despair – to the healing virtues of patience, fidelity, contrition and forgiveness – leading to reconciliation and hope. That of course is too simple. The denouements of *Lear*, *Macbeth* and *Antony and Cleopatra* are far from being wholly pessimistic; a kind of human splendour shines out from the fall of their flawed heroes. 'Ripeness', we are told in *Lear*, 'is all'. There is an ultimate victory of good over evil – however arbitrary it may sometimes appear. Nor do the final comedies blink at man's potentialities for evil or self-destruction; but their final message is very different, echoing Julian of Norwich; that whatever disasters people may bring upon themselves and others, or fate may have in store for them, 'All thing shall be well . . . Thou shalt see thyself that all manner thing shall be well'.[12] Stylistically, the change from *Coriolanus* to *Pericles* is as great as that between *Love's Labour's Lost* and *Romeo and Juliet*, or *Richard II* and *Henry IV*.

Pericles, as I have said, survives only in a pirated, plainly corrupted text – omitted from the First Folio presumably because its editors were unable to trace a better. And yet we know the play was a great success when first produced in its original form in 1608; and, when further London performances were prevented by the plague, the pirated text appeared in a record number of printed quartos – three before Shakespeare's death in 1616, and a further three between then and 1635. Late in 1608, there was published moreover a prose version of the story, based in part on Shakespeare's play by George Wilkins, as today a successful film is often followed by a 'book of the film', in obvious response to popular demand. Wilkins' treatment carries the title of 'The Painfull Adventures of Pericles Prince of Tyre. Being the true History of the Play of Pericles, as it was lately presented by the worthy and ancient Poet John Gower', and is accompanied by a woodcut of Gower, which I believe may be a portrait of Shakespeare in that role. If so, it would, of course, be unique as a representation of him in action as a player. That he played the role is (to my own mind at least) beyond doubt. I have already written of his fondness for the old English poets, and Gower would have been familiar to him, not only from his published verse, but from his tomb in Southwark, where he is shown reclining with his head resting on a pile of his books (Plate 8), and from which, in the opening speech of the play, he is imagined as rising.

> To sing a song that old was sung,
> From ashes ancient Gower is come,
> Assuming man's infirmities,
> To glad your ear, and please your eyes.

It is another, and one of the best, of Shakespeare's presenter roles, and the archaism of the rhyming couplets that he speaks is, of course, a deliberate impersonation of Gower – not, perhaps, without a touch of affectionate satire. It may be this assumed manner of speech – along with the simplicity of the play's story-telling and the rarity of its stage productions until comparatively recent times – that has led scholars into theories of multiple authorship (once so fashionable in respect of his earlier work) in which the best of the scenes are attributed to Shakespeare and the rest to some other less accomplished hand or hands. But having both directed and acted in the play, I can only say that no such division of authorship is apparent on closer acquaintance, and in almost every scene one finds images, characters and snatches of dialogue that have Shakespeare's unique impress upon them:

> The blind mole casts
> Copp'd hills towards heaven, to tell the earth is throng'd
> By man's oppression, and the poor worm doth die for't.
> (I.i.101–3)

The wise old counsellor, Helicanus (a beautiful part for Heminges) in an exchange with Pericles in a rare moment of anger:

Pericles: Helicanus
        Thou hast mov'd us; what seest thou in our looks?
Helicanus: An angry brow, dread lord.
Pericles: If there be such a dart in princes' frowns,
        How durst thy tongue move anger to our face?
Helicanus: How dares the plants look up to heaven, from whence
        They have their nourishment?
Pericles: Thou know'st I have power
        To take thy life from thee.
Helicanus: I have ground the axe myself;
        Do you but strike the blow.
                            (I.ii.51–9)

And the humour of the three down-to-earth but kindly

Fishermen who find and succour Pericles when he has been cast ashore after shipwreck:

> *Fisherman 3*: Master, I marvel how the fishes live in the sea.
> *Fisherman 1*: Why, as men do a-land: the great ones eat up the little ones. I can compare our rich misers to nothing so fitly as to a whale: a' plays and tumbles, driving the poor fry before him, and at last devours them all at a mouthful. Such whales have I heard on a'th' land, who never leave gaping till they swallow'd the whole parish, church, steeple, bells and all. (II.i.26–34)

– all three examples from the first two acts, which are generally denied to Shakespeare.

I said earlier of *Timon of Athens* that the most likely reason for its remaining unfinished is that the Globe, for which it was planned, was closed by the plague; that it had missed its moment. That may have been true but is not, I think, the whole explanation. It is possible also that in the course of writing *Timon*, Shakespeare tired of its protagonist's imprecations upon a corrupt and ungrateful world, and felt the need to refresh his spirit in that other world of folk-tale and myth from which he had already drawn in *All's Well* and *Measure for Measure*, but had never as yet wholly succeeded in reconciling with his more realist aims of holding the mirror up to nature and the complexities of human personality and behaviour. For *Pericles*, while starting from a situation of impending degradation and evil, soon escapes with its hero into the story of an epic journey encompassing the Mediterranean world of its time – vaguely that of the post-classical, early Middle Ages.

Pericles' fortunes rise and fall. He marries a king's daughter and has a child by her he names Marina, but his wife is thought to have died in giving birth to her during a storm at sea, and in course of time Marina is lost to him also. But he is the antithesis of Timon in that in face of all the disasters that befall him, he refuses to be overcome or embittered by them. At the climax of an earlier storm that has wrecked his ship and cast him ashore, he has a speech that recalls Lear but also marks a significant

difference in their respective attitudes to the forces of nature that
threaten them both:

> Yet cease your ire, you angry stars of heaven!
> Wind, rain, and thunder, remember, earthly man
> Is but a substance that must yield to you;
> And I, as fits my nature, do obey you . . .

> Let it suffice the greatness of your powers
> To have bereft a prince of all his fortunes;
> And having thrown him from your wat'ry grave,
> Here to have death in peace is all he'll crave.
>
> (II.i.1–11)

– this again from the supposedly non-Shakespearean second act.
But no one, so far as I am aware, has sought to deny Shakespeare
the final act of the play in which all that Pericles has seemingly
lost is restored to him, with its beautiful and moving recognition
scene on board a ship at anchor, in which he and Marina find
each other again.

> O Helicanus, strike me, honour'd sir!
> Give me a gash, put me to present pain,
> Let this great sea of joys rushing upon me
> O'erbear the shores of my mortality,
> And drown me with their sweetness. O, come hither,
> Thou that beget'st him that did thee beget;
> Thou wast born at sea, buried at Tharsus,
> And found at sea again. O Helicanus,
> Down on thy knees! thank the holy gods as loud
> As thunder threatens us: this is Marina.
>
> (V.1.190–9)

The story is very old, deriving from that of Apollonius of Tyre,
but it is Gower's version of it in his *Confessio Amantis* that
Shakespeare gives us, with interesting correspondences to the
medieval Saints' play of *Mary Magdalene*. Shakespeare's original
contribution is in his introduction of the themes of patience,
redemption through suffering, loss and recovery, which was to set
the keynote for his later romances.[13] The text abounds in verbal

obscurities, irregularities of rhythm and rhyme, mislineation, prose printed as verse and verse as prose – mainly arising from its having been 'reported', that is to say, surreptitiously taken down in a form of shorthand by a publisher's nark during one of its first performances at the Globe in 1608. The wonder is that so much that is good has been preserved.

Of its eighteen named roles (five of them female) and some dozen other speaking parts, only Pericles and Helicanus continue through the whole of the action, the rest being confined to particular scenes or sections of the play, which makes it readily amenable to doubling. As Pericles, Burbage would have been mature for the dashing young prince of the first three acts, but perfectly cast in the fourth, with Condell perhaps doubling the two kings of contrasting character, the evil Antiochus of Act 1 with the affable Simonides of Act 2, and Armin as Fisherman and Bawd.

The sea is never far away in the play; nor is the sound of music which, as in a similar situation in *Lear*, accompanies Pericles' awakening from a near-fatal lethargy. I would like to see it performed in an amphitheatre open to the sky and, if possible, near to the sea. It is a play for the summer.

The first recorded performance of *Cymbeline* was that seen by Forman at the Globe before September 1611, probably in April of that year; but the consensus of recent scholarly opinion accords with that of Chambers in putting its composition two years earlier in 1608/9. Though intended for the Globe, it could not have been performed there until 1610 at the earliest. The probability is that it was premiered during the long tour of 1609/10, and acted at court in the Christmas season of 1609.[14]

It is an extraordinary play that has evoked wildly variant responses from the critics, ranging from Dr Johnson's – that though it has 'many just sentiments, some natural dialogues, and some pleasing scenes',

> they are obtained at the expense of much incongruity. To remark the folly of the fiction, the absurdity of the conduct, the confusion of the names, and manners of different times, and the impossibility of the events in any system of life, were to waste criticism upon unresisting imbecility, upon faults too evident for detection, and too gross for aggravation –

to Hazlitt's 'one of the most delightful of Shakespeare's historical plays', and Swinburne's rhapsodical praise of Imogen as 'woman above all Shakespeare's women . . . the woman best beloved in all the world of song and all the tide of time'.[15]

The plot of *Cymbeline* is put together by Shakespeare from an incongruous selection of historical, pseudo-historical, and fictional sources including Geoffrey of Monmouth, Holinshed and Boccaccio's *Decameron*. It has a strongly fairy-tale atmosphere. There is an intemperate king (Cymbeline), practised upon by a malign, hypocritical Queen, stepmother to Imogen, Cymbeline's only daughter; a flawed hero in Posthumus whom Imogen has married in defiance of her father's wishes, and who is banished in consequence; the story of Posthumus' wager in Rome with a smooth, Italian villain named Iachimo on the question of Imogen's chastity, with unfortunate consequences that take up most of Act 2; an appropriately named boaster called Cloten, son to the Queen by a previous marriage, whom the King had wanted Imogen to marry; a tale of two princes, Cymbeline's sons, stolen as infants from the cradle, growing up in a cave in the Welsh mountains unaware of their true identity, thinking the man who has brought them up, a banished lord named Belarius, to be their father – and quite a lot more. The scene shifts between Cymbeline's palace, Rome, and the Welsh mountains, and the whole is set in a context of political strife between Britain and Rome, culminating in a Roman invasion. One point that all the critics and commentators agree upon is that it is very entertaining. And at the centre of it all is the courageous, faithful Imogen – the truest and most appealing of the many fine roles that Shakespeare created for his boy actors.

His own role, of course, would have been that of the King. Who else at this time might have undertaken it? For though the company's original apprentices would by now have been in their twenties and thirties, and there were plenty of young recruits to take their places – Ostler, Underwood and Field among them – there are no recorded replacements for the older men, and with the loss of Pope, Phillips and Sly, those who were left would have been hard-pressed to cover all the more mature parts in the plays. As a player, Shakespeare would have been more valuable to the company in this period of its history than perhaps ever before. Posthumus needs to be more of an age with Imogen, and would

have gone to one of the younger men – perhaps Field (Plate 17).
With Lowin as Iachimo, Condell as Pisanio, Armin doubling as
Cloten and the First Gaoler, and Heminges as Jupiter in
Posthumus' vision, Burbage would have been most valuably
employed as Belarius who, having previously abducted the King's
sons, returns with them in Act 4 to save the British cause from
defeat.

In spite of its moments of near-tragedy and horror, the play
has more humour in it than may appear on the page, and the
smiles that greet the more improbable coincidences of the final
scene, as Shakespeare weaves his magic in bringing the play's
disparate elements into a coherent unity, would not, I think, have
surprised or displeased him. The scene is one of his most brilliant
technical achievements. But what gradually arises in the audience
is not just admiration for the dramatist's skill but also a
deepening sense of genuine wonder: that out of such a mishmash
of mixed intentions, disordered emotions and strange events, the
good and the just should be seen to prevail.

The Winter's Tale, deriving as it does in the main from a prose
romance by Robert Greene first published in 1588, is a more
simply organised, co-ordinated play than *Cymbeline*; but, as its
title suggests, explores the same territory of folk-tale and
romance. It has many parallels with *Pericles*: at the centre of both,
there is a wide gap of time in which infants grow up; in each, a
ruler believes mistakenly his wife to be dead, and there is a royal
daughter, separated from her father, who is finally reunited with
him.[16] Shakespeare's themes, as in all his plays of the period, are
of the loss of harmony through human frailty and sin; its recovery
by means of an acceptance of suffering, and sincere contrition; of
death and regeneration. All this is worked out in terms of the
play's theatrical life on the stage, in which music and dance play a
prominent role. The rhythms and texture of the verse, and the
imagery that it employs, affect the auditors' emotions at a deep,
subliminal level. However improbable the stories may appear on
the page, they are peopled by men and women of real flesh and
blood. Leontes, King of Sicilia, is jealous of his wife, Hermione's
affection for his friend and guest Polixenes, King of Bohemia.
Jealousy in Shakespeare's plays is nearly always murderous.
Leontes commands Camillo, one of his lords, to poison
Polixenes, but Camillo warns the intended victim and procures

his escape. Hermione is imprisoned and gives birth to a daughter, whom Leontes orders should be taken to some desert place, beyond his dominions, and there abandoned. The story of Hermione's vindication and her seeming death, of Leontes' repentance and the eventual restoration to him of both his wife and the daughter, Perdita, he had abandoned, must be left to the playgoer to enjoy in the theatre. It is a beautiful play that carries the audience with it every step of the way – I would say a perfect one if there were not an even better to come.

Probably written in the latter part of 1610, it was seen by Forman at the Globe on 15 May 1611 and performed at court on 5 November of that year, having been toured to Shrewsbury and doubtless other towns west. Like *Pericles*, it has eighteen named roles (six of them female) but offers less scope for doubling. If, as I have previously suggested, Burbage played Ford in the *Merry Wives* and Othello, he would have been on familiar ground with Leontes, and brought to it the passion and commitment the character demands. There is no immediately obvious part for Shakespeare – or rather, there are several that might have been his, and we must make a difficult choice between them. Polixenes is of an age with Leontes, and this, of course, would not have been the first occasion when Burbage and he had played together as kings. The small chorus role of Time is another possibility as standing, both in character and function, apart from the rest of the action. Carrying an hourglass, he introduces the second half of the play (Acts 4 and 5), speaking antique rhyming couplets reminiscent of Gower, announcing a lapse in time of sixteen years. It offers a nostalgic indulgence in theatrical cliché Shakespeare would have enjoyed, and the speech has several allusions that hint at a parallel identity for the speaker as author:

> Your patience this allowing,
> I turn my glass, and give *my scene* such growing
> As you had slept between . . .
> A shepherd's daughter,
> And what to her adheres, which follows after,
> Is *th' argument* of Time.

But Time is not the only character to use imagery deriving from the drama. Camillo, the wise old man who serves in turn both

Leontes and Polixenes as counsellor, tells Florizel, Polixenes' son and Perdita's lover, when contriving their flight together,

> it shall so be my care
> To have you royally appointed, as if
> *The scene you play were mine.*   (IV.iv.592–4)

And a little later, Perdita responds to his advice to disguise herself with,

> I see the play so lies
> That I must bear a part.   (655–6)

Camillo, the fourth largest role with 300 lines, opens the play with a visiting Bohemian lord and is there (largely silent) at the end. It is one of Shakespeare's 'old man' roles, and also bears the character of a benevolent contriver in the mould of Friar Laurence and the Duke of *Measure for Measure*. When we look at the likeliest allocation of other principal parts, we find it supports this casting, for Polixenes requires little more than kingly bearing and authority which Condell would have been able to supply, and Time would have fitted what little we know of Cowley's ecentric but more limited talents. Heminges is usually relegated to a solely managerial function in this later period of the company's history on the basis of a report (in a popular ballad) of his being distressed and 'stuttering' when the Globe burnt down in 1613; but if a man is not allowed to show distress and stutter when a theatre in which he has just been acting and has a substantial financial stake, burns down before his eyes without being judged as 'past it' as an actor, it would be a poor outlook for a good many of us! The Old Shepherd who finds Perdita as a baby and brings her up as his daughter would have been an excellent part for him. With Armin as his clownish son and Lowin as the roguish pedlar Autolycus, all the senior men would thus have been well used. The two mature women's parts (Hermione and her doughty friend and ally Paulina) would probably have gone to Tooley and Cooke, and there remains scope for both the older apprentices and hired men in doubling the various Lords and Gentlemen, and for the younger recruits as Mamillius (Leontes' young son who dies of grief for his mother),

Perdita and her sister shepherdesses, with Field perhaps as Florizel.

I said earlier that in writing these final plays Shakespeare was feeling his way to a more consistent reconciliation of the folkloric material that had always attracted him (now more than ever) with his other, realist aims of fidelity to nature and psychological truth and, if we read the plays in sequence, we see evidence of his growing confidence in achieving just that. The process culminates in *The Tempest*, which can make good claim to be his most beautifully constructed play. Its earliest recorded performance was at court at Hallowmas (1 November) before the King in 1611,[17] but there is nothing to suggest that this was its premiere – though it may have been. In the best of conditions, first nights are chancy, nervous occasions, and in 1611 *The Tempest* was to open the season. In the busy banqueting hall at Whitehall where the play was given, there cannot have been much time or opportunity to rehearse. Without previews or follow-up performances, when faults could be corrected or the staging improved, this, like nearly all Shakespeare's court performances, was a one-off affair before the company's patron, who was also of course the King. Instinct and experience tell me that the players would have made very sure they were well practised to cope with any emergencies or unforeseen responses and that here, as on prior occasions of a similar kind, the play had been premiered elsewhere – perhaps on the Shrewsbury tour of that year and possibly also in private performance at Blackfriars, which at last was available to use by the company.

The Tempest is too well known to require more than a sentence or two of description. The action begins with a shipwreck – echoing those of *Pericles* and the *Winter's Tale* – in which a party of noblemen including Antonio, usurping Duke of Milan, and his ally the King of Naples are cast on the shore of a remote island whch they believe to be uninhabited. But here, as we learn in the second scene, Prospero, the rightful ruler of Milan, is already in occupation with his daughter Miranda, and is responsible for having raised the tempest by use of the magical power he has acquired in exile to bring those who had usurped his duchy, and consigned him and his infant daughter to the mercies of the sea twelve years before, within reach of his vengeance. These events, that at an earlier period of Shakespeare's writing would probably have occupied an act at least in chronicle form, he here condenses into a duologue between Prospero and the now twelve-year-old Miranda (of which Prospero has by far the greater part) that recapitulates the past and brings it on stage in the most masterly way. As Roy Walker has written of the Peter Brook production in the 1950s, which he describes as a breakthrough in theatrical understanding of the play, 'the brief opening scene on a ship heaving wildly in a storm at sea became the image of a storm in the mind of a man who has suffered notorious wrong and nursed his anger through long years of exile on bitter fantasies of superhuman revenge'.[18]

So much for the initial situation of disharmony and loss. The action that follows is a profound meditation on the conflict of good and evil – both in the souls of men and human affairs – expressed in purely theatrical terms. As such, it defies interpretation of the allegorical or symbolical kind which so many critics (and some directors) have attempted to impose on it. Of all Shakespeare's plays, it makes the most insistent call to be seen and heard for what it is rather than 'read' for what it represents; it represents only itself, and we should be more than content with that. And yet all the themes I have mentioned as filling Shakespeare's mind in these last romances are here: loss of harmony and its recovery, the final victories of forgiveness over revenge, love over hate, life over death. If taken at this spiritual level throughout – as I am sure that it was under Shakespeare's firm hand as 'instructor' – 'questions of credibility are not answered, they simply never arise. This is a contest of ape and essence for possession of a man's soul, played out like a master-game of chess. The final disclosure of Ferdinand and Miranda at chess becomes . . . a summing of what has been happening throughout . . . the war-game has ended in a love-match'.[19]

Though it was once supposed that by Prospero's breaking of his magician's staff and drowning of his book, as well as by his epilogue –

> Now my charms are all o'erthrown,
> And what strength I have's mine own,
> Which is most faint . . .

> As you from crimes would pardon'd be,
> Let your indulgence set me free.

– Shakespeare was signalling his retirement from the stage, it is virtually certain that the part was played by Burbage; his own role was probably that of Alonso, King of Naples, whose grief at what he believes to be the loss of his son Ferdinand in the wreck is poignantly expressed in his silences and refusal to be comforted. 'You cram these words into mine ears against/The stomach of my sense', he complains in his one substantial speech in this earlier part of the play.

> O thou mine heir
> Of Naples and of Milan, what strange fish
> Hath made his meal on thee? (II.i.102–9)

With little more than a hundred lines, he is there as usual at both beginning and end. It was another of Shakespeare's kingly roles. The play is remarkable (among many things) for the originality of the two semi-human creatures Shakespeare invents as ministers of Prospero's magic. Ariel is described as an 'airy spirit'; Caliban as a 'salvage and deformed slave'. King and courtiers are not the only survivors of the tempest. Stephano is a 'drunken butler' and his companion, Trinculo, a professional jester. And one of Shakespeare's master strokes is to keep all three groups – Prospero and Miranda, the usurping duke and his party, and the two comic servants – apart from each other until the final act. With Ariel, Miranda, Ferdinand, and the masqueing spirits going to apprentices or hired men, there would have been little need for doubling. I see Condell as Antonio, Lowin as Caliban, and Cowley as Stephano. There is another charming 'old man' part for Heminges in Gonzalo and, in Trinculo, a last and very funny jester for Armin.

Like *Pericles*, the play is never far from the sea, nor from the sounds of music, for as Caliban explains,

> the isle is full of noises,
> Sounds and sweet airs, that give delight, and hurt not.
> Sometimes a thousand twangling instruments

Will hum about mine ears; and sometimes voices,
That, if I then had wak'd after long sleep,
Will make me sleep again . . .   (III.ii.133–8)

There is little more to be said of Shakespeare's final years with the company. As a writer, he was apparently content to let his younger colleagues – notably John Fletcher – have their day in supplying the new plays that would still have been required. He was roped in, however, to contribute to *Henry VIII* (first recorded in performance on the occasion of the destruction of the first Globe in June 1613) and *The Two Noble Kinsmen*, which may date from the latter part of that year. But there is not the slightest indication that he had ceased to act; nor is there any sign in the actor lists or other records of the company during these years of the introduction of an actor of comparable age and experience who could have taken over his customary roles in those earlier plays of his we know to have been still in the repertoire or revived in the period: *Macbeth* in 1611; *Much Ado About Nothing, The Tempest, The Winter's Tale, Henry IV, Othello* and *Julius Caesar* – all revived in 1613 as part of the festivities surrounding the marriage of Princess Elizabeth to the Elector Palatine.

I say he had been roped in to contribute scenes to *Henry VIII* but it may have been he who did the roping in; for if we look at the particular scenes that have been most usually attributed to him (I.i and ii; II.iii and iv; III.ii to line 203; and V.i) we find that all but two feature Wolsey and, in sum, contain nearly all of that role, and certainly the best of it. With Burbage as Buckingham and Lowin as Henry (in which we are told by a Restoration writer he was instructed by Shakespeare) he was the obvious choice to play the Cardinal. And having agreed to do so, might he not also have felt, with justification, that he could produce some rather better lines to speak than Fletcher had been able to do, and gone on to rewrite, not only his own lines as Wolsey, but the whole of the scenes in which he appeared – and one or two others as well? Fletcher was adept at rhetorical speeches, but was he as good as this?

Nay then, farewell!
I have touched the highest point of all my greatness,
And from that full meridian of my glory

I haste now to my setting. I shall fall
Like a bright exhalation in the evening,
And no man see me more.   (III.ii.222–7)

Similar questions arise in relation to the *Two Noble Kinsmen*, though here the division of scenes between the two authors appears to have been more deliberately planned. But again we notice that those scenes generally attributed to Shakespeare (the whole of Act I; III.i; and V.i, iii and iv) contain the most and the best of a particular character – Theseus, Duke of Athens; but, in this instance, it is not only the one most likely to have been played by Shakespeare (he is 'kingly', present from the start, speaks the closing lines, and is of optimum size) but one he had played before in *Midsummer Night's Dream*, where he had been accompanied, as here, by Hippolyta, queen of the Amazons and his wife to be.

The company continued to tour. In 1614, they were back in Coventry, and in April 1615 were recorded in Nottingham,[20] which, so far as we know (and that is very little), was the furthest north they were ever to travel. I see no reason whatever to doubt that Shakespeare was as usual in company with his fellows, playing his usual parts in their recent successes. Though none of their titles were recorded, they performed seven plays at court in the holiday season of 1613/14, sixteen in 1614/15, and a further fifteen in 1615/16. Many of these, of course, would have been revivals.

It was probably in November or December of 1615 that Shakespeare gave instructions for the drafting of his will. This is generally assumed to have been executed in Stratford by the Warwick solicitor, Francis Collins, but the handwriting remains to be positively identified and may belong instead to any number of others including Collins' clerk and Shakespeare himself; nor do we have any evidence as to where it was written. If Shakespeare had summoned Collins for the purpose, it is more likely to have been to London, where he would then have been working, than to Stratford. As Shakespeare attests in the opening preamble that he is in 'perfect health & memorie god be praysed', there are no grounds for believing that he was ill at the time.

The holiday season at court extended that winter from 1 November 1615 to 12 February 1616 (Shrove Tuesday, the last

day before Lent), with a final performance on 1 April (Easter
Monday). According to John Ward, who was Vicar of Stratford
from 1662 to 1681 – just early enough to have met Shakespeare's
younger daughter Judith before her death at the age of seventy-
seven – and writing nearly half a century before Rowe,
'Shakespear, Drayton, and Ben Jhonson, had a merry meeting,
and itt seems drank too hard, for Shakespear died of a feavour
there contracted'.[21] Such a meeting could only, of course, have
occurred in London, and it was just of the kind that we might
expect a group of theatre friends and colleagues to enjoy together
at the conclusion of a busy season. As such, it may well have
taken place on the evening of Shrove Tuesday or quite shortly
afterwards. Shakespeare had probably intended to return to
Stratford for the first few weeks of Lent, as was his custom, and
the fever would have hurried him home. Did John Robinson, his
lodger at Blackfriars, seeing his state of health, accompany him?
It would be good to think so, and certainly someone of that name
was present in Stratford a few weeks later to witness his will. It
was not until 25 March that Collins was summoned to the
bedside to make those amendments to the earlier draft
consequent upon Judith's marriage to the Stratford vintner
Thomas Quiney in the previous month. A need for some haste at
that point is indicated by the use of the draft for all but the first of
the will's three pages, with small corrections and additions being
made between the lines. Shakespeare's bequests of money to
John Heminges, Richard Burbage and Henry Condell – whom he
describes as 'my ffellowes', not *former* fellows – to buy them rings,
remain unaltered. When, on 1 April, his old company came
together in London to give the final performance of the season
for the King at Whitehall, their thoughts would all have been with
him. He was to linger on for another three weeks, and died on his
birthday, 23 April. He was just fifty-two.

THIRTEEN

The Man Shakespeare

Shakespeare was the least of an egotist it was possible to be. He was nothing in himself; but he was all that others were, or that they could become. He not only had in himself the germs of every faculty and feeling, but he could follow them by anticipation, intuitively, into all their conceivable ramifications, through every change of fortune, or conflict of passion, or turn of thought. He had 'a mind reflecting ages past', and present . . . He had only to think of anything in order to become that thing, with all the circumstances belonging to it.

William Hazlitt, 1818[1]

When, in the 1890s, the historian William Cory visited Wilton House, home of the earls of Pembroke, he was told of the letter that an earlier Lady Pembroke had written to her son, asking him to bring James I from Salisbury to see *As You Like It*, and telling him 'we have the man Shakespeare with us'; a curious expression if we did not know that by 'man' in this context was meant an actor as Shakespeare had been first a 'Chamberlain's man' and then a 'King's man', for this is how he was generally known in his time. In 1592, Chettle was to speak of him as 'exelent in the qualitie he professes', and 'qualitie' in such a context was used of the *acting* profession. In 1602, when York Herald challenged the grant to his father and himself by Garter King-of-Arms of a coat of arms and the right to call themselves gentlemen, it was on the grounds that the author of some two dozen of the finest plays in the English language, including *Romeo and Juliet*, *Henry V* and *Hamlet*, was merely a player, as a sketch in his notes of the arms in question, with the words 'Shakespeare the Player' underneath them, makes abundantly clear.[2]

In the first chapter we discovered how – precisely as player – he was to remain invisible to so many of his contemporaries, and especially the literary establishment of his day to whom, if he was known at all, it was chiefly as 'sweet Mr Shakespeare', the author of *Venus and Adonis* and the Sonnets. But how *much* of a player was he, and how important was the fact of his profession to *him*? It will be clear from the preceding chapters that it took up a very great deal of his time and his life, and was important enough for him to have abandoned a promising career as narrative and lyric poet, aiming at publication, in order to pursue this other profession, devoting all his energies to the writing, production and performance of plays for the looked-down-upon public theatres of his day. For the three activities hung together, and I doubt that he ever stopped to distinguish them in his own mind, or to think of his acting career as separate from his writing career, or his writing and acting careers as separate from his responsibilities for their production and the 'instruction' of his fellows. He was not, as generally envisaged and presented by academic authors, a great dramatist who did some acting on the side; he was not a university, part-time or amateur actor, happy enough to indulge himself on the stage for a few months, or even for one or two years, in order to gain experience before getting on with the serious business of life, which, in his case, is assumed to have been the writing of plays; but a full-time, wholly committed, professional player and man of the theatre for whom the text of a play was not an end in itself (like any other book) but a means to an end – a performance on stage with himself as author, enabler and player. Contrary to Rowe's unfounded assertion, and the statements of those who have accepted it at face value, he was not a dramatist who became an actor for a time and, having made his pile, gave it up to enjoy rural retirement and the 'Conversation of his Friends', but an actor who became a dramatist, and never stopped performing, even after he had stopped writing plays, until fatal illness intervened.

He was not unique in that total commitment. I have presented him in his dual capacity of Player Poet as heir to an ancient European tradition of performing poets and minstrels; but we could find his fellows also among the great dramatists of classical Greece and Rome who were equally involved in the staging and performance of their works, and doubtless those in other periods and cultures who, like him, were written down in their own time on account of that involvement as 'merely players'. Nor was he unique in this respect among his contemporaries. Among Shakespeare's fellows, Robert Armin and Nathan Field are both known to have written and published successful plays and, among the dramatists, Jonson – possibly Marlowe also – spent some years as players. But the man whose career parallels that of Shakespeare most nearly is Thomas Heywood, a prolific and popular dramatist whose distinguished career as a player can be traced in the records between 1598 and 1619, but who, as late as 1640, was told in an epigram that 'grovelling on the stage' did not become his then advanced years.[3] 'Grovelling' was how the literati of his time thought about acting, and how many of their successors have continued to think until comparatively recent times (some still do). Little wonder then that Shakespeare's first biographers had so little to say about his acting, and contrived his entrance into that profession as late as possible and his exit from it as early as possible.

It was not so much the activity of acting itself that presented such people with a problem, but the fact that it was done for money (hence the 'grovelling'); that Shakespeare and his fellows were professionals. Shakespeare's professionalism is summed up in his title and status of 'sharer'. It is a concept that, even today, some academics find hard to take hold of. It means, of course, that he shared in the profits of the enterprise – so much is clear; but it also implies a willingness to share in its work – in every aspect of its work; and if he was allowed, indeed encouraged, by reason of his immense contributions as author and instructor, to take a somewhat smaller part in the performance of the plays than his gifts as a player would otherwise have merited, that is not to say that he would ever have expected to be excused from involvement altogether; or, more importantly, would have *wanted* to be so excused. Nor, as has been seriously proposed, would he have been left at home to write another masterpiece while his fellows slogged their way around the country earning the company's bread. Nor would he have *wanted* to be!

How *good* a player was he, and how good were his fellows? For the answer to both questions, we only need to look again at Shakespeare's professionalism. He would only have cast himself in certain parts if he had felt his talents as a player were equal to them – and his fellows agreed. He would not have written the parts that he did for his fellows if they were beyond their capacity to perform. Dramatists do not write good plays for bad or indifferent actors and, if they do, the results can only be disastrous for both: the better the play, the worse the result. Good actors and good direction can make a poor play appear much better than it is; bad or indifferent actors can only drag a good play down. One has sat through too many bad or inadequate performances of Shakespeare's plays to make any mistake about this. An unactable play is a bad play. Shakespeare was not writing for posterity, for some future generation of super-actors who would one day, hopefully, attain the skills his writing required, but for his fellows in the then and there: for Burbage, Cowley, Sly and the rest, and the results were put to the test in the immediate term. They were not found wanting. The 'devil of progress in the arts' would have it that what was seen on the stage of the Globe, or in the provincial guildhalls in which the company performed four hundred years ago, was necessarily inferior to what we might see today at Stratford or the National; but why should we believe it? The players were speaking in an idiom and at a pace much nearer to the rhythms of natural speech in their time than their modern successors, and in a style of verse to which both they and their audience were more thoroughly attuned. They were trained from an early age in the technical disciplines required; today they are not, and are too often left to pick them up for themselves wherever they can. The spaces in which they acted were generally more intimate (even when larger) than they are today, and the theatres more designed for hearing than seeing. Audiences, if less inhibited in expressing their approval and disapproval, were better and more practised listeners, and more practised also, perhaps, in using their imaginations.

I have said that actors develop with the parts they are given to play, and as they develop, the dramatist is encouraged to challenge them further. Burbage at twenty or thirty would not have been able to meet the challenge of Othello or Lear any more than Shakespeare would have been able to write those plays at a similar age. By the 1600s, they could and they did. They developed together, along with the rest of their fellows, in a unique theatrical partnership of poet and players.

So much for 'the man Shakespeare'. What of 'Shakespeare the man'? To see him, to try to understand him as a player, takes us some of the way in dispelling the invisibility that often surrounds him, but we have further to go before we can greet him as a fellow human being, and displace the myth. Players, though they have an indefinable something about them they recognise in each other, are as individually different in character and personality as the members of any other profession or craft. What kind of person was he? Gentle or forceful? Quietly confident in his own genius or restlessly ambitious? Extrovert or introvert? Religious or sceptical? A devoted husband or a bit of a rake?

Having come with me so far, year by year, through the various turns of Shakespeare's career, and the detailed history of the company of which he was a member for the final twenty years of his life, the reader may agree with me in saying that the characteristic that most impresses itself on one's mind is his apparently limitless energy. To write thirty-six plays of such variety, scope and achievement; to have at least a guiding hand – probably a decisive hand – in shaping their realisation on stage; acting in most, if not all of them, travelling hundreds of miles in each year to take them to halls large and small throughout the country; to build with his fellows their own theatre in London, to see it destroyed, and build it again within a year – is to leave one without any doubt whatsoever of his exceptional energy and commitment. It was, I believe, a contained energy, and a quiet but deep-seated commitment to the theatre he loved. I cannot imagine that he ever wasted his energy in shouting or railing to get what he wanted, however important he felt it to be. 'Some others raile', Davies tells us,

> but raile as they thinke fit
> Thou hast no rayling, but, a raigning Wit.

His plays are suffused with his wit – even the tragedies; the light that it throws flickers low in *Coriolanus* and goes out in *Timon*, but otherwise is always there. He was a naturally witty man, who liked always to see the humorous side of things, and was never over-solemn about his work or anything else. He had learnt how 'to care and not to care'.

'Shakespeare was the least of an egotist it was possible to

be . . . He had only to think of anything in order to become that thing, with all the circumstances belonging to it.' This, of course, is where his writing and acting joined hands: the ability to enter into his characters and by living within them, to give them life. In both, he was drawing on the same mental and intuitive resources, applying them in different ways. If I am not to be accused of attempting to pluck out the heart of his mystery, I must leave it there. It goes without saying that he was acutely sensitive to the people around him – endlessly curious, ever receptive of their thoughts, feelings and experiences, and all this acquired understanding, as well as what he could obtain from books, was fed into that fund of knowledge from which his creative imagination drew. He was in love with the English language.

We have Chettle's word (although at second hand) for his 'uprightness of dealing, which argues his honesty', and Aubrey's that 'he was not a company keeper' and 'wouldnt be debauched'. The distinction of his mind was, I believe, reflected in his outward manners and appearance in such a way as to make his casting as kings and royal personages almost inevitable, and to draw from John Davies the statement I have quoted that, were it not for his association with the stage, he might have been 'companion for a King' and 'King among the meaner sort'; the latter he surely was. He had the rare gift of 'presence' on stage.

But he was too good an actor to allow himself to become typecast in such roles, and contrived in his writing to give himself also parts such as Friar Laurence, Adam and Pandarus which enabled him to extend his acting range in a number of other directions. If, as we have seen, the one characteristic that all his roles hold in common is a certain detachment from the central action of the plays, the detachment lay in the plays' conceptual structure – providing time and opportunity to exercise his directorial function in their rehearsal – rather than his performance of them, which was as whole-hearted and committed as that of Burbage in *Hamlet* or *Lear*.

In religion, the invariably sympathetic treatment that he gives to the many friars and nuns who feature in the plays, and the detailed knowledge he betrays of their orders and ways of life – in striking contrast to his fellow dramatists (Marlowe and Greene in particular) who routinely hold them up to parody and ridicule – tells us that he was Catholic in his sympathies. Nor did he ever seek to conceal them – even from his royal patrons. Doubtless he obeyed the law when he had to; not otherwise. I see no reason to doubt the unequivocal statement by an Anglican minister of honest repute that 'He dyed a papist'.[4] To what degree he had lived as one, we have insufficient information to judge.

He was not a saint, and was not without faults, but we have no knowledge of what they were. We know that he was late in paying his rates, but so are a good many others for various reasons. He would not have been human had he not been tempted to mitigate the long periods of celibacy that he spent away from Anne – in London or elsewhere on his travels – by an occasional sexual adventure, but if he did indulge himself in that way, we have no evidence of it, or that he was ever anything but faithful to her – despite the 'second-best bed' of his will, which probably had some special, personal significance for them both.

One other thing we know from the plays, that strangely enough has not been much remarked on or appreciated, is the interest and confidence he had in the young, as demonstrated by the opportunities he provided for the young apprentices of the company to shine in his plays – more than any other dramatist then, before or since. He loved music, played the lute, and saw music and dance in combination as the supreme expression of that ultimate harmony in the universe that he thought about and longed for all his life; a longing that became a faith, and one that permeates the last romances, 'that all thing shall be well and all manner of thing shall be well'.

He knew very little of his aristocratic patrons and the other famous men and women of his day; he was most at home with his fellows, and they, apart from his family and one or two of his Stratford neighbours, were the only people to be named in his will. To them he was simply and proudly, 'Our Shakespeare'.

Appendix A

Recollections of (1) *Tamburlaine the Great*, (2) *The Jew of Malta*, (3) *The Spanish Tragedy*, (4) *Soliman and Perseda*, (5) *Arden of Faversham*, and (6) *Edward I* in Shakespeare's early plays (*Titus Andronicus, The Taming of the Shrew, Henry VI,* and *Richard III*).

SECTION 1: TAMBURLAINE

PART ONE

Meander at I.i.41:
. . . misled by dreaming prophecies

Clarence at R3: I.i.54:
He hearkens after prophecies
and dreams

Cosroe at II.i.1 – opening line of scene:

Thus far are we towards Theridamus

*K. Edward at 3H6: V.iii.1 –
opening line of scene:*
Thus far our fortune keeps an
upward course

Meander at II.ii.22:
This country swarms with vile outrageous
men

Gloucester at 1H6: III.i.11:
The manner of thy vile
outrageous crimes

Meander at II.ii.73:
Fortune herself doth sit upon our crests

Stanley at R3: V.iii.80:
Fortune and Victory sit upon
thy helm
Richard at V.iii.352:
Upon them! Victory sits on our
helms

Theridamus at II.v.58–60:
I think the pleasure they enjoy in heaven
Cannot compare with kingly joys in earth;
To wear a crown . . .

Richard at 3H6: I.ii.29–31:
How sweet a thing it is to wear
a crown,
Within whose circuit is Elysium
And all that poets feign of bliss
and joy

Tamburlaine at II.vii.28–9
The perfect bliss and sole felicity,
The sweet fruition of an earthly crown

King of Morocco at III.i.51–2:
For neither rain can fall upon the earth,
Nor sun reflex his virtuous beams thereon

Pucelle at 1H6: V.iv.87–8:
May never glorious sun reflex
his beams
Upon the country where you
make abode

Agydas at III.ii.85–7:
         . . . the late-felt frowns
That sent a tempest to my daunted thoughts,
And makes my soul divine her overthrow

Clarence at R3: I.iv.44:
O then began the tempest in my
soul

Tamburlaine at III.iii.44–5:
I that am term'd the Scourge and Wrath
of God,
The only fear and terror of the world

*French General (of Talbot) at 1H6:
IV.ii.15–16:*
Thou ominous and fearful owl
of death,
Our nation's terror and their
bloody scourge

Bejazeth at III.iii.236–8:
Now will the Christian miscreants be glad,
Ringing with joy their superstitious bells
And making bonfires for my overthrow

York at 2H6: V.i.3:
Ring bells aloud; burn bonfires
clear and bright

Tamburlaine at IV.ii.8–9:
The chiefest god, first mover of that sphere
Enchas'd with thousands ever-shining lamps

K. Henry at 2H6: III.iii.19:
O thou eternal Mover of the
heavens

Tamburlaine at IV.iv.29–31:
I glory in the curses of my foes,
Having the power from the empyreal heaven
To turn them all upon their proper heads

Buckingham at R3: V.i.20–2:
That high All-seer which I
dallied with
Hath turn'd my feigned prayer
on my head,
And given in earnest what I
begg'd in jest

First Virgin at V.ii.18–19:
Pity old age, within whose silver hairs
Honour and reverence evermore have reign'd

K. Henry at 2H6: V.i.162:
Old Salisbury, shame to thy
silver hair

PART TWO

Sigismund at I.ii.5–6:
I here present thee with a naked sword;
Wilt thou have war, then shake this blade
  at me

Clifford at 2H6: IV.viii.16, 18:
Who hateth him [the King] . . .
Shake he his weapon at us, and
  pass by

Callapine at 1.iii.41–2:
And, as thou rid'st in triumph through the
The pavement underneath thy chariot
  wheels . . .

Gloucester at 2H6: II.iv.11, 13–14:
  streets, The abject people . . .
That erst did follow thy proud
  chariot wheels
When thou didst ride in triumph
  through the streets

Tamburlaine at I.iv.19:
. . . all the wealthy kingdoms I subdu'd

Cardinal at 2H6: I.i.153:
. . . all the wealthy kingdoms of
  the west

Tamburlaine at I.iv.25–31:
Their hair . . .
Which should be like the quills of
  porcupines
As black as jet, and hard as iron or steel,
Bewrays they are too dainty for the wars.
Their fingers made to quaver on a lute,
Their arms to hang about a lady's neck,
Their legs to dance and caper in the air

York [of Cade] at 2H6:
III.i.362–5:
  . . . his thighs with darts
Were almost like a sharp-quill'd
  porpentine
And, in the end being rescu'd, I
  have seen
Him caper like a wild Morisco

Richard at R3: I.i.12–13:
He capers nimbly in a lady's
  chamber
To the lascivious pleasing of a
  lute

Tamburlaine at II.iv.1, 7:
Black is the beauty of the brightest day . . .
Ready to darken earth with endless night

Bedford at 1H6: I.i.1:
Hung be the heavens with
  black, yield day to night

Theridamus at II.iv.121:
If words might serve, our voice hath
  rent the air

Edward at 2H6: V.i.139:
Ay, noble father, if our words
  will serve

Olympia [to Theridamus] at IV.ii.33–5:
        . . . draw your sword
Making a passage for my troubled soul,
Which beats against this prison to get out

Clarence at R3: I.iv.36–8:
. . . often did I strive
To yield the ghost, but still the
  envious flood
Stopp'd in my soul, and would
  not let it forth

Stage direction at IV.iii.1:
Enter Tamburlaine, drawn in his chariot
by the Kings of Trebizon and Soria, with bits
in their mouths, reins in his left hand, and
in his right hand a whip with which he
scourgeth them

Exeter at 1H6: I.i.19, 22:
Upon a wooden coffin we
　attend . . .
Like captives bound to a
　triumphant car

Tamburlaine at IV.iii.20–1:
　　　　　　　　　　. . . draw
My chariot swifter than the racking clouds

Richard at 3H6: II.i.26–7:
Three glorious suns . . .
Not separated with the racking
　clouds

Orcanes at IV.iii.32:
O thou that sway'st the region under earth

Pucelle at 1H6: V.iii.10–11:
. . . ye familiar spirits that are
　cull'd
Out of the powerful regions
　under earth

Orcanes at IV.iii.42:
Haling him headlong to the lowest hell

Bedford at 1H6: I.i.149:
I'll hale the Dauphin headlong
　from his throne

Amyras at V.iii.250:
Meet heaven and earth, and here let all
things end

Young Clifford at 2H6: V.ii.40, 42:
O let the vile world end . . .
Knit heaven and earth together

SECTION 2: THE JEW OF MALTA

Prologue to the play is spoken by 'Machevill'

Richard at 3H6: III.ii.193:
　　　　　　　　　　I can . . .
. . . set the murderous
　Machiavel to school

Barabas at I.ii.197–8:
And henceforth wish for an eternal night,
That clouds of darkness may enclose my flesh

Margaret at R3: I.iii.267–9:
Witness my son, now in the
　shade of death,
Whose bright out-shining
　beams thy cloudy wrath
Hath in eternal darkness folded
　up

Barabas at I.ii.241–2:
. . . Things past recovery
Are hardly cur'd with exclamations

Richard at R3: II.ii.103:
But none can help our harms
　by wailing them

Barabas at II.iii.20–1:
We Jews can fawn like spaniels when
we please,
And when we grin, we bite

Margaret at R3: I.iii.289–90:
O Buckingham, take heed of
    yonder dog!
Look when he fawns, he bites

Ferneze [of his son] at III.ii.11–12:
. . . My Lodowick slain!
These arms of mine shall be thy sepulchre

Talbot [of his son] at 1H6: IV.vii.32:
Now my old arms are young
    Talbot's grave
*Father [of his son] at 3H6:
II.v.114–15*:
These arms of mine shall be thy
    winding-sheet;
My heart, sweet boy, shall be
    thy sepulchre

Ferneze at III.ii.35:
And with my prayers pierce impartial heavens

Margaret at R3: I.iii.195:
Can curses pierce the clouds
    and enter heaven?

Ferneze at III.v.2–4:
Ferneze: What wind drives you thus
    into Malta-road?
Basso: The wind that bloweth all the world
    besides,
Desire of gold

Hortensio at Shr.: I.ii.47ff.:
Hortensio: . . . what happy gale
Blows you to Padua here from
    old Verona?
Petruchio: Such wind as scatters
    young men through the world
To seek their fortunes farther
    than at home

Calymath [to Ferneze and others] at V.ii.1–2:
Now vail your pride, you captive Christians,
And kneel for mercy to your conquering foe

Katherina at Shr.: V.ii.177–8:
Then vail your stomachs, for it is
    no boot,
And place your hands below
    your husband's foot

SECTION 3: THE SPANISH TRAGEDY

Ghost of Andrea at I.i.12–13:
But in the harvest of my summer joys
Death's winter nipped the blossoms of my
    bliss

Gloucester at 2H6: II.iv.1–4:
Thus sometimes hath the
    brightest day a cloud;
And after summer evermore
    succeeds
Barren winter, with his wrathful
    nipping cold:
So cares and joys abound, as
    seasons fleet

Ghost of Andrea at I.i.27–8:
Then was the ferryman of hell content
To pass me over to the slimy strand

Clarence at R3: I.iv.31–2:
     . . . reflecting gems,
That woo'd the slimy bottom of
  the deep

Ghost of Andrea at I.i.55–6:
In keeping on my way to Pluto's court,
Through dreadful shades of ever-glooming
  night

Clarence at R3: I.iv.45–7:
I pass'd . . .
With that sour ferryman which
  poets write of,
Unto the kingdom of perpetual
  night

Ghost of Andrea at I.i.65, 71:
Where bloody Furies shakes their whips
of steel . . .
And all foul sins with torments overwhelmed

Clarence at R3: I.iv.57–9:
'Seize on him, Furies! Take him
  into torment!'
With that, methoughts, a legion
  of foul fiends
Environ'd me, and howled in
  my ears

Viceroy at I.iii.5:
Then rest we here awhile in our unrest

Duchess of York at R3: IV.iv.29:
Rest thy unrest on England's
  lawful earth

Hieronimo at III.xiii.29:
Thus therefore will I rest me in unrest

Aaron at Tit.:IV.ii.31:
But let her rest in her unrest
  awhile

Horatio at I.iv.36:
III.ii.338–9:
There laid him down and dewed him with
  my tears

Q. Margaret at 2H6:

     . . . Give me thy hand
That I may dew it with my tears

Ghost of Andrea at I.v.1:
Come we for this from depth of underground

Hume at 2H6: I.ii.79:
A spirit rais'd from depth of
  under ground

Pedringano at II.i.89:
I swear to both by Him that made us all

Richard at 3H6: II.ii.124:
By Him that made us all, I am
  resolv'd

King of Spain at II.iii.17–18:
I'll grace her marriage with an uncle's gift,
And this it is: in case the match go forward . . .

Q. Margaret [of a proposed marriage] at 3H6: III.iii.58:
If that go forward, Henry's
  hope is done

Lorenzo [murdering Horatio] at II.iv.55:
Ay, thus and thus! These are the fruits of love

K. Edward [in another sense] at 3H6: III.ii.58:
But stay thee – 'tis the fruits of love I mean

Lorenzo [of Bel-imperia] at II.iv.63:
Come, stop her mouth. Away with her

Chiron [to Lavinia] at Tit.: II.iii.185:
Nay, then, I'll stop your mouth

Hieronimo at II.v.17:
O speak, if any spark of life remain

Richard at 3H6: V.vi. 66–7:
If any spark of life be yet remaining,
Down, down to hell

Hieronimo at II.v.46:
Sweet lovely rose, ill-plucked before thy time

Q. Margaret at 3H6: V.v.60:
How sweet a plant have you untimely cropp'd

Hieronimo at II.v.53:
Seest thou those wounds that yet are bleeding fresh?

Lady Anne at R3: I.ii.55–6:
                    . . . See, see dead Henry's wounds
Open their congeal'd mouths and bleed afresh

Ghost of Andrea at II.vi.4–6:
                    . . . Bel-imperia,
On whom I doted more than all the world
Because she loved me more than all the world

Chiron at Tit.: II.i.71–2:
I care not, I, knew she and all the world:
I love Lavinia more than all the world

Pedringano at III.iii.16:
Here therefore will I stay and take my stand

1 Watchman at 3H6: IV.iii.1:
Come on, my masters, each man take his stand

Pedringano at III.iii.37:
Who first lays hand on me, I'll be his priest *[meaning to kill him; administer the last rites]*

Suffolk [in same sense] at 2H6: III.i.272:
Say but the word and I will be his priest

Lorenzo at III.iv.78:
Now stands our fortune on a tickle point

York at 2H6: I.i.216–17:
                    . . . the state of Normandy
Stands on a tickle point

Hieronimo at III.vii.32–3 [reading letter]:
. . . I write, as mine extremes required,
That you would labour my delivery

Clarence at R3: I.iv.235–6:
. . . he . . . swore with sobs
That he would labour my delivery

Bel-imperia at III.ix.12:
Well, force perforce, I must constrain myself

York at 2H6: I.i.259:
And force perforce I'll make
  him yield the crown

Lorenzo at III.x.1:
Boy, talk no further; thus far things go well
[opening line of scene]

K. Edward at 3H6: V.iii.1:
Thus far our fortune keeps an
  upward course
[opening line of scene]

Portingale 1 at III.xi.1–3:
Portingale 1: By your leave, sir.
Hieronimo: Good leave have you. Nay, I
pray you go,
For I'll leave you, if you can leave me, so

K. Edward at 3H6: III.ii.33–5:
K. Edward: Lords, give us
  leave . . .
Richard: Ay, good leave have
  you, for you will have leave
Till youth take leave and leave
  you to the crutch

Hieronimo at III.xii.31:

. . . Hieronimo, beware; go by, go by

Sly at Shr.: Induction.i.7
[deliberate quotation]:
Go by, Saint Jeronimy, go to thy
  cold bed and warm thee

Hieronimo at II.v.1–2:
What outcries pluck me from my naked bed,
And chill my throbbing heart with trembling fear

Hieronimo at III.xii.70–1:
Give me my son . . .
Away! I'll rip the bowels of the earth
He diggeth with his dagger

Titus at Tit.: IV.iii.5, 11–12:
She's gone, she's fled. Sirs, take
  to your tools . . .
Tis you must dig with mattock
  and with spade
And pierce the inmost centre of
  the earth

Hieronimo at III.xiii.86–7:
He draweth out a bloody napkin
O no, not this! Horatio, this was thine,
And when I dyed it in your dearest blood . . .

Q. Margaret at 3H6: I.iv.79–81:
Look, York, I stain'd this napkin
  with the blood
That valiant Clifford with his
  rapier's point
Made issue from the bosom of
  the boy

Hieronimo at IV.iv.122–4:
And here behold this bloody handkercher,
blood of my sweet Which at Horatio's death
I weeping dipped
Within the river of his bleeding wounds.

York at 3H6: I.iv.157–9:
This cloth thou dipp'dst in boy,
And I with tears do wash the
  blood away
Keep thou the napkin . . .

Hieronimo at III.xiv.118:
Pocas palabras, mild as the lamb
[*pocas palabras* is Spanish for 'few words']

Sly at Shr.: Induction.i.5:
Therefore *paucas pallabris*, let
the world slide

SECTION 4: SOLIMAN AND PERSEDA

Erastus at I.iv.136:
As storms that fall amid a sun shine day

Richard at 3H6: II.i.187:
Ne'er may he live to see a
sunshine day

Erastus at II.i.189,212:
. . . bid them bring some store of crowns with
them . . . What store of crowns have you
brought?

Son at 3H6: II.v.56-7
This man . . .
May be possessed with some
store of crowns

Ferdinando [to Erastus] at II.i.244:
Dasell mine eyes, or ist Lucinas chaine?

Edward at 3H6: II.i.25:
Dazzle mine eyes, or do I see
three suns?

Piston [to Erastus] at II.i.291-2:
Hetherto all goes well; but, if I be taken –
I, marry, sir, then the case is altered . . .

Warwick at 3H6: IV.ii.1:
Trust me, my lord, all hitherto
goes well
K. Edward at 3H6: IV.iii.31:
Ay, but the case is alter'd

Erastus at III.i.85-7:
As ayre bred Eagles, if they once perceive

That any of their broode but close their sight
When they should gase against the glorious
Sunne

Richard at 3H6: II.i.91-2:
Nay, if thou be that princely
eagle's bird,
Show thy descent by gazing
'gainst the sun

Perseda at V.iv.67:
A kisse I graunt thee, though I hate thee
deadlie

Q. Margaret at 3H6: I.iv.84-5:
Alas, poor York! but that I hate
thee deadly, I should lament . . .

SECTION 5: ARDEN OF FAVERSHAM

Mosby at i.325:
The rancorous venom of thy mis-swol'n
heart

Aaron at Tit.: V.iii.13:
The venomous malice of my
swelling heart

Franklin [alone on stage] at iv.45:
Then fix his sad eyes on the sullen earth

Eleanor at 2H6: I.ii.5:
Why are thine eyes fix'd to the
sullen earth

Black Will [to Alice] at xiv.79:
Patient yourself; we cannot help it now

Titus [to Tamora] at Tit.: I.i.121:
Patient yourself, madam, and
   pardon me

Mosby at xiv.96–7:
     . . . will you two
Perform the complot that I have laid?

Tamora at Tit.: II.iii.264–5:
     . . . too late I bring this
fatal writ,
The complot of this timeless
   tragedy

Alice at xiv.310:
Ah, neighbours, a sudden qualm came
over my heart

Gloucester at 2H6: I.i.54:
Some sudden qualm hath
   struck me at the heart

SECTION 6: EDWARD I

Lluellen at iv.20–1 (ll.853–4):
Tell them the Chaines that Mulciber erst made,
To tie Prometheus lims to Caucasus . . .

Aaron at Tit.: II.i.16–17
And faster bound to Aaron's
   charming eyes
Than is Prometheus tied to
   Caucasus

Edward at x.201 (l. 1796):
Fast to those lookes are all my fancies tide

Appendix B

Conjectural Programme of Performances of 'harey the vi' at the Rose between 3 March 1592 and 31 January 1593 (based on Henslowe's Diary in Foakes and Rickert, pp. 16–20)

General note: A play was performed on every weekday with the exception of Good Friday (24 March) and two other days, drawing on a repertoire of 23 plays performed in varying sequence and at varying intervals, the same play being rarely repeated in any one week. The longer intervals between performances of 'harey the vi' on 16 and 28 March, 21 April and 4 May (11 and 12 days respectively against an average elsewhere of 5) are interpreted as allowing for a more extended period of rehearsal in which the following play in the trilogy was brought up to scratch. (I assume that the leading roles would already have been familiar to the actors who played them from their having previously toured in the plays.) Performances took place in the afternoons.

Date	Interval between performances		Henslowe's share of the takings	
Friday, 3 March 1592		FIRST PERFORMANCE, Henry VI, Part 1	£3 16s 8d	
Tuesday, 7 March	3 days	SECOND PERFORMANCE, Part 1	£3	
Saturday, 11 March	3 days	THIRD PERFORMANCE, Part 1	£2 7s 6d	
Thursday, 16 March	4 days	FOURTH PERFORMANCE, Part 1	£1 11s 6d	(1)
Tuesday, 28 March (Easter Tuesday)	11 days	FIRST PERFORMANCE, Henry VI, Part 2	£3 8s	
Wednesday, 5 April	7 days	SECOND PERFORMANCE, Part 2	£2 1s	
Thursday, 13 April	7 days	THIRD PERFORMANCE, Part 2	£1 6s	(2)
Friday, 21 April	7 days	FOURTH PERFORMANCE, Part 2	£1 13s	
Thursday, 4 May (Ascension Day)	12 days	FIRST PERFORMANCE, Henry VI. Part 3	£2 16s	(3)

				(4)
Sunday, 7 May	2 days	SECOND PERFORMANCE, Part 3	£1 2s	
Sunday, 14 May (Whit Sunday)	6 days	THIRD PERFORMANCE, Part 3	£2 10s	
Friday, 19 May	4 days	FOURTH PERFORMANCE, Part 3	£1 10s	
Thursday, 25 May	5 days	FIFTH PERFORMANCE, Part 3	£1 4s	
Monday, 12 June	17 days	New sequential cycle begins with FIFTH PERFORMANCE OF Henry VI, Part 1	£1 12s	
Monday, 19 June	6 days	FIFTH PERFORMANCE, Henry VI, Part 2	£1 11s	
Thursday, 22 June		Season interrupted by riots in City		
Friday, 29 December	6 months	Season resumes		
Tuesday, 16 January 1593	New cycle begins with (?) SIXTH PERFORMANCE of Henry VI, Part 1	£2 6s		
Wednesday, 31 January	14 days	(?) SIXTH PERFORMANCE of Henry VI, Part 2	£1 6s	
Wednesday, 7 February		Season interrupted by plague and abandoned		

Notes to Appendix B

1. To produce a regular sequence of four performances for each of the trilogy in this early part of the season, Henslowe's 'harey' is here interpreted as referring to *Henry VI*. Note diminishing returns with each repeat of Part 1.

2. Again, note diminishing returns.

3. This, and the performances on 7, 14 and 25 May were consecutive with 'titus and vespacia'. On 4 and 25 May, 'harey the vi' followed 'titus'; on 7 and 14 May, it preceded 'titus'. Performances of these plays are often linked also with 'Jeronimo' (*The Spanish Tragedy*) or *The Jew of Malta*. All six plays belonged primarily to the Admiral's.

4. Either Henslowe has mistaken the date or, exceptionally, the play was performed on a Sunday, as in the following week on Whit Sunday.

Appendix C

Correspondences in word, image or thought between Plays of 1593/4 and the Sonnets

Section 1: The Two Gentlemen of Verona

Proteus at I.i.42–3:

Yet writers say: as in the sweetest bud
The eating canker dwells

Sonnet 70.7:

For canker vice the sweetest buds doth love

Sonnet 35.4:

And loathsome canker lives in sweetest bud

Lucetta at I.ii.139:

I see things too, although you judge I wink

Sonnet 43.1:

When most I wink, then do mine eyes best see

Speed and Valentine at II.i.65–8:

Speed: If you love her, you cannot see her.
Valentine: Why?
Speed: Because Love is blind. O that you had mine
eyes, or your own eyes had the lights they were wont
to have

Sonnet 137.1–2:

Thou blind fool, Love, what dost thou to mine eyes
That they behold and see not what they see?

Sonnet 148.1–2:

O me, what eyes hath love put in my head,
Which have no correspondence with true sight!

(See also 113.1–4)

Proteus at II.ii.16–18:

　　　　　　What, gone without a word?
Ay, so true love should do: it cannot speak,
For truth hath better deeds than words to grace it

Sonnet 69.8–10:

. . . seeing farther than the eye hath shown.
They look into the beauty of thy mind,
And that in guess they measure by thy deeds

Section 2: The Comedy of Errors

Adriana at II.i.87–8:

His company must do his minions grace,
Whilst I at home starve for a merry look

Adriana at II.ii.110–11:

Ay, ay, Antipholus, look strange and frown,
Some other mistress hath thy sweet aspects

Adriana at II.ii.119–23:

How comes it now, my husband, O, how comes it,
That thou are then estranged from thyself? –
Thyself I call it, being strange to me,
That undividable, incorporate,
Am better than thy dear self's better part

Antipholus of Syracuse at III.ii.47–51:

Sing, siren, for thyself, and I will dote;
Spread o'er the silver waves thy golden hairs,
And as a bed I'll take thee, and there lie,
And in that glorious supposition think
He gains by death that hath such means to die

Antipholus of Syracuse at III.ii.61–2:

It is thyself, mine own self's better part,
Mine eye's clear eye, my dear heart's dearer heart

Sonnet 47.3:

When that mine eye is famished for a look

Sonnet 75.9–10:

Sometime all full with feasting on your sight,
And by and by clean starved for a look

Sonnet 89.8:

I will acquaintance strangle and look strange

Sonnet 39.1–4:

O, how thy worth with manners may I sing
When thou art all the better part of me?
What can mine own praise to mine own self bring,
And what is't but mine own when I praise thee?

Sonnet 92.9–12:

Thou canst not vex me with inconstant mind,
Since that my life on thy revolt doth lie.
O, what a happy title do I find,
Happy to have thy love, happy to die!

Sonnet 46.12–14:

The clear eye's moiety and the dear heart's part:
As thus – mine eye's due is thy outward part,
And my heart's right thy inward love of heart

Section 3: Edward III

Lodowick at II.i.10–12:

His cheeks put on their scarlet ornaments,
But no more like her oriental red
Than brick to coral or live things to dead

King Edward at II.i.143–6:

Compar'st thou her to the pale queen of night,
Who, being set in dark, seems therefore light?
What is she, when the sun lifts up his head,
But like a fading taper, dim and dead?

King Edward at II.i.164–5:

Who smiles upon the basest weed that grows,
As lovingly as on the fragrant rose

Warwick at II.i.450–1:

Dark night seems darker by the lightning flash;
Lilies that fester smell far worse than weeds

Sonnet 142.5–7:

. . . not from those lips of thine,
That have profaned their scarlet ornaments
And sealed false bonds of love as oft as mine

Sonnet 7.1–4:

Lo, in the orient when the gracious light
Lifts up his burning head, each under eye
Doth homage to his new-appearing sight,
Serving with looks his sacred majesty

Sonnet 94.11–12:

But if that flower with base infection meet,
The basest weed outbraves his dignity

Sonnet 95.1–3:

How sweet and lovely dost thou make the shame
Which, like a canker in the fragrant rose,
Doth spot the beauty of thy budding name

Sonnet 94.13–14 (continues from above)

For sweetest things turn sourest by their deeds;
Lilies that fester smell far worse than weeds

Plot 1: Romeo and Juliet (characters in approximate order of appearance)

ACTOR	ACT 1 (1-4)	MASQUE (1.5)	ACT 2	ACT 3	ACT 4	ACT 5 (1-2)	TOMB (5.3)	(Notes)
S1 (Shakespeare)	CHORUS		CHORUS/FRIAR	FRIAR	FRIAR	FRIAR	FRIAR	
S2 (Sly?)	SAMPSON	CAP SERV		Tyb man	CAP SERV		WATCH	(1)
HM1	GREGORY	CAP SERV		Tyb man	CAP SERV		CAP SERV	
HM2 (Sincler?)	ABRAM	Masquer		Mont man		APOTHECARY/BALTHASAR	Mont man	(2)
S3 (Cowley?)	BALTHASAR	Masquer		Mont man			BALTHASAR	
S4 (Condell?)	BENVOLIO	Masquer	BENVOLIO	BENVOLIO			Benvolio	
HM3	TYBALT	TYBALT		TYBALT/		FRIAR JOHN	WATCH	
S5 (Pope?)	CAPULET	CAPULET		CAPULET	CAPULET		CAPULET	
A1	L CAPULET	L CAPULET		L CAPULET	L CAPULET		L CAPULET	(3)
S6 (Heminges?)	MONTAGU	Masquer		MONTAGU			MONTAGU	
A2	L MONTAGU	ANTHONY		L MONTAGU			WATCH	(3)
S7 (Phillips?)	PRINCE	Masquer		PRINCE			PRINCE	(4)
A3	ROMEO	ROMEO	ROMEO	ROMEO		ROMEO	ROMEO	
A4	PARIS	Masquer		PARIS	PARIS		PARIS	
A5	NURSE	NURSE	NURSE	NURSE	NURSE		Nurse	
A6	JULIET	JULIET	JULIET	JULIET	JULIET		JULIET	
S8 (Burbage?)	MERCUTIO	MERCUTIO/	MERCUTIO	MERCUTIO/			Watch	
A7		POTPAN		Tyb man	Cap serv		Cap serv	
S9 (Bryan?)		COUSIN CAP/		CITIZEN			Watch	
S10 (Kempe)	CAP SERV (?)	Masquer	PETER	Peter	PETER		Peter	(5)
A8	Prince's train	'Susan G'/		Prince's train	Cap serv		Prince's train	(6)
A9	Prince's train	'Nell'/		Prince's train	Cap serv		Page to Paris	
A10	Prince's train	'Rosaline'/		Mercutio's page	Cap serv		Mon man	
Musicians 3+	Citizens	Musicians		Citizens	MUSICIANS			
Extras 5+	Citizens	Torchbearers		Citizens			Prince's train	

Notes

1. Sampson and Gregory remain in character while playing all Capulet servants and Tybalt's men.
2. Abram and Balthasar remain in character while playing Montagu men. As masquers, their faces remain covered throughout the scene.
3. The older women's roles are played by senior apprentices, some of whom may have become hired men.
4. All the mute masquers are disguised by masks and cloaks.
5. Kempe (as Peter) may also have played the illiterate Capulet servant of Act 1, Scene 2.
6. Susan Grindstone, Nell and Rosaline are brought on stage to provide dancing partners for the masquers.

Plot 2: *Henry V (sharers listed first)*

ACTOR	1.1	1.2	2.1	2.2	2.3	2.4	3.1	3.2	3.3	3.4	3.5	3.6	3.7	4.1	4.2	4.3	4.4	4.5	4.6	4.7	4.8	5.1	5.2	Notes
S1 (Shakespeare)	CHO	Bed	CHO	BED			CHO		Bed					CHO	Bed	Bed			Bed	Bed		CHO	BUR	(1)
S2 (Burbage)		HEN	HEN	HEN			HEN		HEN			HEN		HEN		HEN			HEN	HEN	HEN		HEN	
S3 (Phillips?)		WES	WES	WES			Wes	MAC	MAC							WES		BOU	·	Bou			WES	
S4 (Hemings?)		EXE	EXE	EXE		EXE	Exe		Exe					BAT		EXE			EXE	EXE	EXE		EXE	
S5 (Pope?)			PIS		PIS			PIS	Prs			PIS		PIS		Pis	PIS					PIS	EPI	(2)
S6 (Cowley?)			NYM		NYM			NYM	Nym					ERP		Erp			Her	Her	HER		lor	
S7 (Sly?)			BAR		BAR			BAR	Bar					WIL						WIL	WIL		lor	
S8 (Condell?)	CAN	CAN				FrK					FrK	MON			GRA	MON				MON			FrK	(3)
S9 (Armin?)	ELY	ELY		SCR				FLU				FLU		FLU						FLU	FLU	FLU	lor	(4)
HM1 (Sincler?)		Cla		Cla		DAU			sol		DAU		DAU		DAU		FER	DAU	sol	sol	sol		Ca	
HM2		AMB		CAM		CON		JAM	Jam		CON		CON		CON			CON	sol	sol			Hun	
HM3		Glo	Glo	Glo		Bri	Glo		GOV		BRI	GLO		GLO		GLO		Glo	Glo	GLO	Glo	Glo	Glo	
HM4		att		GRE		MES		GOW	Gow			GOW		GOW		Gow				GOW	GOW	GOW	Gow	
A1 (Gilburne?)		War	War	War		MES					Ram	sol	RAM	COU	RAM	SAL		RAM		War	WAR		War	(5)
A2		Amb				Ber					Orl	sol	ORL		MES				Orl	Orl	sol		ALI	
A3			HOS		HOS					ALI					ORL	YOR		ORL		Orl	sol		ISA	
A4			BOY		BOY			Boy		KAT							BOY		pri	pri	sol		KAT	(6)
Mute extras (3+)		att	sol	sol		att	sol		cit			sol	sol	sol	sol				sol	sol	sol		att	(7)

Section 4: Love's Labour's Lost

Princess at II.i.13–16:

Good Lord Boyet, my beauty, though but mean,
Needs not the painted flourish of your praise:
Beauty is bought by judgement of the eye,
Not utter'd by base sale of chapmen's tongues

Princess at IV.i.1–2:

Was that the king, that spurr'd his horse so hard
Against the steep-up rising of the hill?

Berowne at IV.iii.230–7:

Of all complexions the cull'd sovereignty
Do meet, as at a fair, in her fair cheek;
Where several worthies make one dignity,
Where nothing wants that want itself doth seek.
Lend me the flourish of all gentle tongues, –
Fie, painted rhetoric! O! she needs it not:
To things of sale a seller's praise belongs;
She passes praise; then praise too short doth blot.

Sonnet 21.1–2, 13–14:

So is it not with me as with that Muse,
Stirred by a painted beauty to his verse . . .
    Let them say more that like of hearsay well;
    I will not praise that purpose not to sell

Sonnet 7.5:

And having climbed the steep-up heavenly hill

Sonnet 82.5–14:

Thou are as fair in knowledge as in hue,
Finding thy worth a limit past my praise;
And therefore art enforced to seek anew
Some fresher stamp of the time-bettering days.
And do so, love; yet when they have devised
What strained touches rhetoric can lend,
Thou, truly fair, wert truly sympathized
In true plain words by thy true-telling friend:
    And their gross painting might be better used
    Where cheeks need blood; in thee it is abused.

Appendix D

Conjectural Doubling Plots

1. Romeo and Juliet

2. Henry V

3. Troilus and Cressida

KEY

CAPITALS denote character speaks in scene

Lower-case letters denote character is mute in scene

S = Sharer

HM = Hired Man

HM/A = Hired Man or Apprentice

A = Apprentice

PM = Player-musician

Extras are drawn from stage keepers, tiremen and gatherers (stage, wardrobe and box-office staff)

Notes

1. Shakespeare would have been able to slip in and out of the scenes in which Bedford appears (including 3.1 and 4.1) with a minimum of fuss; he is always at hand to swell a scene and add the odd line when required. A change of costume to armour as the action moves from England to France would have been equally appropriate to Bedford and Chorus. He would have changed to a robe for Burgundy. Bedford is named in the initial stage direction to 5.2 but is not among those deputed to negotiate the details of the treaty, as he would surely have been if Shakespeare had finally intended him to be present. Huntingdon (a mute character who appears nowhere else in the play) looks like a late substitution.

2. The Epilogue goes to Pope as Pistol in the same way that the Epilogue to *Henry IV* had gone to Kempe as Falstaff. Both refer to the author as a separate person, which would have come strangely from Shakespeare.

3. Montjoy, as herald, is the voice of the French King. 'Where is Montjoy the herald?', asks the King at 3.5.36. Where indeed? 'Speed him hence/Let him greet England with our sharp defiance'. And on his first appearance in the following scene, Montjoy, having identified himself by his habit, begins, 'Thus says my king' (3.6.117). I am indebted for this and other doubles to John Barton, who directed me in both parts for the Elizabethan Theatre Company in 1953.

4. I have assumed that by 1599 Armin would have become a sharer.

5. In the Folio text of the opening stage direction to 3.7, Rambures appears as 'Gebon', and 'Ge' is given the first line of 4.5, in which Rambures also appears but is otherwise silent. 'Gebon' may have been Shakespeare's approximation of the name of Samuel Gilburne, mentioned in Phillips' will of 1605 as his 'late apprentice'. Apprentices 1, 2 and 3 would all have been drawn from the company's older apprentices, some of whom may by this time have achieved the status of hired men. There are indications that those who played girls' parts in their young years sometimes grew up to play older women on occasion, but usefully could double these with male roles.

6. The only boy actor required in the cast. Like Apprentice 2, he would have needed some knowledge of French.

7. The extras fit in as attendants, soldiers, citizens or French prisoners as required.

Plot 3: Troilus and Cressida (sharers listed first as in 1603 patent)

ACTOR	1.1	1.2	1.3	2.1	2.2	2.3	3.1	3.2	3.3	4.1	4.2	4.3	4.4	4.5	5.1	5.2	5.3	5.4	5.5	5.6	5.7	5.8	5.9	5.10	5.11	Notes
S1 Fletcher	AEN	Aen	AEN							AEN	AEN	Aen	AEN	AEN	AEN	AEN									AEN	(1)
S2 Shakespeare	PAN	PAN					PAN	PAN		PAN	PAN		PAN				PAN			Myr	Myr		Myr		PAN	(2)
S3 Burbage	PRO		ULY			ULY			ULY					ULY	ULY				ULY					ULY		
S4 Phillips			AGA			AGA			AGA					AGA	AGA				AGA					AGA		
S5 Heminges																							Myr			(3)
S6 Condell		Hec		PRI	HEC				CAL					HEC	HEC	CAL	HEC	HEC		HEC	HEC		HEC			(4)
S7 Sly		Hls	MEN		HLS				MEN					MEN	MEN							MEN	Myr			(5)
S8 Armin		ALE	THE	THE		THE			THE									THE				THE	Myr			
S9 Cowley		sol	NES			NES			NES					NES	NES				NES	Myr			NES	NES		
HM Lowin	TRO	Tro			TRO			TRO			TRO	TRO	TRO	TRO		TRO	TRO	TRO		TRO	TRO				TRO	
HM/A 1				ACH		ACH			ACH					ACH	ACH				ACH	ACH			ACH			(6)
HM/A 2		sol		AJA		AJA			AJA					AJA	AJA				AJA	AJA	AJA			AJA		(7)
HM/A 3		sol		PAT		PAT			PAT					PAT	PAT				Pat		Myr					
HM/A 4			Dio			DIO			DIO	DIO		Dio	DIO	DIO	DIO	DIO		DIO	DIO	DIO			DIO			(8)
HM/A 5		Par			PAR		PAR			PAR			PAR	PAR								PAR			PAR	
A1	Boy							BOY		tor		tor	att	att					sol	sol		sol				(9)
A2		CRE			CAS			CRE			CRE		CRE	CRE		CRE	CAS					BAS			Bas	
A3		sol					HEL												sol	sol		sol	sol			
PM 1		Dei					SER			DEI		DEI		tru			AND		sol						Dei	
PM2		Ant					mus		Ant	Ant		Ant	tru								Myr	tru			Ant	

Notes

1. Fletcher was appointed a King's servant by the patent of 1603, and being known to the King – having previously appeared with a company of English players on tour in Scotland – is listed first. He seems not to have joined the company on a permanent basis but, in this plague year of 1603, I think it at least possible that he went with them on tour.

2. There is no necessity for Shakespeare to double until Act 5, when he would have been needed as a Myrmidon. The Myrmidons wear distinctive cloaks and concealing helmets, possibly masks.

3. Heminges has only two scenes as Priam. As Company Manager, he would have had much to do off-stage – especially on tour. But he too would have been needed as a Myrmidon.

4. Calchas has nothing to say in 2.3, and I have left him offstage. In 5.2 we hear his voice from off; he does not appear.

5. When doubling Trojan and Greek characters (as Sly briefly does here), any possibility of confusion is avoided by the use of distinctive costumes and armour for the opposing armies. There is no need for Helenus to be present in 4.5, or for Menelaus in 5.10, though both are named in stage-directions by some editors.

6. John Lowin may have been brought in as a replacement for Thomas Pope, who was ill when the 1603 patent was drawn up, and died later this year.

7. The apprentices who play the younger male roles (HM/A 1 to 5) have been with the company since its formation in 1594. They would now have been in their middle to late twenties, and some would have achieved their 'freedom' and been employed as hired men.

8. I have hesitated as to whether to include Patroclus among the older apprentices or the boys. He is addressed by Achilles as 'sweet Patroclus', and by Thersites as 'boy', 'fool' and ruder terms. He has the gift of mimicry and is old enough to enjoy kissing Cressida. He kisses her twice.

9. I have assumed that A2 has some instrumental skill and doubles as a musician in 3.1. Player-musician 1 is young enough to play Andromache. PM 2 is an older man with a good presence but is mute throughout. Both need to be expert trumpeters.

Abbreviations

The following abbreviations are used in the notes that follow. Other works and sources are cited in full on first reference to them in each set of notes. Place of publication is London except where otherwise stated.

Bentley, JCS	G.E. Bentley, *The Jacobean and Caroline Stage*, 7 vols., Oxford, 1941–68
Bentley, PDST	G.E. Bentley, *The Profession of Dramatist in Shakespeare's Time, 1590–1642*, Princeton, 1971
Bentley, PPST	G.E. Bentley, *The Profession of Player in Shakespeare's Time, 1590–1642*, Princeton, 1984
Chambers, ES	E.K. Chambers, *The Elizabethan Stage*, 4 vols., Oxford, 1923
Chambers, WS	E.K. Chambers, *William Shakespeare, A Study of Facts and Problems*, 2 vols., Oxford, 1930
Fripp	Edgar I. Fripp (ed.), *Minutes and Accounts of the Corporation of Stratford-upon-Avon and Other Records, 1553–1620*, vols 2 and 3, 1924–6
Halliwell-Phillipps	J.O. Halliwell-Phillipps, *The Visits of Shakespeare's Company of Actors to the Provincial Cities and Towns of England*, Brighton, 1887
Jonson	*Ben Jonson*, ed. C.H. Herford, P. and E. Simpson, 11 vols, Oxford, 1925–52
MLR	*Modern Language Review*
MSC	*Malone Society Collections*
II, Part 3	for 'Players at Ipswich', ed. E.K. Chambers, pp. 258–84, Oxford, 1931
VII	*Records of Plays and Players in Kent, 1450–1642*, ed. G.E. Dawson, Oxford, 1965
XI	*Records of Plays and Players in Norfolk and Suffolk, 1330–1642*, ed. John Wasson, Oxford, 1980–1
MSR	*Malone Society Reprints*
Murray	John Tucker Murray, *English Dramatic*

	Companies, 1558–1642, 2 vols, 1910, reprinted New York, 1963
Nungezer	Edwin Nungezer, *A Dictionary of Actors*, New York, 1929, reprinted 1968
PMLA	*Publications of the Modern Language Association of America*
REED	*Records of Early English Drama*. General editor: A.F. Johnston. Toronto, 1979 –
Bristol	*Bristol*, ed. Mark C. Pilkington, 1997
Cambridge	*Cambridge*, ed. A.H. Nelson, 2 vols, 1989
Coventry	*Coventry*, ed. R.W. Ingram, 1981
Cumb, West, Glos	*Cumberland, Westmorland, Gloucestershire*, ed. A. Douglas and P. Greenfield, 1986
Devon	*Devon*, ed. John M. Wasson, 1986
Hereford and	*Herefordshire, Worcestershire*, ed. David N. Klausner,
Worcester	1990
Newcastle	*Newcastle upon Tyne*, ed. J.J. Anderson, 1982
Norwich	*Norwich 1540–1642*, ed. David Galloway, 1984
Shropshire	*Shropshire*, ed. J.A.B. Somerset, 2 vols, 1994
Somerset	*Somerset including Bath*, ed. James Stokes, with R.J. Alexander, 2 vols, 1996
Schoenbaum, CDL	S. Schoenbaum, *William Shakespeare, A Compact Documentary Life*, Oxford, 1977
Schoenbaum, SL	S. Schoenbaum, *Shakespeare's Lives*, Oxford, revd edn, 1993
Southworth, EMM	John Southworth, *The English Medieval Minstrel*, Woodbridge, 1989
Southworth, F & J	John Southworth, *Fools and Jesters at the English Court*, Stroud, 1998
SQ	*Shakespeare Quarterly*
SS	*Shakespeare Survey*
Wills	E.A.J. Honigmann and Susan Brock, *Playhouse Wills, 1558–1642*, Manchester and New York, 1993

Notes

Chapter 1: The Invisible Man

1. Schoenbaum, CDL, p. 315.
2. Quoted from Chambers, WS, II, pp. 228–30.
3. I am drawing here on Bentley, PDST, pp. 38–9.
4. *Ibid.*, pp. 51–3.
5. *Ibid.*, pp. 50–1.
6. For the harper-poets, see Southworth, EMM, chapters 3 and 7.
7. See H.C. Gardiner, *Mysteries' End*, Yale, 1946 (reprinted Anchor, 1967).
8. Quoted from *Harrison's Description of England in Shakspere's Youth*, ed. F.F. Furnivall with additions by Mrs C.C. Stopes, IV (Supplement, 1908), p. 367.
9. From *Microcosmos* in *The Complete Works of John Davies of Hereford*, ed. A.B. Grosart (1878), I, p. 82. Davies qualifies this statement in the next line with, 'Yet generous yee are in minde and moode'.
10. Bentley describes the effect of the Jonson and Shakespeare folios on the reputation of dramatists as a rise 'from an exceedingly low status to a moderately low one'; *op. cit.* (n. 3), p. 57. For the Bodleian copy referred to below, see Schoenbaum (n. 1), p. 315.
11. Letter to Richard Woodhouse of 27 October 1818, in *The Letters of John Keats*, ed. Maurice Buxton Forman (Oxford, 3rd edn, 1947), pp. 227–8.
12. Jorge Luis Borges, *Labyrinths* (Penguin, 1970), pp. 284–5.
13. As quoted by Kenneth Muir in *Shakespeare the Professional and Related Studies* (1973) from Florence E. Hardy, *Life of Thomas Hardy* (1962), p. 341.

Chapter 2: Killing the Calf

1. Quoted from Schoenbaum, SL, p. 120.
2. *Letters and Papers of Henry VIII* (HMSO), III, Part 2, p. 1100.
3. Schoenbaum, CDL, p. 74.
4. Fripp, III, p. 170.

5. Quoted from Schoenbaum, CDL, p. 47.

6. Quoted from Chambers, WS, II, p. 189.

7. I have been drawing here on the actors' biographies in Chambers, ES, II, pp. 295–350. See also Bentley's study of apprenticeship in PPST. Professor Bentley writes (p. 122): 'there is no doubt that the acting troupes used the apprentice system to train and hold their boy actors'.

8. Shakespeare, *Works*, ed. Rowe (1709), I, p. v.

9. Shakespeare, *Works*, ed. Malone (1821), II, Section IX. Malone concludes (p. 166): 'All these circumstances decidedly prove, in my apprehension, that this anecdote is a mere fiction. . . . It is, I think, much more probable, that his own lively disposition made him acquainted with some of the principal performers who visited Stratford . . . and that there he first determined to engage in that profession.'

10. John Dover Wilson, *The Essential Shakespeare, A Biographical Adventure* (Cambridge, 1937), pp. 42–3.

11. For the distinction between the two, see Chambers, WS, II, pp. 84–5.

12. Bentley, PPST, p. 26.

Chapter 3: The Apprentice

1. *The Essential Shakespeare, A Biographical Adventure* (Cambridge, 1937), p. 43.

2. The municipal year in Stratford ran from Michaelmas (29 September) to Michaelmas, and the Chamberlains' accounts were presented retrospectively. Confusingly, however, certain entries are found to be subsequent to the accounting periods to which they are attributed. For dates throughout the chapter, I draw on Fripp, II and III, and Murray, I, pp. 43–57.

3. *The Statutes of the Realm*, ed. A. Luders *et al.*, IV, Part 1 (1819), p. 591. Also in Chambers, ES, IV, p. 270.

4. REED: *Cumb, West, Glos*, pp. 362–3.

5. For Essex' and Berkeley's men, see Chambers, ES, II, pp. 102–4. Robert Devereux, second earl of Essex, had a company from 1581 which visited Stratford in 1583–4 and 1587. Berkeley was named at Stratford as 'Bartlett' or 'Bartlite'.

6. On the occasion of their first visit in 1569, when John Shakespeare was Mayor and therefore in a position to determine the amount of their reward, they received a mere

shilling in contrast to the thirteen shillings awarded later to Leicester's players. But in subsequent years, though remaining well below the level that Leicester's continued to command, their rewards were to rise to a more respectable 3s 4d or 5s. As I explain in Chapter 10, the mayor's reward was only a part of the income they would expect to receive in the course of such visits.

7. REED: *Coventry*, pp. 293, 298.

8. For Gloucester, see REED: *Cumb, West, Glos*, p. 309; for Leicester, Murray, II, p. 302; and for Coventry, REED: *Coventry*, p. 302.

9. For a full and revealing account of the dispute that gave rise to these records, see Chambers, ES, II, pp. 221–4.

10. *Ibid.*, p. 223.

Chapter 4: Admiral's Man

1. *The Life and Times of William Shakespeare* (1988), p. 61.

2. Unlike non-dramatic poetry, which often circulated in manuscript before publication, playscripts were jealously guarded by the companies that had commissioned and owned them to protect them from rival companies and pirates.

3. For Kent towns, see MSC VII under appropriate towns and dates; for Ipswich, MSC II, Part 3, p. 274; other towns, Murray, I, p. 141.

4. Murray, I, p. 112. Plays and players were regarded by Puritans as in direct competition with Protestant preachers of sermons (given in the afternoons when plays were performed in the open-air theatres) and thus in league with the 'papists'.

5. Murray, I, pp. 141–2.

6. Chambers, ES, II, p. 135.

7. Jonson, VI, p. 16.

8. Jonson, VIII, pp. 56–7.

9. See William A. Armstrong, 'Shakespeare and the Acting of Edward Alleyn' in SS 7 (1954, reprinted 1974), pp. 82–9.

10. J.C. Maxwell in his 1961 Arden edition stated that 'there does not seem to be anything that flatly contradicts a date of about 1589/90' (p. xxiv). Eugene M. Waith in his Oxford edition of 1984 concludes that 'by a conservative estimate, it was first performed in the years 1590–2' (p. 20). Jonathan Bate, in his Arden edition of 1995 (pp. 69–79) is alone among the play's recent editors in dating its first performance to as late as 1594. I return to consider the

play's performance history in the following chapter.

11. He is mentioned by name as visiting Worcester in REED: *Hereford and Worcester*, pp. 494, 499. For Shakespeare's use of other actors' names (subsequently to find their way into the Folio texts of his plays), see Alison Gaw, 'Actors' Names in Basic Shakespeare Texts' in PMLA 40 (1925), pp. 530–50; and Karl P. Wentersdorf, 'Actors' Names in Shakespearean Texts' in *Theatre Studies* (1976/7), pp. 18–30.

12. 'Par', which appears as a speech prefix at IV.ii.71, is probably meant to indicate the player of the Pedant, and may be either an abbreviation for Thomas Parsons, who was acting with the Admiral's in 1598, or a reference to William Parr, recorded in a 'plot' of *Tamar Cam*, a lost play performed by the Admiral's in 1602, who is 'not known to have been associated with any company except this one and its derivatives' (Bentley, JCS, II, p. 520). He was to become a personal friend of Alleyn's. Similarly, 'Fel', prefixing the one-line role of the Haberdasher at IV.iii.63, is likely to have been William Felle, who is described in *Henslowe's Diary*

in 1599 as William Bird's 'man'; Bird was a member of the Admiral's company in 1597, and both he and his man (apprentice?) may go back to this earlier time. Among the many named servants of Petruchio in IV.i, 'Peter' is given several short speeches and, as Dover Wilson pointed out, is almost certainly the first name of an actor as he makes another, speechless entrance at IV.iv.68 as a servant to Tranio. The forename is rare among players of the time. He may be Alleyn's servant, Peter, sent with a message and a horse to Henslowe in 1593 (*Henslowe's Diary*, ed. Greg, II, p. 302). For such a large cast all available supernumeraries would have been roped in. The still rarer 'Curtis' – improbably given to the steward of Petruchio's estate near Verona – is more than likely that of the actor Curtis Greville, who is later recorded as a King's man, playing small parts in *The Two Noble Kinsmen* of 1613 (Chambers, WS, I, p. 530). See also the New Cambridge edition of the play, ed. Sir Arthur Quiller–Couch and John Dover Wilson (Cambridge, 1928, reprinted 1968), pp. 115–20, and for biographies of the actors named, Chambers, ES, II, pp. 295–350.

13. Andrew S. Cairncross in his Arden edition of *Henry VI, Part One* (1962), p. xli.

14. Edward Hall, *The Union of the Two Noble and Illustre Famelies of Lancastre and Yorke* (1548), as quoted by Cairncross, *op. cit.*, p. xlii.

15. See Chambers, ES, II, pp. 137–8.

16. MSC II, Part 3, p. 276. Only the fiscal year is stated (1589/90), but from the position of the entries in the Chamberlain's accounts, they appear to have taken place no earlier than the end of October and would probably therefore have followed the City prohibition of 5 November. They received £1 for the first performance and 10s for the second.

17. Chambers, WS, I, p. 41; II, p. 306.

18. Chambers, WS, I, pp. 48–9.

19. The plot, which was found among Alleyn's papers at Dulwich, relates to a somewhat earlier revival of the play at the Theatre or Curtain in 1590/1.

20. These are all commonly described as 'minor players', but Spencer at least was famous enough in his day to be mentioned by Thomas Heywood in his *Apology for Actors* of 1612 along with Singer, Pope, Phillips and Sly: that 'though they be dead, their deserts yet live in the remembrance of many' (p. 43). Though Shakespeare only names them as playing very small, unnamed parts, they may of course have doubled these with larger roles that he had no particular reason to record.

21. That Howard was willing to supply such a document indicates that he took a closer interest in his players, and was more helpful to them, than is often suggested.

22. See Willem Schrickx, 'English Actors at the Courts of Wolfenbüttel, Brussels and Graz during the Lifetime of Shakespeare' in SS 33 (1980), pp. 153–9.

23. Quoted from Chambers, WS, II, p. 253.

24. The texts of Shakespeare's plays as memorially reconstructed by actors in pirated editions, such as the quartos of *Henry VI, Parts Two and Three (First Part of the Contention* and *The true Tragedie)*, are mainly of this approximate kind.

25. Nicholas Rowe in the biographical introduction to Shakespeare, *Works* (1709) I, p. vi.

26. See F.S. Boas (ed.), *The Works of Thomas Kyd* (Oxford, 1901), pp. lxxviii–lxxx, and Eugene M. Waith's introduction to his Oxford edition of *Titus* (1984), pp. 37–8. For the use that Shakespeare made of it in his later writings, Boas, pp. lxxxii–iii. Shakespeare may also have acted in an old play about Hamlet (the so-called *Ur-Hamlet*), possibly by Kyd, that was being performed in 1589, and in which the Ghost wore a visard (mask) and cried 'like an oister wife, "Hamlet, revenge"'. A later performance of it was given by a combination of the Admiral's and Chamberlain's men in a small theatre at Newington Butts on 11 June 1594, in which Shakespeare is likely to have taken part, and this may have influenced his own later treatment of the story more directly. See Chambers, WS, I, pp. 411–12.

27. It was not licensed for publication till 1592, and the only surviving copies date from 1599. See Boas (n. 26 above), pp. liv–lxi.

28. *The Life and Times of William Shakespeare* (1988), p. 62.

29. Scene 5, 1–9; Cf. *Macbeth*, ll.i.49–64; also *The Rape of Lucrece*, ll. 162–8.

30. In his introduction to the text of the play in *Three Elizabethan Domestic Tragedies* (Penguin English Library, 1969), p. 25.

31. For the Faversham visits, see Murray, I, p. 141; MSC VII, p. 62. The visit of 1586 appears in Murray and Chambers (ES, II, p. 135) only. I cannot do justice to the case for Shakespeare's authorship here. The usual tests fail in that being so early nothing of the play would have been known to Heminges and Condell, or to Mears; nor does it appear to have been revived by the Chamberlain's men. It is true that it is quite unlike anything else that Shakespeare was to write; but in a curious way, this may also be taken as an argument in its favour, for how often did Shakespeare ever repeat himself?

32. F.G. Fleay, *A Chronicle History of the Life and Work of William Shakespeare* (1886), p. 14; *King Edward the First by George Peele 1593*, ed. W.W. Greg, MSR (1911), ll. 759–62; my italics.

33. Chambers, ES, III, pp. 460–1.

34. In Elizabethan drama, a shaking of weapons is usually taken as a gesture of rejection or defiance. In *Tamburlaine*, the Christian general Sigismund presents a

doubtful ally with a naked sword and tells him, 'Wilt thou have war, then shake this blade at me;/If peace, restore it to my hands again' (2 *Tam*: I.ii.6–7); Tamburlaine defies Mahomet by burning his sacred books and challenging him to send his vengeance 'on the head of Tamburlaine/That shakes his sword against thy majesty' (2 *Tam*: V.i.193–4). In Shakespeare (according to Onions), the commonest meanings of 'shake' are 'lay aside, get rid of, discard', and in *Henry VI*, Old Clifford instructs those of Cade's rebels who hate the king and 'honours not his father/Henry the Fifth . . . Shake he his weapon at us, and pass by' (2H6: IV.viii.16–18). He has not many takers.

35. Chambers, as n. 33 above.

Chapter 5: The Rose, 1592

1. As quoted by Eugene M. Waith in his Oxford edition of *Titus* (1984), p. 12.

2. Quoted from the Arden edition of *Henry VI, Part 1*, ed. Andrew S. Cairncross (1962, reprinted 1986), p. xxxviii.

3. *Henslowe's Diary*, ed. R.A. Foakes and R.T. Rickert (Cambridge, 1961),

pp. 16–21. According to Chambers (ES, II, p. 139), the fluctuating sum of his takings 'seems to have represented half the amount received for admission to the galleries of the house; the other half, with the payments for entrance to the standing room in the yard, being divided amongst such of the players as had a share in the profits'.

4. I have excluded an indeterminate entry of 'harey' on 16 March as this might refer to a play Henslowe names elsewhere as 'harey of cornwell'.

5. The same gloss is given to 'the second pte of tamber' (a lost play called *Tamar Cham*) on 28 April, 'the taner of denmarke' (another lost play) on 23 May, and 'a knacke to know a knave' (on 10 June), which is extant and contains a reference to Titus as having 'made a conquest on the Goths', thus tending to confirm that Shakespeare's *Titus* was already in existence by this date and known to the author of the *Knack* (see Chambers, WS, I, p. 316). Henslowe's 'ne' does not, of course, preclude the possibility that the plays so marked had been premiered out of London. It may simply

mean that they were new to Henslowe, or the Rose.

6. Chambers, WS, I, pp. 318–19; translated from German to English in E. and H. Brennecke, *Shakespeare in Germany 1590–1700* (Chicago, 1964), pp. 18–51.

7. Chambers, ES, II, p. 274.

8. Waith (n. 1 above), pp. 32–3, 39. W.W. Greg noted that 'Mutius seems to be an extra son, for Titus had twenty-five and lost twenty-two, yet brought four to Rome'; quoted from Geoffrey Bullough, *Narrative and Dramatic Sources of Shakespeare* (1966), VI, p. 6, n. 3.

9. Chambers, WS, I, pp. 312–22; II, p. 346.

10. June Schlueter in 'Rereading the Peacham Drawing' in SQ (Summer 1999), pp. 171–83.

11. *Henslowe's Diary* (n. 3 above), p. 21.

12. Perhaps as a hangover from the old revision theory of the plays' origins, whereby it was believed that Parts 2 and 3 were written in advance of Part 1 for another company, Pembroke's men, and published by them as *The First part of the Contention betwixt the two famous Houses of Yorke and Lancaster* and *The true Tragedie of Richard Duke of Yorke*, which Shakespeare was thought to have later revised. However, in 1929 Peter Alexander convincingly demonstrated that the *Contention* and the *True Tragedie* were, in fact, memorial reconstructions of Shakespeare's plays pirated by actors – probably a break-away group from the Admiral's/Strange's alliance following the closure of the Rose season in February 1593. There is no evidence that Shakespeare had anything to do with Pembroke's men as either author or actor. Cf. similarly comprehensive references to Parts 1 and 2 of *Henry IV* as simply *Henry IV* as noted by A.R. Humphreys in his Arden edition of Part 2 of that play (1966), p. xvi.

13. I derive these, and the figures that follow, from Chambers, ES, II, pp. 121–2.

14. Strange's men were at Oxford on 6 October and Coventry on 1 November; the Admiral's at Leicester on 19 December. While Strange's were performing at Hampton Court for the Queen on 31 December and 1 January 1593, the Admiral's were back at the Rose in the *Knack to Know a Knave* (on 31 December) and the *Jew of Malta* (on 1 January). This suggests that, though in alliance, the companies had

retained performance right in the smaller-cast plays in their respective repertoires while joining forces only, perhaps, for the bigger productions, which would certainly have included *Titus* and the *Henry VI* plays.

15. I agree, however, with Chambers that, in view of Henslowe's manifest imprecision in his use of titles, it is not inconceivable that the play performed as *Buckingham* by Sussex's men at the Rose when the theatres reopened at the end of 1593 was Shakespeare's *Richard III*. It opened on 30 December, and three more performances were given in January 1594. If Buckingham is not the lead role in Shakespeare's play, it is the second lead. The fact that Sussex's company also gave two performances of 'titus & andronicous' (undoubtedly Shakespeare's *Titus*) in the same short season (it closed on 6 February) suggests that the prompt-books of both *Titus* and *Richard III* had been retained by Henslowe on the breaking of the Admiral's/ Strange's alliance (as he may have been entitled to do), and passed by him to Sussex's men for performance a year later. See Chambers, WS, I, pp. 303–4, 497–8; *Henslowe's*

Diary (n. 3 above), pp. 20–1.

16. Prologue to the *Jew of Malta* at the Cockpit theatre, 1633, in *Works of Christopher Marlowe*, ed. C.F. Tucker Brooke (Oxford, 1910), p. 239.

17. V.iii.136. T.W. Baldwin in his *Organization and Personnel of the Shakespearean Company* (Princeton, 1927) gives the part to Heminges, the older actor of the later Chamberlain's company; but we need to remember that at this early date Shakespeare's fellows, including Heminges, Brian and Pope, cannot have been a great deal older than he was. Alleyn was younger, and Heminges went on to outlive him by fourteen years. It was a young company throughout.

18. As quoted by Chambers, WS, II, p. 188. Was Nashe's 'Tragedian' Edward Alleyn? As principal player of the company and foremost tragedian of his day, it would seem more than likely. But if so, he was much smaller in stature than his imposing portrait at Dulwich (Plate 7) suggests. For, on first meeting Talbot, the Countess of Auvergne – expecting 'some Hercules/ A second Hector' – is surprised to find a person she is

overheard to describe as 'a silly dwarf', 'this weak and writhled shrimp' (II.iii.18–22). The part is usually assigned to Burbage, but there is no evidence that he was one of the company at this date. In view of the quarrel between Alleyn and Richard's father, James, that had brought the company to the Rose in the first place, it is most unlikely that he was.

19. From *Greenes Groats-worth of Wit* (1592) as quoted by Chambers, WS, II, p. 188.

20. From *Epistle* to *Kind-Harts Dreame* (n.d.); quoted by Chambers, WS, II, p. 189.

21. Quoted by J.C. Maxwell in his Arden edition of *Titus* (1953, 3rd edn of 1961), p. xxxiv.

22. In his 1962 Arden edition of *1 Henry VI*, p. xxviii.

23. At San Francisco in 1903, and again in 1935 (including *Richard III*); at Stratford in 1906 by Sir Frank Benson; by the Birmingham Repertory Theatre (*2 and 3 Henry VI*) in 1952, and later (*1 to 3 Henry VI*) at the Old Vic; by the RSC in heavily adapted versions by John Barton and Peter Hall as *The Wars of the Roses* in 1963; and again by the RSC, including *Richard III* but extensively edited to form three plays as *The Plantagenets* by Adrian Noble, in 1988/9.

The British theatre has yet to do justice to the four plays of the tetralogy by performing them in due sequence and in full. Perhaps the new, restored Globe will oblige?

24. *Johnson on Shakespeare*, ed. Walter Raleigh (Oxford, 1908, reprinted 1965), pp. 144, 136.

25. Hereward T. Price, *Construction in Shakespeare* (Michigan, 1951), p. 26, as quoted by Cairncross (n. 2 above), p. xli.

Chapter 6: The Player Poet

1. Quoted from Schoenbaum, SL, p. 182.

2. J.F. Goodridge, *Piers the Ploughman* (Penguin Classics, 1966 edn), p. 9.

3. For *Richard II*, III.ii.155–6; *Macbeth*, V.v.24–8; *Richard III*, V.v.23, 40–1.

4. For Sly, *Taming of the Shrew*, Ind., ii, 69–70; Demetrius, *Midsummer Night's Dream*, IV.i.192–4; Prospero, *Tempest*, IV.i.156–8.

5. For an account of their medieval history, see Southworth, EMM, chapters 3 and 7.

6. For the rehearsal of new plays, none of the players was provided with a complete copy of the text (as yet unpublished), but only with a transcript of their own

speeches and cues. Once the actors had learnt their lines, these would often have been discarded. It may have been some of these that Bevis and his fellows got hold of and incorporated in their pirated versions of the plays. For the company, see Chambers, ES, II, p. 128; Mary Edmond, 'Pembroke's Men' in *Review of English Studies*, NS, Vol. XXV, No. 98 (1974), pp. 129–30.

7. The wording is given in full by Chambers, WS, II, pp. 312–13.

8. Chambers, ES, IV, pp. 164–5.

9. Quoted from Chambers, WS, I, pp. 543–4.

10. The unreliable Davenant is credited by Rowe with a story that Southampton had given to Shakespeare 'a thousand pounds, to enable him to go through with a Purchase which he heard he had a mind to' (cited in Schoenbaum, SL, p. 65). Even if essentially true, the amount of the gift has been inflated beyond credibility in the retelling. In 1605, Edward Alleyn valued his 'share of aparell' in the Admiral's at £100 (Chambers, ES, II, p. 298). Southampton's gift could hardly have been more than that, and may have been less.

11. See Leech's introduction to his 1969 Arden edition of the play, pp. xxvi–xxx.

12. Professor T.W. Baldwin betrays his ignorance of the actor's craft when he opines that Shakespeare chose such roles because they required of him 'comparatively little acting to do' (*Organization and Personnel of the Shakespearean Company*, Princeton, 1927, p. 262). One has only to see how poorly they are played in some modern productions to realise how mistaken the Professor was in his estimate of their inherent difficulty.

13. When the Ephesian Dromio and his master try unsuccessfully to gain admittance to their house (in III.i), we hear the voice of the Syracusan Dromio from within (either imitated by an actor backstage or spoken upstage by his twin), but there is no need for them to appear together. The only occasion on which they meet is in the final scene, where clearly look-alike doubles are required, but Antipholus and Dromio of Syracuse, who are the last to arrive on stage, have only 26 lines between them in the rest of the play, and the scene is kept as short as Shakespeare could reasonably make it, with the Abbess having all the

longer speeches. By then, the light in an open-air performance on Innocents' Day in the winter would have been failing. If it is objected that the audience would be initially confused by such doubling, the answer is that they are meant to be confused, and it is from that general confusion that the essential humour of the play arises.

14. See the account printed by R.A. Foakes in his Arden edition of 1962, pp. 115–17.

15. *The Sonnets and A Lover's Complaint* (Penguin, 1986), p. 11. My italics.

16. *Shakespeare, The poet in his world* (1978, University Paperback edn, 1980), p. 79.

17. Chambers, WS, I, p. 515.

18. For a detailed study of these, see Eric Sams, *Shakespeare's Edward III* (New Haven and London, 1996), pp. 185–7 and notes.

19. For a deeper relationship between them, see Kerrigan (n. 15 above), pp. 293–5.

20. For a detailed synopsis and more sympathetic appreciation of the play and its themes, see Sams (n. 18 above), pp. 3–12.

21. See ll. 111, 793–4, 1660–6, 1720, and notes on these lines by John Roe in his New Cambridge edition of *The Poems* (Cambridge, 1992).

22. Chambers, WS, I, p. 546. Sir Edmund comments (*ibid.*, pp. 61–2): 'A super-subtle criticism detects a great advance in the poet's intimacy with his patron between the two addresses, which I am bound to say is not apparent to me'. If, as I believe, Shakespeare had received a financial reward from Southampton for *Venus and Adonis*, any increase of warmth discernible in the second letter is adequately explained, for then his patron could indeed be said to have made an investment in Shakespeare's future, so that 'what I have to doe is yours, being part in all I have' becomes no more than the literal truth of his situation at the time.

23. To play with conviction a Princess of France or one of her ladies was not something that any intelligent choirboy or page could pick up in a matter of days or weeks; it was the result of years of continuous instruction from as early an age as eight. Though the London theatres had been closed since February 1593, the companies had continued to tour so the apprentices' training need not have been interrupted.

24. Chambers, WS, I, pp. 331–2.

Chapter 7: Chamberlain's Man

1. *A Life of William Shakespeare* (1923), pref., p. ix; quoted from Schoenbaum, SL, pp. 505–6.

2. Chambers, ES, II, p. 193. When, in July 1596, Henry Carey died and was succeeded as Lord Hunsdon by his son, Sir George Carey, and as Chamberlain by Lord Cobham, the company was to be known briefly once more as Lord Hunsdon's. It was only in March 1597, when Cobham died and was succeeded in turn by Sir George in his father's old office as Chamberlain, that the company was able to resume its former title.

3. Chambers, WS, II, p. 314.

4. He may, however, have appeared as the young Richard (afterwards Gloucester) in Part 3 of *Henry VI* at the Theatre before the dispute with Alleyn, and thus have prepared the ground for one of the most famous of his later roles, that of Richard III in Shakespeare's play.

5. A full account of the latter dispute is given by Chambers in ES, II, pp. 387–93.

6. *The Works of Thomas Nashe*, ed. R.B. McKerrow, revised F.P. Wilson (Oxford, 1958), III, p. 341.

7. That the *Knacke* was an Admiral's play, and that it was the Admiral's company that Kempe had joined on his return from the continent (not Strange's, as is usually stated), is proven by performance records for 31 December 1592 and 1 January 1593, for on those dates the *Knacke* and the *Jew of Malta* (another Admiral's play) were in performance at the Rose while Strange's were performing at court; see *Henslowe's Diary*, ed. Foakes and Rickert, p. 19, and Chambers, WS, II, p. 311.

8. On negative evidence, Chambers (ES, II, p. 340) assumes he was a Strange's man, though the record he quotes from an inventory of costumes belonging to the Admiral's in March 1598 after he had transferred to the Chamberlain's ('Perowes sewt, which Wm Sley were') indicates the contrary.

9. For biographical information, above and below, I have drawn mainly on Chambers, ES, II, pp. 295–350, and WS, II, pp. 71–87; Nungezer, *Dictionary*; and Bentley, JCS, II. For the players' wills, see *Wills*.

10. See Bentley, PPST, p. 221, para 2. In the *Seven Deadly Sins*, 'Mr Bryan' plays the part of a Councillor to Burbage's

leading role as Goboduc, and Warwick in a concluding scene with Henry VI and Sincler as his Keeper. (Was Warwick Bryan's part in *Henry VI, Part 3* as the Keeper was Sincler's?) In another plot (for *The Battle of Alcazar, c.* 1598), a 'Mr Charles' has three supporting roles, and 'Mr Sam', six (*ibid.*, pp. 213, 230–1).

11. See Bentley, PPST, pp. 118–26. William Trigg, a leading player of women's roles in the Caroline period, was thirteen or fourteen when apprenticed to John Heminges for a period of twelve years to learn 'la arte d'une Stage player'; he would thus have been twenty-five or twenty-six before achieving his freedom. Some of the guilds (and the Grocers may have been one of them) withheld enfranchisement until the apprentice was twenty-four – as ordained by the Statute of Artificers of 1563, Section 19.

12. In 1597, Henslowe 'bought' a boy, James Bristow, for £8 – presumably from a player to whom James had initially been apprenticed on payment of a premium – and received 3*s* a week from the Admiral's in respect of his services; Chambers, ES, II, pp. 153, 155.

13. In the Induction to Marston's *The Malcontent* of 1603, Condell appears under his own name, and is asked for as 'Harry Condell' (Revels edn, l. 11.) Beeston went on to a successful career as actor-manager in the Jacobean and Caroline theatre. He is thought to have provided information to John Aubrey regarding Shakespeare's mode of life in the time they had worked together as Chamberlain's men. To this I return.

14. In 1592, he is recorded as a Pembroke's man (Mary Edmond in *Review of English Studies*, 25, 1974, p. 131), but in 1593 the company had collapsed on the road, which may have prompted his move to the Chamberlain's and change of occupation.

15. See n. 11 above. Heminges had probably achieved his freedom of the Grocers by performing at their feasts – a means of entry for which there is long precedent among entertainers. Among other Chamberlain's men and 'principal actors' known to have enjoyed the freedom of one or other of the London guilds were Robert Armin and John Lowin of the Goldsmiths, John Shank of the Weavers, and James

Burbage of the Joiners. Robert Armin (who succeeded Kempe in his clown roles) is on record as apprenticing another player in the same craft, as Heminges had apprenticed Cooke. There is no evidence that any of these men practised at any time the crafts of which they were nominally 'free'.

16. See *Wills*, pp. 94–6.

17. *Ibid.*, pp. 73, 80. The specific mention of Sandes' 'Indenture' is interesting in view of what has been said above (n. 15). Chambers (WS, II, p. 85) reluctantly allows that Phillips may have been a member of the London Company of Minstrels and Musicians, and that Sandes may have followed him into that indistinct profession; but the ability to play musical instruments was, if not *de rigueur*, common among players of the time, and Phillips could just as easily have been free of any one of the guilds, and used it (as Heminges had done) to hold his apprentice. To have taken over from him in the way that he did, Sly must have belonged to the same guild.

18. Among later recruits to be named in the Folio as sharers and principal actors were John Lowin (from 1603), William Ostler (1610), Nathan Field (1615, a former pupil of Ben Jonson's) – all of whom we shall meet again in later chapters – John Underwood (1608), Richard Robinson (1611) and John Rice (before 1607, another of Heminges' apprentices). Of these, Ostler, Field, Underwood and Robinson had begun their careers as children in one of the royal chapels or Queen's Revels, and joined the King's men as adolescents.

19. The text of neither part of the *Seven Deadly Sins* has survived. Though described by Henslowe in his *Diary* as 'Four Plays in One', it is clear from the plot that the second part comprised only three plays, preceded by a Prologue, in which Pride, Wrath and Covetousness (presumably the subjects of Part 1) are ejected from the stage by Envy, Sloth and Lechery, the subjects of Part 2. It is at this point that Henry VI (as played, I believe, by Shakespeare), who has been asleep, perhaps dreaming, in a tent, wakes up and is joined by J. Sincler as the Keeper. The Prologue's author may here have been drawing on Act 3, Scene 1 of Shakespeare's *Henry VI, Part 3*, which also features Henry VI and Sincler as a Keeper,

and for an Epilogue – in which Henry is joined by others including 'warders' and Warwick, played by Bryan – made use of other speeches from that play.

20. The player-musicians included William Tawyer, the trumpeter of the *Dream* (V.i.125) and Jack Wilson, the lutenist and singer of 'Sigh no more, ladies' in *Much Ado* (II.iii.36); but we cannot claim these two as necessarily original members of the company as their names (unlike those previously cited from rogue directions and speech prefixes) are more likely to derive from the prompt books of later revivals than from Shakespeare's original manuscripts. See Alison Gaw, 'Actors' Names in Basic Shakespearean Texts' in PMLA, 40 (1925), pp. 532–3.

21. When, in the early 1950s, the then directors of the Old Vic (Michel Saint-Denis, Glen Byam Shaw and George Devine) had proposed a similar organisational structure for the company that was intended to form the basis for a future National Theatre, incorporating a school and youth theatre (the Young Vic) which were already in existence, the Old Vic governors were advised by various well-known theatre people of the time that such a structure, though long established and notably successful in other European capitals, would be inimical to 'English theatrical tradition', and in consequence it was shamefully abandoned; an indication of the depth of ignorance prevailing at the time (and which regrettably still largely prevails both in and out of the profession) concerning our own theatrical history in the period of its finest achievements.

22. See Bentley, PDST, *passim*.

23. Chambers, ES, IV, p. 316. He concedes that 'where heretofore they began not their Plaies till towardes fower a clock, they will now begin at two, & have don betwene fower and five, and will nott use anie Drumes or trumpettes att all for the callinge of peopell together . . .'.

24. Chambers, WS, II, p. 319; for the amount, ES, IV, pp. 164–5. As the Admiral's were also paid for a court performance on the 28th and, as previously stated, the Chamberlain's performance of the *Comedy of Errors* at Grays Inn was given on the same evening, the second of the two

Greenwich dates is usually taken to be a mistake for the 27th. This may be so; but the *Comedy* is Shakespeare's shortest play, and the distance between Greenwich and the City is not so great as to make it impossible for the players to have gone by river from an afternoon performance at Greenwich to Grays Inn where, we are told, the audience did not arrive until 9 p.m. and where the festivities were further delayed by a 'disordered Tumult and Crowd upon the stage' (*Gesta Grayoram*, as quoted by R.A. Foakes in his Arden edition of the play, pp. 115–17). The Admiral's performance may have followed that of the Chamberlain's on the same evening. The Christmas season was harvest-time for the players and they would have needed to make the most of it.

25. It is sometimes supposed that it is easier and more practicable to double parts that are similar in age, diction, character or appearance than those which are contrasting in one or more of these respects; as an actor himself, Shakespeare would have known that the opposite is true. The more different the parts, the easier it is for the actor to make the necessary distinctions between them by drawing on contrasting facets of his own personality. If he is able to do this, there is also less risk of confusing the audience. In a non-naturalistic theatre such as Shakespeare's, in which 'doubling' (by which is meant playing more than one part, perhaps three or more) is an accepted convention, there is no requirement for the actor to conceal his identity when performing duplicate roles; simply to make them true to themselves in all their differences.

26. Of the other five plays that open with a Prologue (*Henry IV, Part 2, Henry V, Henry VIII, Troilus and Cressida*, and *Pericles*), all but *Troilus* end with a formal Epilogue.

27. I am indebted to T.J.B. Spencer's defence of the Friar in his Penguin edition of the play (1967), pp. 8, 36. The character may have been based by Shakespeare on one of the recusant priests he had met with in Stratford during the period of his father's return to the Catholicism of his youth in the late 1570s or early '80s. Cf. Greene's paltry treatment of the thirteenth-century English Franciscan, Roger Bacon, in his *Friar*

Bacon and Friar Bungay of about 1589.

28. As quoted by William A. Armstrong, 'Actors and Theatres', in SS 17 (1964), p. 196.

29. From Preface by Rhenanus to *Speculum Aistheticum* of 1613, as cited and translated by David Klein, 'Notes on "Did Shakespeare Produce His Own Plays?"' in MLR 57 (October 1962), p. 556. For other references to the poet's function at rehearsals, see Klein, pp. 556–60.

30. See Bentley, PPST, pp. 113–16.

31. He was the author of a number of published jigs – a lost performance art involving characterisation and song, as well as dance. Marston's *Scourge of Villainy* (Satire XI.31) of 1598 has the lines,

A hall, a hall!
Room for the spheres, the orbs celestial
Will dance Kempe's jig (Nungezer, p. 218) that echo Capulet's,

A hall, a hall, give room! And foot it, girls!
More light, you knaves, and turn the tables up. (I.v.26–7)

32. In the course of an English Heritage survey by Simon Blatherwick, as reported in *The Times* of 11 January 1999, p. 3.

33. Chambers, WS, II, p. 252. According to the way it is punctuated, these phrases can be, and sometimes are, interpreted as meaning 'Lived in Shoreditch; wouldn't be debauched, and, if invited [to be debauched], replied he was in pain'. But is anyone normally *invited* to be debauched? And if someone was so invited, would they normally excuse themselves by saying they were *in pain*? I find it easier to believe that Shakespeare was often in pain in writing his plays.

34. Chambers, WS, I, p. 356. My italics.

35. Introduction to his Penguin edition of 1967, p. 13.

36. For the court performances, Chambers, WS, II, p. 321.

37. Chambers, WS, II, p. 320; MSC 2, Part 3, p. 279. The amount of their reward was twice as much as that received by the Queen's, and four times that by the Admiral's men in 1596/7.

38. My personal experience suggests that if one can get the play started in the right way, even at the cost of a disproportionate amount of rehearsal time, the chances of its staying on course to the end are vastly improved. To

have Shakespeare on stage for both opening and concluding scenes would have been double insurance!

39. On the basis of some lines in *Hamlet*, Professor Baldwin (*Organization and Personnel of the Shakespearean Company*, Princeton, 1927, pp. 230ff.) proposed that each of the players had a set line of parts ('player king', 'adventurous knight', 'humorous man' etc.) that was consistently adhered to in the casting of the plays. Apart from the thin man, Sincler (in a category of his own), and to some extent Kempe or Armin as clowns and Shakespeare in his kingly parts, there is no real evidence of this; nor does the theory take into account the frequent necessity for doubling, especially in the histories. Great credit is nevertheless due to Baldwin who, virtually alone among serious scholars, attempted to throw some much-needed light on the matter. Though my own suggestions as to casting rarely accord with his, I have consulted them throughout, and am indebted to his discussion of the problems.

40. Andrew Gurr, in his New Cambridge edition of *Richard II* of 1984, among other scholars, dates the play to 1595 partly on the basis of a letter written by Sir Edward Hoby on 7 December of that year to Lord Burleigh, inviting him to 'visit poore Channon rowe where as late as it shal please you a gate for your supper shal be open: & K. Richard present him selfe to your vewe' (pp. 1–2). Hoby is known to have been a collector of historical portraits, and the letter reads to me more like an invitation to view a recent acquisition of that kind (not necessarily of the *second* Richard) than a two or three-hour performance of Shakespeare's play, of which Burleigh and Hoby were apparently to be the only auditors. How late would the players have been expected to remain in waiting for Burleigh? and how late would Burleigh have been expected to stay?

41. See Chambers, WS, I, p. 373: *The Merchant of Venice*, ed. John Russell Brown (Arden edn, 1955, reprinted 1964), pp. xxv–vii.

42. It is interesting to find that nearly all of Shakespeare's Balthasars (in the *Comedy of Errors, Romeo*, and here) are obvious doubles for one or other of the sharers. The Balthasar of *Much Ado* is the exception.

43. The attitude of Elizabethan playwrights to the Jews in general is more complex than is often supposed; nor were they unaware or uncritical of hypocrisy in the behaviour of Christians towards them. In Robert Wilson's *Three Ladies of London*, a popular morality of the 1580s, the Jew Gerontus is depicted as a paragon of upright dealing and generosity, in pointed contrast to Mercatore, a Christian merchant who, having borrowed money of the Jew, seeks to avoid repayment by fraud, perjury in a Turkish court, and finally apostasy. Gerontus is so appalled by the merchant's willingness to deny his religion that he remits the debt as, in Shakespeare's play, Antonio remits a part of the fine imposed on Shylock. Mercatore later boasts that he has 'cosen'd' the Jew. The Turkish judge in the case concludes that 'Jews seek to excel in Christianity and Christians in Jewishness'. The text of the play is in Dodsley's *Old English Plays*, ed. W.C. Hazlitt, VI (1874).

44. The skilful use that Shakespeare makes of the natural dimming of light in the late afternoon of autumn and winter days in the theatres where his plays were performed has not always been noticed or appreciated. The hour at which his final scenes are said to take place is often found to correspond, more or less exactly, with the actual time a 2 o'clock performance would by then have reached in the theatre. In the *Comedy of Errors*, the Duke's doom on Egeon is timed to take effect at five in the evening and that is the hour of its final scene; the play of the Nine Worthies in Act 5 of *Love's Labour's Lost* is intended, as Holofernes says, for the 'posterior of the day'; and when, in the last act of the *Tempest*, Prospero asks of Ariel, 'How's the day?', the spirit replies, 'On the sixth hour'. Sometimes, as in the *Merchant*, candles and other lights are introduced, and I see no reason to doubt that they were practical. In Act 5 of *Romeo*, Paris and Romeo enter the darkness of the cemetery accompanied by torchbearers, and the Friar carries a lantern. The fairies in Act 5 of the *Dream* are commanded, 'Through the house give glimmering light/By the dead and drowsy fire' and, as the New Cambridge edition notes, this is explained by a stage direction in the Bad Quarto

text of the *Merry Wives* (probably descriptive of performance) instructing the pretend fairies of that play to enter with 'waxen tapers on their heads', which, as Mistress Page explains, 'at the very instant of Falstaff's and our meeting, they will at once display to the night' (V.iii.14–16). (If the tapers were fixed to their heads with bands, both sets of fairies would have been free to dance 'hand-in-hand'.) The final scene of *Othello* begins with Desdemona asleep in bed and the entrance of Othello 'with a light'. These are not just tokens to the audience that a degree of darkness is to be imagined, but more probably actual lights that on a shadowed stage would both have illumined the action to some extent and, more importantly, added to the atmosphere that Shakespeare wished to create.

45. The year is given by Chambers (in WS, II, p. 321) under a heading of 1597 but, as he points out elsewhere, the Faversham visit must have been in 1596 because the company is named there as Lord Hunsdon's players and it was only known by that title between 22 July 1596, when the first Lord Hunsdon died, and 5 March 1597, when his son succeeded him as Chamberlain. See also MSC VII, p. 63, where the entry is correctly placed in 1595/6.

46. Victorian scholars liked to date *King John* to this year because they thought that Shakespeare's rather idealised portrait of young Arthur in that play was his memorial to Hamnet; but I am one of those who consider that if *John* had been completed after rather than before his son's death, he would have written about Arthur in a different way, or perhaps not at all.

47. Chambers, WS, II, p. 321. The dates were 26 and 27 December, 1 and 6 January, and 6 and 8 February. The three pairs of dates suggest that three plays were given, and each in turn repeated a day or two later, to allow more of the Queen's household and guests to see them than could easily be accommodated at a single performance.

48. I am indebted here to Baldwin, who assigns it with probability to Condell.

Chapter 8: He that Plays the King

1. From *The Scourge of Folly*, Epigram 159, in *The Complete*

Works of John Davies of Hereford, ed. Alexander B. Grosart (2 vols, privately printed, 1878), II, p. 26.

2. From *Microcosmos* (1603) in *Complete Works* (*op. cit.*), I, p. 82.

3. From *Speculum Proditori* in *Complete Works* (note 1 above), II, p. 18.

4. From *Scourge of Folly*, Epigram 180, *Complete Works*, II, p. 28.

5. I have previously suggested that the play was originally written for the Admiral's/Strange's alliance at the Rose in 1592/3. When revived by Shakespeare for the Chamberlain's in 1595/6, it became necessary to reduce its length and the number of its roles. It is now generally accepted as probable that the prompt-book of this revised text was somehow lost (perhaps on tour) and, Shakespeare's original manuscript not being readily to hand, was reconstructed from memory by the actors, including Shakespeare, for its publication in the Quarto edition of 1597. By 1623, Shakespeare's manuscript had resurfaced and was used by Heminges and Condell in combination with the published Quarto for their fuller version of the play in the First Folio. See Antony Hammond's introduction to his Arden edition of 1981, pp. 1–50.

6. See previous note. Hammond describes Clarence as a 'gift' part: 'Into his dream Shakespeare poured the most impassioned, lyrically active verse in the play. Most other characters are assigned a single tone of voice, but apart from Richard Clarence alone is allowed the span of the poet's abilities' (Introduction, p. 111). Note also the recollections in the dream speech of the Ghost of Andrea from the *Spanish Tragedy*, as listed in Section 3 of Appendix A. As the ghosts in the last act of *Richard*, including that of Clarence, are not individualised in manner or diction, and announce in a ritual way who they are on appearance, Shakespeare's presence on stage as Richmond, sleeping in his tent, would not have created any difficulty. Probably, the ghosts wore identical shrouds and masks and spoke in diguised spectral voices, and thus could have been played by any of the actors who happened to be available. They are shades from a classical Hades, rather than spirits from a Catholic

Purgatory who (like the Ghost in *Hamlet*) retain much of their human personalities and concerns.

7. Quoted from Geoffrey Bullough, *Narrative and Dramatic Sources of Shakespeare*, IV, p. 148.

8. Of the speech in question (III.i.263ff.), contrary to those who see in it a parody of riddling casuistry, Dr Johnson comments, 'I am not able to discover here any thing inconsequent or ridiculously subtle. The propositions that the voice of the church is the voice of heaven, and that the Pope utters the voice of the church, neither of which Pandulph's auditors would deny, being once granted, the argument used is irresistible; nor is it easy, notwithstanding the gingle, to enforce it with greater brevity or propriety'. I am indebted for this quotation, and other points in my discussion, to John Dover Wilson's introduction to the New Cambridge edition of the play (1936, reprinted 1954), pp. lvii–lxii.

9. For this location, see John Wasson, *Suffolk in the History Plays of Shakespeare*, Xth Harry Clement Memorial Lecture at Keynes Hall, King's College, Cambridge (Suffolk Federation of WEA, 1974), pp. 4–7.

10. For this timing of events, I am drawing on that proposed by A.R. Humphreys in his Arden edition of Part One of *Henry IV* (1960); see especially pp. xiii–xv. For the *Merry Wives*, see following chapter.

11. John Marston in his *Scourge of Villanie* of 1598 speaks of 'Curtaine plaudeties' in connection with *Romeo and Juliet*, which, in 1597, would still have been in the company's repertoire (quoted in Chambers, WS, II, pp. 195–6).

12. The possibility of 'out of town' openings for these and other of Shakespeare's plays was not seriously considered by Chambers, being out of the sphere of his experience of theatre in the period when he wrote, the early 1900s, when such an expedient was rarer than it has since become. There are, however, distinct advantages, as later producers have discovered, in opening plays in the course of a pre-London provincial tour – especially from the point of view of the author, who is thereby enabled to put his work to the test of an audience and introduce whatever changes are required in the light of that

experience in a gradual, unpressured way.

13. This was first proposed by Professor H.D. Gray, 'The Roles of William Kempe', in MLR 25 (1930), pp. 265–7, and taken up by Professor Wilson in *The Fortunes of Falstaff* (Cambridge, 1943), pp. 124–5. The discussion that follows draws (with amendment) on that in Southworth, F & J, pp. 131–3.

14. I am using the term 'buffoon' in the specialised sense of the medieval *scurra*, a type of court fool distinguished by his innate cleverness and talent to amuse, typically literate and belonging to the minor armorial class. For some historical precedents see Southworth, F & J, 'buffoons' as indexed.

15. Chambers, ES, II, p. 326.

16. *Kemps Nine Daies Wonder: Performed in a Morrice from London to Norwich* (1600), ed. G.B. Harrison (Bodley Head Quartos, 1923), p. 3.

Chapter 9: The Globe, 1599–1601

1. From *Theatre of the World* (1969), p. 189.

2. Critics have argued that for him to have done so required Falstaff to reform and that this would have been contrary to the character's essential nature as previously established; but it would have been quite in character for him to have *pretended* reform, and so convinced the king of his sincerity as to be included in his army. In substituting Falstaff for his original name of Oldcastle, Shakespeare was drawing on a minor character in Part One of *Henry VI*, who is denounced as a 'cowardly knight' in that play; but he may also have had it in mind from Holinshed that the historical Fastolfe, a lieutenant in service of the Duke of Exeter, was appointed to command the garrison of Harfleur after its capture by the king, which would have provided ample scope for further backsliding on the part of Sir John. In the event, he had no choice but to insert the scene in which his earlier death is reported by Mistress Quickly (II.iii), and to suppress the fact of Fastolfe's appointment.

3. *The Chronicle History of Henry the fift, With his battell fought at Agin Court in France, Togither with Auntient Pistoll. As it hath bene sundry times playd by the Right honorable the Lord Chamberlaine his servants.*

4. In so doing they sentimentalise Falstaff. He dies of a 'quotidian tertian',

not of a broken heart. However he got there, he is doubtless in Arthur's bosom. Theobald's emendation in Quickly's speech of the Folio's 'and a Table of greene fields' to 'a babbled of green fields' was inspirational but may have been mistaken, as a slight rearrangement of the speech renders it unnecessary without changing a word: 'For after I saw him fumble with the sheets and play wi'th' flowers, and smile upon his fingers' ends *and a table of green fields*, I knew there was but one way, for his nose was as sharp as a pen . . .'. 'Table' was the Tudor term for small, alabaster plaques depicting devotional subjects, including the decapitated head of St John the Baptist on a salver, of the type manufactured in Nottingham for private use of the laity up to the time of the Reformation. These were brightly painted, and surviving examples on which some traces of paint remain show a green field in the lower background, dotted with daisies (see Francis Cheetham, *English Medieval Alabasters,* Oxford, 1984, pp. 317–32). John the Baptist was of course Sir John's name saint, and he dies calling on God.

5. This sequence of events is supported by his description of himself in the first edition of his *Foole upon Foole* – published in 1600 but written a year or so earlier, as also in his *Quips upon Questions* of similar date – as 'Clonnico de *Curtanio* Snuffe', and in a later edition of *Foole upon Foole* in 1605, as 'Clonnico del *Mondo* Snuffe'. See Chambers, ES, II, p. 300.

6. See II.iv.37 for the 'Roman Brutus'; Fluellen's references to the 'Roman disciplines' and wars in III.ii; to Pompey the Great at IV.i.70; and, most pertinently, the chorus to Act 5, where 'the senators of th'antique Rome/With the plebeians swarming at their heels,/Go forth and fetch their conquering Caesar in' (ll. 26–8).

7. As quoted in David Daniell's Arden edition of 1998, p. 12. The German original is in Chambers, ES, II, pp. 364–5.

8. For Burbage's roles, see Chambers, ES, II, pp. 308–9. In Jonson's actor lists, his name appears in first place in the tragedies, in *Every Man Out of his Humour* (1599), *Volpone* (1605?), and *The Alchemist* (1610), but in only sixth place in the earlier *Every Man in his Humour* (1598) behind Shakespeare,

Phillips, Condell, Sly and Kempe.

9. This would have given particular point to Caesar's line, 'The skies are painted with unnumbered sparks' (III.i.63); and it may be significant that, in the night before the murder when the conspirators are due to meet, the skies are covered with cloud so that Brutus is unable to tell the time from 'the progress of the stars'; he is losing his way.

10. Quoted by Alan Brissenden in his Oxford edition of the play (1993), p. 1.

11. Quoted from Chambers, WS, II, p. 278.

12. *The Life and Times of William Shakespeare* (1988), p. 209.

13. There is some confusion in the Folio text as to the relative heights of Rosalind and Celia. At I.ii.262, Celia is said to be the taller of the two, but at I.iii.111 Rosalind claims to be 'more than common tall', while at IV.iii.87 Celia is described as 'low'. This may indicate a change of cast during what is likely to have been an extended run or, perhaps to share the load, the two young actors involved exchanged roles on occasion.

14. There is only one difficult change: from Jaques to Frederick between II.vii and

III.i, which would require Jaques to make an early exit from II.vii – perhaps at the end of his 'seven ages' speech or during Amiens' song. Or was there a pause in the action at this point?

15. For more about Armin, see Leslie Hotson, *Shakespeare's Motley* (1952), pp. 84–128; Charles S. Felver, *Robert Armin, Shakespeare's Fool* (Kent State University Bulletin, Research Series V, Ohio, 1961; Southworth, F & J, for Armin, pp. 133–6, and Stone, 139–40. My quotation is from Armin's preface to his 1608 edition of the *Two Maids of More-clacke:* 'I commit it into your hands to be scan'd, and you shall find verse, as well blancke, as crancke, yet in the prose let it passe for currant. I would have againe inacted *John* myselfe, but *Tempora mutantur in illis.* . . .'

16. Some scholars have found inconsistency in his early scenes as to the kind of fool Touchstone is intended to be; on his first entrance, for example, he is referred to by Celia as a 'natural'; but this is surely Celia's attempt at a deliberate put-down, which the clown takes in his stride and immediately demonstrates is unfounded. The part as written was, I believe,

conceived from the start as for Armin. In view of his skill as a singer, which he had demonstrated in the *Two Maids*, it is odd, however, that he is not given any songs to sing.

17. It probably comprised doublet and hose, and was of the kind supplied by the Queen to her court fools Hoyden and Shenton in 1574/5, which included 'canyons' (thigh-fitting extensions of trunk hose, reaching to the knee), doublets of striped sackcloth, and a coat of wrought velvet, 'paned' in red, green and yellow (see Southworth, F & J, p. 113 and Chapter 17, 'The Fools' Motley').

18. For Dennis, see Chambers, WS, II, p. 263.

19. In *Shakespeare versus Shallow* (1931), pp. 119–22.

20. Chambers, WS, I, p. 434.

21. See Hibbard's introduction to his Penguin edition of the play (1973), pp. 48–50. A further point that Professor Hibbard makes in support of this hypothesis is Shakespeare's treatment of the Welsh parson, Sir Hugh Evans. Shakespeare's Welsh parts in the period form a sequence which I have earlier traced from *Richard II* to *Henry V* and associated with the arrival and advance in the company of Robert Armin. Hibbard points out that not only do the parts become progressively bigger and more important, but they also become more obviously Welsh. The Welsh Captain of *Richard II* is the smallest and betrays no trace of an accent; Glendower is susceptible to being spoken with a Welsh lilt but his pronunciation is not apparent in the writing; Fluellen, with his confusion of 'p's and 'b's, 'look you's' and verbal repetitions is unmistakably Welsh, and Sir Hugh goes further in the same comedic direction: 'Trib, trib, fairies. Come. And remember your parts. Be pold, I pray you. Follow me into the pit, and when I give the watch-'ords, do as I pid you. Come, come; trib, trib' (V.iv). 'Evans', the Professor concludes, 'must be the last term in the series; and *The Merry Wives of Windsor* must have followed *Henry V*' (*ibid.*, p. 49). It should also be noticed that there is no trace of Sir Hugh's peculiarities of pronunciation in his part as satyr in the masque, and that in a similar way Quickly's malapropisms and other idiosyncrasies of speech disappear from her lines as the Fairy Queen, indicating

that the masque was written first, and for a different occasion.

22. See Hibbard, *op. cit.*, pp. 42–6; and H.J. Oliver in his Arden edition of 1971, pp. lxvii–lxx.

23. A clue to the actors playing the Host and, less certainly, Falstaff, is provided by the 'bad' quarto text (Q1) published in 1602, which most editors agree is a pirated report of a performance supplied in part by two of the original performers, identified by the exceptional accuracy with which their lines are reported. As only two actors, Kit Beeston and John Duke, are known to have left the company between 1598 (when they are listed by Jonson as appearing in *Every Man in his Humour*) and 1602, by which time they had joined Queen Anne's men – and it is hardly conceivable that any others would have risked their employment in such a way for what was doubtless a paltry fee – the finger of suspicion points to them. Were they, in fact, fired for their disloyalty? If the suspects are so obvious to modern editors four hundred years later, they would have been even more apparent to their fellows at the time. Interestingly, Oliver (n.

22 above, p. xxvii, n. 2) suggests that the actor who played the Host may also have understudied Falstaff which, if so, would let one of them off the hook!

24. For the dating of *Hamlet*, see Chambers, WS, I, pp. 423–4; Harold Jenkins, Arden edition (1982), pp. 1–13. For *Twelfth Night*, Chambers, WS, I, p. 405; Leslie Hotson, *The First Night of 'Twelfth Night'* (1954).

25. As quoted in Chambers, WS, II, p. 265.

26. Levi (n. 12 above), p. 218.

27. Quoted from Chambers, ES, II, p. 309. But the casting is not without its problems; there is a discrepancy of age. The impression we get of the character from all that is said about him in the earlier part of the play is of a very young man; a fellow-student and contemporary of Rosencrantz and Guildenstern at Wittenberg at a time when university education normally began earlier and finished sooner than it does today. He is consistently referred to as 'young Hamlet'; and yet, in Act 5, the Grave-digger tells us that he came to his work thirty years ago – 'that very day that young Hamlet was born' (V.i.143); and, in the midst of the duel, Gertrude comments to Claudius that

Hamlet is 'fat and scant of breath' (V.ii.290), which, even if 'fat' is interpreted as 'out of condition', is a strange thing to say of an eighteen or nineteen-year-old youth who assures Horatio of his 'continual practice' (V.II.207). It sounds very much as if Shakespeare had originally intended the part for a much younger actor but, in the course of writing the play, changed his mind, and decided (whatever the reason) to give it to the 33-year-old Burbage.

28. *Shakespeare and the Idea of the Play* (1962), pp. 158–9.

29. In his 1982 Arden edition, p. 479, citing Schlegel.

30. The role would have gone to one of Shakespeare's senior fellows – probably Phillips or Heminges – who would have had experience of the earlier, more rhetorical style of verse employed by Kyd and Marlowe, and had worked with Alleyn, its finest exponent. But if a memory of Alleyn was present to the player – and had been present also perhaps to Shakespeare when he wrote it – it is far more likely to have been intended as a tribute than a parody. See William Armstrong, 'Shakespeare and the Acting of Edward Alleyn' in SS 7 (1954), pp. 82–9.

31. G.B. Harrison, in his notes to the Penguin edition of 1937, p. 170, goes so far as to say that 'Both the attack on the ranting tragedian and the conceited clown are directed against individuals', and that 'The latter is obviously Will Kempe'; whereas there is not a scrap of evidence to suggest that any such 'ranting tragedian' would have been tolerated for a moment in the Chamberlain's company, or that Kempe was either conceited or had ever indulged in the sort of behaviour Hamlet is deploring.

32. *Johnson on Shakespeare*, ed. Walter Raleigh (Oxford, 1908, 1965 edn), p. 93.

33. I have been drawing here on Leslie Hotson (n. 24 above), p. 180 and *passim*, and remain unconvinced by the objections to Hotson's hypothesis made in recent editions of the play. Chambers dates it before *Hamlet* to 1600/1 (WS, I, pp. 404–7). It may be, as T.W. Craik remarks, 'downright simplicity' to suggest, along with John Downes in 1708, that it was called *Twelfth Night* because 'it was got up on purpose to be Acted on Twelfth Night' (Arden, 1975, p. xxxiv); perhaps I am very simple, but this still seems to

me the most likely
explanation.

34. Cf. Sir Toby's reference to
Andrew as playing the viol-de-
gamboys (I.iii.25) and (in
relation to his hair) 'I hope to
see a housewife take thee
between her legs and spin it
off' (I.iii.99–101), with the
passage in the Induction to
Marston's *The Malcontent*
(1604), in which Sincler
features under his own name
and, when Sly invites him to
sit between his legs, refuses on
the grounds that 'the audience
then will take me for a viol-de-
gamboy, and think that you
play upon me' (Revels edition,
1975, p. 9, ll. 20–1). Some
academics dismiss the
possibility of Sincler having
played the role because it is
too important for a 'small-
part' or 'bit' player. But, as in
any half-decent repertory
company, members of the
Chamberlain's were allowed,
and doubtless encouraged, to
develop, and the parts that
Shakespeare wrote for them
were as small or as large as he
wanted them to be.

35. I am indebted for this idea to
John Harrison's production at
the Nottingham Playhouse in
January 1957, with designs by
Voytek, in which I had the
good fortune to play Sir
Andrew.

Chapter 10: Travelling Man

1. From *Early English Stages,
1300 to 1660*, Vol. 2
(1576–1660), Part 1 (1963),
p. 183.

2. H.E. Salter, *Oxford Council
Acts, 1583–1626* (Oxford,
1928), p. 382. For this
possibility, see Chambers, ES,
II, pp. 205–7.

3. Chambers, WS, II, pp. 326–7.

4. *Ibid.*, pp. 327–8.

5. For this dating, see
Chambers, WS, I, pp. 443,
451. David Bevington
suggests late in 1601 for
Troilus (Arden edition of 1998,
p. 11), and G.K. Hunter,
1603/4 for *All's Well* (Arden,
1959, p. xxv).

6. Chambers, ES, II, p. 208; my
italics.

7. I am indebted for these figures
to the table given by Professor
Leeds Barroll in his *Politics,
Plague, and Shakespeare's
Theater, The Stuart Years*
(Ithaca and London, 1991),
p. 223.

8. As cited above (n. 6); again,
my italics.

9. As Glynne Wickham
discovered, the great majority
of performances by players in
general in the period,
including all localities, were
given indoors. See *Early
English Stages* (n. 1 above),
pp. 176–9.

10. According to the records collated by Chambers (WS, II, pp. 319–43), they were at Richmond in 1595, 1598/9, 1600 and 1602/3; at Greenwich in 1594, 1605/6, 1611/12 and 1613; at Hampton Court in 1603/4 and 1605/6; and at Wilton in 1603.

11. Stanley Wells, Gary Taylor *et al.*, *William Shakespeare, A Textual Companion* (Oxford, 1987), p. 90.

12. The Oxford editors argue that during the summer months of July and August, 'the smart set left London for their country estates' and that Queen Elizabeth chose this time of year for her annual progresses; but I doubt that the movements of the 'smart set' – or, for that matter, the court – had much effect on business at the Globe, which was a popular theatre seating upwards of 2000 people and largely dependent for its success on a popular audience, most of whom would have had to cross the river to get to it. There is, of course, no evidence for the scholarly assumption that Shakespeare did not accompany his fellows on tour. How would he have been replaced as player in such a tight-knit ensemble,

operating without subsidy and with only occasional help from its patrons? Precise dates for the companies' appearances in provincial towns are so infrequent that it is unsafe to draw any firm conclusions from them, but they do not uphold the Oxford editors' claim that, ignoring plague years, 'the summer months account for almost every datable reference to a provincial performance by a London company [?] with which Shakespeare was – or may have been – associated'. On a cursory survey, I find the Admiral's men at Ipswich on 20 February 1586 and 26 May 1587, and at Shrewsbury on 3 February 1592. Strange's men were at Exeter on 17 April 1580, and Leicester's (another contender for the title of Shakespeare's first company) at Exeter on 23 March 1586, at Maidstone on 23 January 1587, Dover on 4 March, Bristol between 9 and 15 April, and Plymouth on 15 May of the same year. Conversely, the Admiral's were at the Rose throughout the summers of 1597 and 1598, in which years they appear not to have travelled at all. In February 1600, they bought a drum and trumpets to 'go into the country', but were back at the Rose between 2 March and 13 July. For the later, plague-free period between 1611 and 1625 (focusing on a single city), the Prince's men were at Coventry on 7 November 1614 and 13 December 1622; the King's men on 10 January 1620; and Lady Elizabeth's men on 4 January 1618, 5 January 1620, and 24 January 1622; all these were so-called 'London companies'.

13. The great majority of court performances recorded at Whitehall or outlying palaces are found to occur in the Christmas holiday period between 26 December and Shrove Tuesday, the eve of the Lenten season, during which playing was inhibited in the City – though not necessarily in the county of Surrey, where the Globe and most other public playhouses were situated. It follows, therefore, that at Christmas each year, through January to the beginning of Lent in February or March, the players would necessarily have been stationed in or about London, but that, until the opening of the Blackfriars indoor playhouse in 1609, performances at the Globe would have been restricted in most years by the severity of the weather. The evidence for Lent is ambiguous but in general suggests – at least in the Stuart period – a cessation of playing (see Barroll, n. 7 above, pp. 211–16). Shakespeare may have used this opportunity to pay what Aubrey claimed to have been an annual visit to his home in Stratford (Chambers, WS, II, p. 253). But, if he did, he would have needed to be back in London for the final weeks of Lent to oversee rehearsals for a short Easter season at the Globe, as in 1611 (Chambers, *ibid.*, pp. 337–41) – plague and weather permitting. This, I propose, is likely to have normally been followed by a spring tour to one of the nearer English regions (as in 1612 when the company were at New Romney in Kent on 21 April), a summer season at the Globe (as in July 1601, and 1613 until 29 June when the Globe burnt down), and a further, more lengthy tour in the autumn (as in 1594, when the players were at Marlborough in September, and in 1597 at Bristol between 11 and 17 September), before returning to the capital as usual for Christmas.

14. See Barroll (n. 7 above), p. 19, and the table shown on p.

173. Cf. the plague records given by Chambers in ES, IV, pp. 345–51.

15. See Chambers, WS, II, pp. 336–42.

16. *Ibid.*, pp. 328–9.

17. See *The Counties of Britain, A Tudor Atlas by John Speed*, with commentaries by Alasdair Hawkyard (paperback edn, 1995), p. 77.

18. REED: *Devon*, p. 267.

19. I am indebted here, as elsewhere throughout the chapter, to Robert Tittler's *Architecture and Power, The Town Hall and the English Urban Community, c. 1500–1640* (Oxford, 1991); see especially pp. 139–50 and, for a partial listing of civic halls in the period, 160–8.

20. For the text of the proclamation, Chambers, ES, IV, pp. 263–4.

21. See Willis's account quoted above, p. 23. The same appears to have been true at Newcastle upon Tyne, where there are several references to rewards for 'free' plays, which (perhaps in compensation for the loss of a gathering) seem especially generous, ranging from 40s to £3. In 1593, the Earl of Sussex' men were awarded 'full paymente of £3 for playing a free play commanded by mr maiore' but only 20s is entered in the accounts (REED: *Newcastle*, p. 92). If the play was free, who contributed the remaining £2? The councillors? As payments to other companies are, however, equally generous as those that are said to be free, I infer that all such mayors' plays in Newcastle were probably free so far as the public was concerned. In Leicester, and perhaps elsewhere, the councillors (the '24' and the '48') were certainly expected to contribute to the reward (see Chambers, ES, I, pp. 334–5).

22. REED: *Somerset*, I, p. 14.

23. REED: *Cumb, West, Glos*, pp. 306–7.

24. REED: *Norwich*; see, for examples, pp. 90 (2 days), 115 (4 days), 117 (3 days), 142 (3 days in one week, 5 in the next), 156 (a week).

25. Compare Henslowe's daily taking at the Rose which, for typical periods in 1595, varied between 3s and 73s, averaging (according to Dr Greg's calculations) 30s. These amounts, of course, represent only his share of the total box office receipts as the theatre's owner. If the company (the Admiral's) received an equal or slightly greater share than Henslowe, we see that the difference between the daily income of a company on tour and one in London was not so

great and, on occasion, may even have been to the advantage of the tourists. (The King's men and the Admiral's are not, however, strictly comparable as the King's owned their own theatre in London which the Admiral's did not.) See Chambers, ES, II, pp. 142–3.

26. As a Worcester's man in 1581/2 and June 1583; as Admiral's man in February and again in May 1586, and twice more with the same company in 1589/90; and with the Chamberlain's (perhaps as suggested earlier in the *Dream*) in 1595. For these records, see 'Players at Ipswich', ed. Chambers, in MSC II, Part 3, pp. 272–81.

27. On this point, with specific reference to Ipswich, see Wickham (n. 1 above), pp. 178–9, and for touring venues generally in the period, 176–90.

28. Chambers (ES, I, p. 335) points out that the rewards entered in the accounts are generally round sums; 'where they are broken, they probably went to make up the results of the "gatherings" to round sums'. If, as elsewhere, the gathering at the mayor's play in Ipswich exceeded the reward, it could easily have resulted in a payment of £3

for that single performance.

29. See John Wasson, *Suffolk in the History Plays of Shakespeare* (Xth Harry Clement Memorial Lecture at Keynes Hall, King's College, Cambridge, 15 June 1974, published by Suffolk WEA, 1974), pp. 3–4. There were thirteen borough towns in Suffolk in the period, of which only four have retained records of payments to players, and of those, all four record visits by companies of which Shakespeare was a member. As Professor Wasson asks, 'Could Shakespeare by some accident have visited only those boroughs which were going to preserve their records?' (p. 4).

30. REED: *Coventry*, pp. 393–4.

31. At Faversham in 1596/7, a wagon belonging to 'Lord Bartlettes [i.e. Berkeley's] players' was misused by 'certen persons', who were fined 15*s* 9*d* for their offence (Murray, II, p. 274).

32. MSC XI, p. 163.

33. *Ibid.*, pp. 196–8.

34. Since the 1940s, the building has been in private hands, and is not open to visitors. See Barry L. Wall, *Sudbury through the Ages* (Ipswich, n.d.), pp. 44–7.

35. REED: *Cambridge*, I, pp. 403–4.

36. *Ibid.*, II, pp. 723–7, including plans of the hall, since demolished.

37. *Ibid.*, I, pp. 290–1.

38. Sometimes referred to familiarly as 'the Mayor's house', as quoted, for example, in REED: *Coventry*, p. 567. It had also been used for rehearsals of the *Corpus Christi* plays. The same identification of the mayor's house with the Guildhall may also be true elsewhere, though the former is usually interpreted by REED editors as a separate building. When, for example, in this year of 1603, James I visited Newcastle on his way south, and was officially received in the 'Mayors house, where he was richly entertained' (REED: *Newcastle*, p. 140), it is surely the Guildhall that was meant.

39. See William Cooper, *Henley-in-Arden, An Ancient Market Town and its Surroundings* (1946, reprinted with illustrations, Buckingham, 1992), pp. 74–5.

40. REED: *Shropshire*, II, p. 382.

41. REED: *Cumb, West, Glos*, pp. 306–7.

42. REED: *Bristol*, p. 85. I take the 'mayers courte' to refer to the 'yelde hall' or Guildhall mentioned in the previous entry, relating to the same occasion. The building has since been demolished.

43. REED: *Cumb, West, Glos*, p. 300.

44. REED: *Bristol*, p. 115.

45. REED: *Cumb, West, Glos*, p. 299.

46. MSC II, Part 3, p. 263.

47. REED: *Bristol*, p. 112.

48. *Ibid.*, p. 122.

49. Murray, II, p. 310; REED: *Devon*, p. 46.

50. REED: *Coventry*, p. 374; REED: *Cumb, West. Glos*, pp. 298, 300.

51. As Chambers notes (WS, II, p. 329), the order of entries at Oxford appears not to have been chronological, so we can infer nothing from the lowly position of the relevant entry on the page, especially as it is the only report of a visit by players in the year.

52. REED: *Somerset*, I, p. 19; II, pp. 490–1.

53. See Wickham (n. 1 above), pp. 186–90.

54. See Salter (n. 2 above), pp. xxiv–v, 26, 386. Neither the Bath nor Oxford guildhalls survive to the present.

55. Quoted from Barroll (n. 7 above), p. 110.

56. Chambers, WS, II, p. 329.

57. *Ibid.*

58. Barroll (n. 7 above), p. 113.

59. Chambers, WS, II, pp. 329–30.

60. Chambers, ES, IV, pp. 168–9.

61. As any actor who has taken part in a 'fit-up' tour of this kind will confirm, the rewards to be obtained from playing in the audience's familiar surroundings, where they come together as an existing community, rather than in a theatre where the actor is on familiar ground and the audience are visitors to it and unknown to each other, are very special, and compensate for the rigours of travel and generally spartan nature of conditions backstage.

62. G.K. Hunter in his Arden edition of 1959 (as reprinted, 1967), pp. xviii–xxv; Chambers, WS, I, pp. 449–52.

63. As suggested by W.J. Lawrence in *Shakespeare's Workshop* (Oxford, 1928), p. 60.

64. See Chambers' early essay on the play, dating from the period 1904/8, reprinted in his *Shakespeare: a Survey* (1925), pp. 200–7.

65. Chambers, WS, I, p. 438.

66. David Bevington in his Arden edition of 1998, p. 19.

67. See E.A.J. Honigmann, 'Shakespeare suppressed: the unfortunate history of *Troilus and Cressida*' in *Myriad-minded Shakespeare: Essays on the tragedies, problem comedies and Shakespeare the man* (London and New York, 1989, 2nd edn, 1998), pp. 112–29.

68. Chambers, WS, II, pp. 216–17.

69. As quoted by Bevington (n. 66 above), p. 4.

70. *Johnson on Shakespeare*, ed. W. Raleigh (Oxford, 1908, reprinted 1965), p. 184.

71. As quoted by Schoenbaum, CDL, p. 315.

72. See, for example, Oscar James Campbell, *Shakespeare's Satire* (Hamden and London, 1943, reprinted New York, 1963), pp. 98–120.

Chapter 11: King's Man

1. From *Mythical Sorrows of Shakespeare* (1934), pp. 27–8, as quoted by Schoenbaum, SL, p. 527.

2. For these and subsequent plague figures, see Leeds Barroll, *Politics, Plague and Shakespeare's Theater* (Ithaca and London, 1991), pp. 223–6.

3. Quoted from Chambers, ES, IV, pp. 168–9.

4. See Barroll (n. 2 above), pp. 49, 59. It is not certain that any of them were actually required to walk in the procession.

5. For Lowin's roles, see Chambers, WS, II, pp. 72, 263–4; ES, II, pp. 328–9.

6. The Barnstaple accounts covered the period 1604/5, and were dated from Michaelmas to Michaelmas. We know, however, with unusual accuracy, that the company were at Oxford on 9 October 1605, having travelled from London where the playhouses had only recently been closed. Almost certainly, therefore, the visit to Barnstaple would have taken place in the previous year at Michaelmas 1604. See REED: *Devon*, pp. xii–xiii, 48. For Oxford, see also n. 10 below.

7. Quoted from Chambers, ES, II, p. 309.

8. Though it is clear from the first scene in the convent (I.iv) that she is still merely a postulant to the Poor Clares (a strictly enclosed contemplative order) and would not at that stage have been clothed in its habit or vowed to its rule, some modern directors have insisted on dressing Isabella as a fully fledged nun, which has the unfortunate effect of making the Duke's tentative proposal of marriage in the final act appear, not only mistimed (which it is, as he himself realises immediately afterwards), but positively sacrilegious, which it is not.

9. For these dates and titles, see Chambers, WS, II, pp. 331–2.

10. H.E. Salter, *Oxford Council Acts, 1583–1626* (Oxford, 1928), p. 390.

11. REED: *Cambridge*, II, p. 985; Halliwell-Phillipps, p. 27.

12. Chambers (WS, I, pp. 468, 475) gives a date 'early in 1606' for both plays; Kenneth Muir (Arden, 1972 edn, pp. xiii–xxii) puts *Macbeth* between 1603 and 1606, inclining to the latter date, and *Lear* (Arden, 1972, p. xxi) a year earlier to the winter of 1604/5.

13. I have written more largely of Armin, including this particular casting, in Southworth, F & J, pp. 133–6 and n. 35.

14. When the present book was at an advanced stage of writing, there appeared Professor Park Honan's biography (*Shakespeare, A Life*, Oxford, 1998) reporting on recent computer studies involving the lexicon or vocabulary of Shakespeare's *dramatis personae*, which appear to confirm his playing of Duncan as well as a number of other roles that I have proposed as his on different grounds in previous chapters; namely, Chorus in *Henry V*, Friar Laurence and Chorus in *Romeo and Juliet*, Theseus in the *Dream*, Leonato in *Much*

Ado, the title role in *Henry IV*, the King in *All's Well*, Adam in *As You Like It* and the Ghost in *Hamlet*. See Honan, pp. 204–5 and n. 10.

15. *Wills*, pp. 72–5.
16. For these dates, see Chambers, WS, II, p. 333, and Barroll (n. 2), p. 148.
17. MSC VII, pp. 117, 65, 49.
18. For this dating, see Chambers, WS, I, pp. 476–8.
19. Extracted from Dekker's *Work for Armorers* (printed 1609), as quoted by Barroll (n. 2 above), p. 176.
20. Chambers, WS, II, pp. 335–6; ES, IV, pp. 174–6.
21. *The Life and Times of William Shakespeare* (1988), p. 279.
22. Quoted from Chambers, ES, II, p. 331.
23. See Philip Brockbank's Arden edition of 1976, pp. 24–9; Chambers, WS, I, pp. 478–80.
24. Chambers, WS, I, pp. 482–3.
25. Chambers, WS, II, p. 18.

Chapter 12: Blackfriars

1. Nicholas Rowe, 'Some Account of the Life . . . of Mr William Shakespeare' in Shakespeare, *Works*, ed. Rowe (1709), I, p. xxxv, as quoted by Schoenbaum, CDL, p. 279.
2. *Wills*, pp. 8–9.
3. See Chambers, WS, II, pp.

154–69, quoting from 166.
4. REED: *Coventry*, p. 373; for Marlborough, Halliwell-Phillipps, p. 29.
5. MSC II, Part 3, pp. 282–4; Nathaniel Bacon, *The Annalls of Ipswiche: The Lawes, Customes and Government of the Same* (1654), ed. W.H. Richardson (Ipswich, 1884), p. 434.
6. MSC VII, pp. 88, 141.
7. Chambers, WS, II, p. 336.
8. *Ibid.*
9. *Ibid.*, pp. 337–42.
10. *Ibid.*, pp. 341–4.
11. Chambers, WS, I, p. 86.
12. Dame Julian of Norwich, *Revelations of Divine Love*, Chapter 32.
13. See F.D. Hoeniger's introduction to his Arden edition of 1963, especially pp. lxxxvi–xci.
14. Chambers, WS, I, pp. 484–7; see also J.M. Nosworthy's Arden edition of 1955, pp. xiv–xvii.
15. As quoted by Nosworthy (*op. cit.*), pp. xl–xlii.
16. Here, and througout this section, I am indebted to J.H.P. Pafford's Arden edition of 1963.
17. Chambers, WS, II, p. 342.
18. In a personal communication to the author.
19. *Ibid.*
20. Chambers, WS, II, p. 345.
21. *Ibid.*, p. 250.

Chapter 13: The Man Shakespeare

1. From *Lectures on the English Poets* (1818), pp. 92–3, as quoted in Schoenbaum, SL, pp. 185–6.
2. See Schoenbaum, CDL, pp. 227–32.
3. *To Mr Thomas Heywood*
   Thou hast writ much and art admir'd by those
   Who love the easie ambling of thy prose;

   But yet thy pleasingest flight was somewhat high,
   When thou didst touch the angels Hyerarchie;
   Fly that way still, it will become thy age
   And better please then groveling on the stage.

   Quoted from Nungezer, *Dictionary*, p. 191.
4. Archdeacon Richard Davies, for whom see Chambers, WS, II, pp. 255–7.

Further Reading

Numerous biographies of Shakespeare and books about his plays are published every year, and most have something useful to say as well as much that is debatable. The following very selective list is of those I have found most useful in writing my own, or relate in a particular way to its themes.

Leeds Barroll, *Politics, Plague and Shakespeare's Theatre, The Stuart Years*, Ithaca and London, 1991.

G.E. Bentley, *The Jacobean and Caroline Stage*, 7 vols, Oxford, 1941–68 – especially Vol. 2 for the information it contains about the later careers of Shakespeare's fellows.

G.E. Bentley, *The Profession of Player in Shakespeare's Time, 1590–1642*, Princeton, 1984.

E.K. Chambers, *William Shakespeare, A Study of Facts and Problems*, 2 vols, Oxford, 1930 – the essential reference work.

Christopher Devlin, *Hamlet's Divinity and Other Essays*, London, 1963 – for the religious background to the plays.

Peter Levi, *The Life and Times of William Shakespeare*, London, 1988 – a poet's biography.

Kenneth Muir, *Shakespeare the Professional and Related Studies*, London, 1973 – especially the lead essay.

S. Schoenbaum, *William Shakespeare, A Compact Documentary Life*, Oxford, 1977.

Ian Wilson, *Shakespeare: The Evidence*, London, 1993.

Index

Shakespeare's plays, and also those that are anonymous or of disputed authorship, are indexed under their titles; other plays under the name of their main author. Principal entries are indicated by bold type, illustrations by italics.

Abingdon, Oxon., 28
Adams, J. Quincy, quoted 84
Admiral, the, see Howard, Lord Charles
Admiral's men, 25, 29, 30–45, 50, 51, 57, 61, 78, 86–8, 92, 199, 206
    see also Howard, Lord Charles; Admiral's/Strange's alliance; Prince's men
Admiral's/Strange's alliance **35–6, 46** 49, 85–6, 88, 91
Aesop (Aesopus Claudius), Roman tragic actor, 32
Alexander, Peter, cited 55, 200
Allen, John (of Sudbury), 186
Alleyn, Edward, player, 18, **26–9, 31–2** *Plate 7*, 33, 34–7, 40, 44, 46, **50–1**, **61–2**, 85, 86, 87, 94, 120
Alleyn (née Woodward), Joan, 61, quoted 192–3
Alleyn, John (Edward's elder brother), 33–4, 86
All's Well that Ends Well, 177, **195–9**
Andrewes, Richard, player, 26
Anne of Denmark, Queen, 194, 204, 206, 243
    see also Queen's men
Antony and Cleopatra, 219, **222–4**
Apollonius of Tyre, 237

apprentices and apprenticeship, 18–21, 24–31, 89–95
    see also boy players, quality of; and under names of individual boys
Arden, Edward, 17–18
Arden of Faversham, 46–8
Ariosto, Lodovico, I *Suppositi*, 32
Armada, the, 33–4
Armin, Robert, player and author, 19, 115, **148–9**, **157–8**, 161–2, **173**, 198, 211, 213, 216, 218, 238, 240, 242, 245
    Foole upon Foole, 148, 158
    History of the Two Maids of More-clacke, 148, 158, 173, *Plate 21*
    Quips for Questions, 158
As You Like It, 105, **153–9**, 193–4
Aubrey, John, 14, 38, 102

Baddeley, Angela, 163
Baldwin, T.W., cited 94
Bale, John, *King Johan*, 125
Barnstaple, Devon, 191, 207, 221
Barton-on-the-Heath, Warwicks., 32–3
Bath, 31, 134, 182–3, 190, **192**
Beeston, Christopher, player, 90–1, 102, 156, 218
Beeston, William (Christopher's son), player, 102
Belt, T., apprentice player, 90, 92

Bentley, E.C., quoted 3
Berkeley's men, 24
Betterton, Thomas, 164
Bevis, George, player, 36, 61
Bible, the, 3–4
Blackfriars
    estate, 103, 109, 177
    Gatehouse, 229–30
    Priory, 104
    theatre, 83, 229, 233
Boccaccio's *Decameron*, 239
Bodley, Sir Thomas, quoted 2
Borges, Jorge Luis, quoted 8–9
Borromeo, St Charles, 17
boy players, quality of, 100–1, 102,
        156–7, 173
    see also apprentices and
        apprenticeship; and under
        names of individual boys
Bradbrook, Muriel, quoted 76
Bradstreet, John, player 37
Bridgwater, Som., 28
Bristol, 134, 190–1
    Guildhall, 191
Brook, Peter, 54–5, 244
Brooke, Arthur, author of Romeus,
        97
Brooke, Sir William, Lord Cobham;
        Lord Chamberlain, 1596/7,
        97
Browne, Edward, player, 26
Browne, Robert, player, 26–7, 28–9,
        34, 35, 37, 61, 231
Browning, Robert, quoted 58
Bryan, George, player, 35, 61, 87–8,
        105, 108, 133, 148
Burbage, Cuthbert (Richard's elder
        brother), 86, 92, 143
Burbage, James (Richard's father),
        player, 46, 86, 104, 109, 134
Burbage, Richard, player, 18, 46, 61,
        86–7, *Plate 6*, 92, 98, 101, 105,
        108, 112, 118, 120, 123, 126,
        128, 137, 143, 150–1, 156,
        157, 161, **166**, 172, 194, 198,
        206, **210**, 213, 215, 218, 222,

        225, 229, 230, 238, 240, 241,
        245, 246, 248
Burghley, Lord (William Cecil), 64,
        188

Cairncross, Andrew, quoted 55
Cambridge, 30, 104, **187–8**, 214
    Guildhall, 188
Campion, Thomas, 17
Carey, Sir George *see* Hunsdon,
        Lord
Carey, Henry, *see* Hunsdon, Lord
Carleton, Dudley, quoted 194
Catesby, Sir William, 18
Cecil, Robert, earl of Salisbury, 2
Chamberlain's men, 81, 82, **84–114**,
        passim to 178, 191 (1576), 199
    see also King's men; Hunsdon's
        men
Chambers, E.K. (Sir Edmund),
        cited 31, 34, 44, 47–8, 64,
        106, 160, 195, 197, 206, 226,
        228–9, 238
Charles I (as Duke of York), 221
Charles II, 9
Chaucer, Geoffrey, *The Canterbury
        Tales*, 58, 79
Chettle, Henry, 18, **53–4**
    Troilus and Cressida, 199
Children of the Chapel Royal, 222,
        229
Cobham, Lord, *see* Brooke, Sir
        William
Coleridge, Samuel Taylor, quoted
        201
College of Heralds, 17, 162, 249
Collins, Francis, 247–8
Comedy of Errors, The, 59, **69–72**,
        96, 213
Condell, Henry, player, 88, 90, 91,
        211, 216, 218, 238, 240, 242,
        245, 248
    see also Heminges and Condell (as
        editors)
*Contention, First part of the, betwixt
        the two famous Houses of Yorke*

and Lancaster (pirated text of *Henry VI, Part 2*), 61

Cooke, Alexander ('Saunder'), player, 19, **91–2**, 207, 211, 216, 218, 242

Cooke, Thomas, player, 26

Coriolanus, 219, **224–6**

Corpus Christi (mystery) plays, 4

Cory, William, 249

Countess of Essex's men, 24

Court, the players at,
 Greenwich, 61, 218
 Hampton Court, 194, 218
 Richmond, 103, 177
 Whitehall, 110, 171, 175, 177, 194, 209, 211, 221, 232, 243, 248
 Wilton, 193–4
 Windsor, 134, 159

Coventry, 4, 25, 30, 31, 182, 185, **188–9**, 191, 221, 232, 247
 St Mary's Guildhall, 188–9, *Plate 22*

Cowley, Richard, player 88, 93, 105, 108, 162, 173, 211, 213, 216, 218, 242, 245

Cross Keys inn (theatre), 95–6, 104

Crosse, Samuel, player, 92–3, 207

Curtain theatre, 109, 134, 141, **142**

Cymbeline, 110, 158, 232, 233, **238–40**

Davies, John, of Hereford, 6, 38 **115–18**, 223, 253,

Dekker, Thomas, quoted 220, 221

de la Casa, John, quoted 5

Denmark, 87
 king of, 218

Dennis, John, 159

Derby's men, 23–4

director, Shakespeare as, 51, 56, **100–2**, 250

Doncaster, Yorks., 28

Donne, John, 2–3

'double-mirror' effect, 52, 169–70

doubles and doubling, 39, 71, 99, 108, 122–3, 136, 146, 148, 150, 165–6, 216, 217, 238
 see also Appendix D

Dover, Kent, 30, 134, 219

dramatists, low status of, 2–3

Drayton, Michael, 248

Droeshout, Martin, and his engraving, ??, 1, 6

Duke, John, player, 93

Dunwich, Suffolk, 221

Eccleston, William, player, 92, 198

Edmans, John, player, 92

Edward III, 77–8

Edward VI, 22

Elector Palatine, 246

Elizabeth, Princess (daughter of James I), 246
 see also Lady Elizabeth's men

Elizabeth I, Queen, *passim* (as Queen) to 159, 170–1, 175–7
 see also Queen's men

Englische Comedien und Tragedien, 47

Essex, Earl of (Robert Devereux, 2nd earl), 144, 175–7
 see also Essex's men; Countess of Essex's men

Essex's men, 192

Eucharist, the, 4

Exeter, 33

Famous Victories of Henry the fifth, The, 146

Faversham, Kent, 30, 42, 43, 110, 219
 Market Hall, 110

Ferdinando, Lord Strange, 24, 85
 see also Strange's men

Field, Nathan, player, 19, 240 *Plate 17*, 243, 251

Field, Richard, 62

First Folio (1623), **1–2**, 6, 9–10, 36, 54, 69, 88, 93, 144, 201, 227, 234
 see also Heminges and Condell (as editors)

Fleay, F.G., cited 44
Flecknoe, Richard, *Short Discourse of the English Stage*, quoted 100–1
Fletcher, John, 246–7
Fletcher, Lawrence, player, 218, 277 n.1
Folkestone, Kent, 30, 233
Forman, Simon, 233
Fortune theatre, 144
Frankfort Autumn Fair, 48
Friendship Cult, 65
Fuller, Thomas, 13–14, 18

Garnet, Fr Henry, 218
Gascoigne, George, 32
gatherings, 23, **183–4**, 185, 186, 188, 192, **194**, 221–2
Geoffrey of Monmouth, 239
Germany, 27, 37, 47–8, 61
Gilburne (Gebon?), Samuel, player, 19, **93**, 216, 218
Globe theatre, 83, 91, **142–4**, *Plate 19*, 145, 153, 157, *passim* to end but see especially 178, 195, 199–200, 230
Gloucester, 23, 26, 184, 190, 191
Booth (Bothall) or town hall, 23
Goodridge, J.F., quoted 58
Gough (née Phillips), Elizabeth, 92
Gough, Robert, player, 19, **92**, 198, 216, 217–8
Gower, John, 58, *Plates 8* and *24*, 234
Confessio Amantis, 58, 237
Great Freeze, 219
Greene, Robert, 50, **52–3**, 240
Friar Bacon and Friar Bungay, 50
Groats-worth of Wit, 52–3
Orlando Furiosa, 50
Grocers, London Company of, 91–2 and n. 15
Grooms of the Chamber, 84, 148, 206–7
guildhalls, 23

see also town halls, and under relevant cities or towns
Gunpowder Plot, 214

Hadleigh, Suffolk, 185–6
Guildhall, 186
Hall, Edward, quoted 34
Hamlet, 14, 41, 115, **163–70**, 192, 199
Hardy, Thomas, quoted 10
harper-poets, 3, 59–60
see also minstrels
Harryson, William, player, 26
Hatcher, John, 188
Hathaway, Anne, *see* Shakespeare, Anne
Hazlitt, William, cited 152, 239
Heminges, John, player, 18–19, 61, **87–88**, 91, 93–4, 101–2, 105, 110, 133, 143, 158, 193, 194, 198, 207, 211, 213, 216, 218, 221, 230, 235, 240, **242**, 245, 248
as editor, *see also* under Heminges and Condell
Heminges and Condell (as editors), **1–2**, 4, 18, 54, 88, 201, 227
see also First folio
Henley-in-Arden, Warwicks., 189–90
Market House or Town Hall, 189
Henry, Prince (son of James I), 206
see also Prince's men
Henry IV, 42, 106, **133–4**, **134–141**, 246
Part I, 135
Part 2, 138–141, 145
Henry V, 141, **144–9**, 213
Henry VI, 15, 33–4, 36, 40, 41, **50**, **51–3**, **54–55**, 84–5, **119**
'harey the vi' (Henslowe), 47, 50, 52–3
Henry VI, Part 1, 39, 50, 51
Henry VI, Part 2, 15, 55, 61, 62
Henry VI, Part 3, 39, 51, 61, 62

Henry VI/Richard III tetralogy, 54, 59

Henry VIII (with Fletcher), 230, 246–7

Henslowe, Philip, 46–50, 61, 78, 84–5, 86
  Diary, 46–7, 178

Herbert, Henry, 2nd earl of Pembroke, 60
  see also Pembroke's men

Herbert, William, 3rd earl of Pembroke, 193

Heywood, Thomas, player and author, 50–1, 88, 251
  Apology for Actors, 88

Hibbard, G.R., cited 160

hired men, 89–90, 93, 148

Holinshed, Raphael, 42, 146, 239

Holland, 35
  see also Low countries

Holland, John, player, 36–7

Honigmann, E.A.J. (with Susan Brock), quoted 228

Hotson, Leslie, quoted 159–60

housekeepers, 143, 230

Howard, Lord Charles, of Effingham, Lord Admiral, 29, 33–7, 64, 86
  see also Admiral's men

Hunsdon, Lord (Lord Chamberlain)
  1585–96: Henry Carey, 1st Lord Hunsdon, 85, 95–6, 103, 133–4
  1597–1603: Sir George Carey, 2nd Lord Hunsdon, 103, 109–10, 133–4, 170–1, 177
  see also Chamberlain's men; Hunsdon's men

Hunsdon's men
  1564–85: 85
  1596–97: 133–4

Hunter, G.K., cited 195

Hythe, Kent, 28, 30, 221, 232

Innocents' Day, 72, 96, 213

interludes and interluders, 3, 33, 65

Ipswich, Suffolk, 28, 30, 31, 35, 104, 182, **184–5**, 191, 221, 232
  Moot or Guildhall, 104, *Plate 23*

Jackson, John, 230

James I, 19, 78, 83, 177–8, **205–6**, **208–9**, **211–12**, 219, 243, 248
  see also King's men

Jeffes, Anthony (Humphrey's younger brother), player, 36–7

Jeffes, Humphrey, player, 37

Jenkins, Harold, quoted 167–8

jigs, 140, **149–50**, **153**

Johnson, Dr Samuel, quoted 55, 154, 170, 201, 238

Johnson, William, 230

Jones, Richard, player, 26, 29, 34, 37

Jonson, Ben, 1–2, 6, 13–14, 16, 31, 37, 200, 203, 248
  The Alchemist, 92
  Bartholomew Fair, 31
  Eastward Ho! 2, 200
  Every Man Out of his Humour, 141, 213
  The Isle of Dogs, 134, 142
  The Poetaster, 222
  Sejanus, 194, 207
  Volpone, 214

Julian of Norwich, 234

Julius Caesar, **149–53**, 246

Keats, John, quoted 8

Kempe, William, player, 61, **66–7**, 71, 81, 82, **87**, *Plate 20*, 98, 101, **105**, 108, 111, **113**, 115, 123, 126, 133, **137–41**, 143

Kerrigan, John, quoted 75

King John, 106, **123–7**

King Lear, 130, **214–6**, *Plate 14*, 219, 233–4

King's men (formerly Chamberlain's), **178**, 179, 181 *passim* to end

Knack to Know a Knave, The, 28, **87**

Kyd, Thomas, 41

Soliman and Perseda, 41–2
The Spanish Tragedy (Jeronimo), 30, 39, **40–1**, 50, 164

Lady Elizabeth's men, 183, 185
  see also Elizabeth, Princess
Lambarde, William, 176
Lambert, Joan (Shakespeare's aunt), 33
Langland's *Piers Plowman*, 58
Leech, Clifford, cited 66, 69
Leicester (town), 26, 27, 28, 30, 31, 183–4, 191, 195
Leicester, Earl of (Robert Dudley), 24, 35, 188–9
  see also Leicester's men
Leicester's men, 23–4, 30, 35, 87, 87–8, 186, 190, 191
Levi, Peter, quoted 30, 43, 156, 222
Lewis Frederick of Württemberg, Prince, 232
Livy, 79
Lodge, Thomas, 154
London and vicinity
  City, 31, 35, 47, 77, 95–6, 178
  Cripplegate, 227, 229, 231
  Grays Inn, 72, 96
  Mortlake, 193
  Shoreditch, 46, 97, 102
  Southwark, 43, 143, 193, 227, 229
  see also Blackfriars; Court
Longshank, see Peele's *Edward I*
Lord Chamberlain, see Hunsdon, Lord; Brooke, Sir William
  see also Chamberlain's men
Lord Chandos' men, 148
Lord Compton's men, 191
Lords of Misrule, 171, 172
Love's Labour's Lost, **81–3**, 96, 213
Low Countries, 27, 87, 88
  see also Holland
Lowin, John, player, 207, *Plate 13*, 213, 216, 240, 242, 245, **246**
Lucy, Sir Thomas, 19, 43
Lydgate, John, 79

Lyly, John, 65
Lynn, Ralph, 70

Macbeth, 2, 59, 214–15, **216–17**, *Plate 15*, 233
Maidstone, Kent, 28, 85, 219
Maldon, Essex, **182–4**
  Moot Hall, 183, *Plate 12*
Malone, Edmond, 19
Manningham, John, Diary, 177
Marlborough, Wilts., 95, 134, 218, 221, 232
Marlowe, Christopher, 30, 52–4
  The Jew of Malta, 30, 40, 51
  Massacre at Paris, 50
  Tamburlaine the Great, 30, 31, **39–40**
Marston, John, 203
  The Malcontent, 205
Martin Marprelate controversy, 35, 82
Mary Magdalene (medieval Saints' play), 237
Mary, Queen
  as princess, 14
  as queen, 22
Master of the Revels, 85, 171
mayor's (or bailiff's) play, 23, **183–4**, 185, 190, 194
Measure for Measure, 42, 208–9, **211–13**
Merchant of Venice, The, **106–9**, *Plate 9*, 122, 213
Meres, Francis, in *Palladis Tamia*, 69, 111
Merry Wives of Windsor, The, 134, 141, 153–4, **159–63**, *Plate 11*, 211
Midsummer Night's Dream, A, 59, 96, **102–4**, 194
minstrels, 5, **59–60**
  see also harper-poets
Morgann, Maurice, quoted 46
Morris, Brian, cited 32
Motley (designers), 163
Mountjoy, Christopher, 229

Much Ado About Nothing, 93, 105, **111–14**, 160, 246
music in the plays, 101, 109, **153**, 159, 170–1, 238

Nashe, Thomas, 52, 81, 87
  Almond for a Parrat, 87
  Pierce Penilesse his Supplication to the Divell, 52
Newington Butts theatre, 61, 86
New Romney, Kent, 221, 232, 233
Norwich, 28, 31, 141, 184
Nottingham, 247

Oldys, William, quoted 155
Olivier, Laurence, 54–5
Orford Castle, Suffolk, 125–6
Orsino, Don Virginio, 170–1
Ostler (née Heminges), Thomasine, 222–3
Ostler, William, player, 19, 211, **222–3**
Othello, **208–11**, 232, 246
Ovid, 79
Oxford (city), 180, 182, **192**, 214, 218, 221, 232
  Guildhall, 192
Oxford's (Lord) men, 30, 186, 188

Painter's *Pallace of Pleasure*, 79
Pateson, William, player, 26
Peacham drawing, *Plate 16*, 48–9
Peele, George, 44
  Edward I, 44
Pembroke's men, 60–1, 66, 91, 134
  see also Herbert, Henry, 2nd earl of Pembroke
Percy, Bishop Thomas, quoted 46
Pericles, 58, 60, 158, 227, 231, **234–8**
Persons, Robert, 17–18
Phillips, Augustine, player, 19, 61, **88**, 92, 93, 101, 143, 157, 176, 193, 207, 211, **217–8**
plague, 50, 60, 85, **177–8**, 180–1, 182, 192–3, 204–5, 206, 207,

214, 218, 219–20, 229, 231, **232–3**
Platter, Thomas, 149–50, 153
Plautus' *Menaechmi*, 69
'play metaphor', **119–20**, 121–2, 130–3, 144–5, 157, 167–70
player-musicians, 94 and note
players, disdain for, **5–6**, 18, 74–5, 116–8, 187–8, 250–1
'plots', 90
Plutarch, 149, 222
Plymouth, 28, 183
Pope, Thomas, player, 19, 35, 61, 87–8, 92, 98, 105, 110, 133; for his death, 143, 162
  Appendix D, Plot 3, n. 6
Powlton, Thomas, player, 26
Price, H.T., quoted 56
Prince's (Prince Henry's, formerly Admiral's) men, 206
Privy Council, 37, 47, 61, 134, 214
publication of plays, 4–5, 60, 134
Puritans, 31, 76–7, 94, 134, 232

Queen's men
  of Elizabeth I: 20, 22, 30, 35
  of Anne of Denmark (formerly Worcester's), 206
Queen's Revels (children's company), 89
Quiney, Thomas, 248

Rape of Lucrece, The, 65, **79–80**
Red Bull theatre, 220
Redman, Joyce, 163
Rhenanus, Johannes, quoted 101
Rice, John, player, 19
Richard II, 59, 106, **128–33**, 135, 175–6
Richard III, 40, 50, 62, 84, **120–3**, 134
Righter, Anne, quoted 167, 168–9
Rigg, Diana, 79
Roberts, Master (publisher), 199, 200
Robinson, John, 230, 248

Robinson, Richard, player, 19
rogues and vagabonds, 5, 22
Romeo and Juliet, 96, **97–102**
Roscius (Roman actor), 31–2, 119
Rose theatre, 24, 36, 42, *Plate 4*,
    46–50
Rowe, Nicholas, 19, 164, 228, 231
Royal Corps of Trumpets and
    Drums, 219
Rutland, Earl of, 230
Rye, Sussex, 134
Rylands, George, cited 55

Sackville, Thomas, player, 37
Saffron Walden, Essex, 214
Salisbury, Earl of, see Cecil, Robert
Sandes, James, player, 93, 218
Schlueter, June, cited 15, 156
Shakespeare (née Hathaway) Anne,
    20, 24–5, 25–6, 255
Shakespeare, Edmund (younger
    brother), 92, 226–7
Shakespeare, Edward (nephew),
    227
Shakespeare, Hamnet (son), 110
Shakespeare, Henry (uncle), 15
Shakespeare, John (father), 16,
    17–18, 20, 162
Shakespeare, Judith (second
    daughter), 13, 189, 248
Shakespeare (née Arden), Mary,
    mother, 16, 231–2
Shakespeare, Susanna (elder
    daughter), 20, 26, 112, 248
sharers, 18, 20–1, 86–90, 101, 148,
    251
    see also under names of individual
        players
Shaw, Glen Byam, 163
Shrewsbury, 182, **190**, 232, 233
    Booth Hall, 190
Sincler, John ('Sinklo'), player, 33,
    36–7, 71–2, 98, 105, 108, 115,
    126, 136, 162, 173, 205
'Sinklo', *see* Sincler, John
Sir John Oldcastle (early version of

Shakespeare's *Henry IV*),
    133–4
    see Henry IV
Sisson, C.J., quoted 204
Sly, William, player, 33, *Plate 5*, 88,
    93, 126, 162, 211, 213, 216,
    218, 231
Slye, John, interluder, 33
Somerset, William, 3rd earl of
    Worcester, 22, 26, 28
    see also Worcester's men
Sonnets, 65, 66, 71, **72–7**, 80
    Sonnet 111, 5–6, 74
    Sonnet 121, 74
Southampton (Hants), 26, 28, 31,
    34
Southampton, Earl of, see
    Wriothesley, Henry
Spencer, Gabriel, player, 36–7
Stafford, 232
Stanley, 4th earl of Derby, 23–4
    see Derby's men
Steevens, George, quoted 13, 155
Stone, a professional fool, 158
Strange's men, 24, 35–6, 46, 50, 61,
    85, 88, 191
    see also Ferdinando, Lord Strange;
        Admiral's/Strange's alliance
Stratford-upon-Avon and vicinity,
    13–21, 22–6, 28, 162, 189,
    214, 231–2
    Guildhall, 16–17, 23
    Holy Trinity church, 6, 16, 26
    Henley Street, 16, 17
    King's New School, 16, *Plate 3*
    New Place, 189
    Shakespeare memorial bust, 6–7
        Plate 2
    Shambles, 14–15
    Snitterfield, 15
Street, Peter, 142, 144
Sturgess, Keith, cited 43
Sudbury, Suffolk, **186–7**, 232
    Old Moot Hall, Plate 18
Swinburne, Algernon Charles,
    quoted 238–9

Taming of a Shrew, The (pirated text of Shakespeare's play), 31, 91
*Taming of **The** Shrew, The* **32–3**, 40, 41, 59, 61, 85, 92, 96
Tarlton, Richard, player and playwright, 19, 22, 35
  Seven Deadly Sins, 19, 36, 86, 90–4
Tempest, The, 2, 59, 233, **243–6**
Theatre, the, 46, 86, **97**, **102**, 104, 109, 128, **134**, 142–3
theatres, *see* Blackfriars, Cross Keys, Curtain, Fortune, Globe, Newington Butts, Red Bull, Rose
Thorndike, Sybil, 79
Thorpe, Thomas, 74–5
Timon of Athens, 226
Titus Andronicus, 33, 38, 41, **47–50**, **50–1**, **54–5**, 61, **84–5**, 96
  'titus and vespacia' (Henslowe), 47–50
Tooley, Nicholas, player, 19, **92**, 156, 207, 211, 216, 218, 242
tours and touring, 28, 30–1, 61, 94, 104, 151, **180–95**, 207, 214, 219, 221–2, 231–2, 233, 247
  seasonal pattern, 179–80, notes 12 and 13
  town halls or houses, 23, 178, 196
  see also guildhalls and under names of relevant towns or cities
Trigg, William, player, 91 and note
Troilus and Cressida, 177, **199–203**
Troublesome Reign of King John, The, 125
Troy (anon. play at the Rose), 199
True Tragedie of Richard, Duke of Yorke, The (pirated text of *Henry VI*, Part 3), 61
Tunstall, James, player, 26, 29, 34
Twelfth Night, 2, 105, **170–4**, 177
Two Gentlemen of Verona, The, **65–9**, 96
Two Noble Kinsmen, The (with Fletcher), 58, 233, 246, 247
type-casting, 103, 113–4, 115–6

Underwood, John, player, 19

Venus and Adonis, **62–4**
Very Lamentable Tragedy of Titus Andronicus and the Haughty Empress, A, *see* under *Titus Andronicus*, 'titus and vespacia'
Vice of the moralities, 40, 120, 122–3
Vincent, Thomas, player and prompter, 90–1

Walker, Roy, quoted 244
Walsingham, Sir Francis, 30
Ward, John, 248
Warwick's men, 22
'We three', image of, 172, *Plate 10*
Wells, Stanley, cited 103
Whateley, Anne, 25
Wickham, Glynne, quoted 175
Wilkins, George, 234
Willis, R., quoted 23
Wilson, John Dover, quoted 22, 24–5, 54, 137–8
Wilton, Wilts., 193–4
Winchester, Hants, 233
Winter's Tale, The, 233, 240, 243, 246
Wise, Andrew, 134
Woodward, Joan, *see* Alleyn, Joan
Worcester, Earl of, *see* Somerset, William
Worcester's men, 22–9, 90–1, 93, 206
  see also Queen's men
Wordsworth, William, quoted 58
Wriothesley, Henry, earl of Southampton, 63–5, 73, 75, 80

Yates, Frances A., quoted 142, 144, 153
York, 28, 31

DATE DUE